A Traveler at

Theodore Dreiser

Alpha Editions

This edition published in 2024

ISBN : 9789357966658

Design and Setting By
Alpha Editions
www.alphaedis.com
Email - info@alphaedis.com

As per information held with us this book is in Public Domain.
This book is a reproduction of an important historical work. Alpha Editions uses the best technology to reproduce historical work in the same manner it was first published to preserve its original nature. Any marks or number seen are left intentionally to preserve its true form.

Contents

CHAPTER I BARFLEUR TAKES ME IN HAND .... - 1 -
CHAPTER II MISS X. .... - 11 -
CHAPTER III AT FISHGUARD .... - 17 -
CHAPTER IV SERVANTS AND POLITENESS .... - 23 -
CHAPTER V THE RIDE TO LONDON .... - 27 -
CHAPTER VI THE BARFLEUR FAMILY .... - 35 -
CHAPTER VII A GLIMPSE OF LONDON .... - 43 -
CHAPTER VIII A LONDON DRAWING-ROOM .... - 50 -
CHAPTER IX CALLS .... - 56 -
CHAPTER X SOME MORE ABOUT LONDON .... - 60 -
CHAPTER XI THE THAMES .... - 69 -
CHAPTER XII MARLOWE .... - 74 -
CHAPTER XIII LILLY: A GIRL OF THE STREETS .... - 88 -
CHAPTER XIV LONDON; THE EAST END .... - 100 -
CHAPTER XV ENTER SIR SCORP .... - 106 -
CHAPTER XVI A CHRISTMAS CALL .... - 115 -
CHAPTER XVII SMOKY ENGLAND .... - 134 -
CHAPTER XVIII SMOKY ENGLAND (*continued*) .... - 141 -
CHAPTER XIX CANTERBURY .... - 147 -
CHAPTER XX EN ROUTE TO PARIS .... - 154 -
CHAPTER XXI PARIS! .... - 164 -
CHAPTER XXII A MORNING IN PARIS .... - 175 -
CHAPTER XXIII THREE GUIDES .... - 186 -
CHAPTER XXIV "THE POISON FLOWER" .... - 193 -
CHAPTER XXV MONTE CARLO .... - 200 -
CHAPTER XXVI THE LURE OF GOLD! .... - 207 -

CHAPTER XXVII WE GO TO EZE .... - 216 -
CHAPTER XXVIII NICE .... - 226 -
CHAPTER XXIX A FIRST GLIMPSE OF ITALY .... - 232 -
CHAPTER XXX A STOP AT PISA .... - 240 -
CHAPTER XXXI FIRST IMPRESSIONS OF ROME .... - 247 -
CHAPTER XXXII MRS. Q. AND THE BORGIA FAMILY - 256 -
CHAPTER XXXIII THE ART OF SIGNOR TANNI .... - 265 -
CHAPTER XXXIV AN AUDIENCE AT THE VATICAN .. - 271 -
CHAPTER XXXV THE CITY OF ST. FRANCIS .... - 278 -
CHAPTER XXXVI PERUGIA .... - 287 -
CHAPTER XXXVII THE MAKERS OF FLORENCE .... - 292 -
CHAPTER XXXVIII A NIGHT RAMBLE IN FLORENCE - 299 -
CHAPTER XXXIX FLORENCE OF TO-DAY .... - 305 -
CHAPTER XL MARIA BASTIDA .... - 314 -
CHAPTER XLI VENICE .... - 325 -
CHAPTER XLII LUCERNE .... - 329 -
CHAPTER XLIII ENTERING GERMANY .... - 335 -
CHAPTER XLIV A MEDIEVAL TOWN .... - 345 -
CHAPTER XLV MY FATHER'S BIRTHPLACE .... - 355 -
CHAPTER XLVI THE ARTISTIC TEMPERAMENT .... - 359 -
CHAPTER XLVII BERLIN .... - 365 -
CHAPTER XLVIII THE NIGHT-LIFE OF BERLIN .... - 375 -
CHAPTER XLIX ON THE WAY TO HOLLAND .... - 385 -
CHAPTER L AMSTERDAM .... - 391 -
CHAPTER LI "SPOTLESS TOWN" .... - 397 -
CHAPTER LII PARIS AGAIN .... - 401 -
CHAPTER LIII THE VOYAGE HOME .... - 407 -

CHAPTER I
BARFLEUR TAKES ME IN HAND

I HAVE just turned forty. I have seen a little something of life. I have been a newspaper man, editor, magazine contributor, author and, before these things, several odd kinds of clerk before I found out what I could do.

Eleven years ago I wrote my first novel, which was issued by a New York publisher and suppressed by him, Heaven knows why. For, the same year they suppressed my book because of its alleged immoral tendencies, they published Zola's "Fecundity" and "An Englishwoman's Love Letters." I fancy now, after eleven years of wonder, that it was not so much the supposed immorality, as the book's straightforward, plain-spoken discussion of American life in general. We were not used then in America to calling a spade a spade, particularly in books. We had great admiration for Tolstoi and Flaubert and Balzac and de Maupassant at a distance—some of us—and it was quite an honor to have handsome sets of these men on our shelves, but mostly we had been schooled in the literature of Dickens, Thackeray, George Eliot, Charles Lamb and that refined company of English sentimental realists who told us something about life, but not everything. No doubt all of these great men knew how shabby a thing this world is—how full of lies, make-believe, seeming and false pretense it all is, but they had agreed among themselves, or with the public, or with sentiment generally, not to talk about that too much. Books were always to be built out of facts concerning "our better natures." We were always to be seen as we wish to be seen. There were villains to be sure—liars, dogs, thieves, scoundrels—but they were strange creatures, hiding away in dark, unconventional places and scarcely seen save at night and peradventure; whereas we, all clean, bright, honest, well-meaning people, were living in nice homes, going our way honestly and truthfully, going to church, raising our children believing in a Father, a Son and a Holy Ghost, and never doing anything wrong at any time save as these miserable liars, dogs, thieves, et cetera, might suddenly appear and make us. Our books largely showed us as heroes. If anything happened to our daughters it was not their fault but the fault of these miserable villains. Most of us were without original sin. The business of our books, our church, our laws, our jails, was to keep us so.

I am quite sure that it never occurred to many of us that there was something really improving in a plain, straightforward understanding of life. For myself, I accept now no creeds. I do not know what truth is, what beauty is, what love is, what hope is. I do not believe any one absolutely and I do not doubt any one absolutely. I think people are both evil and well-intentioned.

While I was opening my mail one morning I encountered a now memorable note which was addressed to me at my apartment. It was from an old literary friend of mine in England who expressed himself as anxious to see me immediately. I have always liked him. I like him because he strikes me as amusingly English, decidedly literary and artistic in his point of view, a man with a wide wisdom, discriminating taste, rare selection. He wears a monocle in his right eye, à la Chamberlain, and I like him for that. I like people who take themselves with a grand air, whether they like me or not—particularly if the grand air is backed up by a real personality. In this case it is.

Next morning Barfleur took breakfast with me; it was a most interesting affair. He was late—very. He stalked in, his spats shining, his monocle glowing with a shrewd, inquisitive eye behind it, his whole manner genial, self-sufficient, almost dictatorial and always final. He takes charge so easily, rules so sufficiently, does so essentially well in all circumstances where he is interested so to do.

"I have decided," he observed with that managerial air which always delights me because my soul is not in the least managerial, "that you will come back to England with me. I have my passage arranged for the twenty-second. You will come to my house in England; you will stay there a few days; then I shall take you to London and put you up at a very good hotel. You will stay there until January first and then we shall go to the south of France—Nice, the Riviera, Monte Carlo; from there you will go to Rome, to Paris, where I shall join you,—and then sometime in the spring or summer, when you have all your notes, you will return to London or New York and write your impressions and I will see that they are published!"

"If it can be arranged," I interpolated.

"It *can* be arranged," he replied emphatically. "I will attend to the financial part and arrange affairs with both an American and an English publisher."

Sometimes life is very generous. It walks in and says, "Here! I want you to do a certain thing," and it proceeds to arrange all your affairs for you. I felt curiously at this time as though I was on the edge of a great change. When one turns forty and faces one's first transatlantic voyage, it is a more portentous event than when it comes at twenty.

*   *   *   *   *

I shall not soon forget reading in a morning paper on the early ride downtown the day we sailed, of the suicide of a friend of mine, a brilliant man. He had fallen on hard lines; his wife had decided to desert him; he was badly in debt. I knew him well. I had known his erratic history. Here on this morning when I was sailing for Europe, quite in the flush of a momentary literary victory, he was lying in death. It gave me pause. It brought to my mind the Latin phrase, "*memento mori.*" I saw again, right in the heart of this hour of brightness, how grim life really is. Fate is kind, or it is not. It puts you ahead, or it does not. If it does not, nothing can save you. I acknowledge the Furies. I believe in them. I have heard the disastrous beating of their wings.

When I reached the ship, it was already a perfect morning in full glow. The sun was up; a host of gulls were on the wing; an air of delicious adventure enveloped the great liner's dock at the foot of Thirteenth Street.

Did ever a boy thrill over a ship as I over this monster of the seas?

In the first place, even at this early hour it was crowded with people. From the moment I came on board I was delighted by the eager, restless movement of the throng. The main deck was like the lobby of one of the great New York hotels at dinner-time. There was much calling on the part of a company of dragooned ship-stewards to "keep moving, please," and the enthusiasm of farewells and inquiries after this person and that, were delightful to hear. I stopped awhile in the writing-room and wrote some notes. I went to my stateroom and found there several telegrams and letters of farewell. Later still, some books which had been delivered at the ship, were brought to me. I went back to the dock and mailed my letters, encountered Barfleur finally and exchanged greetings, and then perforce soon found myself taken in tow by him, for he wanted, obviously, to instruct me in all the details of this new world upon which I was now entering.

At eight-thirty came the call to go ashore. At eight fifty-five I had my first glimpse of a Miss E., as discreet and charming a bit of English femininity as one would care to set eyes upon. She was an English actress of some eminence whom Barfleur was fortunate enough to know. Shortly afterward a Miss X. was introduced to him and to Miss E., by a third acquaintance of Miss E.'s, Mr. G.—a very direct, self-satisfied and aggressive type of Jew. I noticed him strolling about the deck some time before I saw him conversing with Miss E., and later, for a moment, with Barfleur. I saw these women only for a moment at first, but they impressed me at once as rather attractive examples of the prosperous stage world.

It was nine o'clock—the hour of the ship's sailing. I went forward to the prow, and watched the sailors on B deck below me cleaning up the final details of loading, bolting down the freight hatches covering the windlass and the like. All the morning I had been particularly impressed with the cloud of gulls fluttering about the ship, but now the harbor, the magnificent wall of lower New York, set like a jewel in a green ring of sea water, took my eye. When should I see it again? How soon should I be back? I had undertaken this voyage in pell-mell haste. I had not figured at all on where I was going or what I was going to do. London—yes, to gather the data for the last third of a novel; Rome—assuredly, because of all things I wished to see Rome; the Riviera, say, and Monte Carlo, because the south of France has always appealed to me; Paris, Berlin—possibly; Holland—surely.

I stood there till the *Mauretania* fronted her prow outward to the broad Atlantic. Then I went below and began unpacking, but was not there long before I was called out by Barfleur.

"Come up with me," he said.

We went to the boat deck where the towering red smoke-stacks were belching forth trailing clouds of smoke. I am quite sure that Barfleur, when he originally made his authoritative command that I come to England with him, was in no way satisfied that I would. It was a somewhat light venture on his part, but here I was. And now, having "let himself in" for this, as he would have phrased it, I could see that he was intensely interested in what Europe would do to me—and possibly in what I would do to Europe. We walked up and down as the boat made her way majestically down the harbor. We parted presently but shortly he returned to say, "Come and meet Miss E. and Miss X. Miss E. is reading your last novel. She likes it."

"I saw Mr. G. conversing with Miss E."

I went down, interested to meet these two, for the actress—the talented, good-looking representative of that peculiarly feminine world of art—appeals to me very much. I have always thought, since I have been able to reason about it, that the stage is almost the only ideal outlet for the artistic temperament of a talented and beautiful women. Men?—well, I don't care so much for the men of the stage. I acknowledge the distinction of such a temperament as that of David Garrick or Edwin Booth. These were great actors and, by the same token, they were great artists—wonderful artists. But in the main the men of the stage are frail shadows of a much more real thing—the active, constructive man in other lines.

On the contrary, the women of the stage are somehow, by right of mere womanhood, the art of looks, form, temperament, mobility, peculiarly suited to this realm of show, color and make-believe. The stage is fairyland and they are of it. Women—the women of ambition, aspiration, artistic longings—act, anyhow, all the time. They lie like anything. They never show their true colors—or very rarely. If you want to know the truth, you must see through their pretty, petty artistry, back to the actual conditions behind them, which are conditioning and driving them. Very few, if any, have a real grasp on what I call life. They have no understanding of and no love for philosophy. They do not care for the subtleties of chemistry and physics. Knowledge—book knowledge, the sciences—well, let the men have that. Your average woman cares most—almost entirely—for the policies and the abstrusities of her own little world. Is her life going right? Is she getting along? Is her skin smooth? Is her face still pretty? Are there any wrinkles? Are there any gray hairs in sight? What can she do to win one man? How can she make herself impressive to all men? Are her feet small? Are her hands pretty? Which are the really nice places in the world to visit? Do men like this trait in women? or that? What is the latest thing in dress, in jewelry, in hats, in shoes? How can she keep herself spick and span? These are all leading questions with her—strong, deep, vital, painful. Let the men have knowledge, strength, fame, force—that is their business. The real man, her man, should have some one of these things if she is really going to love him very much. I am talking about the semi-artistic woman with ambition. As for her, she clings to these poetical details and they make her life. Poor little frail things—fighting with every weapon at their command to buy and maintain the courtesy of the world. Truly, I pity women. I pity the strongest, most ambitious woman I ever saw. And, by the same token, I pity the poor helpless, hopeless drab and drudge without an idea above a potato, who never had and never will have a look in on anything. I know—and there is not a beating feminine heart anywhere that will contradict me—that they are all struggling to buy this superior masculine strength against which they can lean, to which they can fly in the hour of terror. It is no answer to my statement, no contradiction of it, to say that the strongest men crave the sympathy of the tenderest women. These are complementary facts and my statement is true. I am dealing with women now, not men. When I come to men I will tell you all about them!

Our modern stage world gives the ideal outlet for all that is most worth while in the youth and art of the female sex. It matters not that it is notably unmoral. You cannot predicate that of any individual case until afterward. At any rate, to me, and so far as women are concerned, it is distinguished, brilliant, appropriate, important. I am always interested in a well recommended woman of the stage.

What did we talk about—Miss E. and I? The stage a little, some newspapermen and dramatic critics that we had casually known, her interest in books and the fact that she had posed frequently for those interesting advertisements which display a beautiful young woman showing her teeth or holding aloft a cake of soap or a facial cream. She had done some of this work in the past—and had been well paid for it because she was beautiful, and she showed me one of her pictures in a current magazine advertising a set of furs.

I found that Barfleur, my very able patron, was doing everything that should be done to make the trip comfortable without show or fuss. Many have this executive or managerial gift. Sometimes I think it is a natural trait of the English—of their superior classes, anyhow. They go about colonizing so efficiently, industriously. They make fine governors and patrons. I have always been told that English direction and English directors are thorough. Is this true or is it not? At this writing, I do not know.

Not only were all our chairs on deck here in a row, but our chairs at table had already been arranged for—four seats at the captain's table. It seems that from previous voyages on this ship Barfleur knew the captain. He also knew the chairman of the company in England. No doubt he knew the chief steward. Anyhow, he knew the man who sold us our tickets. He knew the head waiter at the Ritz—he had seen him or been served by him somewhere in Europe. He knew some of the servitors of the Knickerbocker of old. Wherever he went, I found he was always finding somebody whom he knew. I like to get in tow of such a man as Barfleur and see him plow the seas. I like to see what he thinks is important. In this case there happens to be a certain intellectual and spiritual compatibility. He likes some of the things that I like. He sympathizes with my point of view. Hence, so far at least, we have got along admirably. I speak for the present only. I would not answer for my moods or basic change of emotions at any time.

Well, here were the two actresses side by side, both charmingly arrayed, and with them, in a third chair, the short, stout, red-haired Mr. G.

I covertly observed the personality of Miss X. Here was some one who, on sight, at a glance, attracted me far more significantly than ever Miss E. could. I cannot tell you why, exactly. In a way, Miss E. appeared, at moments and from certain points of view—delicacy, refinement, sweetness of mood—the more attractive of the two. But Miss X., with her chic face, her dainty little chin, her narrow, lavender-lidded eyes, drew me quite like a magnet. I liked a certain snap and vigor which shot from her eyes and which I could feel represented our raw American force. A foreigner will not, I am afraid, understand exactly what I mean; but there is something about the American climate, its soil, rain, winds, race spirit, which produces a raw, direct incisiveness of soul in its children. They are strong, erect, elated, enthusiastic. They look you in the eye, cut you with a glance, say what they mean in ten thousand ways without really saying anything at all. They come upon you fresh like cold water and they have the luster of a hard, bright jewel and the fragrance of a rich, red, full-blown rose. Americans are wonderful to me—American men and American women. They are rarely polished or refined. They know little of the subtleties of life—its order and procedures. But, oh, the glory of their spirit, the hope of them, the dreams of them, the desires and enthusiasm of them. That is what wins me. They give me the sense of being intensely, enthusiastically, humanly alive.

Miss X. did not tell me anything about herself, save that she was on the stage in some capacity and that she knew a large number of newspaper men, critics, actors, et cetera. A chorus girl, I thought; and then, by the same token, a lady of extreme unconventionality.

I think the average man, however much he may lie and pretend, takes considerable interest in such women. At the same time there are large orders and schools of mind, bound by certain variations of temperament, and schools of thought, which either flee temptation of this kind, find no temptation in it, or, when confronted, resist it vigorously. The accepted theory of marriage and monogamy holds many people absolutely. There are these who would never sin—hold unsanctioned relations, I mean—with any woman. There are others who will always be true to one woman. There are those who are fortunate if they ever win a single woman. We did not talk of these things but it was early apparent that she was as wise as the serpent in her knowledge of men and in the practice of all the little allurements of her sex.

Barfleur never ceased instructing me in the intricacies of ship life. I never saw so comforting and efficient a man.

"Oh"—who can indicate exactly the sound of the English "Oh"—"Oh, *there* you are." (His *are* always sounded like *ah*.) "Now let me tell you something. You are to dress for dinner. Ship etiquette requires it. You are to talk to the captain some—tell him how much you think of his ship, and so forth; and you are not to neglect the neighbor to your right at table. Ship etiquette, I believe, demands that you talk to your neighbor, at least at the captain's table—that is the rule, I think. You are to take in Miss X. I am to take in Miss E." Was it any wonder that my sea life was well-ordered and that my lines fell in pleasant places?

After dinner we adjourned to the ship's drawing-room and there Miss X. fell to playing cards with Barfleur at first, afterwards with Mr. G., who came up and found us, thrusting his company upon us perforce. The man amused me, so typically aggressive, money-centered was he. However, not he so much as Miss X. and her mental and social attitude, commanded my attention. Her card playing and her boastful accounts of adventures at Ostend, Trouville, Nice, Monte Carlo and Aix-les-Bains indicated plainly the trend of her interests. She was all for the showy life that was to be found in these places—burning with a desire to glitter—not shine—in that half world of which she was a smart atom. Her conversation was at once showy, naïve, sophisticated and yet unschooled. I could see by Barfleur's attentions to her, that aside from her crude Americanisms which ordinarily would have alienated him, he was interested in her beauty, her taste in dress, her love of a certain continental café life which encompassed a portion of his own interests. Both were looking forward to a fresh season of it—Barfleur with me—Miss X. with some one who was waiting for her in London.

I think I have indicated in one or two places in the preceding pages that Barfleur, being an Englishman of the artistic and intellectual classes, with considerable tradition behind him and all the feeling of the worth-whileness of social order that goes with class training, has a high respect for the conventions—or rather let me say appearances, for, though essentially democratic in spirit and loving America—its raw force—he still clings almost pathetically, I think, to that vast established order, which is England. It may be producing a dying condition of race, but still there is something exceedingly fine about it. Now one of the tenets of English social order is that, being a man you must be a gentleman, very courteous to the ladies, very observant of outward forms and appearances, very discreet in your approaches to the wickedness of the world—but nevertheless you may approach and much more, if you are cautious enough.

After dinner there was a concert. It was a dreary affair. When it was over, I started to go to bed but, it being warm and fresh, I stepped outside. The night was beautiful. There were no fellow passengers on the promenade. All had retired. The sky was magnificent for stars—Orion, the Pleiades, the Milky Way, the Big Dipper, the Little Dipper. I saw one star, off to my right as I stood at the prow under the bridge, which, owing to the soft, velvety darkness, cast a faint silvery glow on the water—just a trace. Think of it! One lone, silvery star over the great dark sea doing this. I stood at the prow and watched the boat speed on. I threw back my head and drank in the salt wind. I looked and listened. England, France, Italy, Switzerland, Germany—these were all coming to me mile by mile. As I stood there a bell over me struck eight times. Another farther off sounded the same number. Then a voice at the prow called, "All's well," and another aloft on that little eyrie called the crow's nest, echoed it. "All's well." The second voice was weak and quavering. Something came up in my throat—a quick unbidden lump of emotion. Was it an echo of old journeys and old seas when life was not safe? When Columbus sailed into the unknown? And now this vast ship, eight hundred and eighty-two feet long, eighty-eight feet beam, with huge pits of engines and furnaces and polite, veneered first-cabin decks and passengers!

CHAPTER II
MISS X.

IT was ten o'clock the next morning when I arose and looked at my watch. I thought it might be eight-thirty, or seven. The day was slightly gray with spray flying. There was a strong wind. The sea was really a boisterous thing, thrashing and heaving in hills and hollows. I was thinking of Kipling's "White Horses" for a while. There were several things about this great ship which were unique. It was a beautiful thing all told—its long cherry-wood, paneled halls in the first-class section, its heavy porcelain baths, its dainty staterooms fitted with lamps, bureaus, writing-desks, washstands, closets and the like. I liked the idea of dressing for dinner and seeing everything quite stately and formal. The little be-buttoned call-boys in their tight-fitting blue suits amused me. And the bugler who bugled for dinner! That was a most musical sound he made, trilling in the various quarters gaily, as much as to say, "This is a very joyous event, ladies and gentlemen; we are all happy; come, come; it is a delightful feast." I saw him one day in the lobby of C deck, his legs spread far apart, the bugle to his lips, no evidence of the rolling ship in his erectness, bugling heartily. It was like something out of an old medieval court or a play. Very nice and worth while.

Absolutely ignorant of this world of the sea, the social, domestic, culinary and other economies of a great ship like this interested me from the start. It impressed me no little that all the servants were English, and that they were, shall I say, polite?—well, if not that, non-aggressive. American servants— I could write a whole chapter on that, but we haven't any servants in America. We don't know how to be servants. It isn't in us; it isn't nice to be a servant; it isn't democratic; and spiritually I don't blame us. In America, with our turn for mechanics, we shall have to invent something which will do away with the need of servants. What it is to be, I haven't the faintest idea at present.

Another thing that impressed and irritated me a little was the stolidity of the English countenance as I encountered it here on this ship. I didn't know then whether it was accidental in this case, or national. There is a certain type of Englishman— the robust, rosy-cheeked, blue-eyed Saxon—whom I cordially dislike, I think, speaking temperamentally and artistically. They are too solid, too rosy, too immobile as to their faces, and altogether too assured and stary. I don't like them. They offend me. They thrust a silly race pride into my face, which isn't necessary at all and which I always resent with a race pride of my own. It has even occurred to me at times that these temperamental race differences could be quickly adjusted only by an appeal to arms, which is sillier yet. But so goes life. It's foolish on both sides, but I mention it for what it is worth.

After lunch, which was also breakfast with me, I went with the chief engineer through the engine-room. This was a pit eighty feet deep, forty feet wide and, perhaps, one hundred feet long, filled with machinery. What a strange world! I know absolutely nothing of machinery—not a single principle connected with it—and yet I am intensely interested. These boilers, pipes, funnels, pistons, gages, registers and bright-faced register boards speak of a vast technique which to me is tremendously impressive. I know scarcely anything of the history of mechanics, but I know what boilers and feed-pipes and escape-pipes are, and how complicated machinery is automatically oiled and reciprocated, and there my knowledge ends. All that I know about the rest is what the race knows. There are mechanical and electrical engineers. They devised the reciprocating engine for vessels and then the turbine. They have worked out the theory of electrical control and have installed vast systems with a wonderful economy as to power and space. This deep pit was like some vast, sad dream of a fevered mind. It clanked and rattled and hissed and squeaked with almost insane contrariety! There were narrow, steep, oil-stained stairs, very hot, or very cold and very slippery, that wound here and there in strange ways, and if you were not careful there were moving rods and wheels to strike you. You passed from bridge to bridge under whirling wheels, over clanking pistons; passed hot containers; passed cold ones. Here men were standing, blue-jumpered assistants in oil-stained caps and gloves—thin caps and thick gloves—watching the manœuvers of this vast network of steel, far from the passenger life of the vessel. Occasionally they touched something. They were down in the very heart or the bowels of this thing, away from the sound of the water; away partially from the heaviest motion of the ship; listening only to the clank, clank and whir, whir and hiss, hiss all day long. It is a metal world they live in, a hard, bright metal world. Everything is hard, everything fixed, everything regular. If they look up, behold a huge, complicated scaffolding of steel; noise and heat and regularity.

I shouldn't like that, I think. My soul would grow weary. It would pall. I like the softness of scenery, the haze, the uncertainty of the world outside. Life is better than rigidity and fixed motion, I hope. I trust the universe is not mechanical, but mystically blind. Let's hope it's a vague, uncertain, but divine idea. We know it is beautiful. It must be so.

The wind-up of this day occurred in the lounging- or reception-room where, after dinner, we all retired to listen to the music, and then began one of those really interesting conversations between Barfleur and Miss X. which sometimes illuminate life and make one see things differently forever afterward.

It is going to be very hard for me to define just how this could be, but I might say that I had at the moment considerable intellectual contempt for the point of view which the conversation represented. Consider first the American attitude. With us (not the established rich, but the hopeful, ambitious American who has nothing, comes from nothing and hopes to be President of the United States or John D. Rockefeller) the business of life is not living, but achieving. Roughly speaking, we are willing to go hungry, dirty, to wait in the cold and fight gamely, if in the end we can achieve one or more of the seven stars in the human crown of life—social, intellectual, moral, financial, physical, spiritual or material supremacy. Several of the forms of supremacy may seem the same, but they are not. Examine them closely. The average American is not born to place. He does not know what the English sense of order is. We have not that national *esprit de corps* which characterizes the English and the French perhaps; certainly the Germans. We are loose, uncouth, but, in our way, wonderful. The spirit of God has once more breathed upon the waters.

Well, the gentleman who was doing the talking in this instance and the lady who was coinciding, inciting, aiding, abetting, approving and at times leading and demonstrating, represented two different and yet allied points of view. Barfleur is distinctly a product of the English conservative school of thought, a gentleman who wishes sincerely he was not so conservative. His house is in order. You can feel it. I have always felt it in relation to him. His standards and ideals are fixed. He knows what life ought to be—how it ought to be lived. You would never catch him associating with the rag-tag and bobtail of humanity with any keen sense of human brotherhood or emotional tenderness of feeling. They are human beings, of course. They are in the scheme of things, to be sure. But, let it go at that. One cannot be considering the state of the underdog at any particular time. Government is established to do this sort of thing. Statesmen are large, constructive servants who are supposed to look after all of us. The masses! Let them behave. Let them accept their state. Let them raise no undue row. And let us, above all things, have order and peace.

One of those really interesting conversations between Barfleur and Miss X.

This is a section of Barfleur—not all, mind you, but a section.

Miss X.—I think I have described her fully enough, but I shall add one passing thought. A little experience of Europe—considerable of its show places—had taught her, or convinced her rather, that America did not know how to live. You will hear much of that fact, I am afraid, during the rest of these pages, but it is especially important just here. My lady, prettily gowned, perfectly manicured, going to meet her lover at London or Fishguard or Liverpool, is absolutely satisfied that America does not know how to live. She herself has almost learned. She is most comfortably provided for at present. Anyhow, she has champagne every night at dinner. Her equipment in the matter of toilet articles and leather traveling bags is all that it should be. The latter are colored to suit her complexion and gowns. She is scented, polished, looked after, and all men pay her attention. She is vain, beautiful, and she thinks that America is raw, uncouth; that its citizens of whom she is one, do not know how to live. Quite so. Now we come to the point.

It would be hard to describe this conversation. It began with some "have you been's," I think, and concerned eating-places and modes of entertainment in London, Paris and Monte Carlo. I gathered by degrees, that in London, Paris and elsewhere there were a hundred restaurants, a hundred places to live, each finer than the other. I heard of liberty of thought and freedom of action and pride of motion which made me understand that there is a free-masonry which concerns the art of living, which is shared only by the initiated. There was a world in which conventions, as to morals, have no place; in which ethics and religion are tabooed. Art is the point. The joys of this world are sex, beauty, food, clothing, art. I should say money, of course, but money is presupposed. You must have it.

"Oh, I went to that place one day and then I was glad enough to get back to the Ritz at forty francs for my room." She was talking of her room by the day, and the food, of course, was extra. The other hotel had been a little bit quiet or dingy.

I opened my eyes slightly, for I thought Paris was reasonable; but not so—no more so than New York, I understood, if you did the same things.

"And, oh, the life!" said Miss X. at one point. "Americans don't know how to live. They are all engaged in doing something. They are such beginners. They are only interested in money. They don't know. I see them in Paris now and then." She lifted her hand. "Here in Europe people understand life better. They know. They know before they begin how much it will take to do the things that they want to do and they start out to make that much—not a fortune—just enough to do the things that they want to do. When they get that they retire and *live*."

"And what do they do when they live?" I asked. "What do they call living?"

"Oh, having a nice country-house within a short traveling distance of London or Paris, and being able to dine at the best restaurants and visit the best theaters once or twice a week; to go to Paris or Monte Carlo or Scheveningen or Ostend two or three or four, or as many times a year as they please; to wear good clothes and to be thoroughly comfortable."

"That is not a bad standard," I said, and then I added, "And what else do they do?"

"And what else should they do? Isn't that enough?"

And there you have the European standard according to Miss X. as contrasted with the American standard which is, or has been up to this time, something decidedly different, I am sure. We have not been so eager to live. Our idea has been to work. No American that I have ever known has had the idea of laying up just so much, a moderate amount, and then retiring and living. He has had quite another thought in his mind. The American—the average American—I am sure loves power, the ability to do something, far more earnestly than he loves mere living. He wants to be an officer or a director of something, a poet, anything you please for the sake of being it—not for the sake of living. He loves power, authority, to be able to say, "Go and he goeth," or, "Come and he cometh." The rest he will waive. Mere comfort? You can have that. But even that, according to Miss X., was not enough for her. She had told me before, and this conversation brought it out again, that her thoughts were of summer and winter resorts, exquisite creations in the way of clothing, diamonds, open balconies of restaurants commanding charming vistas, gambling tables at Monte Carlo, Aix-les-Bains, Ostend and elsewhere, to say nothing of absolutely untrammeled sex relations. English conventional women were frumps and fools. They had never learned how to live; they had never understood what the joy of freedom in sex was. Morals—they are built up on a lack of imagination and physical vigor; tenderness—well, you have to take care of yourself; duty—there isn't any such thing. If there is, it's one's duty to get along and have money and be happy.

CHAPTER III
AT FISHGUARD

WHILE I was lying in my berth the fifth morning, I heard the room steward outside my door tell some one that he thought we reached Fishguard at one-thirty.

I packed my trunks, thinking of this big ship and the fact that my trip was over and that never again could I cross the Atlantic for the first time. A queer world this. We can only do any one thing significantly once. I remember when I first went to Chicago, I remember when I first went to St. Louis, I remember when I first went to New York. Other trips there were, but they are lost in vagueness. But the first time of any important thing sticks and lasts; it comes back at times and haunts you with its beauty and its sadness. You know so well you cannot do that any more; and, like a clock, it ticks and tells you that life is moving on. I shall never come to England any more for the first time. That is gone and done for—worse luck.

So I packed—will you believe it?—a little sadly. I think most of us are a little silly at times, only we are cautious enough to conceal it. There is in me the spirit of a lonely child somewhere and it clings pitifully to the hand of its big mama, Life, and cries when it is frightened; and then there is a coarse, vulgar exterior which fronts the world defiantly and bids all and sundry to go to the devil. It sneers and barks and jeers bitterly at times, and guffaws and cackles and has a joyous time laughing at the follies of others.

Then I went to hunt Barfleur to find out how I should do. How much was I to give the deck-steward; how much to the bath-steward; how much to the room-steward; how much to the dining-room steward; how much to "boots," and so on.

"Look here!" observed that most efficient of all managerial souls that I have ever known. "I'll tell you what you do. No—I'll write it." And he drew forth an ever ready envelope. "Deck-steward—so much," it read, "Room steward—so much—" etc.

I went forthwith and paid them, relieving my soul of a great weight. Then I came on deck and found that I had forgotten to pack my ship blanket, and a steamer rug, which I forthwith went and packed. Then I discovered that I had no place for my derby hat save on my head, so I went back and packed my cap. Then I thought I had lost one of my brushes, which I hadn't, though I did lose one of my stylo pencils. Finally I came on deck and sang coon songs with Miss X., sitting in our steamer chairs. The low shore of Ireland had come into view with two faint hills in the distance and these fascinated me. I thought I should have some slight emotion on seeing land again, but I didn't. It was gray and misty at first, but presently the sun came out beautifully clear and the day was as warm as May in New York. I felt a sudden elation of spirits with the coming of the sun, and I began to think what a lovely time I was going to have in Europe.

Miss X. was a little more friendly this morning than heretofore. She was a tricky creature—coy, uncertain and hard to please. She liked me intellectually and thought I was able, but her physical and emotional predilections, so far as men are concerned, did not include me.

We rejoiced together singing, and then we fought. There is a directness between experienced intellects which waves aside all formalities. She had seen a lot of life; so had I.

She said she thought she would like to walk a little, and we strolled back along the heaving deck to the end of the first cabin section and then to the stern. When we reached there the sky was overcast again, for it was one of those changeable mornings which is now gray, now bright, now misty. Just now the heavens were black and lowering with soft, rain-charged clouds, like the wool of a smudgy sheep. The sea was a rich green in consequence—not a clear green, but a dark, muddy, oil-green. It rose and sank in its endless unrest and one or two boats appeared—a lightship, anchored out all alone against the lowering waste, and a small, black, passenger steamer going somewhere.

"I wish my path in life were as white as that and as straight," observed Miss X., pointing to our white, propeller-churned wake which extended back for half a mile or more.

"Yes," I observed, "you do and you don't. You do, if it wouldn't cost you trouble in the future—impose the straight and narrow, as it were."

"Oh, you don't know," she exclaimed irritably, that ugly fighting light coming into her eyes, which I had seen there several times before. "You don't know what my life has been. I haven't been so bad. We all of us do the best we can. I have done the best I could, considering."

"Yes, yes," I observed, "you're ambitious and alive and you're seeking—Heaven knows what! You would be adorable with your pretty face and body if you were not so—so sophisticated. The trouble with you is—"

"Oh, look at that cute little boat out there!" She was talking of the lightship. "I always feel sorry for a poor little thing like that, set aside from the main tide of life and left lonely—with no one to care for it."

"The trouble with you is," I went on, seizing this new remark as an additional pretext for analysis, "you're romantic, not sympathetic. You're interested in that poor little lonely boat because its state is romantic; not pathetic. It may be pathetic, but that isn't the point with you."

"Well," she said, "if you had had all the hard knocks I have had, you wouldn't be sympathetic either. I've suffered, I have. My illusions have been killed dead."

"Yes. Love is over with you. You can't love any more. You can like to be loved, that's all. If it were the other way about—"

I paused to think how really lovely she would be with her narrow lavender eyelids; her delicate, almost retroussé, little nose; her red cupid's-bow mouth.

"Oh," she exclaimed, with a gesture of almost religious adoration. "I cannot love any one person any more, but I can love love, and I do—all the delicate things it stands for."

"Flowers," I observed, "jewels, automobiles, hotel bills, fine dresses."

"Oh, you're brutal. I hate you. You've said the cruelest, meanest things that have ever been said to me."

"But they're so."

"I don't care. Why shouldn't I be hard? Why shouldn't I love to live and be loved? Look at my life. See what I've had."

"You like me, in a way?" I suggested.

"I admire your intellect."

"Quite so. And others receive the gifts of your personality."

"I can't help it. I can't be mean to the man I'm with. He's good to me. I won't. I'd be sinning against the only conscience I have."

"Then you have a conscience?"

"Oh, you go to the devil!"

But we didn't separate by any means.

They were blowing a bugle for lunch when we came back, and down we went. Barfleur was already at table. The orchestra was playing Auld Lang Syne, Home Sweet Home, Dixie and the Suwannee River. It even played one of those delicious American rags which I love so much—the Oceana Roll. I felt a little lump in my throat at Auld Lang Syne and Dixie, and together Miss X. and I hummed the Oceana Roll as it was played. One of the girl passengers came about with a plate to obtain money for the members of the orchestra, and half-crowns were universally deposited. Then I started to eat my dessert; but Barfleur, who had hurried off, came back to interfere.

"Come, come!" (He was always most emphatic.) "You're missing it all. We're landing."

I thought we were leaving at once. The eye behind the monocle was premonitory of some great loss to me. I hurried on deck—to thank his artistic and managerial instinct instantly I arrived there. Before me was Fishguard and the Welsh coast, and to my dying day I shall never forget it. Imagine, if you please, a land-locked harbor, as green as grass in this semi-cloudy, semi-gold-bathed afternoon, with a half-moon of granite scarp rising sheer and clear from the green waters to the low gray clouds overhead. On its top I could see fields laid out in pretty squares or oblongs, and at the bottom of what to me appeared to be the east end of the semi-circle, was a bit of gray scruff, which was the village no doubt. On the green water were several other boats—steamers, much smaller, with red stacks, black sides, white rails and funnels—bearing a family resemblance to the one we were on. There was a long pier extending out into the water from what I took to be the village and something farther inland that looked like a low shed.

This black hotel of a ship, so vast, so graceful, now rocking gently in the enameled bay, was surrounded this hour by wheeling, squeaking gulls. I always like the squeak of a gull; it reminds me of a rusty car wheel, and, somehow, it accords with a lone, rocky coast. Here they were, their little feet coral red, their beaks jade gray, their bodies snowy white or sober gray, wheeling and crying—"my heart remembers how." I looked at them and that old intense sensation of joy came back—the wish to fly, the wish to be young, the wish to be happy, the wish to be loved.

But, my scene, beautiful as it was, was slipping away. One of the pretty steamers I had noted lying on the water some distance away, was drawing alongside—to get mails, first, they said. There were hurrying and shuffling people on all the first cabin decks. Barfleur was forward looking after his luggage. The captain stood on the bridge in his great gold-braided blue overcoat. There were mail chutes being lowered from our giant vessel's side, and bags and trunks and boxes and bales were then sent scuttling down. I saw dozens of uniformed men and scores of ununiformed laborers briskly handling these in the sunshine. My fellow passengers in their last hurrying hour interested me, for I knew I should see them no more; except one or two, perhaps.

While we were standing here I turned to watch an Englishman, tall, assured, stalky, stary. He had been soldiering about for some time, examining this, that and the other in his critical, dogmatic British way. He had leaned over the side and inspected the approaching lighters, he had stared critically and unpoetically at the gulls which were here now by hundreds, he had observed the landing toilet of the ladies, the material equipment of the various men, and was quite evidently satisfied that he himself was perfect, complete. He was aloof, chilly, decidedly forbidding and judicial.

Finally a cabin steward came hurrying out to him.

"Did you mean to leave the things you left in your room unpacked?" he asked. The Englishman started, stiffened, stared. I never saw a self-sufficient man so completely shaken out of his poise.

"Things in my room unpacked?" he echoed. "What room are you talking about? My word!"

"There are three drawers full of things in there, sir, unpacked, and they're waiting for your luggage now, sir!"

"My word!" he repeated, grieved, angered, perplexed. "My word! I'm sure I packed everything. Three drawers full! My word!" He bustled off stiffly. The attendant hastened cheerfully after. It almost gave me a chill as I thought of his problem. And they hurry so at Fishguard. He was well paid out, as the English say, for being so stalky and superior.

Then the mail and trunks being off, and that boat having veered away, another and somewhat smaller one came alongside and we first, and then the second class passengers, went aboard, and I watched the great ship growing less and less as we pulled away from it. It was immense from alongside, a vast skyscraper of a ship. At a hundred feet, it seemed not so large, but more graceful; at a thousand feet, all its exquisite lines were perfect—its bulk not so great, but the pathos of its departing beauty wonderful; at two thousand feet, it was still beautiful against the granite ring of the harbor; but, alas, it was moving. The captain was an almost indistinguishable spot upon his bridge. The stacks—in their way gorgeous—took on beautiful proportions. I thought, as we veered in near the pier and the ship turned within her length or thereabouts and steamed out, I had never seen a more beautiful sight. Her convoy of gulls was still about her. Her smoke-stacks flung back their graceful streamers. The propeller left a white trail of foam. I asked some one: "When does she get to Liverpool?"

"At two in the morning."

"And when do the balance of the passengers land?" (We had virtually emptied the first cabin.)

"At seven, I fancy."

Just then the lighter bumped against the dock. I walked under a long, low train-shed covering four tracks, and then I saw my first English passenger train—a semi-octagonal-looking affair—(the ends of the cars certainly looked as though they had started out to be octagonal) and there were little doors on the sides labeled "First," "First," "First." On the side, at the top of the car, was a longer sign: "Cunard Ocean Special—London—Fishguard."

CHAPTER IV
SERVANTS AND POLITENESS

RIGHT here I propose to interpolate my second dissertation on the servant question and I can safely promise, I am sure, that it will not be the last. One night, not long before, in dining with a certain Baron N. and Barfleur at the Ritz in New York this matter of the American servant came up in a conversational way. Baron N. was a young exquisite of Berlin and other European capitals. He was one of Barfleur's idle fancies. Because we were talking about America in general I asked them both what, to them, was the most offensive or objectionable thing about America. One said, expectorating; the other said, the impoliteness of servants. On the ship going over, at Fishguard, in the train from Fishguard to London, at London and later in Barfleur's country house I saw what the difference was. Of course I had heard these differences discussed before *ad lib.* for years, but hearing is not believing. Seeing and experiencing is.

On shipboard I noticed for the first time in my life that there was an aloofness about the service rendered by the servants which was entirely different from that which we know in America. They did not look at one so brutally and critically as does the American menial; their eyes did not seem to say, "I am your equal or better," and their motions did not indicate that they were doing anything unwillingly. In America—and I am a good American—I have always had the feeling that the American hotel or house servant or store clerk—particularly store clerk—male or female—was doing me a great favor if he did anything at all for me. As for train-men and passenger-boat assistants, I have never been able to look upon them as servants at all. Mostly they have looked on me as an interloper, and as some one who should be put off the train, instead of assisted in going anywhere. American conductors are Czars; American brakemen and train hands are Grand Dukes, at least; a porter is little less than a highwayman; and a hotel clerk—God forbid that we should mention him in the same breath with any of the foregoing!

However, as I was going on to say, when I went aboard the English ship in question I felt this burden of serfdom to the American servant lifted. These people, strange to relate, did not seem anxious to fight with me. They were actually civil.

They did not stare me out of countenance; they did not order me gruffly about. And, really, I am not a princely soul looking for obsequious service. I am, I fancy, a very humble-minded person when traveling or living, anxious to go briskly forward, not to be disturbed too much and allowed to live in quiet and seclusion.

The American servant is not built for that. One must have great social or physical force to command him. At times he needs literally to be cowed by threats of physical violence. You are paying him? Of course you are. You help do that when you pay your hotel bill or buy your ticket, or make a purchase, but he does not know that. The officials of the companies for whom he works do not appear to know. If they did, I don't know that they would be able to do anything about it. You can not make a whole people over by issuing a book of rules. Americans are free men; they don't want to be servants; they have despised the idea for years. I think the early Americans who lived in America after the Revolution—the anti-Tory element—thought that after the war and having won their nationality there was to be an end of servants. I think they associated labor of this kind with slavery, and they thought when England had been defeated all these other things, such as menial service, had been defeated also. Alas, superiority and inferiority have not yet been done away with—wholly. There are the strong and the weak; the passionate and passionless; the hungry and the well-fed. There are those who still think that life is something which can be put into a mold and adjusted to a theory, but I am not one of them. I cannot view life or human nature save as an expression of contraries—in fact, I think that is what life is. I know there can be no sense of heat without cold; no fullness without emptiness; no force without resistance; no anything, in short, without its contrary. Consequently, I cannot see how there can be great men without little ones; wealth without poverty; social movement without willing social assistance. No high without a low, is my idea, and I would have the low be intelligent, efficient, useful, well paid, well looked after. And I would have the high be sane, kindly, considerate, useful, of good report and good-will to all men.

Years of abuse and discomfort have made me rather antagonistic to servants, but I felt no reasonable grounds for antagonism here. They were behaving properly. They weren't staring at me. I didn't catch them making audible remarks behind my back. They were not descanting unfavorably upon any of my fellow passengers. Things were actually going smoothly and nicely and they seemed rather courteous about it all.

Yes, and it was so in the dining-saloon, in the bath, on deck, everywhere, with "yes, sirs," and "thank you, sirs," and two fingers raised to cap visors occasionally for good measure. Were they acting? Was this a fiercely suppressed class I was looking upon here? I could scarcely believe it. They looked too comfortable. I saw them associating with each other a great deal. I heard scraps of their conversation. It was all peaceful and genial and individual enough. They were, apparently, leading unrestricted private lives. However, I reserved judgment until I should get to England, but at Fishguard it was quite the same and more also. These railway guards and porters and conductors were not our railway conductors, brakemen and porters, by a long shot. They were different in their attitude, texture and general outlook on life. Physically I should say that American railway employees are superior to the European brand. They are, on the whole, better fed, or at least better set up. They seem bigger to me, as I recall them; harder, stronger. The English railway employee seems smaller and more refined physically—less vigorous.

But as to manners: Heaven save the mark! These people are civil. They are nice. They are willing. "Have you a porter, sir? Yes, sir! Thank you, sir! This way, sir! No trouble about that, sir! In a moment, sir! Certainly, sir! Very well, sir!" I heard these things on all sides and they were like balm to a fevered brain. Life didn't seem so strenuous with these people about. They were actually trying to help me along. I was led; I was shown; I was explained to. I got under way without the least distress and I began actually to feel as though I was being coddled. Why, I thought, these people are going to spoil me. I'm going to like them. And I had rather decided that I wouldn't like the English. Why, I don't know; for I never read a great English novel that I didn't more or less like all of the characters in it. Hardy's lovely country people have warmed the cockles of my heart; George Moore's English characters have appealed to me. And here was Barfleur. But the way the train employees bundled me into my seat and got my bags in after or before me, and said, "We shall be starting now in a few minutes, sir," and called quietly and pleadingly—not yelling, mind you—"Take your seats, please," delighted me.

I didn't like the looks of the cars. I can prove in a moment by any traveler that our trains are infinitely more luxurious. I can see where there isn't heat enough, and where one lavatory for men and women on any train, let alone a first-class one, is an abomination, and so on and so forth; but still, and notwithstanding, I say the English railway service is better. Why? Because it's more human; it's more considerate. You aren't driven and urged to step lively and called at in loud, harsh voices and made to feel that you are being tolerated aboard something that was never made for you at all, but for the employees of the company. In England the trains are run for the people, not the people for the trains. And now that I have that one distinct difference between England and America properly emphasized I feel much better.

CHAPTER V
THE RIDE TO LONDON

AT last the train was started and we were off. The track was not so wide, if I am not mistaken, as ours, and the little freight or goods cars were positively ridiculous—mere wheelbarrows, by comparison with the American type. As for the passenger cars, when I came to examine them, they reminded me of some of our fine street cars that run from, say Schenectady to Gloversville, or from Muncie to Marion, Indiana. They were the first-class cars, too—the English Pullmans! The train started out briskly and you could feel that it did not have the powerful weight to it which the American train has. An American Pullman creaks audibly, just as a great ship does when it begins to move. An American engine begins to pull slowly because it has something to pull—like a team with a heavy load. I didn't feel that I was in a train half so much as I did that I was in a string of baby carriages.

Miss X. and her lover, Miss E. and her maid, Barfleur and I comfortably filled one little compartment; and now we were actually moving, and I began to look out at once to see what English scenery was really like. It was not at all strange to me, for in books and pictures I had seen it all my life. But here were the actual hills and valleys, the actual thatched cottages, and the actual castles or moors or lovely country vistas, and I was seeing them!

As I think of it now I can never be quite sufficiently grateful to Barfleur for a certain affectionate, thoughtful, sympathetic regard for my every possible mood on this occasion. This was my first trip to this England of which, of course, he was intensely proud. He was so humanly anxious that I should not miss any of its charms or, if need be, defects. He wanted me to be able to judge it fairly and humanly and to see the eventual result sieved through my temperament. The soul of attention; the soul of courtesy; patient, long-suffering, humane, gentle. How I have tried the patience of that man at times! An iron mood he has on occasion; a stoic one, always. Gentle, even, smiling, living a rule and a standard. Every thought of him produces a grateful smile. Yet he has his defects—plenty of them. Here he was at my elbow, all the way to London, momentarily suggesting that I should not miss the point, whatever the point might be, at the moment. He was helpful, really interested, and above all and at all times, warmly human.

We had been just two hours getting from the boat to the train. It was three-thirty when the train began to move, and from the lovely misty sunshine of the morning the sky had become overcast with low, gray—almost black—rain clouds. I looked at the hills and valleys. They told me we were in Wales. And, curiously, as we sped along first came Wordsworth into my mind, and then Thomas Hardy. I thought of Wordsworth first because these smooth, kempt hills, wet with the rain and static with deep gray shadows, suggested him. England owes so much to William Wordsworth, I think. So far as I can see, he epitomized in his verses this sweet, simple hominess that tugs at the heart-strings like some old call that one has heard before. My father was a German, my mother of Pennsylvania Dutch extraction, and yet there is a pull here in this Shakespearian-Wordsworthian-Hardyesque world which is precisely like the call of a tender mother to a child. I can't resist it. I love it; and I am not English but radically American.

I understand that Hardy is not so well thought of in England as he might be—that, somehow, some large conservative class thinks that his books are immoral or destructive. I should say the English would better make much of Thomas Hardy while he is alive. He is one of their great traditions. His works are beautiful. The spirit of all the things he has done or attempted is lovely. He is a master mind, simple, noble, dignified, serene. He is as fine as any of the English cathedrals. St. Paul's or Canterbury has no more significance to me than Thomas Hardy. I saw St. Paul's. I wish I could see the spirit of Thomas Hardy indicated in some such definite way. And yet I do not. Monuments do not indicate great men. But the fields and valleys of a country suggest them.

At twenty or thirty miles from Fishguard we came to some open water—an arm of the sea, I understood—the Bay of Bristol, where boats were, and tall, rain-gutted hills that looked like tumbled-down castles. Then came more open country—moorland, I suppose—with some sheep, once a flock of black ones; and then the lovely alternating hues of this rain-washed world. The water under these dark clouds took on a peculiar luster. It looked at times like burnished steel—at times like muddy lead. I felt my heart leap up as I thought of our own George Inness and what he would have done with these scenes and what the English Turner has done, though he preferred, as a rule, another key.

At four-thirty one of the charming English trainmen came and asked if we would have tea in the dining-car. We would. We arose and in a few moments were entering one of those dainty little basket cars. The tables were covered with white linen and simple, pretty china and a silver tea-service. It wasn't as if you were traveling at all. I felt as though I were stopping at the house of a friend; or as though I were in the cozy corner of some well-known and friendly inn. Tea was served. We ate toast and talked cheerfully.

This whole trip—the landscape, the dining-car, this cozy tea, Miss X. and her lover, Miss E. and Barfleur—finally enveloped my emotional fancy like a dream. I realized that I was experiencing a novel situation which would not soon come again. The idea of this pretty mistress coming to England to join her lover, and so frankly admitting her history and her purpose, rather took my mind as an intellectual treat. You really don't often get to see this sort of thing. I don't. It's Gallic in its flavor, to me. Barfleur, being a man of the world, took it as a matter of course—his sole idea being, I fancy, that the refinement of personality and thought involved in the situation were sufficient to permit him to tolerate it. I always judge his emotion by that one gleaming eye behind the monocle. The other does not take my attention so much. I knew from his attitude that ethics and morals and things like that had nothing to do with his selection of what he would consider interesting personal companionship. Were they interesting? Could they tell him something new? Would they amuse him? Were they nice—socially, in their clothing, in their manners, in the hundred little material refinements which make up a fashionable lady or gentleman? If so, welcome. If not, hence. And talent! Oh, yes, he had a keen eye for talent. And he loves the exceptional and will obviously do anything and everything within his power to foster it.

Having started so late, it grew nearly dark after tea and the distant landscapes were not so easy to descry. We came presently, in the mist, to a place called Carmarthen, I think, where were great black stacks and flaming forges and lights burning wistfully in the dark; and then to another similar place, Swansea, and finally to a third, Cardiff—great centers of manufacture, I should judge, for there were flaming lights from forges (great, golden gleams from open furnaces) and dark blue smoke, visible even at this hour, from tall stacks overhead, and gleaming electric lights like bright, lucent diamonds.

I never see this sort of place but I think of Pittsburgh and Youngstown and the coke ovens of western Pennsylvania along the line of the Pennsylvania Railroad. I shall never forget the first time I saw Pittsburgh and Youngstown and saw how coke was fired. It was on my way to New York. I had never seen any mountains before and suddenly, after the low, flat plains of Indiana and Ohio, with their pretty little wooden villages so suggestive of the new life of the New World, we rushed into Youngstown and then the mountains of western Pennsylvania (the Alleghanies). It was somewhat like this night coming from Fishguard, only it was not so rainy. The hills rose tall and green; the forge stacks of Pittsburgh flamed with a red gleam, mile after mile, until I thought it was the most wonderful sight I had ever seen. And then came the coke ovens, beyond Pittsburgh mile after mile of them, glowing ruddily down in the low valleys between the tall hills, where our train was following a stream-bed. It seemed a great, sad, heroic thing then, to me,—plain day labor. Those common, ignorant men, working before flaming forges, stripped to the waist in some instances, fascinated my imagination. I have always marveled at the inequalities of nature—the way it will give one man a low brow and a narrow mind, a narrow round of thought, and make a slave or horse of him, and another a light, nimble mind, a quick wit and air and make a gentleman of him. No human being can solve either the question of ability or utility. Is your gentleman useful? Yes and no, perhaps. Is your laborer useful? Yes and no, perhaps. I should say obviously yes. But see the differences in the reward of labor—physical labor. One eats his hard-earned crust in the sweat of his face; the other picks at his surfeit of courses and wonders why this or that doesn't taste better. I did not make my mind. I did not make my art. I cannot choose my taste except by predestined instinct, and yet here I am sitting in a comfortable English home, as I write, commiserating the poor working man. I indict nature here and now, as I always do and always shall do, as being aimless, pointless, unfair, unjust. I see in the whole thing no scheme but an accidental one—no justice save accidental justice. Now and then, in a way, some justice is done, but it is accidental; no individual man seems to will it. He can't. He doesn't know how. He can't think how. And there's an end of it.

But these queer, weird, hard, sad, drab manufacturing cities—what great writer has yet sung the song of them? Truly I do not recall one at present clearly. Dickens gives some suggestion of what he considered the misery of the poor; and in "Les Miserables" there is a touch of grim poverty and want here and there. But this is something still different. This is creative toil on a vast scale, and it is a lean, hungry, savage, animal to contemplate. I know it is because I have studied personally Fall River, Patterson and Pittsburgh, and I know what I'm talking about. Life runs at a gaunt level in those places. It's a rough, hurtling world of fact. I suppose it is not any different in England. I looked at the manufacturing towns as we flashed by in the night and got the same feeling of sad commiseration and unrest. The homes looked poor and they had a deadly sameness; the streets were narrow and poorly lighted. I was eager to walk over one of these towns foot by foot. I have the feeling that the poor and the ignorant and the savage are somehow great artistically. I have always had it. Millet saw it when he painted "The Man with the Hoe." These drab towns are grimly wonderful to me. They sing a great diapason of misery. I feel hunger and misery there; I feel lust and murder and life, sick of itself, stewing in its own juice; I feel women struck in the face by brutal men; and sodden lives too low and weak to be roused by any storm of woe. I fancy there are hungry babies and dying mothers and indifferent bosses and noble directors somewhere, not caring, not knowing, not being able to do anything about it, perhaps, if they did. I could weep just at the sight of a large, drab, hungry manufacturing town. I feel sorry for ignorant humanity. I wish I knew how to raise the low foreheads; to put the clear light of intellect into sad, sodden eyes. I wish there weren't any blows, any hunger, any tears. I wish people didn't have to long bitterly for just the little thin, bare necessities of this world. But I know, also, that life wouldn't be as vastly dramatic and marvelous without them. Perhaps I'm wrong. I've seen some real longing in my time, though. I've longed myself and I've seen others die longing.

Between Carmarthen and Cardiff and some other places where this drab, hungry world seemed to stick its face into the window, I listened to much conversation about the joyous side of living in Paris, Monte Carlo, Ostend and elsewhere. I remember once I turned from the contemplation of a dark, sad, shabby world scuttling by in the night and rain to hear Miss E. telling of some Parisian music-hall favorite—I'll call her Carmen—rivaling another Parisian music-hall favorite by the name of Diane, let us say, at Monte Carlo. Of course it is understood that they were women of loose virtue. Of course it is understood that they had fine, white, fascinating bodies and lovely faces and that they were physically ideal. Of course it is understood that they were marvelous mistresses and that money was flowing freely from some source or other—perhaps from factory worlds like these—to let them work their idle, sweet wills. Anyhow they were gambling, racing, disporting themselves at Monte Carlo and all at once they decided to rival each other in dress. Or perhaps it was that they didn't decide to, but just began to, which is much more natural and human.

As I caught it, with my nose pressed to the carriage window and the sight of rain and mist in my eyes, Carmen would come down one night in splendid white silk, perhaps, her bare arms and perfect neck and hair flashing priceless jewels; and then the fair Diane would arrive a little later with her body equally beautifully arrayed in some gorgeous material, her white arms and neck and hair equally resplendent. Then the next night the gowns would be of still more marvelous material and artistry, and more jewels—every night lovelier gowns and more costly jewels, until one of these women took all her jewels, to the extent of millions of francs, I presume, and, arraying her maid gorgeously, put all the jewels on her and sent her into the casino or the ballroom or the dining-room—wherever it was—and she herself followed, in—let us hope—plain, jewelless black silk, with her lovely flesh showing voluptuously against it. And the other lady was there, oh, much to her chagrin and despair now, of course, decked with all her own splendid jewels to the extent of an equally large number of millions of francs, and so the rivalry was ended.

It was a very pretty story of pride and vanity and I liked it. But just at this interesting moment, one of those great blast furnaces, which I have been telling you about and which seemed to stretch for miles beside the track, flashed past in the night, its open red furnace doors looking like rubies, and the frosted windows of its lighted shops looking like opals, and the fluttering street lamps and glittering arc lights looking like pearls and diamonds; and I said: behold! these are the only jewels of the poor and from these come the others. And to a certain extent, in the last analysis and barring that unearned gift of brain which some have without asking and others have not at all, so they do.

It was seven or eight when we reached Paddington. For one moment, when I stepped out of the car, the thought came to me with a tingle of vanity—I have come by land and sea, three thousand miles to London! Then it was gone again. It was strange—this scene. I recognized at once the various London types caricatured in *Punch*, and *Pick Me Up*, and *The Sketch*, and elsewhere. I saw a world of cabs and 'busses, of porters, gentlemen, policemen, and citizens generally. I saw characters—strange ones—that brought back Dickens and Du Maurier and W. W. Jacobs. The words "Booking Office" and the typical London policeman took my eye. I strolled about, watching the crowd till it was time for us to board our train for the country; and eagerly I nosed about, trying to sense London from this vague, noisy touch of it. I can't indicate how the peculiar-looking trains made me feel. Humanity is so very different in so many little unessential things—so utterly the same in all the large ones. I could see that it might be just as well or better to call a ticket office a booking office; or to have three classes of carriages instead of two, as with us; or to have carriages instead of cars; or trams instead of street railways; or lifts instead of elevators. What difference does it make? Life is the same old thing. Nevertheless there was a tremendous difference between the London and the New York atmosphere—that I could see and feel.

"A few days at my place in the country will be just the thing for you," Barfleur was saying. "I sent a wireless to Dora to have a fire in the hall and in your room. You might as well see a bit of rural England first."

He gleamed on me with his monocled eye in a very encouraging manner.

We waited about quite awhile for a local or suburban which would take us to Bridgely Level, and having ensconced ourselves first class—as fitting my arrival—Barfleur fell promptly to sleep and I mused with my window open, enjoying the country and the cool night air.

CHAPTER VI
THE BARFLEUR FAMILY

I AM writing these notes on Tuesday, November twenty-eighth, very close to a grate fire in a pretty little sitting-room in an English country house about twenty-five miles from London, and I am very chilly.

We reached this place by some winding road, inscrutable in the night, and I wondered keenly what sort of an atmosphere it would have. The English suburban or country home of the better class has always been a concrete thought to me—rather charming on the whole. A carriage brought us, with all the bags and trunks carefully looked after (in England you always keep your luggage with you), and we were met in the hall by the maid who took our coats and hats and brought us something to drink. There was a small fire glowing in the fireplace in the entrance hall, but it was so small—cheerful though it was—that I wondered why Barfleur had taken all the trouble to send a wireless from the sea to have it there. It seems it is a custom, in so far as his house is concerned, not to have it. But having heard something of English fires and English ideas of warmth, I was not greatly surprised.

"I am going to be cold," I said to myself, at once. "I know it. The atmosphere is going to be cold and raw and I am going to suffer greatly. It will be the devil and all to write."

I fancy this is a very fair and pretty example of the average country home near London, and it certainly lacks none of the appointments which might be considered worthy of a comfortable home; but it is as cold as a sepulcher, and I can't understand the evolved system of procedure which has brought about any such uncomfortable state and maintains it as satisfactory. These Britons are actually warm when the temperature in the room is somewhere between forty-five and fifty and they go about opening doors and windows with the idea that the rooms need additional airing. They build you small, weak coal fires in large, handsome fireplaces, and then if the four or five coals huddled together are managing to keep themselves warm by glowing, they tell you that everything is all right (or stroll about, at least, looking as though it were). Doors are left open; the casement windows flung out, everything done to give the place air and draughtiness.

"Now," said my host, with his usual directness of speech, as I stood with my back to the hall fireplace, "I think it is best that you should go to bed at once and get a good night's rest. In the morning you shall have your breakfast at whatever hour you say. Your bath will be brought you a half or three-quarters of an hour before you appear at table, so that you will have ample time to shave and dress. I shall be here until eleven-fifteen to see how you are getting along, after which I shall go to the city. You shall have a table here, or wherever you like, and the maid will serve your luncheon punctually at two o'clock. At half past four your tea will be brought to you, in case you are here. In the evening we dine at seven-thirty. I shall be down on the five fifty-two train."

So he proceeded definitely to lay out my life for me and I had to smile. "That vast established order which is England," I thought again. He accompanied me to my chamber door, or rather to the foot of the stairs. There he wished me pleasant dreams. "And remember," he cautioned me with the emphasis of one who has forgotten something of great consequence, "this is most important. Whatever you do, don't forget to put out your boots for the maid to take and have blacked. Otherwise you will disrupt the whole social procedure of England."

It is curious—this feeling of being quite alone for the first time in a strange land. I began to unpack my bags, solemnly thinking of New York. Presently I went to the window and looked out. One or two small lights burned afar off. I undressed and got into bed, feeling anything but sleepy. I lay and watched the fire flickering on the hearth. So this was really England, and here I was at last—a fact absolutely of no significance to any one else in the world, but very important to me. An old, old dream come true! And it had passed so oddly—the trip—so almost unconsciously, as it were. We make a great fuss, I thought, about the past and the future, but the actual moment is so often without meaning. Finally, after hearing a rooster crow and thinking of Hamlet's father—his ghost—and the chill that invests the thought of cock-crow in that tragedy, I slept.

* * * * *

Morning came and with it a knocking on the door. I called, "Come in." In came the maid, neat, cleanly, rosy-cheeked, bringing a large tin basin—very much wider than an American tub but not so deep—a large water can, full of hot water, towels and the like. She put the tub and water can down, drew a towel rack from the wall nearby, spread out the towels and left.

I did not hear her take the boots, but when I went to the door they were gone. In the afternoon they were back again, nice and bright. I speculated on all this as an interesting demonstration of English life. Barfleur is not so amazingly well-to-do, but he has all these things. It struck me as pleasing, soothing, orderly—quite the same thing I had been seeing on the train and the ship. It was all a part of that interesting national system which I had been hearing so much about.

At breakfast it was quite the same—a most orderly meal. Barfleur was there to breakfast with me and see that I was started right. His face was smiling. How did I like it? Was I comfortable? Had I slept well? Had I slept very well? It was bad weather, but I would rather have to expect that at this season of the year.

I can see his smiling face—a little cynical and disillusioned—get some faint revival of his own native interest in England in my surprise, curiosity and interest. The room was cold, but he did not seem to think so. No, no, no, it was very comfortable. I was simply not acclimated yet. I would get used to it.

This house was charming, I thought, and here at breakfast I was introduced to the children. Berenice Mary Barfleur, the only girl and the eldest child, looked to me at first a little pale and thin—quite peaked, in fact—but afterwards I found her not to be so—merely a temperamental objection on my part to a type which afterwards seemed to me very attractive. She was a decidedly wise, high-spoken, intellectual and cynical little maid. Although only eleven years of age she conversed with the air, the manner and the words of a woman of twenty.

"Oh, yes. Amáyreeka! Is that a nice place? Do you like it?"

I cannot in the least way convey the touch of lofty, well-bred feeling it had—quite the air and sound of a woman of twenty-five or thirty schooled in all the niceties of polite speech. "What a child," I thought. "She talks as though she were affected, but I can see that she is not." Quite different she seemed from what any American child could be—less vigorous, more intellectual, more spiritual; perhaps not so forceful but probably infinitely more subtle. She looked delicate, remote,

Burne-Jonesy—far removed from the more commonplace school of force we know—and I think I like our type better. I smiled at her and she seemed friendly enough, but there was none of that running forward and greeting people which is an average middle-class American habit. She was too well bred. I learned afterward, from a remark dropped at table by her concerning American children, that it was considered bad form. "American children are the kind that run around hotel foyers with big bows on their hair and speak to people," was the substance of it. I saw at once how bad American children were.

Well, then came the eldest boy, Percy Franklin Barfleur, who reminded me, at first glance, of that American caricature type—dear to the newspaper cartoonist—of Little Johnnie Bostonbeans. Here he was—"glawses," inquiring eyes, a bulging forehead, a learned air; and all at ten years, and somewhat undersized for his age—a clever child; sincere, apparently; rather earnest; eager to know, full of the light of youthful understanding. Like his sister, his manners were quite perfect but unstudied. He smiled and replied, "Quite well, thank you," to my amused inquiries after him. I could see he was bright and thoughtful, but the unconscious (though, to me, affected) quality of the English voice amused me here again. Then came Charles Gerard Barfleur, and James Herbert Barfleur, who impressed me in quite the same way as the others. They were nice, orderly children but English, oh, so English!

It was while walking in the garden after breakfast that I encountered James Herbert Barfleur, the youngest; but, in the confusion of meeting people generally, I did not recognize him. He was outside the coach house, where are the rooms of the gardener, and where my room is.

"And which little Barfleur might this be?" I asked genially, in that patronizing way we have with children.

"James Herbert Barfleur," he replied, with a gravity of pronunciation which quite took my breath away. We are not used to this formal dignity of approach in children of so very few years in America. This lad was only five years of age and he was talking to me in the educated voice of one of fifteen or sixteen. I stared, of course.

"You don't tell me," I replied. "And what is your sister's name, again?"

"Berenice Mary Barfleur," he replied.

"Dear, dear, dear," I sighed. "Now what do you know about that?"

Of course such a wild piece of American slang as that had no significance to him whatsoever. It fell on his ears without meaning.

"I don't know," he replied, interested in some fixture he was fastening to a toy bath tub.

"Isn't that a fine little bath tub you have," I ventured, eager to continue the conversation because of its novelty.

"It's a nice little bawth," he went on, "but I wouldn't call it a tub."

I really did not know how to reply to this last, it took me so by surprise;—a child of five, in little breeches scarcely larger than my two hands, making this fine distinction. "We surely live and learn," I thought, and went on my way smiling.

This house interested me from so many other points of view, being particularly English and new, that I was never weary of investigating it. I had a conversation with the gardener one morning concerning his duties and found that he had an exact schedule of procedure which covered every day in the year. First, I believe, he got hold of the boots, delivered to him by the maid, and did those; and then he brought up his coal and wood and built the fires; and then he had some steps and paths to look after; and then some errands to do, I forget what. There was the riding pony to curry and saddle, the stable to clean—oh, quite a long list of things which he did over and over, day after day. He talked with such an air of responsibility, as so many English servants do, that I was led to reflect upon the reliability of English servants in general; and he dropped his h's where they occurred, of course, and added them where they shouldn't have been. He told me how much he received, how much he had received, how he managed to live on it, how shiftless and irresponsible some people were.

"They don't know 'ow to get along, sir," he informed me with the same solemn air of responsibility. "They just doesn't know 'ow to manige, sir, I tyke it; some people doesn't, sir. They gets sixteen or highteen shillin's, the same as me, sir, but hawfter they goes and buys five or six g'uns (I thought he said guns—he actually said gallons) o' beer in the week, there hain't much left fer other things, is there, sir? Now that's no wy, sir, is it, sir? I hawsk you."

I had to smile at the rural accent. He was so simple minded—so innocent, apparently. Every one called him Wilkins—not Mr. Wilkins (as his colleagues might in America) or John or Jack or some sobriquet, but just Wilkins. He was Wilkins to every one—the master, the maid, the children. The maid was Dora to every one, and the nurse, Nana. It was all interesting to me because it was so utterly new.

And then this landscape round about; the feel of the country was refreshing. I knew absolutely nothing about it, and yet I could see and feel that we were in a region of comfortable suburban life. I could hear the popping of guns all day long, here—and thereabouts—this being the open season for shooting, not hunting, as my host informed me; there was no such thing as hunting hereabouts. I could see men strolling here and there together, guns under their arms, plaid caps on their heads, in knee breeches, and leather leggings. I could see, from my writing desk in the drawing-room window, clever-riding English girls bounding by on light-moving horses, and in my limited walks I saw plenty of comfortable-looking country places—suburban homes. I was told by a friend of mine that this was rather a pleasant country section, but that I might see considerable of the same thing anywhere about London at this distance.

"Dora" the maid interested me very much. She was so quiet, so silent and so pretty. The door would open, any time during the day when I was writing, and in she would come to look after the fire, to open or close the windows, to draw the curtains, light the candles and serve the tea, or to call me to luncheon or dinner. Usually I ate my luncheon and drank my four-o'clock tea alone. I ate my evening meal all alone once. It made no difference—my eating alone. The service was quite the same; the same candles were lighted—several brackets on different parts of the table; the fire built in the dining-room. There were four or five courses and wine. Dora stood behind me watching me eat in silence, and I confess I felt very queer. It was all so solemn, so stately. I felt like some old gray baron or bachelor shut away from the world and given to contemplating the follies of his youth. When through with nuts and wine—the final glass of port—it was the custom of the house to retire to the drawing-room and drink the small cup of black coffee which was served there. And on this night, although I was quite alone, it was the same. The coffee was served just as promptly and dignifiedly as though there were eight or ten present. It interested me greatly, all of it, and pleased me more than I can say.

Personally I shall always be glad that I saw some rural aspects of England first, for they are the most characterful and, to me, significant. London is an amazing city and thoroughly English, but the rural districts are more suggestive. In what respects do the people of one country differ from those of another, since they eat, sleep, rise, dress, go to work, return, love, hate, and aspire alike? In little—dynamically, mechanically speaking. But temperamentally, emotionally, spiritually and even materially they differ in almost every way. England is a mood, I take it, a combination of dull colors and atmosphere. It expresses heaven only knows what feeling for order, stability, uniformity, homeliness, simplicity. It is highly individual—more so almost than Italy, France or Germany. It is vital—and yet vital in an intellectual way only. You would say off-hand, sensing the feel of the air, that England is all mind with convictions, prejudices, notions, poetic longings terribly emphasized. The most egotistic nation in the world because, perhaps, the most forcefully intellectual.

How different is the very atmosphere of it from America. The great open common about this house smacked of English individuality, leisure, order, stratification—anything you will. The atmosphere was mistily damp, the sun at best a golden haze. All the bare trees were covered with a thin coating of almost spring-green moss. The ground was springy, dewy. Rooks were in the sky, the trees. Little red houses in the valleys, with combination flues done in quaint individual chimney pots send upward soft spirals of blue smoke. Laborers, their earth-colored trousers strapped just below the knees by a small leather strap, appeared ever and anon; housemaids, spick and span, with black dresses, white aprons, white laces in their hair, becoming streamers of linen made into large trig bows at their backs, appeared at some door or some window of almost every home. The sun glints into such orderly, well-dressed windows; the fields suspire such dewy fragrances. You can encounter hills of sheep, creaking wains, open common land of gorse and wild berries. My little master, smartly clad, dashes by on a pony; my young mistress looks becomingly gay and superior on a Shetland or a cob. A four-year-old has a long-eared white donkey to ride. That is England.

How shall it be said—how described? It is so delicate, so remote, so refined, so smooth, a pleasant land of great verse and great thought.

CHAPTER VII
A GLIMPSE OF LONDON

AFTER a few days I went to London for the first time—I do not count the night of my arrival, for I saw nothing but the railway terminus—and, I confess, I was not impressed as much as I might have been. I could not help thinking on this first morning, as we passed from Paddington, via Hyde Park, Marble Arch, Park Lane, Brook Street, Grosvenor Square, Berkeley Square, Piccadilly and other streets to Regent Street and the neighborhood of the Carlton Hotel, that it was beautiful, spacious, cleanly, dignified and well ordered, but not astonishingly imposing. Fortunately it was a bright and comfortable morning and the air was soft. There was a faint bluish haze over the city, which I took to be smoke; and certainly it smelled as though it were smoky. I had a sense of great life but not of crowded life, if I manage to make myself clear by that. It seemed to me at first blush as if the city might be so vast that no part was important. At every turn Barfleur, who was my ever-present monitor, was explaining, "Now this that we are coming to," or "This that we are passing," or "This is so and so;" and so we sped by interesting things, the city impressing me in a vague way but meaning very little at the moment. We must have passed through a long stretch of Piccadilly, for Barfleur pointed out a line of clubs, naming them—the St. James's Club, the Savile Club, the Lyceum Club, and then St. James's Palace.

I was duly impressed. I was seeing things which, after all, I thought, did not depend so much upon their exterior beauty or vast presence as upon the import of their lineage and connections. They were beautiful in a low, dark way, and certainly they were tinged with an atmosphere of age and respectability. After all, since life is a figment of the brain, built-up notions of things are really far more impressive in many cases than the things themselves. London is a fanfare of great names; it is a clatter of vast reputations; it is a swirl of memories and celebrated beauties and orders and distinctions. It is almost impossible any more to disassociate the real from the fictitious or, better, spiritual. There is something here which is not of brick and stone at all, but which is purely a matter of thought. It is disembodied poetry; noble ideas; delicious memories of great things; and these, after all, are better than brick and stone.

The city is low—universally not more than five stories high, often not more than two, but it is beautiful. And it alternates great spaces with narrow crevices in such a way as to give a splendid variety. You can have at once a sense of being very crowded and of being very free. I can understand now Browning's desire to include "poor old Camberwell" with Italy in the confines of romance.

The thing that struck me most in so brief a survey—we were surely not more than twenty minutes in reaching our destination—was that the buildings were largely a golden yellow in color, quite as if they had been white and time had stained them. Many other buildings looked as though they had been black originally and had been daubed white in spots. The truth is that it was quite the other way about. They had been snow white and had been sooted by the smoke until they were now nearly coal black. And only here and there had the wind and rain whipped bare white places which looked like scars or the drippings of lime. At first I thought, "How wretched." Later I thought, "This effect is charming."

We are so used to the new and shiny and tall in America, particularly in our larger cities, that it is very hard at first to estimate a city of equal or greater rank, which is old and low and, to a certain extent, smoky. In places there was more beauty, more surety, more dignity, more space than most of our cities have to offer. The police had an air of dignity and intelligence such as I have never seen anywhere in America. The streets were beautifully swept and clean; and I saw soldiers here and there in fine uniforms, standing outside palaces and walking in the public ways. That alone was sufficient to differentiate London from any American city. We rarely see our soldiers. They are too few. I think what I felt most of all was that I could not feel anything very definite about so great a city and that there was no use trying.

We were soon at the bank where I was to have my American order for money cashed; and then, after a short walk in a narrow street, we were at the office of Barfleur, where I caught my first glimpse of an English business house. It was very different from an American house of the same kind, for it was in an old and dark building of not more than four stories—and set down in a narrow angle off the Strand and lighted by small lead-paned windows, which in America would smack strongly of Revolutionary days. In fact we have scarcely any such buildings left. Barfleur's private offices were on the second floor, up a small dingy staircase, and the room itself was so small that it surprised me by its coziness. I could not call it dingy. It was quaint rather, Georgian in its atmosphere, with a small open fire glowing in one corner, a great rolltop desk entirely out of keeping with the place in another, a table, a book-case, a number of photographs of celebrities framed, and the rest books. I think he apologized for, or explained the difference between, this and the average American business house, but I do not think explanations are in order. London is London. I should be sorry if it were exactly like New York, as it may yet become. The smallness and quaintness appealed to me as a fit atmosphere for a healthy business.

I should say here that this preliminary trip to London from Bridgely Level, so far as Barfleur was concerned, was intended to accomplish three things: first, to give me a preliminary glimpse of London; second, to see that I was measured and examined for certain articles of clothing in which I was, according to Barfleur, woefully lacking; and third, to see that I attended the concert of a certain Austrian singer whose singing he thought I might enjoy. It was most important that I should go, because he had to go; and since all that I did or could do was merely grist for my mill, I was delighted to accompany him.

Barfleur in many respects, I wish to repeat here, is one of the most delightful persons in the world. He is a sort of modern Beau Brummel with literary, artistic and gormandizing leanings. He loves order and refinement, of course,—things in their proper ways and places—as he loves life. I suspect him at times of being somewhat of a martinet in home and office matters; but I am by no means sure that I am not doing him a grave injustice. A more even, complaisant, well-mannered and stoical soul, who manages to get his way in some fashion or other, if it takes him years to do it, I never met. He surely has the patience of fate and, I think, the true charity of a great heart. Now before I could be properly presented in London and elsewhere I needed a long list of things. So this morning I had much shopping to attend to.

Since the matter of English and American money had been troubling me from the moment I reached that stage on my voyage where I began to pay for things out of my own pocket to the ship's servants, I began complaining of my difficulties now. I couldn't figure out the tips to my own satisfaction and this irritated me. I remember urging Barfleur to make the whole matter clear to me, which he did later. He gave me a typewritten statement as to the relative value of the various pieces and what tips I should pay and how and when at hotels and country houses, and this I followed religiously. Here it is:

In leaving the hotel to-morrow, give the following tips:	
Maid	3/-
Valet	3/-
Gold Braid	1/-
Porter (who looks after telephone)	1/-
Outside Man (Doorman)	1/-

If you reckon at a hotel to give 9d. a day to the maid and the valet, with a minimum of 1/-, you will be doing handsomely. On a visit, on the supposition that they have only maids, give the two maids whom you are likely to come across 2/6 each, when you come away on Monday. (I am speaking of weekends.) Longer periods should be figured at 9d. a day. If, on the other hand, it is a large establishment—butler and footman—you would have to give the butler 10/- and the footman 5/- for a week-end; for longer periods more.

I cannot imagine anything more interesting than being introduced as I was by Barfleur to the social character of London. He was so intelligent and so very nice about it all. "Now, first," he said, "we will get your glasses mended; and then you want a traveling bag; and then some ties and socks, and so on. I have an appointment with you at your tailor's at eleven o'clock, where you are to be measured for your waistcoats, and at eleven-thirty at your furrier's, where you are to be measured for your fur coat," and so on and so forth. "Well, come along. We'll be off."

I have to smile when I think of it, for I, of all people, am the least given to this matter of proper dressing and self-presentation, and Barfleur, within reasonable limits, represents the other extreme. To him, as I have said, these things are exceedingly important. The delicate manner in which he indicated and urged me into getting the things which would be all right, without openly insisting on them, was most pleasing. "In England, you know," he would hint, "it isn't quite good form to wear a heavy striped tie with a frock coat—never a straight black; and we never tie them in that fashion—always a simple knot." My socks had to be striped for morning wear and my collars winged, else I was in very bad form indeed. I fell into the habit of asking, "What now?"

London streets and shops as I first saw them interested me greatly. I saw at once more uniforms than one would ordinarily see in New York, and more high hats and, presumably,—I could not tell for the overcoats—cutaway coats. The uniforms were of mail-men, porters, messenger-boys and soldiers; and all being different from what I had been accustomed to, they interested me—the mail-men particularly, with a service helmet cut square off at the top; and the little messenger boys, with their tambourine caps cocked joyously over one ear, amused me; the policeman's helmet strap under his chin was new and diverting.

In the stores the clerks first attracted my attention, but I may say the stores and shops themselves, after New York, seemed small and old. New York is so new; the space given to the more important shops is so considerable. In London it struck me that the space was not much and that the woodwork and walls were dingy. One can tell by the feel of a place whether it is exceptional and profitable, and all of these were that; but they were dingy. The English clerk, too, had an air of civility, I had almost said servility, which was different. They looked to me like individuals born to a condition and a point of view; and I think they are. In America any clerk may subsequently be anything he chooses (ability guaranteed), but I'm not so sure that this is true in England. Anyhow, the American clerk always looks his possibilities—his problematic future; the English clerk looks as if he were to be one indefinitely.

We were through with this round by one o'clock, and Barfleur explained that we would go to a certain very well-known hotel grill.

The hotel, after its fashion—the grill—was a distinct blow. I had fancied that I was going to see something on the order of the luxurious new hotel in New York—certainly as resplendent, let us say, as our hotels of the lower first class. Not so. It could be compared, and I think fairly so, only to our hotels of the second or third class. There was the same air of age here that there was about our old but very excellent hotels in New York. The woodwork was plain, the decorations simple.

As for the crowd, well, Barfleur stated that it might be smart and it might not. Certain publishers, rich Jewish merchants, a few actors and some Americans would probably be here. This grill was affected by the foreign element. The *maître d'hôtel* was French, of course—a short, fat, black-whiskered man who amused me by his urbanity. The waiters were, I believe, German, as they are largely in London and elsewhere in England. One might almost imagine Germany intended invading England via its waiters. The china and plate were simple and inexpensive, almost poor. A great hotel can afford to be simple. We had what we would have had at any good French restaurant, and the crowd was rather commonplace-looking to me. Several American girls came in and they were good-looking, smart but silly. I cannot say that I was impressed at all, and my subsequent experiences confirm that feeling. I am inclined to think that London hasn't one hotel of the material splendor of the great new hotels in New York. But let that go for the present.

While we were sipping coffee Barfleur told me of a Mrs. W., a friend of his whom I was to meet. She was, he said, a lion-hunter. She tried to make her somewhat interesting personality felt in so large a sea as London by taking up with promising talent before it was already a commonplace. I believe it was arranged over the 'phone then that I should lunch there—at Mrs. W.'s—the following day at one and be introduced to a certain Lady R., who was known as a patron of the arts, and a certain Miss H., an interesting English type. I was pleased with the idea of going. I had never seen an English lady lion-hunter. I had never met English ladies of the types of Lady R. and Miss H. There might be others present. I was also informed that Mrs. W. was really not English but Danish; but she and her husband, who was also Danish and a wealthy broker, had resided in London so long that they were to all intents and purposes English, and in addition to being rich they were in rather interesting standing socially.

After luncheon we went to hear a certain Miss T., an Austrian of about thirty years of age, sing at some important hall in London—Bechstein Hall, I believe it was,—and on the way I was told something of her. It seemed that she was very promising—a great success in Germany and elsewhere as a concert-singer—and that she might be coming to America at some time or other. Barfleur had known her in Paris. He seemed to think I would like her. We went and I heard a very lovely set of songs—oh, quite delightful, rendered in a warm, sympathetic, enthusiastic manner, and representing the most characteristic type of German love sentiment. It is a peculiar sentiment—tender, wistful, smacking of the sun at evening and lovely water on which the moon is shining. German sentiment verges on the mushy—is always close to tears—but anything more expressive of a certain phase of life I do not know.

Miss T. sang forcefully, joyously, vigorously, and I wished sincerely to meet her and tell her so; but that was not to be, then.

As we made our way to Paddington Barfleur, brisk and smiling, asked:

"Were you amused?"

"Quite."

"Well, then this afternoon was not wasted. I shall always be satisfied if you are amused."

I smiled, and we rode sleepily back to Bridgely Level to dine and thence to bed.

CHAPTER VIII
A LONDON DRAWING-ROOM

I RECALL the next day, Sunday, with as much interest as any date, for on that day at one-thirty I encountered my first London drawing-room. I recall now as a part of this fortunate adventure that we had been talking of a new development in French art, which Barfleur approved in part and disapproved in part—the Post-Impressionists; and there was mention also of the Cubists—a still more radical departure from conventional forms, in which, if my impressions are correct, the artist passes from any attempt at transcribing the visible scene and becomes wholly geometric, metaphysical and symbolic.

When I reached the house of Mrs. W., which was in one of those lovely squares that constitute such a striking feature of the West End, I was ushered upstairs to the drawing-room, where I found my host, a rather practical, shrewd-looking Dane, and his less obviously Danish wife.

"Oh, Mr. Der*ri*zer," exclaimed my hostess on sight, as she came forward to greet me, a decidedly engaging woman of something over forty, with bronze hair and ruddy complexion. Her gown of green silk, cut after the latest mode, stamped her in my mind as of a romantic, artistic, eager disposition.

"You must come and tell us at once what you think of the picture we are discussing. It is downstairs. Lady R. is there and Miss H. We are trying to see if we can get a better light on it. Mr. Barfleur has told me of you. You are from America. You must tell us how you like London, after you see the Degas."

I think I liked this lady thoroughly at a glance and felt at home with her, for I know the type. It is the mobile, artistic type, with not much practical judgment in great matters, but bubbling with enthusiasm, temperament, life.

"Certainly—delighted. I know too little of London to talk of it. I shall be interested in your picture."

We had reached the main floor by this time.

"Mr. Der*ri*zer, the Lady R."

A modern suggestion of the fair Jahane, tall, astonishingly lissom, done—as to clothes—after the best manner of the romanticists—such was the Lady R. A more fascinating type—from the point of view of stagecraft—I never saw. And the languor and lofty elevation of her gestures and eyebrows defy description. She could say, "Oh, I am so weary of all this," with a slight elevation of her eyebrows a hundred times more definitely and forcefully than if it had been shouted in stentorian tones through a megaphone.

She gave me the fingers of an archly poised hand.

"It is a pleasure!"

"And Miss H., Mr. Der*riz*er."

"I am very pleased!"

A pink, slim lily of a woman, say twenty-eight or thirty, very fragile-seeming, very Dresden-china-like as to color, a dream of light and Tyrian blue with some white interwoven, very keen as to eye, the perfection of hauteur as to manner, so well-bred that her voice seemed subtly suggestive of it all—that was Miss H.

To say that I was interested in this company is putting it mildly. The three women were so distinct, so individual, so characteristic, each in a different way. The Lady R. was all peace and repose—statuesque, weary, dark. Miss H. was like a ray of sunshine, pure morning light, delicate, gay, mobile. Mrs. W. was of thicker texture, redder blood, more human fire. She had a vigor past the comprehension of either, if not their subtlety of intellect—which latter is often so much better.

Mr. W. stood in the background, a short, stocky gentleman, a little bored by the trivialities of the social world.

"Ah, yes. Daygah! You like Daygah, no doubt," interpolated Mrs. W., recalling us. "A lovely pigture, don't you think? Such color! such depth! such sympathy of treatment! Oh!"

Mrs. W.'s hands were up in a pretty artistic gesture of delight.

"Oh, yes," continued the Lady R., taking up the rapture. "It is saw human—saw perfect in its harmony. The hair—it is divine! And the poor man! he lives alone now, in Paris, quite dreary, not seeing any one. Aw, the tragedy of it! The tragedy of it!" A delicately carved vanity-box she carried, of some odd workmanship—blue and white enamel, with points of coral in it—was lifted in one hand as expressing her great distress. I confess I was not much moved and I looked quickly at Miss H. Her eyes, it seemed to me, held a subtle, apprehending twinkle.

"And you!" It was Mrs. W. addressing me.

"It is impressive, I think. I do not know as much of his work as I might, I am sorry to say."

"Ah, he is marvelous, wonderful! I am transported by the beauty and the depth of it all!" It was Mrs. W. talking and I could not help rejoicing in the quality of her accent. Nothing is so pleasing to me in a woman of culture and refinement as that additional tang of remoteness which a foreign accent lends. If only all the lovely, cultured women of the world could speak with a foreign accent in their native tongue I would like it better. It lends a touch of piquancy not otherwise obtainable.

Our luncheon party was complete now and we would probably have gone immediately into the dining-room except for another picture—by Piccasso. Let me repeat here that before Barfleur called my attention to Piccasso's cubical uncertainty in the London Exhibition, I had never heard of him. Here in a dark corner of the room was the nude torso of a consumptive girl, her ribs showing, her cheeks colorless and sunken, her nose a wasted point, her eyes as hungry and sharp and lustrous as those of a bird. Her hair was really no hair—strings. And her thin bony arms and shoulders were pathetic, decidedly morbid in their quality. To add to the morgue-like aspect of the composition, the picture was painted in a pale bluish-green key.

I wish to state here that now, after some little lapse of time, this conception—the thought and execution of it—is growing upon me. I am not sure that this work which has rather haunted me is not much more than a protest—the expression and realization of a great temperament. But at the moment it struck me as dreary, gruesome, decadent, and I said as much when asked for my impression.

"Gloomy! Morbid!" Mrs. W. fired in her quite lovely accent. "What has that to do with art?"

"Luncheon is served, Madam!"

The double doors of the dining-room were flung open.

I found myself sitting between Mrs. W. and Miss H.

"I was so glad to hear you say you didn't like it," Miss H. applauded, her eyes sparkling, her lip moving with a delicate little smile. "You know, I abhor those things. They *are* decadent like the rest of France and England. We are going backward instead of forward—I am quite sure. We have not the force we once had. It is all a race after pleasure and living and an interest in subjects of that kind. I am quite sure it isn't healthy, normal art. I am sure life is better and brighter than that."

"I am inclined to think so, at times, myself," I replied.

We talked further and I learned to my surprise that she suspected England to be decadent as a whole, falling behind in brain, brawn and spirit and that she thought America was much better.

"Do you know," she observed, "I really think it would be a very good thing for us if we were conquered by Germany."

I had found here, I fancied, some one who was really thinking for herself and a very charming young lady in the bargain. She was quick, apprehensive, all for a heartier point of view. I am not sure now that she was not merely being nice to me, and that anyhow she is not all wrong, and that the heartier point of view is the courage which can front life unashamed; which sees the divinity of fact and of beauty in the utmost seeming tragedy. Piccasso's grim presentation of decay and degradation is beginning to teach me something—the marvelous perfection of the spirit which is concerned with neither perfection, nor decay, but life. It haunts me.

The charming luncheon was quickly over and I think I gathered a very clear impression of the status of my host and hostess from their surroundings. Mr. W. was evidently liberal in his understanding of what constitutes a satisfactory home. It was not exceptional in that it differed greatly from the prevailing standard of luxury. But assuredly it was all in sharp contrast to Piccasso's grim representation of life and Degas's revolutionary opposition to conventional standards.

"I like it," he pronounced. "The note is somber, but it is excellent work"

Another man now made his appearance—an artist. I shall not forget him soon, for you do not often meet people who have the courage to appear at Sunday afternoons in a shabby workaday business suit, unpolished shoes, a green neckerchief in lieu of collar and tie, and cuffless sleeves. I admired the quality, the workmanship of the silver-set scarab which held his green linen neckerchief together, but I was a little puzzled as to whether he was very poor and his presence insisted upon, or comfortably progressive and indifferent to conventional dress. His face and body were quite thin; his hands delicate. He had an apprehensive eye that rarely met one's direct gaze.

"Do you think art really needs that?" Miss H. asked me. She was alluding to the green linen handkerchief.

"I admire the courage. It is at least individual."

"It is after George Bernard Shaw. It has been done before," replied Miss H.

"Then it requires almost more courage," I replied.

Here Mrs. W. moved the sad excerpt from the morgue to the center of the room that he of the green neckerchief might gaze at it.

"I like it," he pronounced. "The note is somber, but it is excellent work."

Then he took his departure with interesting abruptness. Soon the Lady R. was extending her hand in an almost pathetic farewell. Her voice was lofty, sad, sustained. I wish I could describe it. There was just a suggestion of Lady Macbeth in the sleep-walking scene. As she made her slow, graceful exit I wanted to applaud loudly.

Mrs. W. turned to me as the nearest source of interest and I realized with horror that she was going to fling her Piccasso at my head again and with as much haste as was decent I, too, took my leave.

CHAPTER IX
CALLS

IT was one evening shortly after I had lunched with Mrs. W. that Barfleur and I dined with Miss E., the young actress who had come over on the steamer with us. It was interesting to find her in her own rather smart London quarters surrounded by maid and cook, and with male figures of the usual ornamental sort in the immediate background. One of them was a ruddy, handsome, slightly corpulent French count of manners the pink of perfection. He looked for all the world like the French counts introduced into American musical comedy,—just the right type of collar about his neck, the perfect shoe, the close-fitting, well-tailored suit, the mustachios and hair barbered to the last touch. He was charming, too, in his easy, gracious aloofness, saying only the few things that would be of momentary interest and pressing nothing.

Miss E. had prepared an appetizing luncheon. She had managed to collect a group of interesting people—a Mr. T., for instance, whose *bête noire* was clergymen and who stood prepared by collected newspaper clippings and court proceedings, gathered over a period of years, to prove that all ecclesiastics were scoundrels. He had, as he insisted, amazing data, showing that the most perverted of all English criminals were usually sons of bishops and that the higher you rose in the scale of hieratic authority the worse were the men in charge. The delightful part of it all was the man's profound seriousness of manner, a thin, magnetic, albeit candle-waxy type of person of about sixty-five who had the force and enthusiasm of a boy.

"Ah, yes," you would hear him exclaim often during lunch, "I know him well. A greater scoundrel never lived. His father is bishop of Wimbledon"—or, for variation—"his father was once rector of Christ Church, Mayfair."

There was a thin, hard, literary lady present, of the obviously and militantly virgin type. She was at the foot of the table, next to the count, but we fell into a discussion of the English woman's-suffrage activity under his very nose, the while he talked lightly to Barfleur. She was for more freedom for women, politically and otherwise, in order that they might accomplish certain social reforms. You know the type. How like a sympathetic actress, I thought, to pick a lady of this character to associate with! One always finds these opposing types together.

The thing that interested me was to see this charming little actress keeping up as smart a social form as her means would permit and still hoping after years of effort and considerable success to be taken up and made much of. She could not have been made to believe that society, in its last reaches, is composed of dullness and heaviness of soul, which responds to no schools of the unconventional or the immoral and knows neither flights of fancy nor delicacy and tenderness of emotion.

Individuals like Miss E. think, somehow, that if they achieve a certain artistic success they will be admitted everywhere. Dear aspiring little Miss E.! She could hardly have been persuaded that there are walls that are never scaled by art. And morality, any more than immorality or religion, has nothing to do with some other walls. Force is the thing. And the ultimate art force she did not possess. If she had, she would have been admitted to a certain interchange in certain fields. Society is composed of slightly interchanging groups, some members of which enter all, most members of which never venture beyond their immediate individual circle. And only the most catholic minded and energetic would attempt or care to bother with the labor of keeping in touch with more than one single agreeable circle.

Another evening I went with Barfleur to call on two professional critics, one working in the field of literature, the other in art exclusively. I mention these two men and their labors because they were very interesting to me, representing as they did two fields of artistic livelihood in London and both making moderate incomes, not large, but sufficient to live on in a simple way. They were men of mettle, as I discovered, urgent, thinking types of mind, quarreling to a certain extent with life and fate, and doing their best to read this very curious riddle of existence.

These two men lived in charming, though small quarters, not far from fashionable London, on the fringe of ultra-respectability, if not of it. Mr. F. was a conservative man, thirty-two or thirty-three years of age, pale, slender, remote, artistic. Mr. Tyne was in character not unlike Mr. F., I should have said, though he was the older man—artistic, remote, ostensibly cultivated, living and doing all the refined things on principle more than anything else.

It amuses me now when I think of it, for of course neither of these gentlemen cared for me in the least, beyond a mild curiosity as to what I was like, but they were exceedingly pleasant. How did I like London? What did I think of the English? How did London contrast with New York? What were some of the things I had seen?

Hoped for the day when the issue might be tried out physically

I stated as succinctly as I could, that I was puzzled in my mind as to what I did think, as I am generally by this phantasmagoria called life, while Mr. Tyne served an opening glass of port and I toasted my feet before a delicious grate-fire. Already, as I have indicated in a way, I had decided that England was deficient in the vitality which America now possesses—certainly deficient in the raw creative imagination which is producing so many new things in America, but far superior in what, for want of a better phrase, I must call social organization as it relates to social and commercial interchange generally. Something has developed in the English social consciousness a sense of responsibility. I really think that the English climate has had a great deal to do with this. It is so uniformly damp and cold and raw that it has produced a sober-minded race. When subsequently I encountered the climates of Paris, Rome and the Riviera I realized quite clearly how impossible it would be to produce the English temperament there. One can see the dark, moody, passionate temperament of the Italian evolving to perfection under their brilliant skies. The wine-like atmosphere of Paris speaks for itself. London is what it is, and the Englishmen likewise, because of the climate in which they have been reared.

I said something to this effect without calling forth much protest, but when I ventured that the English might possibly be falling behind in the world's race and that other nations— such as the Germans and the Americans—might rapidly be displacing them, I evoked a storm of opposition. The sedate Mr. F. rose to this argument. It began at the dinner-table and was continued in the general living-room later. He scoffed at the suggestion that the Germans could possibly conquer or displace England, and hoped for the day when the issue might be tried out physically. Mr. Tyne good-humoredly spoke of the long way America had to go before it could achieve any social importance even within itself. It was a thrashing whirlpool of foreign elements. He had recently been to the United States, and in one of the British quarterlies then on the stands was a long estimate by him of America's weaknesses and potentialities. He poked fun at the careless, insulting manners of the people, their love of show, their love of praise. No Englishman, having tasted the comforts of civilized life in England, could ever live happily in America. There was no such thing as a serving class. He objected to American business methods as he had encountered them, and I could see that he really disliked America. To a certain extent he disliked me for being an American, and resented my modest literary reputation for obtruding itself upon England. I enjoyed these two men as exceedingly able combatants—men against whose wits I could sharpen my own.

I mention them because, in a measure, they suggested the literary and artistic atmosphere of London.

CHAPTER X
SOME MORE ABOUT LONDON

"LONDON sings in my ears." I remember writing this somewhere about the fourth or fifth day of my stay. It was delicious, the sense of novelty and wonder it gave me. I am one of those who have been raised on Dickens and Thackeray and Lamb, but I must confess I found little to corroborate the world of vague impressions I had formed. Novels are a mere expression of temperament anyhow.

New York and America are all so new, so lustful of change. Here, in these streets, when you walk out of a morning or an evening, you feel a pleasing stability. London is not going to change under your very eyes. You are not going to turn your back to find, on looking again, a whole sky line effaced. The city is restful, naïve, in a way tender and sweet like an old song. London is more fatalistic and therefore less hopeful than New York.

One of the first things that impressed me, as I have said, was the grayish tinge of smoke that was over everything—a faint haze—and the next that as a city, street for street and square for square, it was not so strident as New York or Chicago—not nearly so harsh. The traffic was less noisy, the people more thoughtful and considerate, the so-called rush, which characterizes New York, less foolish. There is something rowdyish and ill-mannered about the street life of American cities. This was not true here. It struck me as simple, sedate, thoughtful, and I could only conclude that it sprang from a less stirring atmosphere of opportunity. I fancy it is harder to get along in London. People do not change from one thing to another so much. The world there is more fixed in a pathetic routine, and people are more conscious of their so-called "betters." In so far as I could judge on so short a notice, London seemed to me to represent a mood—a uniform, aware, conservative state of being, neither brilliant nor gay anywhere, though interesting always. About Piccadilly Circus, Trafalgar Square, Leicester Square, Charing Cross, and the Strand I suppose the average Londoner would insist that London is very gay; but I could not see it. Certainly it was not gay as similar sections in New York are gay. It is not in the Londoner himself to be so. He is solid, hard, phlegmatic, a little dreary, like a certain type of rain-bird or Northern loon, content to make the best of a rather dreary situation. I hope not, but I felt it to be true.

I do not believe that it is given any writer to wholly suggest a city. The mind is like a voracious fish—it would like to eat up all the experiences and characteristics of a city or a nation, but this, fortunately, is not possible. My own mind was busy pounding at the gates of fact, but during all the while I was there I got but a little way. I remember being struck with the nature of St. James's Park which was near my hotel, the great column to the Duke of Marlborough, at the end of the street, the whirl of life in Trafalgar Square and Piccadilly Circus which were both very near. The offices I visited in various nearby streets interested me, and the storm of cabs which whirled by all the corners of the region of my hotel. It was described to me as the center of London; and I am quite sure it was—for clubs, theaters, hotels, smart shops and the like were all here. The heavy trading section was further east along the banks of the Thames, and between that and Regent Street, where my little hotel was located, lay the financial section, sprawling around St. Paul's Cathedral and the Bank of England. One could go out of this great central world easily enough—but it was only, apparently, to get into minor centers such as that about Victoria Station, Kensington, Paddington, Liverpool Street, and the Elephant and Castle.

I may be mistaken, but London did not seem either so hard or foreign to me as New York. I have lived in New York for years and years and yet I do not feel that it is My city. One always feels in New York, for some reason, as though he might be put out, or even thrown out. There is such a perpetual and heavy invasion of the stranger. Here in London I could not help feeling off-hand as though things were rather stable and that I was welcome in the world's great empire city on almost any basis on which I wished myself taken. That sense of civility and courtesy to which I have already so often referred was everywhere noticeable in mail-men, policemen, clerks, servants. Alas, when I think of New York, how its rudeness, in contrast, shocks me! At home I do not mind. With all the others I endure it. Here in London for the first time in almost any great city I really felt at home.

But the distances! and the various plexi of streets! and the endless directions in which one could go! Lord! Lord! how they confounded me. It may seem odd to make separate comment on something so thoroughly involved with everything else in a trip of this kind as the streets of London; but nevertheless they contrasted so strangely with those of other cities I have seen that I am forced to comment on them. For one thing, they are seldom straight for any distance and they change their names as frequently and as unexpectedly as a thief. Bond Street speedily becomes Old Bond Street or New Bond Street, according to the direction in which you are going; and I never could see why the Strand should turn into Fleet Street as it went along, and then into Ludgate Hill, and then into Cannon Street. Neither could I understand why Whitechapel Road should change to Mile End Road, but that is neither here nor there. The thing that interested me about London was that it was endless and that there were no high buildings—nothing over four or five stories as a rule—though now and then you actually find eight- and nine-story buildings—and that it was homey and simple and sad in some respects. I remember thinking how gloomy were some of the figures I saw trudging here and there in the smoke-grayed streets and the open park spaces. I never saw such sickly, shabby, run-down-at-the-heels, decayed figures in all my life—figures from which all sap and juice and the freshness of youth and even manhood had long since departed. Men and women they were who seemed to emerge out of gutters and cellars where could be neither light nor freshness nor any sense of hope or care, but only eloquent misery. "Merciful heaven!" I said to myself more than once, "is this the figure of a man?" That is what life does to some of us. It drains us as dry as the sickled wheat stalks and leaves us to blow in wintry winds. Or it poisons us and allows us to fester and decay within our own skins.

But mostly I have separate, vivid pictures of London—individual things that I saw, idle, pointless things that I did, which cheer and amuse and please me even now whenever I think of them. Thus I recall venturing one noon into one of the Lyons restaurants just above Regent Street in Piccadilly and being struck with the size and importance of it even though it was intensely middle class. It was a great chamber, decorated after the fashion of a palace ball-room, with immense chandeliers of prismed glass hanging from the ceiling, and a balcony furnished in cream and gold where other tables were set, and where a large stringed orchestra played continuously during lunch and dinner. An enormous crowd of very commonplace people were there—clerks, minor officials, clergymen, small shop-keepers—and the bill of fare was composed of many homely dishes such as beef-and-kidney pie, suet pudding, and the like—combined with others bearing high-sounding French names. I mention this Lyons restaurant because there were several quite like it, and because it catered to an element not reached in quite the same way in America. In spite of the lifted eyebrows with which Barfleur greeted my announcement that I had been there, the food was excellent; and the service, while a little slow for a place of popular patronage, was good. I recall being amused by the tall, thin, solemn English head-waiters in frock coats, leading the exceedingly *bourgeois* customers to their tables. The English curate with his shovel hat was here in evidence and the minor clerk. I found great pleasure in studying this world, listening to the music, and thinking of the vast ramifications of London which it represented; for every institution of this kind represents a perfect world of people.

Another afternoon I went to the new Roman Catholic Cathedral in Westminster to hear a fourteenth-century chant which was given between two and three by a company of monks who were attached to the church. In the foggy London atmosphere a church of this size takes on great gloom, and the sound of these voices rolling about in it was very impressive. Religion seems of so little avail these days, however, that I wondered why money should be invested in any such structure or liturgy. Or why able-bodied, evidently material-minded men should concern themselves with any such procedure. There were scarcely a half-dozen people present, if so many; and yet this vast edifice echoes every day at this hour with these voices—a company of twenty or thirty fat monks who seemingly might be engaged in something better. Of religion—the spirit as opposed to the form—one might well guess that there was little.

From the cathedral I took a taxi, and bustling down Victoria Street, past the Houses of Parliament and into the Strand, came eventually to St. Paul's. Although it was only four o'clock, this huge structure was growing dusky, and the tombs of Wellington and Marlborough were already dim. The organist allowed me to sit in the choir stalls with the choristers—a company of boys who entered, after a time, headed by deacons and sub-deacons and possibly a canon. A solitary circle of electric bulbs flamed gloomily overhead. By the light of this we were able to make out the liturgy covering this service—the psalms and prayers which swept sonorously through the building. As in the Roman Catholic Cathedral, I was impressed with the darkness and space and also, though not so much for some reason (temperamental inclination perhaps), with the futility of the procedure. There are some eight million people in London, but there were only twenty-five or thirty here, and I was told that this service was never much more popular. On occasions the church is full enough—full to overflowing—but not at this time of day. The best that I could say for it was that it had a lovely, artistic import which ought to be encouraged; and no doubt it is so viewed by those in authority. As a spectacle seen from the Thames or other sections of the city, the dome of St. Paul's is impressive, and as an example of English architecture it is dignified—though in my judgment not to be compared with either Canterbury or Salisbury. But the interesting company of noble dead, the fact that the public now looks upon it as a national mausoleum and that it is a monument to the genius of Christopher Wren, makes it worth while. Compared with other cathedrals I saw, its chief charm was its individuality. In actual beauty it is greatly surpassed by the pure Gothic or Byzantine or Greek examples of other cities.

One evening I went with a friend of mine to visit the House of Parliament, that noble pile of buildings on the banks of the Thames. For days I had been skirting about them, interested in other things. The clock-tower, with its great round clock-face,—twenty-three feet in diameter, some one told me,—had been staring me in the face over a stretch of park space and intervening buildings on such evenings as Parliament was in session, and I frequently debated with myself whether I should trouble to go or not, even if some one invited me. I grow so weary of standard, completed things at times! However, I did go. It came about through the Hon. T. P. O'Connor, M.P., an old admirer of "Sister Carrie," who, hearing that I was in London, invited me. He had just finished reading "Jennie Gerhardt" the night I met him, and I shall never forget the kindly glow of his face as, on meeting me in the dining-room of the House of Commons, he exclaimed:

"Ah, the biographer of that poor girl! And how charming she was, too! Ah me! Ah me!"

I can hear the soft brogue in his voice yet, and see the gay romance of his Irish eye. Are not the Irish all in-born cavaliers, anyhow?

I had been out in various poor sections of the city all day, speculating on that shabby mass that have nothing, know nothing, dream nothing; or do they? It was most depressing, as dark fell, to return through long, humble streets alive with a home-hurrying mass of people—clouds of people not knowing whence they came or why. And now I was to return and go to dine where the laws are made for all England.

I was escorted by another friend, a Mr. M., since dead, who was, when I reached the hotel, quite disturbed lest we be late. I like the man who takes society and social forms seriously, though I would not be that man for all the world. M. was one such. He was, if you please, a stickler for law and order. The Houses of Parliament and the repute of the Hon. T. P. O'Connor meant much to him. I can see O'Connor's friendly, comprehensive eye understanding it all—understanding in his deep, literary way why it should be so.

As I hurried through Westminster Hall, the great general entrance, once itself the ancient Parliament of England, the scene of the deposition of Edward II, of the condemnation of Charles I, of the trial of Warren Hastings, and the poling of the exhumed head of Cromwell, I was thinking, thinking, thinking. What is a place like this, anyhow, but a fanfare of names? If you know history, the long, strange tangle of steps or actions by which life ambles crab-wise from nothing to nothing, you know that it is little more than this. The present places are the thing, the present forms, salaries, benefices, and that dream of the mind which makes it all into something. As I walked through into Central Hall, where we had to wait until Mr. O'Connor was found, I studied the high, groined arches, the Gothic walls, the graven figures of the general anteroom. It was all rich, gilded, dark, lovely. And about me was a room full of men all titillating with a sense of their own importance—commoners, lords possibly, call-boys, ushers, and here and there persons crying of "Division! Division!" while a bell somewhere clanged raucously.

"There's a vote on," observed Mr. M. "Perhaps they won't find him right away. Never mind; he'll come."

He did come finally, with, after his first greetings, a "Well, now we'll ate, drink, and be merry," and then we went in.

At table, being an old member of Parliament, he explained many things swiftly and interestingly, how the buildings were arranged, the number of members, the procedure, and the like. He was, he told me, a member from Liverpool, which, by the way, returns some Irish members, which struck me as rather strange for an English city.

"Not at all, not at all. The English like the Irish—at times," he added softly.

"I have just been out in your East End," I said, "trying to find out how tragic London is, and I think my mood has made me a little color-blind. It's rather a dreary world, I should say, and I often wonder whether law-making ever helps these people."

He smiled that genial, equivocal, sophisticated smile of the Irish that always bespeaks the bland acceptance of things as they are, and tries to make the best of a bad mess.

"Yes, it's bad,"—and nothing could possibly suggest the aroma of a brogue that went with this,—"but it's no worse than some of your American cities—Lawrence, Lowell, Fall River." (Trust the Irish to hand you an intellectual "You're another!") "Conditions in Pittsburgh are as bad as anywhere, I think; but it's true the East End is pretty bad. You want to remember that it's typical London winter weather we're having, and London smoke makes those gray buildings look rather forlorn, it's true. But there's some comfort there, as there is everywhere. My old Irish father was one for thinking that we all have our rewards here or hereafter. Perhaps theirs is to be hereafter." And he rolled his eyes humorously and sanctimoniously heavenward.

An able man this, full, as I knew, from reading his weekly and his books, of a deep, kindly understanding of life, but one who, despite his knowledge of the tragedies of existence, refused to be cast down.

He was going up the Nile shortly in a house-boat with a party of wealthy friends, and he told me that Lloyd George, the champion of the poor, was just making off for a winter outing on the Riviera, but that I might, if I would come some morning, have breakfast with him. He was sure that the great commoner would be glad to see me. He wanted me to call at his rooms, his London official offices, as it were, at 5 Morpeth

Mansions, and have a pleasant talk with him, which latterly I did.

While he was in the midst of it, the call of "Division!" sounded once more through the halls, and he ran to take his place with his fellow-parliamentarians on some question of presumably vital importance. I can see him bustling away in his long frock coat, his napkin in his hand, ready to be counted yea or nay, as the case might be.

Afterwards when he had outlined for me a tour in Ireland which I must sometime take, he took us up into the members' gallery of the Commons in order to see how wonderful it was, and we sat as solemn as owls, contemplating the rather interesting scene below. I cannot say that I was seriously impressed. The Hall of Commons, I thought, was small and stuffy, not so large as the House of Representatives at Washington, by any means.

In delicious Irish whispers he explained a little concerning the arrangement of the place. The seat of the speaker was at the north end of the chamber on a straight line with the sacred wool sack of the House of Lords in another part of the building, however important that may be. If I would look under the rather shadowy canopy at the north end of this extremely square chamber, I would see him, "smothering under an immense white wig," he explained. In front of the canopy was a table, the speaker's table, with presumably the speaker's official mace lying upon it. To the right of the speaker were the recognized seats of the government party, the ministers occupying the front bench. And then he pointed out to me Mr. Lloyd George, Mr. Bonar Law (Unionist member and leader of the opposition), and Mr. Winston Churchill, all men creating a great stir at the time. They were whispering and smiling in genial concert, while opposite them, on the left hand of the speaker, where the opposition was gathered, some droning M. P. from the North, I understood, a noble lord, was delivering one of those typically intellectual commentaries in which the British are fond of indulging. I could not see him from where I sat, but I could see him just the same. I knew that he was standing very straight, in the most suitable clothes for the occasion, his linen immaculate, one hand poised gracefully, ready to emphasize some rather obscure point, while he stated in the best English why this and this must be done. Every now and then, at a suitable point in his argument, some friendly and equally intelligent member would give voice to a soothing "Hyah! hyah!" or "Rathah!" Of the four hundred and seventy-six provided seats, I fancy something like over four hundred were vacant, their occupants being out in the dining-rooms, or off in those adjoining chambers where parliamentarians confer during hours that are not pressing, and where they are sought at the call for a division. I do not presume, however, that they were all in any so safe or sane places. I mock-reproachfully asked Mr. O'Connor why he was not in his seat, and he said in good Irish:

"Me boy, there are thricks in every thrade. I'll be there whin me vote is wanted."

We came away finally through long, floreated passages and towering rooms, where I paused to admire the intricate woodwork, the splendid gilding, and the tier upon tier of carven kings and queens in their respective niches. There was for me a flavor of great romance over it all. I could not help thinking that, pointless as it all might be, such joys and glories as we have are thus compounded. Out of the dull blatherings of half-articulate members, the maunderings of dreamers and schemers, come such laws and such policies as best express the moods of the time—of the British or any other empire. I have no great faith in laws. To me, they are ill-fitting garments at best, traps and mental catch-polls for the unwary only. But I thought as I came out into the swirling city again, "It is a strange world. These clock-towers and halls will sometime fall into decay. The dome of our own capital will be rent and broken, and through its ragged interstices will fall the pallor of the moon." But life does not depend upon parliaments or men.

CHAPTER XI
THE THAMES

AS pleasing hours as any that I spent in London were connected with the Thames—a murky little stream above London Bridge, compared with such vast bodies as the Hudson and the Mississippi, but utterly delightful. I saw it on several occasions,—once in a driving rain off London Bridge, where twenty thousand vehicles were passing in the hour, it was said; once afterward at night when the boats below were faint, wind-driven lights and the crowd on the bridge black shadows. I followed it in the rain from Blackfriars Bridge, to the giant plant of the General Electric Company at Chelsea one afternoon, and thought of Sir Thomas More, and Henry VIII, who married Anne Boleyn at the Old Church near Battersea Bridge, and wondered what they would think of this modern powerhouse. What a change from Henry VIII and Sir Thomas More to vast, whirling electric dynamos and a London subway system!

Another afternoon, bleak and rainy, I reconnoitered the section lying between Blackfriars Bridge and Tower Bridge and found it very interesting from a human, to say nothing of a river, point of view; I question whether in some ways it is not the most interesting region in London, though it gives only occasional glimpses of the river. London is curious. It is very modern in spots. It is too much like New York and Chicago and Philadelphia and Boston; but here between Blackfriars Bridge and the Tower, along Upper and Lower Thames Street, I found something that delighted me. It smacked of Dickens, of Charles II, of Old England, and of a great many forgotten, far-off things which I felt, but could not readily call to mind. It was delicious, this narrow, winding street, with high walls,—high because the street was so narrow,—and alive with people bobbing along under umbrellas or walking stodgily in the rain. Lights were burning in all the stores and warehouses, dark recesses running back to the restless tide of the Thames, and they were full of an industrious commercial life.

It was interesting to me to think that I was in the center of so much that was old, but for the exact details I confess I cared little. Here the Thames was especially delightful. It presented such odd vistas. I watched the tumbling tide of water, whipped by gusty wind where moderate-sized tugs and tows were going by in the mist and rain. It was delicious, artistic, far more significant than quiescence and sunlight could have made it. I took note of the houses, the doorways, the quaint, winding passages, but for the color and charm they did not compare with the nebulous, indescribable mass of working boys and girls and men and women which moved before my gaze. The mouths of many of them were weak, their noses snub, their eyes squint, their chins undershot, their ears stub, their chests flat. Most of them had a waxy, meaty look, but for interest they were incomparable. American working crowds may be much more chipper, but not more interesting. I could not weary of looking at them.

Here the Thames was especially delightful

Lastly I followed the river once more all the way from Cleopatra's Needle to Chelsea one heavily downpouring afternoon and found its mood varying splendidly though never once was it anything more than black-gray, changing at times from a pale or almost sunlit yellow to a solid leaden-black hue. It looked at times as though something remarkable were about to happen, so weirdly greenish-yellow was the sky above the water; and the tall chimneys of Lambeth over the way, appearing and disappearing in the mist, were irresistible. There is a certain kind of barge which plies up and down the Thames with a collapsible mast and sail which looks for all the world like something off the Nile. These boats harmonize with the smoke and the gray, lowery skies. I was never weary of looking at them in the changing light and mist and rain. Gulls skimmed over the water here very freely all the way from Blackfriars to Battersea, and along the Embankment they sat in scores, solemnly cogitating the state of the weather, perhaps. I was delighted with the picture they made in places, greedy, wide-winged, artistic things.

Finally I had a novel experience with these same gulls one Sunday afternoon. I had been out all morning reconnoitering strange sections of London, and arrived near Blackfriars Bridge about one o'clock. I was attracted by what seemed to me at first glance thousands of gulls, lovely clouds of them, swirling about the heads of several different men at various points along the wall. It was too beautiful to miss. It reminded me of the gulls about the steamer at Fishguard. I drew near. The first man I saw was feeding them minnows out of a small box he had purchased for a penny, throwing the tiny fish aloft in the air and letting the gulls dive for them. They ate from his hand, circled above and about his head, walked on the wall before him, their jade bills and salmon-pink feet showing delightfully.

I was delighted, and hurried to the second. It was the same. I found the vender of small minnows near by, a man who sold them for this purpose, and purchased a few boxes. Instantly I became the center of another swirling cloud, wheeling and squeaking in hungry anticipation. It was a great sight. Finally I threw out the last minnows, tossing them all high in the air, and seeing not one escape, while I meditated on the speed of these birds, which, while scarcely moving a wing, rise and fall with incredible swiftness. It is a matter of gliding up and down with them. I left, my head full of birds, the Thames forever fixed in mind.

I went one morning in search of the Tower, and coming into the neighborhood of Eastcheap witnessed that peculiar scene which concerns fish. Fish dealers, or at least their hirelings, always look as though they had never known a bath and are covered with slime and scales, and here, they wore a peculiar kind of rubber hat on which tubs or pans of fish could be carried. The hats were quite flat and round and reminded me of a smashed "stovepipe" as the silk hat has been derisively called. The peasant habit of carrying bundles on the head was here demonstrated to be a common characteristic of London.

On another morning I visited Pimlico and the neighborhood of Vincent Square. I was delighted with the jumble of life I found there, particularly in Strutton Ground and Churton Street. Horse Ferry Road touched me as a name and Lupus Street was strangely suggestive of a hospital, not a wolf.

It was here that I encountered my first coster cart, drawn by the tiniest little donkey you ever saw, his ears standing up most nobly and his eyes suggesting the mellow philosophy of indifference. The load he hauled, spread out on a large table-like rack and arranged neatly in baskets, consisted of vegetables—potatoes, tomatoes, cabbage, lettuce and the like. A bawling merchant or peddler followed in the wake of the cart, calling out his wares. He was not arrayed in coster uniform, however, as it has been pictured in America. I was delighted to listen to the cockney accent in Strutton Ground where "'Ere you are, Lydy," could be constantly heard, and "Foine potytoes these 'ere, Madam, hextra noice."

In Earl Street I found an old cab-yard, now turned into a garage, where the remnants of a church tower were visible, tucked away among the jumble of other things. I did my best to discover of what it had been a part. No one knew. The ex-cabman, now dolefully washing the wheels of an automobile, informed me that he had "only been workin' 'ere a little wile," and the foreman could not remember. But it suggested a very ancient English world—as early as the Normans. Just beyond this again I found the saddest little chapel—part of an abandoned machine-shop, with a small hand-bell over the door which was rung by means of a piece of common binding-twine! Who could possibly hear it, I reflected. Inside was a wee chapel, filled with benches constructed of store boxes and provided with an altar where some form of services was conducted. There was no one to guard the shabby belongings of the place and I sat down and meditated at length on the curiosity of the religious ideal.

In another section of the city where I walked—Hammersmith—and still another—Seven Kings—I found conditions which I thought approximated those in the Bronx, New York, in Brooklyn, in Chicago and elsewhere. I could not see any difference between the lines of store-front apartment houses in Seven Kings and Hammersmith and Shepherd's Bush for that matter, and those in Flatbush, Brooklyn or the South End of Philadelphia. You saw the difference when you looked at the people and, if you entered a tavern, America was gone on the instant. The barmaid settled that and the peculiar type of idler found here. I recall in Seven Kings being entertained by the appearance of the working-men assembled, their trousers strapped about the knees, their hats or caps pulled jauntily awry. Always the English accent was strong and, at times, here in London, it became unintelligible to me. They have a lingo of their own. In the main I could make it out, allowing for the appearance or disappearance of "h's" at the most unexpected moments.

The street cars in the outlying sections are quite the same as in America and the variety of stores about as large and bright. In the older portions, however, the twisting streets, the presence of the omnibus in great numbers, and of the taxi-stands at the more frequented corners, the peculiar uniforms of policemen, mail-men, street-sweepers (dressed like Tyrolese mountaineers), messenger-boys, and the varied accoutrements of the soldiery gave the great city an individuality which caused me to realize clearly that I was far from home—a stranger in a strange land. As charming as any of the spectacles I witnessed were the Scotch soldiers in bare legs, kilts, plaid and the like swinging along with a heavy stride like Norman horses or—singly—making love to a cockney English girl on a 'bus top perhaps. The English craze for pantomime was another thing that engaged my curious attention and why any reference to a mystic and presumably humorous character known as "Dirty Dick" should evoke such volumes of applause.

CHAPTER XII
MARLOWE

AFTER I had been at Bridgely Level four or five days Barfleur suggested that I visit Marlowe, which was quite near by on the Thames, a place which he said fairly represented the typical small country town of the old school.

"You will see there something which is not so generally common now in England as it was—a type of life which is changing greatly, I think; and perhaps you had better see that now before you see much more."

I promised to go and Barfleur gave positive instructions as to how this was to be achieved. I was to say to the maid when I would be ready. Promptly at that hour one of the boys was to come and escort me to some point in the road where I could see Marlowe. From there I was to be allowed to proceed alone.

"You won't want to be bothered with any company, so just send him back. You'll find it very interesting."

The afternoon had faired up so beautifully that I decided I must go out of doors. I was sick of writing. I gave notice to Dora, the maid, at luncheon that I should want one of the boys for a guide at three o'clock, and at ten minutes of the hour Percy entered my room with the air of a soldier.

"When shall you be ready for your walk to Marlowe?" he asked, in his stately tone.

"In just ten minutes now."

"And have you any objection to our walking to Marlowe with you?"

"Are there two of you?"

"Yes. My brother Charles and myself."

"None whatever. Your father doesn't mind, does he?"

"No, he doesn't mind."

So at three Percy and Charles appeared at the window. Their faces were eager with anticipation and I went at once to get my cap and coat. We struck out along a road between green grass, and although it was December you would have thought it April or May. The atmosphere was warm and tinged with the faintest, most delicate haze. A lovely green moss, very fine, like powdered salt, was visible on the trunks of the trees. Crows were in the air, and robins—an English robin is a solemn-looking bird—on the lawns. I heaved a breath of delight, for after days of rain and chill this burst of golden light was most delicious.

On the way, as I was looking about, I was being called upon to answer questions such as: "Are there any trees like these in Amáyreeka? Do you have such fine weather in Amáyreeka? Are the roads as good as this in Amáyreeka?"

"Quite as good as this," I replied, referring to the one on which we were walking, for it was a little muddy.

The way lay through a patch of nearly leafless trees, the ground strewn thick with leaves, and the sun breaking in a golden shower through the branches. I laughed for joy at being alive—the hour was so fine. Presently, after going down a bank so steep that it was impossible not to run if you attempted to walk fast, we came to an open field, the west border of which was protected by a line of willows skirting the banks of a flume which gave into the Thames somewhere. Below the small bridge over which we passed was fastened a small punt, that quaint little boat so common on the Thames. Beyond that was a very wide field, fully twenty acres square, with a yellow path running diagonally across it and at the end of this path was Marlowe.

In the meantime my young friends insisted on discussing the possibility of war between America and England and I was kept busy assuring them that England would not be able to do anything at all with the United States. The United States was so vast, I said. It was full of such smart people. While England was attempting to do something with its giant navy, we should be buying or building wonderful ships and inventing marvelous machines for destroying the enemy. It was useless to plead with me as they did that England had a great army and we none. "We can get one," I insisted, "oh, a much vaster army than you could."

"And then Can-ee-dah," insisted Percy wisely, "while you would be building your navy or drilling your army, we should be attacking you through Can-ee-dah."

"But Canada doesn't like you," I replied. "And besides it only has six million people."

He insisted that Canada was a great source and hope and I finally said: "Now, I'll tell you what I'll do. You want England to whip the United States, don't you?"

"Yes," echoed both Percy and Charles heartily.

"Very well, then for peace and quiet's sake, I'll agree that it can. England can whip the United States both on sea and land. Now is that satisfactory?"

"Yes," they echoed, unanimously.

"Very well then," I laughed. "It is agreed that the United States is badly beaten everywhere and always by England. Isn't Marlowe lovely?" and fixed my interested gaze on the approaching village.

In the first glimpse of Marlowe some of the most joyous memories of my childhood came back. I don't know whether you as a boy or a girl loved to look in your first reader at pictures of quaint little towns with birds flying above belfries and gabled roofs standing free in some clear, presumably golden air, but I did. And here, across this green field lay a little town, the sweetness of which was most appealing. The most prominent things were an arched bridge and a church, with a square gray belfry, set in a green, tree-grown church-yard. I could see the smooth surface of the Thames running beside it, and as I live, a flock of birds in the sky.

"Are those rooks?" I asked of Percy, hoping for poetry's sake that they were.

"Rooks or crows," he replied, "I don't know which."

"Are there rooks in Amáyreeka?"

"No—there are no rooks."

"Ah, that's something."

I walked briskly because I wanted to reach this pretty scene while the sun was still high, and in five minutes or so we were crossing the bridge. I was intensely interested in the low gray stone houses, with here and there a walk in front with a gate, and a very pretty churchyard lying by the water, and the sylvan loveliness of the Thames itself.

On the bridge I stopped and looked at the water. It was as smooth as glass and tinged with the mellow light which the sun casts when it is low in the west. There were some small boats anchored at a gate which gave into some steps leading up to an inn—The Compleat Angler. On the other side, back of the church was another inn—the Lion and Elk or something like that—and below the bridge, more towards the west, an old man in a punt, fishing. There was a very old man such as I have often seen pictured in *Punch* and the *Sketch*, sitting near the support of the bridge, a short black pipe between his very wrinkled lips. He was clad in thick greenish-brown clothes and heavy shoes and a low flat hat some curate may have discarded. His eyes, which he turned up at me as I passed, were small and shrewd, set in a withered, wrinkled skin, and his hands were a collection of dried lines, like wrinkled leather.

"There," I thought, "is a type quite expressive of all England in its rural form. Pictures of England have been teaching me that all my life."

I went into the church, which was located on the site of one built in the thirteenth century—and on the wall near the door was a list of the resident vicars and their patrons, beginning with some long-since-forgotten soul. The monks and the abbots of the pre-Reformation period were indicated and the wars of the Reformation also. I think that bridge which I had crossed had been destroyed by Cromwell and rebuilt only sixty or seventy years before, but my memory is not good and I will not guarantee these facts.

From the church we went out into the street and found an old stock inside an iron fence, dating from some older day where they punished people after that fashion. We came to a store which was signaled by a low, small-paned window let into a solid gray wall, where were chocolates and candies and foreign-manufactured goods with labels I had never seen before. It is a strange sensation to go away from home and leave all your own familiar patent medicines and candies and newspapers and whiskies and journey to some place where they never saw or heard of them.

Here was Marlowe, and lovely as it was, I kept saying to myself, "Yes, yes, it is delicious, but how terrible it would be to live here! I couldn't. It's a dead world. We have passed so far beyond this." I walked through the pretty streets as smooth and clean as though they had been brushed and between rows of low, gray, winding houses which curved in pretty lines, but for the life of me I could not help swinging between the joy of art for that which is alive and the sorrow for something that is gone and will never be, any more. Everything, everything spoke to me of an older day. These houses—all of them were lower than they need be, grayer than they need be, thicker, older, sadder. I could not think of gas or electricity being used here, although they were, or of bright broad windows, open plumbing, modern street cars, a stock of modern, up-to-date goods, which I am sure they contained. I was impressed by a grave silence which is apathetic to me as nothing else—a profound peace. "I must get out of this," I said to myself, and yet I was almost hugging myself for joy at the same time.

I remember going into one courtyard where an inn might once have been and finding in there a furniture shop, a tin shop, a store room of some kind and a stable, all invisible from the street. Do you recall Dickens' description of busy inn scenes? You came into this one under the chamber belonging to a house which was built over the entry way. There was no one visible inside, though a man did cross the court finally with a wheel spoke in his hand. One of the houses or shops had a little circular cupola on it, quite white and pretty and surmounted by a faded weather cock. "How lovely," I said, "how lovely," but I was as sad as I could be.

In the stores in the main street were always small, many-paned windows. There were no lights as yet and the rooms into which I peered and the private doors gave glimpses of things which reminded me of the poorest, most backward and desolate sections of our own country.

I saw an automobile here and there, not many, and some girls on bicycles,—not very good looking. Say what you will, you could not find an atmosphere like this in an American town, however small, unless it had already been practically abandoned. It would not contain a contented population of three or four hundred. Instead of saloons I saw "wine and spirit merchants" and also "Mrs. Jane Sawyer, licensed wine and spirit dealer." The butcher shops were the most American things I saw, because their ruddy goods were all displayed in front with good lights behind, and the next best things were the candy stores. Dressmakers, milliners, grocers, hardware stores, wine shops, anything and everything—were apparently concealed by solid gray walls or at best revealed by small-paned windows. In the fading afternoon I walked about hunting for schools, some fine private houses, some sense of modernness—but no—it was not there. I noticed that in two directions the town came abruptly to an end, as though it had been cut off by a knife, and smooth, open, green fields began. In the distance you could see other towns standing out like the castellated walls of earlier centuries—but here was an end, sharp, definite, final.

I saw at one place—the end of one of these streets and where the country began—an old gray man in a shabby black coat bending to adjust a yoke to his shoulders to the ends of which were attached two buckets filled with water. He had been into a low, gray, one-story inn entitled, "Ye Bank of England," before which was set a bench and also a stone hitching post. For all the world he looked like some old man in Hardy, wending his fading, reflective way homeward. I said to myself here—England is old; it is evening in England and they are tired.

I went back toward the heart of things along another street, but I found after a time it was merely taking me to another outer corner of the town. It was gray now, and I was saying to my young companions that they must be hurrying on home—that I did not intend to go back so soon. "Say I will not be home for dinner," I told them, and they left after a time, blessed with some modern chocolate which they craved very much.

Before they left, however, we reconnoitered another street and this led me past low, one-story houses, the like of which, I insist, can rarely be duplicated in America. Do you recall the log cabin? In England it is preserved in stone, block after block of it. It originated there. The people, as I went along, seemed so thick and stolid and silent to me. They were healthy enough, I thought, but they were raw, uncouth, mirthless. There was not a suggestion of gaiety anywhere—not a single burst of song. I heard no one whistling. A man came up behind us, driving some cattle, and the oxen were quite upon me before I heard them. But there were no loud cries. He was so ultra serious. I met a man pushing a dilapidated baby carriage. He was a grinder of knives and mender of tinware and this was his method of perambulating his equipment. I met another man pushing a hand cart with some attenuated remnants of furniture in it. "What is that?" I asked. "What is he?"

"Oh, he's somebody who's moving. He hasn't a van, you know."

Moving! Here was food for pathetic reflection.

I looked into low, dark doors where humble little tin and glass-bodied lamps were beginning to flicker.

"Thank God, my life is different from this," I said, and yet the pathos and the beauty of this town was gripping me firmly. It was as sweet as a lay out of Horace—as sad as Keats.

Before a butcher shop I saw a man trying to round up a small drove of sheep. The grayish-yellow of their round wooly backs blended with the twilight. They seemed to sense their impending doom, for they ran here and there, poking their queer thin noses along the ground or in the air and refusing to enter the low, gray entry way which gave into a cobbled yard at the back where were located the deadly shambles they feared. The farmer who was driving them wore a long black coat and he made no sound, or scarcely any.

"Sooey!" he called softly—"Ssh," as he ran here and there—this way and that.

The butcher or his assistant came out and caught one sheep, possibly the bell-wether, by the leg and hauled him backward into the yard. Seeing this, the silly sheep, not recognizing the enforced leadership, followed after. Could there be a more convincing commentary on the probable manner in which the customs and forms of life have originated?

I walked out another long street, quite alone now in the dusk, and met a man driving an ox, also evidently to market.

There was a school in session at one place, a boys' school—low, ancient in its exterior equipment and silent as I passed. It was *out*, but there was no running—no hallooing. The boys were going along chatting rather quietly in groups. I do not understand this. The American temper is more ebullient. I went into one bar—Mrs. Davidge's—and found a low, dark room, with a very small grate fire burning and a dark little bar where were some pewter mugs, some pink-colored glasses and a small brass lamp with a reflector. Mrs. Davidge must have served me herself, an old, slightly hunched lady in a black dress and gray gingham apron. "Can this place do enough business to support her?" I asked myself. There was no one in the shop while I was there.

The charm of Marlowe to me was its extreme remoteness from the life I had been witnessing in London and elsewhere. It was so simple. I had seen a comfortable inn somewhere near the market place and this I was idly seeking, entertaining myself with reflections the while. I passed at one place a gas manufacturing plant which looked modern enough, in so far as its tank was concerned, but not otherwise, and then up one dark street under branches of large trees and between high brick walls, in a low doorway, behind which a light was shining, saw a shovel-hatted curate talking to an old woman in a shawl. All the rest was dark. At another corner I saw a thin old man, really quite reverential looking, with a peaked intelligent face, fine in its lines (like Calvin or Dante or John Knox) and long thin white hair, who was pulling a vehicle—a sort of revised baby carriage on which was, of all things, a phonograph with a high flower-like tin horn. He stopped at one corner where some children were playing in the dark and putting on a record ground out a melody which I did not consider very gay or tuneful. The children danced, but not, however, with the lightness of our American children. The people here seemed either like this old man, sad and old and peaked, with a fine intellectuality apparent, or thick and dull and red and stodgy.

When I reached the market I saw a scene which something—some book or pictures had suggested to me before. Solid women in shawls and flat, shapeless wrecks of hats, and tall shambling men in queer long coats and high boots—drovers they looked like—going to and fro. Children were playing about and laborers were going home, talking a dialect which I could not understand, except in part.

Five men came into the square and stood there under the central gas lamp, with its two arms each with a light. One of them left the others and began to sing in front of various doors. He sang and sang—"Annie Laurie," "Auld Lang Syne," "Sally in our Alley," in a queer nasal voice, going in and coming out again, empty-handed I fancy. Finally he came to me.

"Would you help us on our way?" he asked.

"Where are you going?" I inquired.

"We are way-faring workmen," he replied simply, and I gave him some coppers—those large English "tuppences" that annoyed me so much. He went back to the others and they stood huddled in the square together like sheep, conferring, but finally they went off together in the dark.

At the inn adjacent I expected to find an exceptional English scene of some kind but I was more or less disappointed. It was homey but not so different from old New England life. The room was large with an open fire and a general table set with white linen and plates for a dozen guests or more. A shambling boy in clothes much too big for him came and took my order, turning up the one light and stirring the fire. I called for a paper and read it and then I sat wondering whether the food would be good or bad.

While I was waiting a second traveler arrived, a small, dapper, sandy-haired person, with shrewd, fresh, inquisitive eyes—a self-confident and yet clerkly man.

"Good evening," he said, and I gave him the time of day. He bustled to a little writing table nearby and sat down to write, calling for a pen, paper, his slippers—I was rather puzzled by that demand—and various other things. On sight this gentleman (I suppose the English would abuse me for that word) looked anything but satisfactory. I suspected he was Scotch and that he was cheap minded and narrow. Later something about his manner and the healthy, brisk way in which, when his slippers came, he took off his shoes and put them on—quite cheerful and homelike—soothed me.

"He isn't so bad," I thought. "He's probably a traveling salesman—the English type. I'd better be genial, I may learn something."

Soon the waiter returned (arrayed by this time, remarkable to relate, in a dress suit the size of which was a piece of pure comedy in itself), and brought the stranger toast and chops and tea. The latter drew up to the other end of the table from me with quite an air of appetite and satisfaction.

"They don't usually put us fellows in with you," he observed, stating something the meaning of which I did not grasp for the moment. "Us traveling men usually have a separate dining- and writing-room. Our place seems to be shut up here to-night for some reason. I wouldn't have called for my slippers here if they had the other room open."

"Oh, that's quite all right," I replied, gathering some odd class distinction. "I prefer company to silence. You say you travel?"

"Yes, I'm connected with a house in London. I travel in the south of England."

"Tell me," I said, "is this a typical English town from the point of view of life and business, or is it the only one of its kind? It's rather curious to me."

"It's one of the poorest I know, certainly the poorest I stop at. There is no life to speak of here at all. If you want to see a typical English town where there's more life and business you want to see Canterbury or Maidenhead. No, no, you mustn't judge England by this. I suppose you're traveling to see things. You're not English, I see."

"No, I'm from America. I come from New York."

"I had a strong notion before I came to London to go to America after I left school"—and to have heard him pronounce *school* alone would have settled his identity for those who know the Scotch. "Some of my friends went there, but I decided not. I thought I'd try London instead and I'm glad I did."

"You like it?"

"Oh, yes, from a money point I do. I make perhaps fifty per cent. more than I did in Scotland but I may say, too, it costs me almost fifty per cent. more to live." He said this with a sigh. I could see Scotch thrift sticking out all over him. An interesting little man he proved, very intelligent, very cautious, very saving. You could see early religious training and keen desire to get up in the world in his every gesture.

We fell into a most interesting conversation, to me, for knowing so little of England I was anxious to know more. Despite the littleness of my companion and his clerkly manner I found him entertaining. He wanted to know what I thought of England and I told him—as much as I could judge by a few days' stay. He told me something of London life—its streets, sections and so on and asked a great many questions about America. He had the ability to listen intelligently which is a fine sign. He wanted to know particularly what traveling salesmen receive in America and how far their money goes. He was interested to know the difference between English and American railroads. By this time the meal had ended and we were toasting our toes before the fire. We were quite friendly.

"It's some little distance back to my place and I think I'll be going," I said. "I don't know whether I really know how to get there, but I'll try. I understand there is no direct railroad connection between here and there. I may not be able to find my way at night as it is."

"Well, I'll walk with you a little way if you don't mind," he replied solicitously. "I have nothing else to do."

The idea of companionship soothed me. Walking around alone and standing in the market place looking at the tramping men had given me the blues. I felt particularly lonely at moments, being away from America, for the difference in standards of taste and action, the difference in modes of thought and practice, and the difference in money and the sound of human voices was growing on me. When you have lived in one country all your life and found yourself comfortable in all its ways and notions and then suddenly find yourself out of it and trying to adjust yourself to things that are different in a hundred little ways, it is rather hard.

"That's very nice of you. I'd like to have you," and out we went, paying our bills and looking into a misty night. The moon was up but there was a fairly heavy fog and Marlowe looked sheeted and gray. Because I stated I had not been in any of the public houses and was interested to go, he volunteered to accompany me, though I could see that this was against his principles.

"I don't drink myself," he observed, "but I will go in with you if you want to. Here's one."

We entered and found a rather dimly lighted room,—gas with a mantle over it,—set with small tables and chairs, and a short bar in one corner. Mrs. Davidge's bar had been short, too, only her room was dingier and small. A middle-sized Englishman, rather stout, came out of a rear door, opening from behind the bar, and asked us what we would have. My friend asked for root beer. I noticed the unescapable open fire and the array of pink and green and blue wine glasses. Also the machinery for extracting beer and ale from kegs, a most brassy and glowing sight. Our host sold cigars and there were boards about on the tables for some simple games.

This and a half-dozen other places into which we ventured gave me the true spirit of Marlowe's common life. I recalled at once the vast difference between this and the average American small town saloon. In the latter (Heaven preserve us from it) the trade might be greater or it might not, but the room would be larger, the bar larger, the flies, dirt, odor, abominable. I hope I am not traducing a worthy class, but the American saloon keeper of small town proclivities has always had a kind of horror for me. The implements of his trade have always been so scummy and ill-kept. The American place would be apt to be gayer, rougher, noisier. I am thinking of places in towns of the same size. Our host was no more like an American barkeeper than a bee is like a hornet. He was a peaceful-looking man, homely, family marked, decidedly dull. Your American country barkeeper is another sort, more intelligent, perhaps, but less civil, less sensible and reliable looking. The two places were miles apart in quality and feeling. Here in Marlowe and elsewhere in England, wherever I had occasion to inspect them, the public houses of the small-town type were a great improvement over the American variety. They were clean and homelike and cheerful. The array of brass, the fire, the small tables for games, all pleased me. I took it to be a place more used as a country club or meeting-house than as in our case a grimy, orgiastic resort. If there were drunken men or women in any of the "pubs," this night I did not see them. My Scotch friend assured me that he believed them, ordinarily, to be fairly respectable.

Not knowing my way through the woods adjacent and having spent much time in this way I finally decided to take a train or conveyance of some kind. But there was no train to be had for some time to come. The trains there were did not run my way and no "fly" would convey me, as one bar mistress informed me, because there was a hard hill to climb and the rain which had fallen during the day had made the roads bad. I began to meditate returning to the inn. Finally the lady observed, "I can tell you how to get there, if you want to walk. It's not more than an hour and it is a perfectly good road all the way." She drew with her finger an outline of the twists of the road. "If you're not afraid of a few screech owls, there's nothing to harm you. You go to the bridge up here, cross it and take the first road to your left. When you come to a culvert about a mile out you will find three roads dividing there. One goes down the hollow to somewhere, I forgot the name; one goes up the hill to Bridgely Level, it's a bridle path; and one goes to the right. It's a smooth, even road—that's the one you want."

It was a lovely night. The moon overhead was clear and bright and the fog gave the fields a white eerie look. As we walked, my friend regaled me with what he said was a peculiar custom among English traveling men. At all English inns there is what is known as the traveling men's club. The man who has been present at any inn on any stated occasion for the greatest number of hours or days is *ipso facto*, president of this club. The traveling man who has been there next longest if only for ten minutes less than the first, or more than the third, is vice president. Every inn serves what is known as the traveling man's dinner at twelve o'clock or thereabouts and he who is president by virtue of the qualifications above described, is entitled to sit at the head of the table and carve and serve the roast. The vice president, if there be one, sits at the foot of the table and carves and serves the fowl. When there are two or more traveling men present, enough to provide a president and a vice president for this dinner, there is a regular order of procedure to be observed. The president arriving takes his seat first at the head of the table; the vice president then takes his place at the foot of the table. The president, when the roast beef is served, lifts the cover of the dish and says, "Mr. Vice President, we have here, I see, some roast beef." The vice president then lifts the cover of his dish and says, "Mr. President we have here, I see, some roast goose." "Gentlemen," then says the president, bowing to the others present, "the dinner is for all," and begins serving the roast. The vice president later does his duty in turn. The next day in all likelihood, the vice president or some other becomes president, and so it goes. My little Scotchman was most interested in telling me this, for it appealed to his fancy as it did to mine and I could see he relished the honor of being president in his turn.

It was while he was telling this that we saw before us three paths, the middle one and the one to the right going up through the dark woods, the one to the left merely skirting the woods and keeping out in the light.

"Let's see, it's the left you want, isn't it?" he asked.

"No, it's the right," I replied.

"I think she said the left," he cautioned. "Well, anyhow here's a sign post. You lift me up and I'll read what it says."

It wasn't visible from the ground.

I caught him about the legs and hoisted him aloft and he peered closely at all three signs. He was a dapper, light little man.

"You're right," he said.

We shook hands and wished each other luck. He struck off back along the road he had come in the fog and I mounted musingly through the woods. It was dark and delightfully odorous, the fog in the trees, struck by the moonlight, looking like moving sheeted ghosts. I went on gaily expecting to hear a screech owl but not one sounded. After perhaps fifteen or twenty minutes of walking I came out into the open road and then I found that I really did not know where Bridgely Level was after all. There was no sign.

I went from house to house in the moonlight—it was after midnight—rousing drowsy Englishmen who courteously gave me directions and facing yowling dogs who stood in the open roadway and barked. I had to push one barking guardian out of the way with my hands. All was silent as a church yard. Finally I came to a family of Americans who were newly locating for the winter not far from Bridgely Level and they put me right. I recall the comment of the woman who opened the door: "You're an American, aren't you?" and the interest she took in being sure that I would find my way. When I finally reached my door I paused in the garden to survey the fog-lined valley from which came the distant bark of a dog.

CHAPTER XIII
LILLY: A GIRL OF THE STREETS

I STOOD one evening in Piccadilly, at the dinner hour, staring into the bright shop windows. London's display of haberdashery and gold and silver ornaments interests me intensely. It was drizzling and I had no umbrella; yet that situation soon ceases to annoy one in England. I walked on into Regent Street and stopped under an arc light to watch the home-surging crowds—the clerks, men and women, the boys and girls.

The thought was with me as I walked in the rain, "Where shall I dine? How shall I do it?" I wandered through New Bond Street; and looking idly at the dark stores, as I came back along Piccadilly, I saw two girls, arm in arm, pass by. One of them looked over her shoulder at me and smiled. She was of medium size and simply dressed. She was pretty in the fresh English way, with large, too innocent eyes. The girls paused before a shop window and as I stopped beside them and looked at the girl who had smiled, she edged over toward me and I spoke to her.

"Wouldn't you like to take the two of us?" she asked with that quaint odd accent of the Welsh. Her voice was soft and her eyes were as blue and weak in their force as any unsophisticated girl's might well be.

"This girl isn't hard and vulgar," I said to myself. I suppose we all pride ourselves on knowing something of character in women. I thought I did.

"No," I replied rather directly to her question. "Not to-night. But let's you and I go somewhere for dinner."

"Would you mind givin' my friend a shillin'?" she asked.

"Not at all," I replied. "There you are."

It was a wet night, chill and dreary, and on second thought I made it half-a-crown. The second girl went away—a girl with a thin white face—and I turned to my companion.

"Now," I said, "what shall we do?" It was nearly eight o'clock and I was wondering where I could go with such a girl to dine. Her clothes, I perceived, were a mere patchwork. Her suit was of blue twill, worn shiny. She wore the cheapest kind of a feather boa and her hat was pathetic. But the color of her cheeks was that wonderful apple color of the English and her eyes—really her eyes were quite a triumph of nature—soft and deep blue, and not very self-protective.

"Poor little storm-blown soul," I thought as I looked at her. "Your life isn't much. A vague, conscienceless thing (in the softer sense of that word). You have a chilly future before you."

She looked as though she might be nineteen.

"Let's see! Have you had your dinner?" I asked.

"No, sir."

"Where is there a good restaurant? Not too smart, you know."

"Well, there's L.'s Corner House."

"Oh, yes, where is that? Do you go there yourself, occasionally?"

"Oh, yes, quite often. It's very nice, I think."

"We might go there," I said. "Still, on second thought, I don't think we will just now. Where is the place you go to—the place you take your—friends?"

"It's at No. — Great Titchfield Street."

"Is that an apartment or a hotel?"

"It's a flat, sir, my flat. The lady lets me bring my friends there. If you like, though, we could go to a hotel. Perhaps it would be better."

I could see that she was uncertain as to what I would think of her apartment.

"And where is the hotel? Is that nice?"

"It's pretty good, sir, not so bad."

I smiled. She was holding a small umbrella over her head.

"We had better take a taxi and get out of this rain."

I put up my hand and hailed one. We got in, the driver obviously realizing that this was a street liaison, but giving no sign. London taxi-drivers, like London policemen, are the pink of civility.

This girl was civil, obliging. I was contrasting her with the Broadway and the American type generally—hard, cynical little animals. The English, from prostitutes to queens, must have an innate sense of fair play in the social relationship of live and let live. I say this in all sincerity and with the utmost feeling of respect for the nation that has produced it. They ought to rule, by right of courtesy. Alas, I fear me greatly that the force and speed of the American, his disregard for civility and the waste of time involved, will change all this.

In the taxi I did not touch her, though she moved over near to me in that desire to play her rôle conscientiously line by line, scene by scene.

"Have we far to go?" I asked perfunctorily.

"Not very, only a little way."

"How much ought the cab charge to be?"

"Not more than eight or ten pence, sir." Then, "Do you like girls, sir?" she asked quaintly in a very human effort to be pleasant under the circumstances.

"No," I replied, lying cautiously.

She looked at me uncertainly—a little over-awed, I think. I was surely a strange fish to swim into her net anyhow.

"Very likely you don't like me then?"

"I am not sure that I do. How should I know? I never saw you before in my life. I must say you have mighty nice eyes," was my rather banal reply.

"Do you think so?" She gave me a sidelong, speculative look.

"What nationality are you?" I asked.

"I'm Welsh," she replied.

"I didn't think you were English exactly. Your tone is softer."

The taxi stopped abruptly and we got out. It was a shabby-looking building with a tea- or coffee-room on the ground floor, divided into small rooms separated by thin, cheap, wooden partitions. The woman who came to change me a half sovereign in order that I might pay the driver, was French, small and cleanly looking. She was pleasant and brisk and her whole attitude reassured me at once. She did not look like a person who would conspire to rob, and I had good reason to think more clearly of this as we came out later.

"This way," said my street girl, "we go up here."

And I followed her up two flights of thinly carpeted stairs into a small dingy room. It was clean, after the French fashion.

"It's not so bad?" she asked with a touch of pride.

"No. Not at all."

"Will you pay for the room, please?"

The landlady had followed and was standing by.

I asked how much and found I was to be charged five shillings which seemed a modest sum.

The girl locked the door, as the landlady went out, and began taking off her hat and jacket. She stood before me with half-challenging, half-speculative eyes. She was a slim, graceful, shabby figure and a note of pathos came out unexpectedly in a little air of bravado as she rested one hand on her hip and smiled at me. I was standing in front of the mantelpiece, below which was the grate ready to be fired. The girl stood beside me and watched and plainly wondered. She was beginning to suspect that I was not there on the usual errand. Her eyes, so curiously soft and blue, began to irritate me. Her hair I noticed was brown but coarse and dusty—not well kept. These poor little creatures know absolutely nothing of the art of living or fascination. They are the shabbiest pawns in life, mere husks of beauty and living on husks.

"Sit down, please," I said. She obeyed like a child. "So you're Welsh. What part of Wales do you come from?"

She told me some outlandish name.

"What were your parents? Poor, I suppose."

"Indeed not," she bridled with that quaint country accent. "My father was a grocer. He had three stores."

"I don't believe it," I said mockingly. "You women lie so. I don't believe you're telling me the truth."

It was brutal, but I wanted to get beneath the conventional lies these girls tell, if I could.

"Why not?" Her clear eyes looked into mine.

"Oh, I don't. You don't look to me like the daughter of a man who owned three grocery stores. That would mean he was well-to-do. You don't expect me to believe that, with you leading this life in London?"

She bristled vaguely but without force.

"Believe it or not," she said sullenly. "It's so."

"Tell me," I said, "how much can you make out of this business?"

"Oh, sometimes more, sometimes less. I don't walk every day. You know I only walk when I have to. If I pick up a gentleman and if he gives me a good lot I don't walk very soon again—not until that's gone. I—I don't like to very much."

"What do you call a good lot?"

"Oh, all sorts of sums. I have been given as high as six pounds."

"That isn't true," I said. "You know it isn't true. You're talking for effect."

The girl's face flushed.

"It is true. As I'm alive it's true. It wasn't in this very room, but it was in this house. He was a rich American. He was from New York. All Americans have money. And he was drunk."

"Yes, all Americans may have money," I smiled sardonically, "but they don't go round spending it on such as you in that way. You're not worth it."

She looked at me, but no angry rage sprang to her eyes.

"It's true just the same," she said meekly. "You don't like women, do you?" she asked.

"No, not very much."

"You're a woman-hater. That's what you are. I've seen such."

"Not a woman-hater, no. Simply not very much interested in them."

She was perplexed, uncertain. I began to repent of my boorishness and recklessly lighted the fire (cost—one shilling). We drew up chairs before it and I plied her with questions. She told me of the police regulations which permit a woman to go with a man, if he speaks to her first, without being arrested—not otherwise—and of the large number of women who are in the business. Piccadilly is the great walking-ground, I understood, after one o'clock in the morning; Leicester Square and the regions adjacent, between seven and eleven. There is another place in the East End—I don't recall where—where the poor Jews and others walk, but they are a dreadful lot, she assured me. The girls are lucky if they get three shillings and they are poor miserable drabs. I thought at the time, if she would look down on them, what must they be?

Then, somehow, because the conversation was getting friendly, I fancy, this little Welsh girl decided perhaps that I was not so severe as I seemed. Experience had trained her to think constantly of how much money she could extract from men—not the normal fee, there is little more than a poor living in that, but extravagant sums which produce fine clothes and jewels, according their estimate of these things. It is an old story. Other women had told her of their successes. Those who know anything of women—the street type—know how often this is tried. She told the customary story of the man who picked her up and, having escorted her to her room, offered her a pound when three or four pounds or a much larger sum even was expected. The result was, of course, according to her, dreadful for the man. She created a great scene, broke some pottery over his head, and caused a general uproar in the house. It is an old trick. Your timid man hearing this and being possibly a new or infrequent adventurer in this world, becomes fearful of a scene. Many men are timid about bargaining with a woman beforehand. It smacks too much of the brutal and evil and after all there is a certain element of romance involved in these drabby liaisons for the average man, even if there is none—*as there is none*—for the woman. It is an old, sad, sickening, grim story to most of them and men are fools, dogs, idiots, with rarely anything fine or interesting in their eyes. When they see the least chance to betray one of them, to browbeat and rob or overcharge him in any way and by any trick, they are ready to do it. This girl, Lilly E——, had been schooled by perhaps a hundred experienced advisers of the street as to how this was done. I know this is so, for afterwards she told me of how other women did it.

But to continue: "He laid a sovereign on the table and I went for him," she said.

I smiled, not so much in derision as amusement. The story did not fit her. Obviously it was not so.

"Oh, no, you didn't," I replied. "You are telling me one of the oldest stories of the trade. Now the truth is you are a silly little liar and you think you are going to frighten me, by telling me this, into giving you two or three pounds. You can save yourself the trouble. I don't intend to do it."

I had every intention of giving her two or three if it suited my mood later, but she was not to know this now.

My little Welsh girl was all at sea at once. Her powerless but really sweet eyes showed it. Something hurt—the pathos of her courage and endurance in the face of my contemptuous attitude. I had made fun of her obvious little lies and railed at her transparent tricks.

"I'm a new experience in men," I suggested.

"Men! I don't want to know anything more about them," she returned with sudden fury. "I'm sick of them—the whole lot of them! If I could get out of this I would. I wish I need never see another man!"

I did not doubt the sincerity of this outburst. But I affected not to believe her.

"It's true!" she insisted sullenly.

"You say that, but that's talk. If you wanted to get out, you would. Why don't you get a job at something? You can work."

"I don't know any trade now and I'm too old to learn."

"What nonsense! You're not more than nineteen and you could do anything you pleased. You won't, though. You are like all the others. This is the easy way. Come," I said more gently, "put on your things and let's get out of this."

Obediently and without a word she put on her coat and her bedraggled hat and we turned to the door.

"Look here," I said, "I haven't meant to be unkind. And Heaven knows I've no right to throw stones at you. We are all in a bad mess in this world—you and I, and the rest. You don't know what I'm talking about and it doesn't matter. And now let's find a good quiet restaurant where we can dine slowly and comfortably like two friends who have a lot to talk over."

In a moment she was all animation. The suggestion that I was going to act toward her as though she were a lady was, according to her standards, wildly unconventional.

"Well, you're funny," she replied, laughing; "you really are funny." And I could see that for once, in a long time, perhaps, the faintest touch of romance had entered this sordid world for her.

As we came out, seeing that my attitude had changed so radically, she asked, "Would you get me a box of cigarettes? I haven't any change."

"Surely," I said, and we stepped into a tobacconist's shop. From there we took a taxi to L.'s Corner House, which she seemed to regard as sufficiently luxurious; and from there—but I'll tell this in detail.

"Tell me," I said, after she had given the order, picking something for herself and me; "you say you come from Wales. Tell me the name of a typical mining-town which is nearer London than some of the others—some place which is really poor and hard-worked."

"Well, where I come from was pretty bad," she ventured, giving me some unpronounceable name. "The people haven't got much to live on there."

I wish you might have heard the peculiar purr of her accent.

"And how far is that?"

She gave me the hours from London and the railroad fare in shillings. I think it was about three hours at most.

"And Cardiff's pretty bad," she added. "There's lots of mines there. Very deep ones, too. The people are poor there."

"Have you ever been in a mine?"

"Yes, sir."

I smiled at her civility, for in entering and leaving the room of the house of assignation, she had helped me on and off with my overcoat, quite as a servant might.

I learned a little about Wales through her—its ill-paid life—and then we came back to London. How much did the average street girl really make? I wanted to know. She couldn't tell me and she was quite honest about it.

"Some make more than others," she said. "I'm not very good at it," she confessed. "I can't make much. I don't know how to get money out of men."

"I know you don't," I replied with real sympathy. "You're not brazen enough. Those eyes of yours are too soft. You shouldn't lie though, Lilly. You're better than that. You ought to be in some other work, worse luck."

She didn't answer, choosing to ignore my petty philosophic concern over something of which I knew so little.

We talked of girls—the different kinds. Some were really very pretty, some were not. Some had really nice figures, she said, you could see it. Others were made up terribly and depended on their courage or their audacity to trick money out of men—dissatisfied men. There were regular places they haunted, Piccadilly being the best—the only profitable place for her kind—and there were no houses of ill repute—the police did not allow them.

"Yes, but that can't be," I said. "And the vice of London isn't concentrated in just this single spot." The restaurant we were in—a large but cheap affair—was quite a center, she said. "There must be other places. All the women who do this sort of thing don't come here. Where do they go?"

"There's another place along Cheapside."

It appeared that there were certain places where the girls congregated in this district—saloons or quasi-restaurants, where they could go and wait for men to speak to them. They could wait twenty minutes at a time and then if no one spoke to them they had to get up and leave, but after twenty minutes or so they could come back again and try their luck, which meant that they would have to buy another drink. Meantime there were other places and they were always full of girls.

"You shall take me to that Cheapside place," I suggested. "I will buy you more cigarettes and a box of candy afterwards. I will pay you for your time."

She thought about her traveling companion whom she had agreed to meet at eleven, and finally promised. The companion was to be left to her fate.

While we dined we talked of men and the types they admired. Englishmen, she thought, were usually attracted toward French girls and Americans liked English girls, but the great trick was to get yourself up like an American girl and speak her patois—imitate her slang, because she was the most popular of all.

"Americans and English gentlemen"—she herself made that odd distinction—"like the American girl. I'm sometimes taken for one," she informed me, "and this hat is like the American hats."

It was. I smiled at the compliment, sordid as it may appear.

"Why do they like them?" I asked.

"Oh, the American girl is smarter. She walks quicker. She carries herself better. That's what the men tell me."

"And you are able to deceive them?"

"Yes."

"That's interesting. Let me hear you talk like an American. How do you do it?"

She pursed her lips for action. "Well, I guess I'll have to go now," she began. It was not a very good imitation. "All Americans say 'I guess,'" she informed me.

"And what else?" I said.

"Oh, let me see." She seemed lost for more. "You teach me some," she said. "I knew some other words, but I forget."

For half an hour I coached her in American slang. She sat there intensely interested while I drilled her simple memory and her lips in these odd American phrases, and I confess I took a real delight in teaching her. She seemed to think it would raise her market value. And so in a way I was aiding and abetting vice. Poor little Lilly E——! She will end soon enough.

At eleven we departed for the places where she said these women congregated and then I saw what the London underworld of this kind was like. I was told afterwards that it was fairly representative.

This little girl took me to a place on a corner very close to a restaurant we were leaving—I should say two blocks. It was on the second floor and was reached by a wide stairway, which gave into a room like a circle surrounding the head of the stairs as a center. To the left, as we came up, was a bar attended by four or five pretty barmaids, and the room, quite small, was crowded with men and women. The women, or girls rather, for I should say all ranged somewhere between seventeen and twenty-six, were good looking in an ordinary way, but they lacked the "go" of their American sisters.

The tables at which they were seated were ranged around the walls and they were drinking solely to pay the house for allowing them to sit there. Men were coming in and going out, as were the other girls. Sometimes they came in or went out alone. At other times they came in or went out in pairs. Waiters strolled to and fro, and the etiquette of the situation seemed to demand that the women should buy port wine—why, I don't know. It was vile stuff, tasting as though it were prepared of chemicals and I refused to touch it. I was shown local detectives, girls who worked in pairs, and those lowest of all creatures, the men who traffic in women. I learned now that London closes all its restaurants, saloons, hotel bars and institutions of this kind promptly at twelve-thirty, and then these women are turned out on the streets.

"You should see Piccadilly around one o'clock in the morning," my guide had said to me a little while before, and now I understood. They were all forced out into Piccadilly from everywhere.

It was rather a dismal thing sitting here, I must confess. The room was lively enough, but this type of life is so vacant of soul. It is precisely as though one stirred in straw and sawdust, expecting it to be vigorous with the feel of growing life and freshness, such as one finds in a stalk or tree. It is a world of dead ideals I should say—or, better yet, a world in which ideals never had a chance to grow. The women were the veriest birds of prey, cold, weary, disillusioned, angry, dull, sad, perhaps; the men were victims of carnal desire without the ability to understand how weary and disgusted the women were who sought to satisfy them. No clear understanding of life on either side; no suggestion of delicacy or romance. No subtlety of lure or parade. Rather, coarse, hard bargaining in which robbery and abuse and bitter recrimination play a sodden part. I know of nothing so ghastly, so suggestive of a totally dead spirit, so bitter a comment on life and love and youth and hope as a street girl's weary, speculative, commercial cry of—"Hello, sweetheart!"

From this first place we went to others—not so good, Lilly told me.

It is a poor world. I do not attempt to explain it. The man or woman of bridled passion is much better off. As for those others, how much are they themselves to blame? Circumstances have so large a part in it. I think, all in all, it is a deadly hell-hole; and yet I know that talking is not going to reform it. Life, in my judgment, does not reform. The world is old. Passion in all classes is about the same. We think this shabby world is worst because it is shabby. But is it? Isn't it merely that we are different—used to different things? I think so.

After buying her a large box of candy I hailed a taxi and took my little girl home to her shabby room and left her. She was very gay. She had been made quite a little of since we started from the region of rented rooms. Her purse was now the richer by three pounds. Her opinion had been asked, her advice taken, she had been allowed to order. I had tried to make her feel that I admired her a little and that I was sorry for her a little. At her door, in the rain, I told her I might use some of this experience in a book sometime. She said, "Send me a copy of your book. Will I be in it?"

"Yes."

"Send it to me, will you?"

"If you're here."

"Oh, I'll be here. I don't move often."

Poor little Welsh waif! I thought, how long, how long, will she be "here" before she goes down before the grim shapes that lurk in her dreary path—disease, despair, death?

CHAPTER XIV
LONDON; THE EAST END

AS interesting as any days that I spent in London were two in the East End, though I am sorry to add more drabby details to those just narrated. All my life I had heard of this particular section as grim, doleful, a center and sea of depraved and depressed life.

"Nothing like the East End of London," I have heard people say, and before I left I expected to look over it, of course. My desire to do so was whetted by a conversation I had with the poet, John Masefield, who, if I remember rightly, had once lived in the extreme East End of London, Canningtown. He had talked of the curious physical condition of the people which he described as "bluggy" or stagnant. Little intelligence in the first place, according to him, seemed to be breeding less and less intelligence as time went on. Poverty, lack of wits, lack of ambition were fostering inbreeding. Such things are easy to say. No one can really tell. Even more interesting to me was the proffered information concerning East End amusements—calf-eating contests, canary-singing contests, whiffet races, pigeon-eating contests. I was told it would be hard to indicate how simple-minded the people were in many things and yet how low and dark in their moods, physical and moral. I got a suggestion of this some days later, when I discovered in connection with the police courts that every little while the court-room is cleared in order that terrible, unprintable, almost unbearable testimony may be taken. What he said to me somehow suggested the atmosphere of the Whitechapel murders—those demoniac crimes that had thrilled the world a few years before.

I must confess that my first impression was one of disappointment. America is strident and its typical "East Side" and slum conditions are strident also. There is no voiceless degradation that I have ever seen in America. The East Side of New York is unquestionably one of the noisiest spots in the world, if not the worst. It is so full of children—so full of hope too.

I was surprised to find how distinctly different are the two realms of poverty in New York and London.

On my first visit I took the subway or tube to St. Mary's Station, Whitechapel, and getting out, investigated all that region which lies between there and the Great Eastern Railway Station and Bethnal Green and Shoreditch. I also reconnoitered Bethnal Green.

It was a chill, gray, January day. The London haze was gray and heavy, quite depressing. Almost at once I noticed that this region which I was in, instead of being strident and blatant as in America, was peculiarly quiet. The houses, as in all parts of London, were exceedingly low, two and three stories, with occasional four- and five-story buildings for variation, but all built out of that drab, yellowish-gray brick which when properly smoked has such a sad and yet effective air. The streets were not narrow, as in New York's East Side,—quite the contrary; but the difference in crowds, color, noise, life, was astounding. In New York the East Side streets, as I have said, are almost invariably crowded. Here they were almost empty. The low doors and areaways oozed occasional figures who were either thin, or shabby, or dirty, or sickly, but a crowd was not visible anywhere. They seemed to me to slink along in a half-hearted way and I, for one, experienced no sense of desperado criminality of any kind—only a low despair. The people looked too meek—too law-governed. The policeman must be an immense power in London. Vice?—yes. Poverty?—yes. I saw young boys and girls with bodies which seemed to me to be but half made up by nature—half done. They were ambling, lackadaisical, weary-looking. Low?—yes, in many cases. Filthy?—yes. Savage or dangerous?—not at all. I noticed the large number of cheap cloth caps worn by the men and boys and the large number of dull gray shawls wrapped slatternwise about the shoulders of the women. This world looked sad enough in all conscience, inexpressibly so, but because of the individual houses in many instances, the clean streets and the dark tiny shops, not unendurable—even homey in instances. I ventured to ask a stalwart London policeman—they are all stalwart in London—"Where are the very poor in the East End—the poorest there are?"

"Well, most of these people hereabouts have little enough to live on," he observed, looking straight before him with that charming soldierly air the London policemen have—his black strap under his chin.

I walked long distances through such streets as Old Montague, King Edward, Great Carden, Hope, Brick Lane, Salesworthy, Flower, Dean, Hare, Fuller, Church Row, Cheshire, Hereford,—a long, long list, too long to give here, coming out finally at St. John's Catholic Church at Bethnal Green and taking a car line for streets still farther out. I had studied shops, doorways, areas, windows, with constant curiosity. The only variation I saw to a dead level of sameness, unbroken by trees, green places or handsome buildings of any kind, were factory chimneys and endless charitable institutions covering, apparently, every form of human weakness or deficiency, but looking as if they were much drearier than the thing they were attempting to cure. One of them I remember was an institution for the orphans of seamen, and another a hospital for sick Spanish Jews. The lodging-houses for working-girls and working-boys were so numerous as to be discouraging and so dreary looking that I marveled that any boy or girl should endure to live in them. One could sense all forms of abuse and distress here. It would spring naturally out of so low a grade of intelligence. Only a Dickens, guided by the lamp of genius, could get at the inward spirit of these, and then perhaps it would not avail. Life, in its farthest reaches, sinks to a sad ugly mess and stays there.

One of the places that I came upon in my perambulations was a public washhouse, laundry and bath, established by the London County Council, if I remember rightly, and this interested me greatly. It was near Winchester Street and looked not unlike a low, one-story, factory building. Since these things are always fair indications of neighborhoods, I entered and asked permission to inspect it. I was directed to the home or apartment of a small martinet of a director or manager, quite spare and dark and cockney, who frowned on me quizzically when he opened his door,—a perfect devil of a cheap superior who was for putting me down with a black look. I could see that it was one of the natives he was expecting to encounter.

"I would like to look over the laundry and baths," I said.

"Where do you come from?" he asked.

"America," I replied.

"Oh! Have you a card?"

I gave him one. He examined it as though by some chance it might reveal something concerning me. Then he said if I would go round to the other side he would admit me. I went and waited a considerable time before he appeared. When he did, it was to lead me with a very uncertain air first into the room filled with homely bath closets, where you were charged a penny more or less—according to whether you had soap and towel or not—and where the tubs were dreary affairs with damp-looking wooden tops or flanges, and thence into the washroom and laundry-room, where at this time in the afternoon—about four o'clock—perhaps a score of women of the neighborhood were either washing or ironing.

Dreary! dreary! dreary! Ghastly! In Italy, later, and southern France, I saw public washing under the sky, beside a stream or near a fountain—a broken, picturesque, deliciously archaic fountain in one instance. Here under gray skies, in a gray neighborhood, and in this prison-like washroom was one of the most doleful pictures of life the mind of man could imagine. Always when I think of the English, I want to go off into some long analysis of their character. We have so much to learn of life, it seems to me, and among the first things is the chemistry of the human body. I always marvel at the nature of the fluids which make up some people. Different climates must produce different kinds, just as they produce strange kinds of trees and animals. Here in England this damp, gray climate produces a muggy sort of soul which you find *au naturel* only when you walk among the very poor in such a neighborhood as this. Here in this wash-house I saw the low English *au naturel*, but no passing commentary such as this could do them justice. One would have to write a book in order to present the fine differences. Weakness, lowness of spirit, a vague comprehension of only the simplest things, combined with a certain meaty solidarity, gave me the creeps. Here they were, scrubbing or ironing; strings tied around their protuberant stomachs to keep their skirts up; clothes the color of lead or darker, and about as cheerful; hair gray or brownish-black, thin, unkempt; all of them flabby and weary-looking—about the atmosphere one would find in an American poorhouse.

They washed here because there were no washing facilities in their own homes—no stationary tubs, no hot or cold water, no suitable stoves to boil water on. It was equally true of ironing facilities, the director told me. They came from blocks away.

Some women washed here for whole vicinities—the more industrious ones. And yet few came here at that—the more self-respecting stayed away. I learned this after a long conversation with my guide whose principal commentary was that they were a worthless lot and that you had to watch them all the time. "If you don't," he said in cockney English, "they won't keep things clean. You can't teach 'em scarcely how to do things right. Now and then they gets their hands caught." He was referring to the washing-drums and the mangles. It was a long story, but all I got out of it was that this was a dreary world, that he was sick of his position but compelled to keep it for financial reasons, that he wanted as little as possible to do with the kind of cattle which he considered these people to be and that he would prefer to give it up. There was a touch of socialism in all this—trying to do for the masses—but I argued that perhaps under more general socialistic conditions things would be better; certainly, one would have to secure more considerate feelings on the part of directors and some public approval which would bring out the better elements. Perhaps under truer socialism, however, public wash-houses would not be necessary at all. Anyhow, the cry from here to Bond Street and the Houses of Parliament and the stately world of the Lords seemed infinitely far. What can society do with the sad, shadowy base on which it rests?

I came another day to another section of this world, approaching the East End via Aldgate and Commercial Road, and cutting through to Bethnal Green via Stepney. I found the same conditions—clean streets, low gray buildings, shabby people, a large museum whose chief distinction was that the floor of its central rotunda had been laid by women convicts!—and towering chimneys. So little life existed in the streets, generally speaking, that I confess I was depressed. London is so far flung. There were a great many Jews of Russian, Roumanian and Slavic extraction, nearly all bearing the marks of poverty and ignorance, but looking shrewd enough at that, and a great many physically deteriorated English. The long-bearded Jew with trousers sagging about his big feet, his small derby hat pulled low over his ears, his hands folded tightly across his back, was as much in evidence here as on the East Side in New York. I looked in vain for restaurants or show places of any kind (saloons, moving pictures, etc.).

There were scarcely any here. This whole vicinity seemed to me to be given up to the poorest kind of living—sad, drab, gray. No wonder the policeman said to me: "Most of these people hereabouts have little enough to live on." I'm sure of it. Finally, after a third visit, I consulted with another writer, a reputed authority on the East End, who gave me a list of particular neighborhoods to look at. If anything exceptional was to be detected from the appearance of the people, beyond what I have noted, I could not see it. I found no poor East End costers with buttons all over their clothes, although they once existed here. I found no evidence of the overcrowded home life, because I could not get into the houses to see. Children, it seemed to me, were not nearly so numerous as in similar areas in American cities. Even a police-court proceeding I saw in Avon Square was too dull to be interesting. I was told I might expect the most startling crimes. The two hours I spent in court developed only drunkenness and adultery. But as my English literary guide informed me, only time and familiarity with a given neighborhood would develop anything. I believe this. All I felt was that in such a dull, sordid, poor-bodied world any depth of filth or crime might be reached, but who cares to know?

CHAPTER XV
ENTER SIR SCORP

DURING all my stay at Bridgely Level I had been hearing more or less—an occasional remark—of a certain Sir Scorp, an Irish knight and art critic, a gentleman who had some of the finest Manets in the world. He had given Dublin its only significant collection of modern pictures—in fact, Ireland should be substituted for Dublin, and for this he was knighted. He was the art representative of some great museum in South Africa—at Johannesburg, I think,—and he was generally looked upon as an authority in the matter of pictures.

Barfleur came one evening to my hotel with the announcement that Sir Scorp was coming down to Bridgely Level to spend Saturday and Sunday, that he would bring his car and that together on Sunday we three would motor to Oxford. Barfleur had an uncle who was a very learned master of Greek at that University and who, if we were quite nice and pleasant, might give us luncheon. We were, I found, to take a little side trip on Saturday afternoon to a place called Penn, some twenty or twenty-five miles from Bridgely Level, in Buckinghamshire, whence William Penn had come originally.

Saturday was rainy and gloomy and I doubted whether we should do anything in such weather, but Barfleur was not easily put out. I wrote all morning in my alcove, while Barfleur examined papers, and some time after two Sir Scorp arrived,— a pale, slender, dark-eyed man of thirty-five or thereabouts, with a keen, bird-like glance, a poised, nervous, sensitive manner, and that elusive, subtlety of reference and speech which makes the notable intellectual wherever you find him. For the ten thousandth time in my life, where intellectuals are concerned, I noticed that peculiarity of mind which will not brook equality save under compulsion. Where are your credentials?—such minds invariably seem to ask. How do you come to be what you think you are? Is there a flaw in your intellectual or artistic armor? Let us see. So the duel of ideas and forms and methods of procedure begins, and you are made or unmade, in the momentary estimate of the individual, by your ability to withstand criticism. I liked Sir Scorp as intellectuals go. I liked his pale face, his trim black beard, his slim hands and his poised, nervous, elusive manner.

"Oh, yes. So you're new to England. I envy you your early impression. I am reserving for the future the extreme pleasure of reading you." These little opening civilities always amuse me. We are all on the stage and we play our parts perforce whether we do so consciously or not.

It appeared that the chauffeur had to be provided for, Sir Scorp had to be given a hasty lunch. He seemed to fall in with the idea of a short run to Penn before dark, even if the day were gloomy, and so, after feeding him quickly before the grate fire in the drawing-room, we were off—Sir Scorp, Barfleur, Berenice and Percy—Barfleur's son—and myself. Sir Scorp sat with me in the tonneau and Barfleur and Percy in the front seat.

Sir Scorp made no effort to strike up any quick relationship with me—remained quite aloof and talked in generalities. I could see that he took himself very seriously—as well he might, seeing that, as I understood it, he had begun life with nothing. There were remarks—familiar ones concerning well-known painters, sculptors, architects, and the social life of England.

This first afternoon trip was pleasant enough, acquainting me as it did with the character of the country about Bridgely Level for miles and miles. Up to this time I had been commiserated on the fact that it was winter and I was seeing England under the worst possible conditions, but I am not so sure that it was such a great disadvantage. To-day as we sped down some damp, slippery hillside where the river Thames was to be seen far below twisting like a letter S in the rain, I thought to myself that light and color—summer light and color—would help but little. The villages that we passed were all rain-soaked and preternaturally solemn. There were few if any people abroad. We did not pass a single automobile on the way to Penn and but a single railroad track. These little English villages for all the extended English railway system, are practically without railway communication. You have to drive or walk a number of miles to obtain suitable railway connection.

I recall the sag-roofed, moss-patterned, vine-festooned cottages of once red but now brownish-green brick, half hidden behind high brick walls where curiously clipped trees sometimes stood up in sentinel order, and vines and bushes seemed in a conspiracy to smother the doors and windows in an excess of knitted leafage. Until you see them no words can adequately suggest the subtlety of age and some old order of comfort, once prevailing, but now obsolete, which these little towns and separate houses convey. You know, at a glance, that they are not of this modern work-a-day world. You know at a glance that no power under the sun can save them. They are of an older day and an older thought—the thought perhaps that goes with Gray's "Elegy" and Goldsmith's "Traveller" and "Deserted Village."

That night at dinner, before and after, we fell into a most stirring argument. As I recall, it started with Sir Scorp's insisting that St. Paul's of London, which is a product of the skill of Sir Christopher Wren, as are so many of the smaller churches of London, was infinitely superior externally to the comparatively new and still unfinished Roman Catholic Cathedral of Westminster. With that I could not agree. I have always objected, anyhow, to the ground plan of the Gothic cathedral, namely, the cross, as being the worst possible arrangement which could be devised for an interior. It is excellent as a scheme for three or four interiors—the arms of the cross being always invisible from the nave—but as one interior, how can it compare with the straight-lying basilica which gives you one grand forward sweep, or the solemn Greek temple with its pediment and glorifying rows of columns. Of all forms of architecture, other things being equal, I most admire the Greek, though the Gothic exteriorly, even more than interiorly, has a tremendous appeal. It is so airy and florate.

However, St. Paul's is neither Greek, Gothic, nor anything else very much—a staggering attempt on the part of Sir Christopher Wren to achieve something new which is to me not very successful. The dome is pleasing and the interior space is fairly impressive, but the general effect is botchy, and I think I said as much. Naturally this was solid ground for an argument and the battle raged to and fro,—through Greece, Rome, the Byzantine East and the Gothic realms of Europe and England. We finally came down to the skyscrapers of New York and Chicago and the railway terminals of various American cities, but I shall not go into that. What was more important was that it raised a question concerning the proletariate of England,—the common people from whom, or because of whom, all things are made to rise, and this was based on the final conclusion that all architecture is, or should be, an expression of national temperament, and this as a fact was partly questioned and partly denied, I think. It began by my asking whether the little low cottages we had been seeing that afternoon—the quaint windows, varying gables, pointless but delicious angles, and the battered, time-worn state of houses generally—was an expression of the English temperament. Mind you, I love what these things stand for. I love the simpleness of soul which somehow is conveyed by Burns and Wordsworth and Hardy, and I would have none of change if life could be ordered so sweetly—if it could really stay. Alas, I know it can not. Compared to the speed and skill which is required to manipulate the modern railway trains, the express companies, the hotels, the newspapers, all this is helpless, pathetic.

Sir Scorp's answer was yes, that they were an expression, but that, nevertheless, the English mass was a beast of muddy brain. It did not—could not—quite understand what was being done. Above it were superimposed intellectual classes, each smaller and more enthusiastic and aware as you reach the top. At least, it has been so, he said, but now democracy and the newspapers are beginning to break up this lovely solidarity of simplicity and ignorance into something that is not so nice.

"People want to get on now," he declared. "They want each to be greater than the other. They must have baths and telephones and railways and they want to undo this simplicity. The greatness of England has been due to the fact that the intellectual superior classes with higher artistic impulses and lovelier tendencies generally could direct the masses and like sheep they would follow. Hence all the lovely qualities of England; its ordered households, its beautiful cathedrals, its charming castles and estates, its good roads, its delicate homes, and order and precedences. The magnificent princes of the realm have been able to do so much for art and science because their great impulses need not be referred back to the mass—the ignorant, non-understanding mass—for sanction."

Sir Scorp sprang with ease to Lorenzo, the magnificent, to the princes of Italy, to Rome and the Cæsars for illustration. He cited France and Louis. Democracy, he declared, is never going to do for all what the established princes could do. Democracy is going to be the death of art. Not so, I thought and said, for democracy can never alter the unalterable difference between high and low, rich and poor, little brain and big brain, strength and weakness. It cannot abolish difference and make a level plane. It simply permits the several planes to rise higher together. What is happening is that the human pot is boiling again. Nations are undergoing a transition period. We are in a maelstrom, which means change and reconstruction. America is going to flower next and grandly, and perhaps after that Africa, or Australia. Then, say, South America, and we come back to Europe by way of India, China, Japan and through Russia. All in turn and new great things from each again. Let's hope so. A pretty speculation, anyhow.

At my suggestion of American supremacy, Sir Scorp, although he protested, no doubt honestly, that he preferred the American to any other foreign race, was on me in a minute with vital criticism and I think some measure of insular solidarity. The English do not love the Americans—that is sure. They admire their traits—some of them, but they resent their commercial progress. The wretched Americans will not listen to the wise British. They will not adhere to their noble and magnificent traditions. They go and do things quite out of order and the way in which they should be done, and then they come over to England and flaunt the fact in the noble Britisher's face. This is above all things sad. It is evil, crass, reprehensible, anything you will, and the Englishman resents it. He even resents it when he is an Irish Englishman. He dislikes the German much—fears the outcome of a war from that quarter—but really he dislikes the American more. I honestly think he considers America far more dangerous than Germany. What are you going to do with that vast realm which is "the states"? It is upsetting the whole world by its nasty progressiveness, and this it should not be permitted to do. England should really lead. England should have invented all the things which the Americans have invented. England should be permitted to dictate to-day and to set the order of forms and procedures, but somehow it isn't doing it. And, hang it all! the Americans *are*. We progressed through various other things,—an American operatic manager who was then in London attempting to revise English opera, an American tobacco company which had made a failure of selling tobacco to the English, but finally weariness claimed us all, and we retired for the night, determined to make Oxford on the morrow if the weather faired in the least.

The next morning I arose, glad that we had had such a forceful argument. It was worth while, for it brought us all a little closer together. Barfleur, the children and I ate breakfast together while we were waiting for Scorp to come down and wondering whether we should really go, it was so rainy. Barfleur gave me a book on Oxford, saying that if I was truly interested I should look up beforehand the things that I was to see. Before a pleasant grate fire I studied this volume, but my mind was disturbed by the steadily approaching fact of the trip itself, and I made small progress. Somehow during the morning the plan that Barfleur had of getting us invited to luncheon by his uncle at Oxford disappeared and it turned out that we were to go the whole distance and back in some five or six hours, having only two or three hours for sightseeing.

At eleven Sir Scorp came down and then it was agreed that the rain should make no difference. We would go, anyhow.

I think I actually thrilled as we stepped into the car, for somehow the exquisite flavor and sentiment of Oxford was reaching me here. I hoped we would go fast so that I should have an opportunity to see much of it. We did speed swiftly past open fields where hay cocks were standing drearily in the drizzling rain, and down dark aisles of bare but vine-hung trees, and through lovely villages where vines and small oddly placed windows and angles and green-grown, sunk roofs made me gasp for joy. I imagined how they would look in April and May with the sun shining, the birds flying, a soft wind blowing. I think I could smell the odor of roses here in the wind and rain. We tore through them, it seemed to me, and I said once to the driver, "Is there no law against speeding in England?"

"Yes," he replied, "there is, but you can't pay any attention to that if you want to get anywhere."

There were graceful flocks of crows flying here and there. There were the same gray little moss-grown churches with quaint belfries and odd vine-covered windows. There were the same tree-protected borders of fields, some of them most stately where the trees were tall and dark and sad in the rain. I think an open landscape, such as this, with green, wet grass or brown stubble and low, sad, heavy, gray clouds for sky and background, is as delicious as any landscape that ever was. And it was surely not more than one hour and a half after we left Bridgely before we began to rush through the narrow, winding streets where houses, always brick and stone and red walls with tall gates and vines above them, lined either side of the way. It was old—you could see that, even much that could be considered new in England was old according to the American standard. The plan of the city was odd to me because unlike the American cities, praise be! there was no plan. Not an east and west street, anywhere. Not a north and south one. Not a four- or five-story building anywhere, apparently, and no wood; just wet, gray stone and reddish-brown brick and vines. When I saw High Street and the façade of Queens College I leaped for joy. I can think of nothing lovelier in either marble or bronze than this building line. It is so gentle, so persuasive of beautiful thought, such an invitation to reflection and tender romance. It is so obvious that men have worked lovingly over this. It is so plain there has been great care and pains and that life has dealt tenderly with all. It has not been destroyed or revised and revivified, but just allowed to grow old softly and gracefully.

Owing to our revised plans for luncheon I had several marmalade sandwiches in my hand, laid in an open white paper which Barfleur had brought and passed around, the idea being that we would not have time for lunch if we wished to complete our visit and get back by dark. Sir Scorp had several meat sandwiches in another piece of paper equally flamboyant. I was eating vigorously, for the ride had made me hungry, the while my eyes searched out the jewel wonders of the delicious prospect before me.

"This will never do," observed Sir Scorp, folding up his paper thoughtfully, "invading these sacred precincts in this ribald manner. They'll think we're a lot of American sightseers come to despoil the place."

"Such being the case," I replied, "we'll disgrace Barfleur for life. He has relations here. Nothing would give me greater pleasure."

"Come, Dreiser. Give me those sandwiches."

It was Barfleur, of course.

I gave over my feast reluctantly. Then we went up the street, shoulder to shoulder, as it were, Berenice walking with first one and another. I had thought to bring my little book on Oxford and to my delight I could see that it was even much better than the book indicated.

How shall one do justice to so exquisite a thing as Oxford,—twenty-two colleges and halls, churches, museums and the like, with all their lovely spires, towers, buttresses, ancient walls, ancient doors, pinnacles, gardens, courts, angles and nooks which turn and wind and confront each other and break into broad views and delicious narrow vistas with a grace and an uncertainty which delights and surprises the imagination at every turn. I can think of nothing more exquisite than these wonderful walls, so old that whatever color they were originally, they now are a fine mottled black and gray, with uncertain patches of smoky hue, and places where the stone has crumbled to a dead white. Time has done so much; tradition has done so much; pageantry and memory; the art of the architect, the perfect labor of builder, the beauty of the stone itself, and then nature—leaves and trees and the sky! This day of rain and lowery clouds—though Sir Scorp insisted it could stand no comparison with sunshine and spring and the pathos of a delicious twilight was yet wonderful to me. Grays and blacks and dreary alterations of storm clouds have a remarkable value when joined with so delicate and gracious a thing as perfectly arranged stone. We wandered through alleys and courts and across the quadrangles of University College, Baliol College, Wadham College, Oriel College, up High Street, through Park Street, into the Chapel of Queens College, into the banquet of Baliol and again to the Bodleian Library, and thence by strange turns and lovely gateways to an inn for tea. It was raining all the while and I listened to disquisitions by Sir Scorp on the effect of the personalities, and the theories of both Inigo Jones and Christopher Wren, not only on these buildings but on the little residences in the street. Everywhere, Sir Scorp, enthusiast that he is, found something—a line of windows done in pure Tudor, a clock tower after the best fashion of Jones, a façade which was Wren pure and simple. He quarreled delightfully, as the artist always will, with the atrocity of this restoration or that failure to combine something after the best manner, but barring the worst errors which showed quite plainly enough in such things as the Oxford art gallery and a modern church or two—it was all perfect. Time and tradition have softened, petted, made lovely even the plainest surfaces.

I learned from Barfleur where Walter Pater and Oscar Wilde lived, where Shelley's essay on atheism was burned, and where afterwards a monument was erected to him, where some English bishops were burned for refusing to recant their religious beliefs and where the dukes and princes of the realm were quartered in their college days. Sir Scorp descanted on the pity of the fact, that some, who would have loved a world such as this in their youth, could never afford to come here, while others who were as ignorant as boors and as dull as swine, were for reasons of wealth and family allowed to wallow in a world of art which they could not possibly appreciate. Here as elsewhere I learned that professors were often cads and pedants—greedy, jealous, narrow, academic. Here as elsewhere precedence was the great fetish of brain and the silly riot of the average college student was as common as in the meanest school. Life is the same, be art great or little, and the fame of even Oxford cannot gloss over the weakness of a humanity that will alternately be low and high, shabby and gorgeous, narrow and vast.

The last thing we saw were some very old portions of Christ College, which had been inhabited by Dominican monks, I believe, in their day, and this thrilled and delighted me quite as much as anything. I forgot all about the rain in trying to recall the type of man and the type of thought that must have passed in and out of those bolt-riven doors, but it was getting time to leave and my companions would have none of my lagging delight.

It was blowing rain and as we were leaving Oxford I lost my cap and had to walk back after it. Later I lost my glove! As we rode my mind went back over the ancient chambers, the paneled woodwork, stained glass windows, and high vaulted ceilings I had just seen. The heavy benches and somber portraits in oil sustained themselves in my mind clearly. Oxford, I said to myself, was a jewel architecturally. Another thousand years and it would be as a dream of the imagination. I feel now as if its day were done; as if so much gentle beauty can not endure. I had seen myself the invasion of the electric switch board and the street car in High Street, and of course other things will come. Already the western world is smiling at a solemnity and a beauty which are noble and lovely to look upon, but which cannot keep pace with a new order and a new need.

CHAPTER XVI
A CHRISTMAS CALL

THE Christmas holidays were drawing near and Barfleur was making due preparations for the celebration of that event. He was a stickler for the proper observance of those things which have national significance and national or international feeling behind them. Whatever joy he might get out of such things, much or little, I am convinced that he was much more concerned lest some one should fail of an appropriate share of happiness than he was about anything else. I liked that in Barfleur. It touched me greatly, and made me feel at times as though I should like to pat him on the head.

During all my youth in Indiana and elsewhere I had been fed on that delightful picture, "Christmas in England," concocted first, I believe (for American consumption, anyhow), by Washington Irving, and from him rehashed for magazines and newspaper purposes until it had come to be romance *ad nauseum*. The boar's head carried in by the butler of Squire Bracebridge, the ancient peacock pie with the gorgeous tail feathers arranged at one end of the platter and the crested head at the other, the yule log, the mistletoe berries, and the Christmas choristers singing outside of windows and doors of echoing halls, had vaguely stood their ground and as such had rooted themselves in my mind as something connected with ancestral England. I did not exactly anticipate anything of this kind as being a part of present-day England, or of Barfleur's simple country residence, but, nevertheless, I was in England, and he was making Christmas preparations of one kind or another, and my mind had a perfect right to ramble a little. I think most of all I anticipated another kind of toy from that to which we are accustomed in America.

So many things go to make up that very amiable feast of Christmas when it is successful that I can hardly think now of all that contributed to this one. There was Sir Scorp, of whom by now I had grown very fond, and who was coming here to spend the holidays. There was Gerard Barfleur, a cousin of Barfleur's, a jolly, roystering theatrical manager, who was unquestionably—after Barfleur—one of the most pleasing figures I met in England, a whimsical, comic-ballad-singing, character-loving soul, who was as great a favorite with women and children as one would want to find. He knew all sorts of ladies, apparently, of high and low degree, rich and poor, beautiful and otherwise, and seemed kindly disposed toward them all. I could write a splendid human-interest sketch of Gerard Barfleur alone. There was Mr. T. McT., a pale, thoughtful person, artistic and poetic to his finger tips, curator of one of the famous museums, a lover of Mr. Housman's "A Shropshire Lad," a lover of ancient glass and silver, whose hair hung in a sweet mop over his high, pale forehead, and whose limpid dark eyes shone with a kindly, artistic light. Then there was Barfleur's aunt and her daughter, mother and sister respectively of the highly joyous Gerard Barfleur, and wife and daughter of a famous litterateur. Then, to cap it all, were the total of Barfleur's very interesting household,—housekeeper, governess, maid, cook, gardener, and—last, but not least, the four charming, I might almost say adorable, children.

There, too, was Barfleur, a host in himself. For weeks beforehand he kept saying on occasion as we wandered about London together, "No, we can't go there," or, "You mustn't accept that, because we have reserved that Saturday and Sunday for Christmas at my place," and so nothing was done which might interfere. Being in his hands I finally consulted him completely as to Christmas presents, and found that I was to be limited to very small gifts, mere tokens of good-will, I being his guest. I did manage to get him a supply of his favorite cigarettes, however, unknown to himself,—the ones his clever secretary told me he much preferred,—and had them sent out to the house with some favorite books for the remaining members of the household.

But the man was in such high spirits over the whole program he had laid out for me—winter and spring,—the thought of Paris and the Riviera,—that he was quite beside himself. More than once he said to me, beaming through his monocle, "We shall have a delightful time on the continent soon. I'm looking forward to it, and to your first impressions." Every evening he wanted to take my hastily scribbled notes and read them, and after doing so was anxious to have me do them all just that way, that is, day by day as I experienced them. I found that quite impossible, however. Once he wanted to know if I had any special preference in wines or cordials and I knew very well why he asked. Another time he overheard me make the statement that I had always longed to eat rich, odorous Limburger cheese from Germany.

"Done!" he exclaimed. "We shall have it for Christmas."

"But, Papa," piped up Berenice maliciously, "we don't all have to have it at the same time, do we?"

"No, my dear," replied Barfleur solemnly, with that amazingly patronizing and parental air which always convulsed me, a sort of gay deviltry always lurking behind it.

"Only Mr. Dreiser need have it. He is German and likes it."

I assumed as German a look as I might,—profound, Limburgery.

"And I believe you like Mr. Jones's sausage," he observed on another occasion, referring to an American commodity, which he had heard me say in New York that I liked. "We shall have some of those."

"Are American sausage like English sausage?" inquired young Charles Gerald interestedly.

"Now Heaven only knows," I replied. "I have never eaten English sausages. Ask your father."

Barfleur merely smiled. "I think not," he replied.

"Christmas is certainly looking up," I said to him badgeringly. "If I come out of here alive,—in condition for Paris and the Riviera,—I shall be grateful."

He beamed on me reprovingly.

Well, finally, to make a long story short, the day came, or, at least, the day before. We were all assembled for a joyous Christmas Eve—T. McT., Sir Scorp, Gerard Barfleur, the dearest aunt and the charming cousin, extremely intelligent and artistic women both, the four children, Barfleur's very clever and appealing secretary, and myself. There was a delightful dinner spread at seven-thirty, when we all assembled to discuss the prospects of the morrow. It was on the program, as I discovered, that I should arise, and accompany Barfleur, his aunt, his cousin, and the children to a nearby abbey church, a lovely affair, I was told, on the bank of the Thames hard by the old English town called Bridgely, while Gerard Barfleur, who positively refused to have anything to do with religion of any kind, quality or description, was to go and reconnoiter a certain neighboring household (of which more anon), and to take young James Herbert (he of the "bawth") for a fine and long-anticipated ride on his motor cycle. Lord Scorp and T. McT. were to remain behind to discuss art, perhaps, or literature, being late risers. If there was to be any Santa Claus, which the children doubted, owing to Barfleur's rather grave asseveration to the contrary (there having been a number of reasons why a severely righteous Santa might see fit to remain away), he was not to make his appearance until rather late in the afternoon. Meanwhile we had all adjourned to the general living-room, where a heavy coal fire blazed on the hearth (for once), and candles were lighted in profusion. The children sang songs of the north, accompanied by their governess. I can see their quaint faces now, gathered about the piano. Lord Scorp, McT. and myself indulged in various artistic discussions and badinage; Mrs. Barfleur, the aunt, told me the brilliant story of her husband's life,—a great naturalistic philosopher and novelist,—and finally after coffee, sherry, nuts and much music and songs,—some comic ones by Gerard Barfleur,—we retired for the night.

It is necessary, to prepare the reader properly for the morrow, to go back a few days or weeks, possibly, and tell of a sentimental encounter that befell me one day as I was going for a walk in that green world which encompassed Bridgely Level. It was a most delightful spectacle. Along the yellowish road before me, with its border of green grass and green though leafless trees, there was approaching a most interesting figure of a woman, a chic, dashing bit of femininity,—at once (the presumption, owing to various accompanying details was mine) wife, mother, chatelaine,—as charming a bit of womanhood and English family sweetness as I had yet seen in England. English women, by and large, let me state here, are not smart, at least those that I encountered; but here was one dressed after the French fashion in trig, close-fitting blue, outlining her form perfectly, a little ermine cap of snowy whiteness set jauntily over her ear, her smooth black hair parted demurely over her forehead, a white muff warming her hands, and white spats emphasizing the trim leather of her foot gear. Her eyes were dark brown, her cheeks rosy, her gait smart and tense. I could scarcely believe she was English, the mother of the three-year-old in white and red wool, a little girl, who was sitting astride a white donkey, which, in turn, was led by a trim maid or nurse or governess in somber brown,—but it was quite plain that she was. There was such a wise, sober look about all this smartness, such a taut, buttressed conservatism, that I was enchanted. It was such a delightful picture to encounter of a clear December morning that, in the fashion of the English, I exclaimed, "My word! This is something like!"

I went back to the house that afternoon determined to make inquiries. Perhaps she was a neighbor,—a friend of the family!

Of all the individuals who have an appropriate and superior taste for the smart efforts of the fair sex, commend me to Barfleur. His interest and enthusiasm neither flags nor fails. Being a widower of discretion he knows exactly what is smart for a woman as well as a man, and all you have to do to make him prick up his ears attentively is to mention trig beauty as existing in some form, somewhere,—not too distant for his adventuring.

"What's this?" I can see his eye lighting. "Beauty? A lovely woman? When? Where?"

This day, finding Wilkins in the garden trimming some bushes, I had said, "Wilkins, do you know any family hereabouts that keeps a white donkey?"

Wilkins paused and scratched his ear reflectively. "No, sir! I cawn't say has I do, sir. I might harsk, sir, down in the village, hif you're very hanxious to know."

Be it known by all men that I feed Wilkins amply for all services performed,—hence his interest.

"Never mind for the present, Wilkins," I replied. "I may want to know. If so, I'll ask you."

I knew he would inquire anyhow.

That night at dinner, the family being all present, Barfleur in his chair at the head of the table, the wine at his right, I said mildly—

"I saw the most beautiful woman to-day I have yet seen in England."

Barfleur was just in the act of elevating a glass of champagne to his lips, but he paused to fix me with an inquiring eye.

"Where?" he questioned solemnly. "Were you in the city?"

"Not at all. I rarely, if ever, see them in the city. It was very near here. A most beautiful woman,—very French,—trim figure, small feet, a gay air. She had a lovely three-year-old child with her riding a white donkey."

"A white donkey? Trim, very French, you say? This is most interesting! I don't recall any one about here who keeps a white donkey. Berenice," he turned to his young daughter. "Do you recall any one hereabout who keeps a white donkey?"

Berenice, a wizard of the future, merely smiled wisely.

"I do not, Papa."

"This is very curious, very curious indeed," continued Barfleur, returning to me. "For the life of me, I cannot think of any one who keeps a white donkey. Who can she be? Walking very near here, you say? I shall have a look into this. She may be the holiday guest of some family. But the donkey and child and maid—Young, you say? Percy, you don't remember whether any one hereabout owns a white donkey,—any one with a maid and a three-year-old child?"

Percy smiled broadly. "No, I don't," he said. Barfleur shook his head in mock perturbation. "It's very strange," he said. "I don't like the thought of there being any really striking women hereabout of whom I know nothing." He drank his wine.

There was no more of this then, but I knew that in all probability the subject would come up again. Barfleur inquired, and Wilkins inquired, and as was natural, the lady was located. She turned out to be the wife of a tennis, golf, and aeroplane expert or champion, a man who held records for fast automobiling and the like, and who was independently settled in the matter of means. Mrs. Barton Churchill was her name as I recall. It also turned out most unfortunately that Barfleur did not know her, and could not place any one who did.

"This is all very trying," he said when he discovered this much. "Here you are, a celebrated American author, admiring a very attractive woman whom you meet on the public highway; and here am I, a resident of the neighborhood in which she is living, and I do not even know her. If I did, it would all be very simple. I could take you over, she would be immensely flattered at the nice things you have said about her. She would be grateful to me for bringing you. Presto,—we should be fast friends."

"Exactly," I replied sourly. "You and she would be fast friends. After I am gone in a few days all will be lovely. I shall not be here to protect my interests. It is always the way. I am the cat's paw, the bait, the trap. I won't stand for it. I saw her first, and she is mine."

"My dear fellow," he exclaimed banteringly, "how you go on! I don't understand you at all. This is England. The lady is married. A little neighborly friendship. Hmm."

"Yes, yes," I replied. "I know all about the neighborly friendship. You get me an introduction to the lady and I shall speak for myself."

"As for that matter," he added thoughtfully, "it would not be inappropriate under the circumstances for me to introduce myself in your behalf. She would be pleased, I'm sure. You are a writer, you admire her. Why shouldn't she be pleased?"

"Curses!" I exclaimed. "Always in the way. Always stepping in just when I fancy I have found something for myself."

But nothing was done until Gerard Barfleur arrived a day or two before Christmas. That worthy had traveled all over England with various theatrical companies. Being the son of an eminent literary man he had been received in all circles, and knew comfortable and interesting people in every walk of life apparently, everywhere. Barfleur, who, at times, I think, resented his social sufficiency, was nevertheless prone to call on him on occasion for advice. On this occasion, since Gerard knew this neighborhood almost as well as his cousin, he consulted him as to our lady of the donkey.

"Mrs. Churchill? Mrs. Barton Churchill?" I can still see his interested look. "Why, it seems to me that I do know some one of that name. If I am not mistaken I know her husband's brother, Harris Churchill, up in Liverpool. He's connected with a bank up there. We've motored all over England together, pretty nearly. I'll stop in Christmas morning and see if it isn't the same family. The description you give suits the lady I know almost exactly."

Barfleur

I was all agog. The picture she had presented was so smart. Barfleur was interested though perhaps disappointed, too, that Gerard knew her when he didn't.

"This is most fortunate," he said to me solemnly. "Now if it should turn out that he does know her, we can call there Christmas day after dinner. Or perhaps he will take you."

This came a little regretfully, I think, for Gerard Barfleur accounted himself an equal master with his cousin in the matter of the ladies, and was not to be easily set aside. So Christmas eve it was decided that Gerard should, on the morrow, reconnoiter the Churchill country house early, and report progress, while we went to church. Fancy Barfleur and me marching to church Christmas morning with the children!

Christmas in England! The day broke clear and bright, and there we all were. It was not cold, and as is usual, there was little if any wind. I remember looking out of my window down into the valley toward Bridgely, and admiring the green rime upon the trees, the clustered chimneys of a group of farmers' and working-men's cottages, the low sagging roofs of red tile or thatch, and the small window panes that always somehow suggest a homey simplicity that I can scarcely resist. The

English milkmaid of fiction, the simple cottages, the ordered hierarchy of farmers are, willy nilly, fixtures in my mind. I cannot get them out.

First then, came a breakfast in our best bibs and tuckers, for were we not to depart immediately afterwards to hear an English Christmas service? Imagine Barfleur—the pride of Piccadilly,—marching solemnly off at the head of his family to an old, gray abbey church. As the French say, "I smile." We all sat around and had our heavy English breakfast,—tea, and, to my comfort and delight, "Mr. Jones's sausages." Barfleur had secured a string of them from somewhere.

"Think of it," commented Berenice sardonically. "'Mr. Jones's sausages' for breakfast. Aren't they comic! Do you like them?"

"I most assuredly do."

"And do you eat them every day in A-máy-reeka?" queried Charles Gerard with a touch of latent jesting in his voice.

"When I can afford them, yes."

"They're quite small, aren't they?" commented five-year-old James Herbert.

"Precisely," I replied, unabashed by this fire of inquiry. "That's their charm."

The church that we visited was one of those semi-ancient abbey affairs, done in good English Gothic, with a touch of Tudor here and there, and was located outside the village of Bridgely Level two or three miles from Barfleur's home. I recall with simple pleasure the smug, self-righteous, Sunday-go-to-meeting air with which we all set forth, crossing homey fields via diagonal paths, passing through stiles and along streams and country roads, by demure little cottages that left one breathless with delight. I wish truly that England could be put under glass and retained as a perfect specimen of unconscious, rural poetry—the south of England. The pots and pans outside the kitchen doorways! The simple stoop, ornamented with clambering vines! The reddish-green sagging roofs with their clustered cylindrical chimneypots! When we came to the top of a hill we could see the church in the valley below, nestling beside one bank of the Thames which wound here and there in delightful S's. A square tower, as I recall, rose quaintly out of a surrounding square of trees, grass, grave-stones and box-hedge.

There was much ado in this semi-ancient place as we came up, for Christmas day, of all days, naturally drew forth a history-loving English audience. Choir boys were scurrying here and there, some ladies of solemn demeanor, who looked as if they might be assisting at the service in some way or another, were dawdling about, and I even saw the rector in full canonicals hastening up a gravel path toward a side door, as though matters needed to be expedited considerably. The interior was dark, heavy-beamed, and by no means richly ornamented with stained glass, but redolent of by-gone generations at that. The walls were studded with those customary slabs and memorial carvings with which the English love to ornament their church interiors. A fair-sized, and yet for so large an edifice, meager audience was present, an evidence it seemed to me, of the validity of the protest against state support for the Established Church. There was a great storm of protest in England at this time against the further state support of an institution that was not answering the religious needs of the people, and there had been some discussion of the matter at Barfleur's house. As was natural, the artistically inclined were in favor of anything which would sustain, unimpaired, whether they had religious value or not, all the old cathedrals, abbeys, and neighborhood churches, solely because of their poetic appearance. On the other hand an immense class, derisively spoken of as "chapel people," were heartily in favor of the ruder disposition of the matter. Barfleur in his best Piccadilly clothing was for their maintenance.

To be frank, as charming as was this semi-ancient atmosphere, and possibly suited to the current English neighborhood mood (I could not say as to that), it did not appeal to me as strongly on this occasion as did many a similar service in American churches of the same size. The vestments were pleasing as high church vestments go; the choir, made of boys and men from the surrounding countryside no doubt, was not absolutely villainous but it could have been much better. To tell the truth, it seemed to me that I was witnessing the last and rather threadbare evidences of an older and much more prosperous order of things. Beautiful in its way? Yes. Quaint? Yes. But smacking more of poverty and an ordered system continued past its day than anything else. I felt a little sorry for the old church and the thin rector and the goodly citizens, albeit a little provincial, who clung so fatuously to a time-worn form. They have their place, no doubt, and it makes that sweet, old lavender atmosphere which seems to hover over so much that one encounters in England. Nevertheless life does move on, and we must say good-bye to many a once delightful thing. Why not set these old churches aside as museums or art galleries, or for any other public use, as they do with many of them in Italy, and let the matter go at that? It is not necessary that a service be kept up in them day by day and year by year. Services on special or state occasions would be sufficient. Let by-gones be by-gones, and let the people tax themselves for things they really do want, skating-rinks, perhaps, and moving pictures. They seemed to flourish even in these elderly and more sedate neighborhoods.

Outside in the graveyard, after the services were over and we were idling about a few moments, I found a number of touches of that valiant simplicity in ability which is such a splendid characteristic of the English. Although there were many graves here of the nobility and gentry, dating from as far back as the sixteenth century, there was no least indication so far as I could see, of ostentation, but everywhere simple headstones recording names only, and not virtues,—sometimes, perhaps, a stately verse or a stoic line. I noticed with a kind of English-speaking pride the narrow new-made grave of Sir Robert Hart, the late great English financial administrator of China, who, recently deceased, had been brought over sea to this simple churchyard, to lie here with other members of his family in what I assumed to be the neighborhood of his youth and nativity. It is rather fine, I think, when a nation's sons go forth over the world to render honorable service, each after his capacity, and then come back in death to an ancient and beloved soil. The very obscurity of this little grave with its two-feet, six-inch headstone and flowerless mound spoke more to me of the dignity and ability that is in true greatness of soul than a soaring shaft might otherwise do.

On the way home I remember we discussed Christian Science and its metaphysical merit in a world where all creeds and all doctrines blow, apparently, so aimlessly about. Like all sojourners in this fitful fever of existence Mrs. Barfleur and her daughter and her son, the cheerful Gerard were not without their troubles; so much so that, intelligent woman that she was, and quite aware of the subtleties and uncertainties of religious dogma, she was eager to find something upon which she could lean,—spiritually speaking,—the strong arm, let us say, of an All Mighty, no less, who would perchance heal her of her griefs and ills. I take it, as I look at life, that only the very able intellectually, or the very rock-ribbed and dull materially can front the storms and disasters that beset us, or the ultimate dark which only the gifted, the imaginative, see, without quakes and fears. So often have I noticed this to be true, that those who stand up brave and strong in their youth turn a nervous and anguished eye upon this troubled seeming in later years. They have no longer any heart for a battle that is only rhyme and no reason, and, whether they can conceive why or not, they must have a god. I, for one, would be the last person in the world to deny that everywhere I find boundless evidence of an intelligence or intelligences far superior to my own. I, for one, am inclined to agree with the poet that "if my barque sink, 'tis to another sea." In fact I have always innately presumed the existence of a force or forces that, possibly ordered in some noble way, maintain a mathematical, chemical, and mechanical parity and order in visible things. I have always felt, in spite of all my carpings, that somehow in a large way there is a rude justice done under the sun, and that a balance for, I will not say right, but for happiness is maintained. The world has long since gathered to itself a vast basket of names such as Right, Justice, Mercy, and Truth. My thinking has nothing to do with these. I do not believe that we can conceive what the ultimate significance of anything is, therefore why label it? I have seen good come to the seemingly evil and evil come to the seemingly good. But if a religion will do anybody any good, for Heaven's sake, let him have it! To me it is a case of individual, sometimes of race weakness. A stronger mind could not attempt to define what may not be defined, nor to lean upon what, to infinite mind must be utterly insubstantial and thin air. Obviously there is a vast sea of force. Is it good? Is it evil? Give that to the philosophers to fight over, and to the fearful and timid give a religion. "A mighty fortress is our God," sang Luther. He may be, I do not know.

But to return to Mrs. Barfleur and her daughter and Barfleur's children and Barfleur ambling across the sunny English landscape this Christmas morning. It was a fine thing to see the green patina of the trees, and richer green grass growing lush and thick all winter long, and to see the roofs of little towns like Bridgely Level,—for we were walking on high ground,—and the silvery windings of the Thames in the valley below, whence we had just come. I think I established the metaphysical basis of life quite ably,—for myself,—and urged Mrs. Barfleur to take up Christian Science. I assailed the wisdom of maintaining by state funds the Established Church largely, I think, to irritate Barfleur, and protested that the chapel people had a great deal of wisdom on their side. As we drew near Bridgely Level and Barfleur's country place it occurred to me that Gerard Barfleur had gone to find out if he really knew the lady of the donkey, and I was all anxiety to find out. Barfleur himself was perking up considerably, and it was agreed that first we would have an early afternoon feast, all the Christmas dainties of the day, and then, if Gerard really knew the lady, we were to visit her and then return to the house, where, I now learned, there was to be a Santa Claus. He was to arrive via the courtesy of Gerard Barfleur who was to impersonate him, and on that account, Barfleur announced, we might have to cut any impending visit to our lady short in order not to disappoint the children, but visit we would. Knowing Gerard Barfleur to be a good actor and intensely fond of children,—Barfleur's especially,—I anticipated some pleasure here. But I will be honest, the great event of the day was our lady of the donkey, her white furs, and whether she was really as striking as I had imagined. I was afraid Gerard would return to report that either, (A)—he did not know her, or (B)—that she was not so fascinating as I thought. In either case my anticipated pleasure would come to the ground with a crash. We entered, shall I say, with beating hearts.

Gerard had returned. With Sir Scorp and T. McT. he was now toasting his English legs in front of the fire, and discoursing upon some vanity of the day. At sight of the children he began his customary badinage but I would have none of it. Barfleur fixed him with a monitory eye. "Well," he said, putting the burden of the inquiry on me. "Our friend here has been quite restless during the services this morning. What did you find out?"

"Yes," chimed in Mrs. Barfleur who had been informed as to this romantic encounter, "for goodness' sake tell us. We are all dying to know."

"Yes, tell them," sarcastically interpolated Lord Scorp. "There will be no peace, believe me, until you do."

"To be sure, to be sure," cheerfully exclaimed Gerard, straightening up from jouncing James Herbert. "I know her well. Her sister and her husband are here with her. That little baby is hers, of course. They live just over the hill here. I admire your taste. She is one of the smartest women I know. I told her that you were stopping here and she wants you to come over and see the Christmas tree lighted. We are all invited after dinner."

"Very good," observed Barfleur, rubbing his hands. "Now that is settled."

"Isn't she charming," observed Mrs. G. A. Barfleur, "to be so politely disposed?"

Thereafter the dinner could not come too soon, and by two-thirty we were ready to depart, having consumed Heaven knows how many kinds of wines and meats, English plum-pudding, and—especially for me—real German Limburger. It was a splendid dinner.

Shall I stop to describe it? I cannot say, outside of the interesting English company, that it was any better or any worse than many another Christmas feast in which I have participated. Imagine the English dining-room, the English maid, the housekeeper in watchful attendance on the children, the maid, like a bit of Dresden china, on guard over the service, Barfleur, monocle in eye, sitting solemnly in state at the head of the board, Lord Scorp, T. McT., Gerard Barfleur, his mother, her daughter, myself, the children all chattering and gobbling. The high-sounding English voices, the balanced English phrases, the quaint English scene through the windows,—it all comes back, a bit of sweet color. Was I happy? Very. Did I enjoy myself? Quite. But as to this other matter.

It was a splendid afternoon. On the way over, Barfleur and myself, the others refusing contemptuously to have anything to do with this sentimental affair, had the full story of our lady of the donkey and her sister and the two brothers that they married.

We turned eventually into one of those charming lawns enclosed by a high, concealing English fence, and up a graveled automobile path to a snow-white Georgian door. We were admitted to a hall that at once bore out the testimony as to the athletic prowess of the husbands twain. There were guns, knives, golf-sticks, tennis rackets, automobile togs and swords. I think there were deer and fox heads in the bargain. By a ruddy, sportsmanlike man of perhaps thirty-eight, and all of six feet tall, who now appeared, we were invited to enter, make ourselves at home, drink what we would, whiskey, sherry, ale—a suitable list. We declined the drink, putting up fur coats and sticks and were immediately asked into the billiard room where the Christmas tree and other festivities were holding,—or about to be. Here, at last there were my lady of the donkey and the child and the maid and my lady's sister and alas, my lady's husband, full six feet tall and vigorous and, of all tragic things, fingering a forty-caliber, sixteen-shot magazine pistol which his beloved brother of sporting proclivities had given him as a Christmas present! I eyed it as one might a special dispensation of Providence.

But our lady of the donkey? A very charming woman she proved, intelligent, smiling, very chic, quite aware of all the nice things that had been said about her, very clever in making light of it for propriety's sake, unwilling to have anything made of it for the present for her husband's sake. But that Anglicized French air! And that romantic smile!

We talked—of what do people talk on such occasions? Gerard was full of the gayest references to the fact that Barfleur had such interesting neighbors as the Churchills and did not know it, and that they had once motored to Blackpool together. I shall not forget either how artfully Barfleur conveyed to Mrs. Barton Churchill, our lady of the donkey, that I had been intensely taken with her looks while at the same time presenting himself in the best possible light. Barfleur is always at his best on such occasions, Chesterfieldian, and with an air that says, "A mere protegee of mine. Do not forget the managerial skill that is making this interesting encounter possible." But Mrs. Churchill, as I could see, was not utterly unmindful of the fact that I was the one that had been heralded to her as a writer, and that I had made the great fuss and said all the nice things about her after a single encounter on a country road which had brought about this afternoon visit. She was gracious, and ordered the Christmas tree lighted and had the young heir's most interesting toys spread out on the billiard table. I remember picking up a linen story book, labeled Loughlin Bros., New York.

"From America," I said, quite unwisely I think.

"Oh, yes, you Americans," she replied, eyeing me archly. "Everything comes from America these days, even our toys. But it's rather ungracious to make us admit it, don't you think?"

I picked up a train of cars, and, to my astonishment, found it stamped with the name of a Connecticut firm. I hesitated to say more, for I knew that I was on dangerous ground, but after that I looked at every book or box of blocks and the like, to find that my suspicions were well founded. England gets many of its Christmas toys from America.

Nothing came of this episode except a pleasant introduction for Barfleur, who had all the future before him. I was leaving for Manchester after the new year, and for Paris a week or two later. It was all in vain as I foresaw, that I was invited to call again, or that she hoped to see something of me among her friends in London. I think I said as much to Barfleur with many unkind remarks about the type of mind that manages to secure all merely by a process of waiting. Meantime he walked bravely forward, his overcoat snugly buttoned, his cane executing an idle circle, his monocle on straight, his nose in the air. I could have made away with him for much less.

The last of this very gallant day came in the home of Barfleur himself. As we neared the house we decided to hurry forward and to say that Gerard had remained at the Churchill's for dinner, while he made a wide detour, ending up, I think, in some chamber in the coach house. I did not see him again until much later in the evening, but meantime the children, the relatives, the friends and the family servants were all gathered in the nursery on the second floor. There was much palaver and badinage concerning the fact that Santa Claus had really had such bad reports that he had found it much against his will to come here, early at least. There were some rather encouraging things that had been reported to him later, however, and he had, so some one had heard, changed his mind. Whether there would be little or much for such a collection of ne'er-do-wells was open to question. However if we were all very quiet for a while we should see. I can see Barfleur now in his gala attire, stalking nobly about, and the four little Barfleurs surveying rather incredulously but expectantly the maid, the nurse, the governess, and their father. I wondered what had become of my small mementos and whether my special cigarettes for Barfleur were in safety in Santa Claus's pack. It was small stock, I fear me much, that these well-behaved little English children took in this make-believe, but presently there was a loud hammering at the nursery door, and without a "By your leave," the same was opened and a vigorous, woolly-headed Santa Claus put his rosy face into the chamber.

"Is there any one living here by the name of Percy Franklin Barfleur, or Berenice Barfleur, or James Herbert Barfleur?" I shall not repeat all the names he called in a high falsetto voice, "I've been a long way to-day and I've had a great deal to do, and I haven't had the least assistance from anybody. They're so busy having a good time themselves."

I never saw a redder nose, or more shaggy eye-browed eyes, or a gayer twinkle in them. And the pack that he carried was simply enormous. It could barely be squeezed through the door. As he made his way to the center of the room he looked quizzically about, groaning and squeaking in his funny voice, and wanting to know if the man in the monocle were really Barfleur, and whether the fat lady in the corner were really a nurse, or merely an interloper, and if the four children that had been reported to him as present were surely there. Having satisfied himself on various counts, and evoked a great deal of innocent laughter, to say nothing of awe as to his next probable comment, he finally untied the enormous bag and began to consult the labels.

"Here's a package marked 'Charles Gerard Barfleur.' It's rather large. It's been very heavy to carry all this distance. Can anybody tell me whether he's been a reasonably good child? It's very hard to go to all this trouble, if children aren't really deserving." Then, as he came forward, he added, "He has a very impish look in his eye, but I suppose I ought to let him have it." And so the gift was handed over.

One by one the presents came forth, commented on in this fashion, only the comments varied with the age and the personality of the recipient. There was no lack of humor or intimacy of application, for this Santa Claus apparently knew whereof he spoke.

"Is there a writer in the room by the name of Theodore Dreiser?" he remarked at one time sardonically. "I've heard of him faintly and he isn't a very good writer, but I suppose he's entitled to a slight remembrance. I hope you reform, Mr. Dreiser," he remarked very wisely, as he drew near me. "It's very plain to me that a little improvement could be effected."

I acknowledged the wisdom of the comment.

When my cigarettes were handed to Barfleur, Santa Claus tapped them sapiently. "More wretched cigarettes!" he remarked in his high falsetto. "I know them well! If it isn't one vice that has to be pampered, it's another. I would have brought him pâté de foies gras or wine, if I didn't think this was less harmful. He's very fond of prawns too, but they're very expensive at this time of the year. A little economy wouldn't hurt him." Dora, the maid, and Mrs. A., the nurse, and Miss C., the governess, came in for really brilliant compliments. Lord Scorp was told that an old English castle or a Rembrandt would be most suitable, but that Santa was all out at present, and if he would just be a little more cheerful in the future he might manage to get him one. T. McT. was given books, as very fitting, and in a trice the place was literally littered with wonders. There were immense baskets and boxes of candied fruit from Holland; toys, books and fruit from Barfleur's mother in Rome; more toys and useful presents from ladies in London and the north of England and France and the Isle of Wight,—a goodly company of mementos. It's something to be an attractive widower! I never saw children more handsomely or bountifully provided for—a new saddle, bridle and whip for Berenice's riding pony, curious puzzles, German mechanical toys from Berlin, and certain ornamental articles of dress seemed, by the astonishing bursts of excitement they provoked, exceedingly welcome. Santa now drew off his whiskers and cap to reveal himself as Gerard Barfleur, and we all literally got down on the floor to play with the children. You can imagine, with each particular present to examine, how much there was to do. Tea-time came and went unnoticed, a stated occasion in England. Supper, a meal not offered except on Christmas, was spread about eight o'clock. About nine an automobile took Lord Scorp and T. McT. away, and after that we all returned to the nursery until about ten-thirty when even by the most liberal interpretation of holiday license it was bedtime. We soberer elders (I hope no one sets up a loud guffaw) adjourned to the drawing-room for nuts and wine, and finally, as the beloved Pepys was accustomed to remark, "So to bed."

But what with the abbey church, the discourse on Christian Science, our lady of the donkey, a very full stomach and a phantasmagoria of toys spinning before my eyes, I went to bed thinking of,—well now, what do you suppose I went to bed thinking of?

CHAPTER XVII
SMOKY ENGLAND

FOR years before going to England I had been interested in the north of England—the land, as I was accustomed to think, of the under dog. England, if one could trust one's impression from a distance, was a land of great social contrasts—the ultimate high and the ultimate low of poverty and wealth. In the north, as I understand it, were all of the great manufacturing centers—Sheffield, Leeds, Nottingham, Birmingham, Liverpool, Manchester—a whole welter of smoky cities whence issue tons upon tons of pottery, linen, cotton, cutlery. While I was at Bridgely Level I spoke of my interest in this region to Barfleur, who merely lifted his eyebrows. He knew little or nothing about that northern world. The south of England encompassed his interest. However, Barfleur's cousin, the agreeable Gerard Barfleur, told me soulfully that the north of England must be like America, because it was so brisk, direct, practical, and that he loved it. (He was a confirmed American "rooter" or "booster," we would say over here, and was constantly talking about coming to this country to enter the theatrical business.)

I journeyed northward the last day of the old year to Manchester and its environs, which I had chosen as affording the best picture of manufacturing life. I had been directed to a certain hotel, recommended as the best equipped in the country. I think I never saw so large a hotel. It sprawled over a very large block in a heavy, impressive, smoky-stone way. It had, as I quickly discovered, an excellent Turkish and Russian bath in connection with it and five separate restaurants, German, French, English, etc., and an American bar. The most important travel life of Manchester centered here—that was obvious. I was told that buyers and sellers from all parts of the world congregated in this particular caravanserai. It was New Year's day and the streets were comparatively empty, but the large, showy, heavily furnished breakfast-room was fairly well sprinkled with men whom I took to be cotton operatives. There was a great mill strike on at this time and here were gathered for conference representatives of all the principal interests involved. I was glad to see this, for I had always wondered what type of man it was that conducted the great manufacturing interests in England—particularly this one of cotton. The struggle was over the matter of the recognition of the unions and a slight raise in the wage-scale. These men were very much like a similar collection of wealthy manufacturers in the United States. Great industries seem to breed a certain type of mind and body. You can draw a mental picture of a certain keen, dressy, phlegmatic individual, not tall, not small, round, solid, ruddy—and have them all. These men were so comfortably solid, physically. They looked so content with themselves and the world, so firm and sure. Nearly all of them were between forty-five and sixty, cold, hard, quick-minded, alert. They differed radically from the typical Englishman of the South. It struck me at once that if England were to be kept commercially dominant it would be this type of man, not that of the South, who would keep it so.

And now I could understand from looking at these men why it was that the north of England was supposed to hate the south of England, and vice versa. I had sat at a dinner-table in Portland Place one evening and heard the question of the sectional feeling discussed. Why does it exist? was the question before the guests. Well, the south of England is intellectual, academic, historic, highly socialized. It is rich in military, governmental, ambassadorial and titled life. The very scenery is far more lovely. The culture of the people, because of the more generally distributed wealth, is so much better. In the north of England the poor are very poor and contentious. The men of wealth are not historically wealthy or titled. In many cases they are "hard greedy upstarts like the irrepressible Americans," one speaker remarked. They have no real culture or refinement. They manage to buy their way in from time to time, it is true, but that does not really count. They are essentially raw and brutal. Looking at these men breakfasting quietly, I could understand it exactly. Their hard, direct efficiency would but poorly adjust itself to the soft speculative intellectuality of the south. Yet we know that types go hand in hand in any country with a claim to greatness.

After my breakfast I struck out to see what I could see of the city. I also took a car to Salford, and another train to Stockport in order to gather as quick a picture of the Manchester neighborhood as I could. What I saw was commonplace enough. All of the larger cities of present-day Europe are virtually of modern construction. Most of them have grown to their present great population in the last fifty years. Hence they have been virtually built—not rebuilt—in that time.

Salford, a part of Manchester, was nothing—great cotton and machine works and warehouses. Stockport was not anything either, save long lines of brick cottages one and two stories high and mills, mills, mills, mills. It always astounds me how life repeats itself—any idea in life such as a design for a house—over and over and over. These houses in Salford, Stockport and Manchester proper were such as you might see anywhere in Chicago, St. Louis, Cincinnati, Baltimore—in the cheap streets. I had the sense of being pursued by a deadly commonplace. It all looked as people do when they think very little, know very little, see very little, do very little. I expected to learn that the churches flourished here very greatly and that there was an enormous Sunday school somewhere about. There was—at Stockport—the largest in the world I was told, five thousand students attending. The thing that impressed me most was the presence of the wooden clog or shoe.

In Stockport there was a drab silence hanging over everything—the pathetic dullness of the laborer when he has nothing to do save the one thing he cannot do—think. As it was a Sunday the streets were largely empty and silent—a dreary, narrow-minded, probably religious, conventional world which accepts this blank drabness as natural, ordered, probably even necessary. To the west and the south and the east and the north are great worlds of strangeness and wonder—new lands, new people—but these folks can neither see nor hear. Here they are harnessed to cotton-mills, believing no doubt that God intended it to be so, working from youth to age without ever an inkling of the fascinating ramifications of life. It appalled me.

In some respects I think I never saw so dreary a world as manufacturing England. In saying this I do not wish to indicate that the working conditions are any worse than those which prevail in various American cities, such as Pittsburgh, and especially the minor cities like Lawrence and Fall River. But here was a dark workaday world, quite unfavored by climate, a country in which damp and fogs prevail for fully three-fourths of the year, and where a pall of smoke is always present. I remember reading a sign on one of the railway platforms which stated that owing to the prevalence of fogs the company could not be held responsible for the running of trains on time. I noticed too, that the smoke and damp were so thick everywhere that occasionally the trees on the roadside or the houses over the way would disappear in a lovely, Corot-like mist. Lamps were burning in all stores and office-buildings. Street cars carried head-lamps and dawned upon you out of a hazy gloom. Traffic disappeared in a thick blanket a half block away.

Most of these outlying towns had populations ranging from ninety to a hundred thousand, but in so far as interesting or entertaining developments of civic life were concerned—proportioned to their size—there were none. They might as well have been villages of five hundred or one thousand. Houses, houses, houses, all of the same size, all the same color, all the same interior arrangement, virtually.

Everywhere—in Middleton, Oldham, and Rochdale, which I visited the first day, and in Boulton, Blackburn, and Wigan, which I visited the next—I found this curious multiplication of the same thing which you would dismiss with a glance—whole streets, areas, neighborhoods of which you could say, "all alike."

In Middleton I was impressed with the constant repetition of "front rooms" or "parlors." You could look in through scores of partly open doors (this climate is damp but not cold) and see in each a chest of drawers exactly like every other chest in the town and in the same position relative to the door. Nearly all the round tables which these front rooms contained were covered with pink, patterned, cotton tablecloths. The small single windows, one to each house, contained blue or yellow jardinières set on small tables and containing geraniums. The fireplace, always to the right of the room as you looked in the window, glowed with a small coal fire. There were no other ornaments that I saw. The ceilings of the rooms were exceedingly low and the total effect was one of clean, frugal living.

The great mills bore pleasing names, such as Rob Roy, Tabitha, Marietta, and their towering stacks looked down upon the humbler habitations at their base much as the famous castles of the feudal barons must have looked down upon the huts of their serfs. I was constrained to think of the workaday existence that all this suggested, the long lines of cotton-mill employees going in at seven o'clock in the morning, in the dark, and coming out at six o'clock at night, in the dark. Many of these mills employ a day and a night shift. Their windows, when agleam in the smoke or rain, are like patins of fine gold. I saw them gleaming at the end of dull streets or across the smooth, olive-colored surfaces of mill ponds or through the mist and rain. The few that were running (the majority of them were shut down because of the strike) had a roar like that of Niagara tumbling over its rocks—a rich, ominous thunder. In recent years the mill-owners have abandoned the old low, two-story type of building with its narrow windows and dingy aspect of gray stone, and erected in its stead these enormous structures—the only approach to the American sky-scraper I saw in England. They are magnificent mills, far superior to those you will see to-day in this country, clean, bright and—every one I saw—new. If I should rely upon my merely casual impression, I should say that there were a thousand such within twenty-five miles of Manchester. When seen across a foreground of low cottages, such as I have described, they have all the dignity of cathedrals—vast temples of labor. I was told by the American Consul-General at London that they are equipped with the very latest cotton-spinning machinery and are now in a position to hold their own on equal terms with American competition, if not utterly to defy it. The intricacy and efficiency of the machinery is greater than that employed in our mills. I could not help thinking what a far cry it was from these humble cottages, some few of which in odd corners looked like the simple, thatched huts sacred to Burns and "The Cotter's Saturday Night," to these lordly mills and the lordly owners behind them—the strong, able, ruthless men whom I saw eating in the breakfast-room at the Midland the day before. Think of the poor little girls and boys, principally girls, clattering to and from work in their wooden shoes and, if you will believe it (I saw it at Boulton on a cold, rainy, January day), in thin black shawls and white straw hats, much darkened by continuous wear. One crowd that I observed was pouring out at high noon. I heard a whistle yelling its information, and then a mouse-hole of a door in one corner of the great structure opened, and released the black stream of mill-workers. By comparison, it looked like a small procession of ants or a trickle of black water. Small as it was, however, it soon filled the street. The air was wet, smoky, gray, the windows even at this midday hour gleaming here and there with lights. The factory hands were a dreary mass in the rain, some of them carrying umbrellas, many without them, all the women wearing straw hats and black shawls!

I looked at their faces—pale, waxy, dull, inefficient. I looked at their shapeless skirts hanging like bags about their feet. I looked at their flat chests, their graceless hands, and then I thought of the strong men who know how to use—I hesitate to say exploit—inefficiency. What would these women do if they could not work in the mills? One thing I am sure of: the mills, whatever charges may be brought against their owners in regard to hours, insufficiency of payment, indifference of treatment, are nevertheless better places in which to spend one's working hours than the cottages with their commonplace round of duties. What can one learn washing dishes and scrubbing floors in a cottage? I can see some one jumping up to exclaim: "What can one learn tying commonplace threads in a cotton mill, taking care of eight or nine machines—one lone woman? What has she time to learn?" This—if you ask me; the single thought of organization, if nothing more. The thought that there is such a thing as a great machine which can do the work of fifty or a hundred men. It will not do to say the average individual can learn this method working in a home. It is not true. What the race needs is ideas. It needs thoughts of life and injustice and justice and opportunity or the lack of it kicked into its senseless clay. It needs to be made to think by some rough process or other (gentleness won't do it), and this is one way. I like labor-leaders. I like big, raw, crude, hungry men who are eager for gain—for self-glorification. I like to see them plotting to force such men as I saw breakfasting at the Midland to give them something—and the people beneath them. I am glad to think that the clay whose womankind wears black shawls and straw hats in January has sense enough at last to appoint these raw, angry fellows, who scheme and struggle and fight and show their teeth and call great bitter strikes, such as I saw here, and such as had shut tight so many of these huge solemn mills. It speaks much for the race. It speaks much for *thinking*, which is becoming more and more common. If this goes on, there won't be so many women with drabbly skirts and flat chests. There will still be strong men and weak, but the conditions may not be so severe. Anyhow let us hope so, for it is an optimistic thought and it cheers one in the face of all the drab streets and the drab people. I have no hope of making millionaires of everybody, nor of establishing that futile abstraction, justice; but I do cherish the idea of seeing the world growing better and more interesting for everybody. And the ills which make for thinking are the only things which will bring this about.

CHAPTER XVIII
SMOKY ENGLAND (*continued*)

AT Middleton the mills are majestically large and the cottages relatively minute. There is a famous old inn here, very picturesque to look upon, and Somebody of Something's comfortable manor, but they were not the point for me. In one of its old streets, in the dark doorway of an old house, I encountered an old woman, very heavy, very pale, very weary, who stood leaning against the door post.

"What do you burn here, gas or oil?" I asked, interested to obtain information on almost any topic and seeking a pretext for talking to her.

"Hey?" she replied, looking at me wearily, but making no other move.

"What do you burn?" I asked. "What do you use for light, gas or oil?"

"Ile," she replied heavily. "You'll have to talk very loud. I'm gettin' old and I'm goin' to die pretty soon."

"Oh, no," I said, "you're not old enough for that. You're going to live a long time yet."

"Hey?" she asked.

I repeated what I had said.

"No," she mumbled, and now I saw she had no teeth. "I'm gettin' old. I'm eighty-two and I'm goin' to die. I been workin' in the mills all my life."

"Have you ever been out of Middleton?" I asked.

"Hey?" she replied.

I repeated.

"Yes, to Manchester, Saturdays. Not of late, though. Not in years and years. I'm very sick, though, now. I'm goin' to die."

I could see from her look that what she said was true. Only her exceeding weariness employed her mind. I learned that water came from a hydrant in the yard, that the kitchen floor was of earth. Then I left, noticing as I went that she wore wooden-soled shoes.

In the public square at Boulton, gathered about the city-hall, where one would suppose for the sake of civic dignity no unseemly spectacle would be permitted, was gathered all the paraphernalia of a shabby, eighth-rate circus—red wagons, wild animal and domestic horse tents, the moderate-sized main tent, the side show, the fat woman's private wagon, a cage and the like. I never saw so queer a scene. The whole square was crowded with tents, great and small; but there was little going on, for a drizzling rain was in progress. Can human dullness sink lower? I asked myself, feeling that the civic heart of things was being profaned. Could utmost drabbiness out-drab this? I doubted it. Why should the aldermen permit it? Yet I have no doubt this situation appealed exactly to the imagination of the working population. I can conceive that it would be about the only thing that would. It was just raw and cheap and homely enough to do it. I left with pleasure.

When I came into Oldham on a tram-car from Rochdale, it was with my head swimming from the number of mills I had seen. I have described the kind—all new. But I did not lose them here.

It was the luncheon hour and I was beginning to grow hungry. As I walked along dull streets I noticed several small eating-places labeled "fish, chip, and pea restaurant" and "tripe, trotters, and cow-heels restaurant," which astonished me greatly—really astonished me. I had seen only one such before in my life and that was this same morning in Middleton—a "fish, chip, and pea restaurant"; but I did not get the point sufficiently clearly to make a note of it. The one that I encountered this afternoon had a sign in the window which stated that unquestionably its chips were the best to be procured anywhere and very nourishing. A plate of them standing close by made it perfectly plain that potato chips were meant. No recommendation was given to either the fish or the peas. I pondered over this, thinking that such restaurants must be due to the poverty of the people and that meat being very dear, these three articles of diet were substituted. Here in Oldham, however, I saw that several of these restaurants stood in very central places where the rents should be reasonably high and the traffic brisk. It looked as though they were popular for some other reason. I asked a policeman.

"What is a 'fish, chip, and pea' restaurant?" I asked.

"Well, to tell you the truth," he said, "it's a place where a man who's getting over a spree goes to eat. Those things are good for the stomach."

I pondered over this curiously. There were four such restaurants in the immediate vicinity, to say nothing of the one labeled "tripe, trotters, and cow-heels," which astonished me even more.

"And what's that for?" I asked of the same officer.

"The same thing. A man who's been drinking eats those things."

I had to laugh, and yet this indicated another characteristic of a wet, rainy climate, namely considerable drinking. At the next corner a man, a woman, and a child conferring slightly confirmed my suspicion.

"Come on," said the man to the woman, all at once, "let's go to the pub. A beer'll do you good."

The three started off together, the child hanging by the woman's hand. I followed them with my eyes, for I could not imagine quite such a scene in America—not done just in this way. Women—a certain type—go to the back rooms of saloons well enough; children are sent with pails for beer; but just this particular combination of husband, wife, and child is rare, I am sure.

And such public houses! To satisfy myself of their character I went to three in three different neighborhoods. Like those I saw in London and elsewhere around it, they were pleasant enough in their arrangement, but gloomy. The light from the outside was meager, darkened as it was by smoke and rain. If you went on back into the general lounging-room, lights were immediately turned on, for otherwise it was not bright enough to see. If you stayed in the front at the bar proper it was still dark, and one light—a mantled gas-jet—was kept burning. I asked the second barmaid with whom I conferred about this:

"You don't always have to keep a light burning here, do you?"

"Always, except two or three months in summer," she replied. "Sometimes in July and August we don't need it. As a rule we do."

"Surely, it isn't always dark and smoky like this?"

"You should see it sometimes, if you call this bad," she replied contemptuously. "It's black."

"I should say it's very near that now," I commented.

"Oh, no, most of the mills are not running. You should see it when it's foggy and the mills are running."

She seemed to take a sort of pride in the matter and I sympathized with her. It is rather distinguished to live in an extreme of any kind, even if it is only that of a smoky wetness of climate. I went out, making my way to the "Kafe" Monico, as the policeman who recommended the place pronounced it. Here I enjoyed such a meal as only a third-rate restaurant which is considered first by the local inhabitants would supply.

I journeyed forth once more, interested by the fact that, according to Baedeker, from one point somewhere, *on a clear day*, whenever that might be, six hundred stacks might be seen. In this fog I soon found that it was useless to look for them. Instead I contented myself with noting how, in so many cases, the end of a street, or the sheer dismal length of an unbroken row of houses, all alike, was honored, made picturesque, made grand even, by the presence of the mills, these gloomy monuments of labor.

There is an architecture of manufacture, dreary and shabby as its setting almost invariably is, which in its solemnity, strangeness of outline, pathos and dignity, quite rivals, if it does not surpass, the more heralded forms of the world—its cathedrals, parthenons, Moorish temples and the like. I have seen it often in America and elsewhere where a group of factory buildings, unplanned as to arrangement and undignified as to substance, would yet take on an exquisite harmony of line and order after which a much more pretentious institution might well have been modeled. At Stockport, near Manchester, for instance, on the Mersey, which here is little more than a rivulet, but picturesque and lovely, I saw grouped a half-dozen immense mills with towering chimneys which, for architectural composition from the vantage point of the stream, could not have been surpassed. They had the dignity of vast temples, housing a world of under-paid life which was nevertheless rich in color and enthusiasm. Sometimes I fancy the modern world has produced nothing more significant architecturally speaking, than the vast manufactory. Here in Oldham they were gathered in notable clusters, towering over the business heart and the various resident sections so that the whole scene might well be said to have been dominated by it. They bespeak a world of thought and feeling which we of more intellectual fields are inclined at times to look on as dull and low, but are they? I confess that for myself they move me at times as nothing else does. They have vast dignity—the throb and sob of the immense. And what is more dignified than toiling humanity, anyhow—its vague, formless, illusioned hopes and fears? I wandered about the dull rain-sodden thoroughfares, looking in at the store windows. In one I found a pair of gold and a pair of silver slippers offered for sale—for what feet in Oldham? They were not high in price, but this sudden suggestion of romance in a dark workaday world took my fancy.

At four o'clock, after several hours of such wandering, I returned to the main thoroughfare—the market-place—in order to see what it was the hundred and fifty thousand inhabitants found to entertain them. I looked for theaters and found two, one of them a large moving-picture show. Of a sudden, walking in a certain direction my ears were greeted by a most euphonious clatter—so interwoven and blended were the particular sounds which I recognized at once as coming from the feet of a multitude, shod with wooden-soled clogs. Where were they coming from? I saw no crowd. Suddenly, up a side street, coming toward me down a slope I detected a vast throng. The immense moving-picture theater had closed for the afternoon and its entire audience, perhaps two thousand in all, was descending toward the main street. In connection with this crowd, as with the other at Boulton, I noted the phenomenon of the black or white straw hat, the black or brown shawl, the shapeless skirts and wooden-soled clogs of the women; the dull, commonplace suit and wooden clogs of the men. Where were they going now? Home, of course. These must be a portion of the strikers. They looked to me like typical mill-workers out on a holiday and their faces had a waxy pallor. I liked the sound of their shoes, though, as they came along. It was like the rattle of many drums. They might have been waltzing on a wooden floor. The thing had a swing and a rhythm of its own. "What if a marching army were shod with wooden shoes!" I thought; and then, "What if a mob with guns and swords came clattering so!"

A crowd like this is like a flood of water pouring downhill. They came into the dark main street and it was quite brisk for a time with their presence. Then they melted away into the totality of the stream, as rivers do into the sea, and things were as they had been before.

If there were any restaurants other than the "Kafe" Monico, I did not find them. For entertainment I suppose those who are not religiously minded do as they do in Fall River and elsewhere—walk up and down past the bright shop windows or sit and drink in the public houses, which are unquestionably far more cheerful by night than by day.

The vast majority who live here must fall back for diversion on other things, their work, their church, their family duties, or their vices. I am satisfied that under such conditions sex plays a far more vital part in cities of this description than almost anywhere else. For, although the streets be dull and the duties of life commonplace, sex and the mysteries of temperament weave their spells quite as effectively here as elsewhere, if not more so. In fact, denied the more varied outlets of a more interesting world, humanity falls back almost exclusively on sex. Women and men, or rather boys and girls (for most of the grown women and men had a drudgy, disillusioned, wearied look), went by each other glancing and smiling. They were alert to be entertained by each other, and while I saw little that I would call beauty in the women, or charm and smartness in the men, nevertheless I could understand how the standards of New York and Paris might not necessarily prevail here. Clothes may not fit, fashion may find no suggestion of its dictates, but after all, underneath, the lure of temperament and of beauty is the same. And so these same murky streets may burn with a rich passional life of their own. I left Oldham finally in the dark and in a driving rain, but not without a sense of the sturdy vigor of the place, keen if drab.

CHAPTER XIX
CANTERBURY

IT was not so long after this that I journeyed southward. My plan was to leave London two days ahead of Barfleur, visit Canterbury and Dover, and meet with him there to travel to Paris together, and the Riviera. From the Riviera I was to go on to Rome and he was to return to England.

Among other pleasant social duties I paid a farewell visit to Sir Scorp, who shall appear often hereafter in these pages. During the Christmas holidays at Barfleur's I had become well acquainted with this Irish knight and famed connoisseur of art, and while in London I had seen much of him. Here in his lovely mansion in Cheyne Walk I found him surrounded by what one might really call the grandeur of his pictures. His house contained distinguished examples of Rembrandt, Frans Hals, Van Dyck, Paul Potter, Velasquez, Mancini and others, and as I contemplated him on this occasion he looked not unlike one of the lymphatic cavaliers of Van Dyck's canvases. A pale gentleman, this—very remote in his spirit, very far removed from the common run of life, concerned only with the ultimately artistic, and wishing to be free of everything save the leisure to attend to this. He was not going to leave London, he thought, at this time, except possibly for a short visit to Paris. He was greatly concerned with the problem of finding a dilapidated "cahstle" which he could restore, live in, fill with his pictures and eventually sell, or dedicate to his beloved England as a memorial of himself. It must be a perfect example of Tudor architecture—that he invariably repeated. I gained the impression that he might fill it with interesting examples of some given school or artist and leave it as a public monument.

He urged upon me that I ought to go about the work of getting up a loan exhibit of representative American art, and have it brought to London. He commended me to the joys of certain cities and scenes—Pisa, San Miniato outside of Florence, the Villa Doria at Rome. I had to smile at the man's profound artistic assurance, for he spoke exactly as a grandee recounting the glories of his kingdom. I admired the paleness of his forehead and his hands and cast one longing look at his inestimable Frans Hals. To think that any man in these days should have purchased for little a picture that can in all likelihood be sold for $500,000—it was like walking into Aladdin's cave.

The morning I left it was gray as usual. I had brought in all my necessary belongings from Bridgely Level and installed them in my room at the hotel, packed and ready. The executive mind of Barfleur was on the qui vive to see that nothing was forgotten. A certain type of tie must be purchased for use on the Riviera—he had overlooked that. He thought my outing hat was not quite light enough in color, so we went back to change it. I had lost my umbrella in the excitement, and that had to be replaced. But finally, rushing to and fro in a taxi, loaded like a van with belongings, Barfleur breathing stertorously after each venture into a shop, we arrived at the Victoria Station. Never having been on the Continent before, I did not realize until we got there the wisdom of Barfleur's insistence that I pack as much of my belongings as possible in bags, and as little as possible in trunks. Traveling first class, as most of those who have much luggage do, it is cheaper. As most travelers know, one can take as many as five or six parcels or bags in the compartment with one, and stow them on racks and under the seats, which saves a heavy charge for excess baggage. In some countries, such as Italy, nothing is carried free save your hand-luggage which you take in your compartment with you. In addition the rates are high. I think I paid as much as thirty shillings for the little baggage I had, over and above that which I took in my compartment with me. To a person with a frugal temperament such as mine, that is positively disconcerting. It was my first taste of what I came subsequently to look upon as greedy Europe.

As the train rushed southeastwards I did my best to see the pleasant country through which we were speeding—the region indicated on the map as North Downs. I never saw any portion of English country anywhere that I did not respond to the charming simplicity of it, and understand and appreciate the Englishman's pride in it. It has all the quality of a pastoral poem—the charm of Arcady—fields of sheep, rows of quaint chimney pots and odd houses tucked away among the trees, exquisite moldy and sagging roofs, doorways and windows which look as though loving care had been spent on them. Although this was January, all the leafless trees were covered with a fine thin mold, as green as spring leaves. At Rochester the ruins of an ancient castle came into view and a cathedral which I was not to see. At Faversham I had to change from the Dover express to a local, and by noon I was at Canterbury and was looking for the Fleur-de-lis which had been recommended to me as the best hotel there. "At least," observed Barfleur, quite solemnly to me as we parted, "I think you can drink the wine." I smiled, for my taste in that respect was not so cultivated as his.

Of all the places I visited in England, not excluding Oxford, I believe that Canterbury pleased me most. The day may have had something to do with it. It was warm and gray—threatening rain at times—but at times also the sun came out and gave the old English town a glow which was not unrelated to spring and Paradise. You will have to have a fondness for things English to like it—quaint, two-story houses with unexpected twists to their roofs, and oriel and bay windows which have been fastened on in the most unexpected places and in the strangest fashion. The colors, too, in some instances, are high for England—reds and yellows and blues; but in the main a smoky red-brick tone prevails. The river Stour, which in America would be known as Stour's Creek, runs through the city in two branches; and you find it in odd places, walled in closely by the buildings, hung over by little balconies and doorsteps, the like of which I did not see again until I reached Venice. There were rooks in the sky, as I noticed, when I came out of the railway station; I was charmed with winding streets, and a general air of peace and quiet—but I could not descry the cathedral anywhere. I made my way up High Street—which is English for "Main"—and finally found my recommended inn, small and dark, but in the hands of Frenchmen and consequently well furnished in the matter of food. I came out after a time and followed this street to its end, passing the famous gate where the pilgrims used to sink on their knees and in that position pray their way to the cathedral. As usual my Baedeker gave me a world of information, but I could not stomach it, and preferred to look at the old stones of which the gate was composed, wondering that it had endured so long. The little that I knew of St. Augustine and King Ethelbert and Chaucer and Thomas à Becket and Laud came back to me. I could not have called it sacred ground, but it was colored at least with the romance of history, and I have great respect for what people once believed, whether it was sensible or not.

Canterbury is a city of twenty-eight thousand, with gas-works and railroads and an electric-power plant and moving pictures and a skating-rink. But, though it has all these and much more of the same kind, it nevertheless retains that indefinable something which is pure poetry and makes England exquisite. As I look at it now, having seen much more of other parts of Europe, the quality which produces this indefinable beauty in England is not so much embodied in the individual as in the race. If you look at architectural developments in other countries you have the feeling at times as if certain individuals had greatly influenced the appearance of a city or a country. This is true of Paris and Berlin, Florence and Milan. Some one seems to have worked out a scheme at some time or other. In England I could never detect an individual or public scheme of any kind. It all seemed to have grown up, like an unheralded bed of flowers. Again I am satisfied that it is the English temperament which, at its best, provides the indefinable lure which exists in all these places. I noticed it in the towns about Manchester where, in spite of rain and smoke, the same poetic *hominess* prevailed. Here in Canterbury, where the architecture dates in its variation through all of eight centuries, you feel the dominance of the English temperament which has produced it. To-day, in the newest sections of London—Hammersmith and Seven Kings, West Dulwich and North Finchley—you still feel it at work, accidentally or instinctively constructing this atmosphere which is common to Oxford and Canterbury. It is compounded of a sense of responsibility and cleanliness and religious feeling and strong national and family ties. You really feel in England the distinction of the fireside and the family heirloom; and the fact that a person must always keep a nice face on things, however bad they may be. The same spirit erects bird-boxes on poles in the yard and lays charming white stone doorsteps and plants vines to clamber over walls and windows. It is a sweet and poetic spirit, however dull it may seem by comparison with the brilliant iniquities of other realms. Here along this little river Stour the lawns came down to the water in some instances; the bridges over it were built with the greatest care; and although houses lined it on either side for several miles of its ramblings, it was nevertheless a clean stream. I noticed in different places, where the walls were quite free of any other marks, a poster giving the picture and the history of a murderer who was wanted by the police in Nottingham, and it came to me, in looking at it, that he would have a hard time anywhere in England concealing his identity. The native horror of disorder and scandal would cause him to be yielded up on the moment.

In my wanderings, which were purely casual and haphazard, I finally came upon the cathedral which loomed up suddenly through a curving street under a leaden sky. It was like a lovely song, rendered with great pathos. Over a Gothic gate of exquisite workmanship and endless labor, it soared—two black stone towers rising shapely and ornate into the gray air. I looked up to some lattices which gave into what might have been the belfry, and saw birds perched just as they should have been. The walls, originally gray, had been turned by time and weather into a soft spongy black which somehow fitted in exquisitely with the haze of the landscape. I had a curious sensation of darker and lighter shades of gray—lurking pools of darkness here and there, and brightness in spots that became almost silver. The cathedral grounds were charmingly enclosed in vine-covered walls that were nevertheless worked out in harmonious detail of stone. An ancient walk of some kind, overhung with broken arches that had fallen into decay, led away into a green court which, by a devious process of other courts and covered arches, gave into the cloister proper. I saw an old deacon, or canon, of the church walking here in stately meditation; and a typical English yeoman, his trousers fastened about the knee by the useless but immemorial strap, came by, wheeling a few bricks in a barrow. There were endless courts, it seemed to me, surrounded by two-story buildings, all quaint in design, and housing Heaven-knows-what subsidiary factors of the archiepiscopal life. They seemed very simple habitations to me. Children played here on the walks and grass, gardeners worked at vines and fences, and occasional workmen appeared—men who, I supposed, were connected with the architectural repairs which were being made to the façade. As I stood in the courtyard of the archbishop's house, which was in front and to the left of the cathedral as you faced it, a large blue-gray touring-car suddenly appeared, and a striking-looking ecclesiastic in a shovel hat stepped out. I had the wish and the fancy that I was looking at the archbishop himself—a sound, stern, intellectual-looking person—but I did not ask. He gave me a sharp, inquiring look, and I withdrew beyond these sacred precincts and into the cathedral itself, where a tinny-voiced bell was beginning to ring for afternoon service.

I am sure I shall never forget the interior of Canterbury. It was the first really old, great cathedral that I had seen—for I had not prized very highly either St. Paul's or St. Alban's. I had never quite realized how significant these structures must have been in an age when they were far and away the most important buildings of the time. No king's palace could ever have had the importance of Canterbury, and the cry from the common peasant to the Archiepiscopal see must have been immense. Here really ruled the primate of all England, and here Becket was murdered.

Of all known architectural forms the Gothic corresponds more nearly to the finest impulse in nature itself—that is, to produce the floreated form. The aisles of the trees are no more appealing artistically than those of a great cathedral, and the overhanging branches through which the light falls have not much more charm than some of these perfect Gothic ceilings sustained by their many branching arms of stone. Much had happened, apparently, to the magnificent stained-glass windows which must have filled the tall-pointed openings at different periods, and many of them have been replaced by plain frosted glass. Those that remain are of such richness of color and such delightful variety of workmanship that, seen at the end of long stretches of aisles and ambulatories, they are like splotches of blood or deep indigo, throwing a strange light on the surrounding stone.

I presently fell in tow of a guide. It is said to-day that Americans are more like the Germans than like the English; but from the types I encountered in England I think the variety of American temperaments spring naturally from the mother country. Four more typical New England village specimens I never saw than these cathedral ushers or guides. They were sitting on the steps leading up to the choir, clad in cap and gown, engaged in cheerful gossip.

"Your turn, Henry," said one, and the tallest of the three came around and unlocked the great iron gates which give into the choir. Then began, for my special benefit, a magnificent oration. We were joined, after we had gone a little way, by a party of ladies from Pennsylvania who were lurking in one of the transepts; and nothing would do but my guide must go back to the iron entrance-way to the choir and begin all over. Not a sentence was twisted, not a pause misplaced. "Good heavens," I thought, "he does that every day in the year, perhaps a dozen times a day." He was like a phonograph with but one record, which is repeated endlessly. Nevertheless, the history of the archbishops, the Black Prince, the Huguenot refugees, the carving of the woodwork and the disappearance of the windows was all interesting. After having made the rounds of the cathedral, we came out into the cloister, the corridors of which were all black and crumbling with age, and he indicated the spot and described the manner in which Becket had been stabbed and had fallen. I don't know when a bit of history has moved me so much.

It was the day—the gentle quality of it—its very spring-like texture that made it all so wonderful. The grass in this black court was as green as new lettuce; the pendants and facets of the arches were crumbling into black sand—and spoke seemingly of a thousand years. High overhead the towers and the pinnacles, soaring as gracefully as winged living things, looked down while I faced the black-gowned figure of my guide and thought of the ancient archbishop crossing this self-same turf (how long can be the life of grass?).

When I came outside the gate into the little square or triangle which faces it I found a beautiful statue of the lyric muse—a semi-nude dancing girl erected to the memory of Christopher Marlowe. It surprised me a little to find it here, facing Canterbury, in what might be called the sacred precincts of religious art; but it is suitably placed and brought back to my mind the related kingdom of poetry.

All the little houses about have heavy overhanging eaves and diamond-shaped, lead-paned windows. The walls are thick and whitewashed, ranging in color from cream to brown. They seem unsuited to modern life; and yet they frequently offered small shop-windows full of all the things that make it: picture-postcards, American shoes, much-advertised candy, and the latest books and magazines. I sought a tea-room near by and had tea, looking joyously out against the wall where some clematis clambered, and then wandered back to the depot to get my mackintosh and umbrella—for it was beginning to rain. For two hours more I walked up and down in the rain and dark, looking into occasional windows where the blinds had not been drawn and stopping in taprooms or public houses where rosy barmaids waited on one with courteous smiles.

CHAPTER XX
EN ROUTE TO PARIS

ONE of the things which dawned upon me in moving about England, and particularly as I was leaving it, was the reason for the inestimable charm of Dickens. I do not know that anywhere in London or England I encountered any characters which spoke very forcefully of those he described. It is probable that they were all somewhat exaggerated. But of the charm of his setting there can be no doubt. He appeared at a time when the old order was giving way, and the new—the new as we have known it in the last sixty years—was manifesting itself very sharply. Railroads were just coming in and coaches being dispensed with; the modern hotel was not yet even thought of, but it was impending.

Dickens, born and raised in London, was among the first to perceive the wonder of the change and to contrast it graphically with what had been and still was. In such places as St. Alban's, Marlowe, Canterbury, Oxford, and others, I could see what the old life must have been like when the stage-coach ruled and made the principal highways lively with traffic. Here in Canterbury and elsewhere there were inns sacred to the characters of Dickens; and you could see how charming that world must have appeared to a man who felt that it was passing. He saw it in its heyday, and he recorded it as it could not have been recorded before and can never be again. He saw also the charm of simple English life—the native love of cleanly pots and pans and ordered dooryards; and that, fortunately, has not changed. I cannot think of any one doing England as Dickens did it until there is something new to be done—the old spirit manifested in a new way. From Shakespeare to Dickens the cry is long; from Dickens to his successors it may be longer still.

I was a bit perturbed on leaving Canterbury to realize that on the morrow at this same time I should catch my first glimpse of Paris. The clerk at the station who kept my bags for me noted that I came from New York and told me he had a brother in Wisconsin, and that he liked it very much out there.

I said, "I suppose you will be coming to America yourself, one of these days?"

"Oh, yes," he said; "the big chances are out there. I'll either go to Canada or Wisconsin."

"Well, there are plenty of states to choose from," I said.

"A lot of people have gone from this place," he replied.

It rained hard on the way to Dover; but when I reached there it had ceased, and I even went so far as to leave my umbrella in the train. When I early discovered my loss I reported it at once to the porter who was carrying my belongings.

"Don't let that worry you," he replied, in the calmest and most assuring of English tones. "They always look through the trains. You'll find it in the parcel-room."

Sure enough, when I returned there it was behind the clerk's desk; and it was handed to me promptly. If I had not had everything which I had lost, barring one stick, promptly returned to me since I had been in England, I should not have thought so much of this; but it confirmed my impression that I was among a people who are temperamentally honest.

My guide led me to the Lord Warden Hotel, where I arranged myself comfortably in a good room for the night. It pleased me, on throwing open my windows, to see that this hotel fronted a bay or arm of the sea and that I was in the realm of great ships and sea traffic instead of the noisy heart of a city. Because of a slight haze, not strong enough to shut out the lights entirely, fog-horns and fog-bells were going; and I could hear the smash of waves on the shore. I decided that after dinner I would reconnoiter Dover. There was a review of warships in the harbor at the time; and the principal streets were crowded with marines in red jackets and white belts and the comic little tambourine caps cocked jauntily over one ear. Such a swarm of red-jackets I never saw in my life. They were walking up and down in pairs and trios, talking briskly and flirting with the girls. I fancy that representatives of the underworld of women who prey on this type of youth were here in force.

Much to my astonishment, in this Snargate Street I found a south-of-England replica of the "Fish, Chip, and Pea" institution of the Manchester district. I concluded from this that it must be an all-English institution, and wherever there was much drunkenness there would be these restaurants. In such a port as Dover, where sailors freely congregate, it would be apt to be common; and so it proved.

Farther up High Street, in its uttermost reaches in fact, I saw a sign which read: "Thomas Davidge, Bone-setter and Tooth-surgeon"—whatever that may be. Its only rival was another I had seen in Boulton which ran: "Temperance Bar and Herbal Stores."

The next morning I was up early and sought the famous castle on the hill, but could not gain admission and could not see it for the fog. I returned to the beach when the fog had lifted and I could see not only the castle on the hill, but the wonderful harbor besides. It was refreshing to see the towering cliff of chalk, the pearl-blue water, the foaming surf along the interesting sea walk, and the lines of summer—or perhaps they are winter—residences facing the sea on this one best street. Dover, outside of this one street, was not—to me—handsome, but here all was placid, comfortable, socially interesting. I wondered what type of Englishman it was that came to summer or winter at Dover—so conveniently located between London and Paris.

At ten-thirty this morning the last train from London making the boat for Calais was to arrive and with it Barfleur and all his paraphernalia bound for Paris.

It seems to me that I have sung the praises of Barfleur as a directing manager quite sufficiently for one book; but I shall have to begin anew. He arrived as usual very brisk, a porter carrying four or five pieces of luggage, his fur coat over his arm, his monocle gleaming as though it had been freshly polished, a cane and an umbrella in hand, and inquiring crisply whether I had secured the particular position on deck which he had requested me to secure and hold. If it were raining, according to a slip of paper on which he had written instructions days before I left London, I was to enter the cabin of the vessel which crossed the channel; preëmpt a section of seat along the side wall by putting all my luggage there; and bribe a porter to place two chairs in a comfortable windless position on deck to which we could repair in case it should clear up on the way over. All of this I faithfully did. The chairs had the best possible position behind the deck-house and one of my pieces of luggage was left there as a guarantee that they belonged to me. It looked like rain when the train arrived, and we went below for a sandwich and a cup of coffee; but before the boat left it faired up somewhat and we sat on deck studying the harbor and the interesting company which was to cross with us. Some twenty English school-girls in charge of several severe-looking chaperones were crossing to Paris, either for a holiday, or, as Barfleur suggested, to renew their studies in a Paris school. A duller lot of maidens it would be hard to conceive, and yet some of them were not at all bad-looking. Conservatism and proper conduct were written all over them. Their clothing was severely plain, and their manners were most circumspect. None of that vivacity which characterizes the average American girl would have been tolerated under the circumstances. There was no undue giggling and little, if any, jesting. They interested me, because I instantly imagined twenty American girls of the same age in their place. They would have manifested twenty times the interest and enthusiasm, only in England that would have been the height of bad manners. As it was these English maidens sat in a quaint row all the way over, and disappeared quite conservatively into the train at Calais.

This English steamer crossing the channel to France was a disappointment to me in one way. I had heard for some time past that the old uncomfortable channel boats had been dispensed with and new commodious steamers put in their place. As a matter of fact, these boats were not nearly so large as those that run from New York to Coney Island, nor so commodious, though much cleaner and brighter. If it had rained, as Barfleur anticipated, the cabin below would have been intolerably overcrowded and stuffy. As it was, all the passengers were on the upper deck, sitting in camp chairs and preparing stoically to be sick. It was impossible to conceive that a distance so short, not more than twenty-three or four miles, should be so disagreeable as Barfleur said it was at times. The boat did not pitch to any extent on this trip over. On my return, some three months later, I had a different experience. But now the wind blew fiercely and it was cold. The channel was as gray as a rabbit and offensively bleak. I did not imagine the sea could be so dull-looking, and France, when it appeared in the distance, was equally bleak in appearance. As we drew near Calais it was no better—a shore-line beset with gas tanks and iron foundries. But when we actually reached the dock and I saw a line of sparkling French *facteurs* looking down on the boat from the platform above—presto! England was gone. Gone all the solemnity and the politeness of the porters who had brought our luggage aboard, gone the quiet civility of ship officers and train-men, gone the solid doughlike quiescence of the whole English race. It seemed to me on the instant as if the sky had changed and instead of the gray misty pathos of English life—albeit sweet and romantic—had come the lively slap-dash of another world. These men who looked down on us with their snappy birdlike eyes were no more like the English than a sparrow is like a great auk. They were black-haired, black-eyed, lean, brown, active. They had on blue aprons and blue jumpers and a kind of military cap. There was a touch of scarlet somewhere, either in their caps or their jackets, I forget which; and somewhere near by I saw a French soldier—his scarlet woolen trousers and lead-blue coat contrasting poorly, so far as *éclat* goes, with the splendid trimness of the British. Nevertheless he did not look inefficient, but raw and forceful, as one imagines the soldiers of Napoleon should be. The vividness of the coloring made up for much, and I said at once that I would not give France for fifty million Englands. I felt, although I did not speak the language, as though I had returned to America.

It is curious how one feels about France, or at least how I feel about it. For all of six weeks I had been rejoicing in the charms and the virtues of the English. London is a great city—splendid—the intellectual capital of the world. Manchester and the north represent as forceful a manufacturing realm as the world holds, there is no doubt of that. The quaintness and sweetness of English country life is not to be surpassed for charm and beauty. But France has fifty times the spirit and enthusiasm of England. After London and the English country it seems strangely young and vital. France is often spoken of as decadent—but I said to myself, "Good Lord, let us get some of this decadence, and take it home with us. It is such a cheerful thing to have around." I would commend it to the English particularly.

On the way over Barfleur had been giving me additional instructions. I was to stay on board when the boat arrived and signal a facteur who would then come and get my luggage. I was to say to him, "*Sept colis*," whereupon he would gather up the bundles and lead the way to the dock. I was to be sure and get his number, for all French facteurs were scoundrels, and likely to rob you. I did exactly as I was told, while Barfleur went forward to engage a section, first class, and to see that we secured places in the dining-car for the first service. Then he returned and found me on the dock, doing my best to keep track of the various pieces of luggage, while the facteur did his best to secure the attention of a customs inspector.

It was certainly interesting to see the difference between the arrival of this boat at Calais and the similar boat which took us off the *Mauretania* at Fishguard. There, although the crowd which had arrived was equally large, all was peaceful and rather still. The porters went about their work in such a matter-of-fact manner. All was in apple-pie order. There was no shouting to speak of. Here all was hubbub and confusion, apparently, although it was little more than French enthusiasm. You would have fancied that the French guards and facteurs were doing their best to liberate their pent-up feelings. They bustled restlessly to and fro; they grimaced; they reassured you frequently by look and sign that all would be well, must be so. Inside of five minutes,—during which time I examined the French news-stand and saw how marvelously English conservatism had disappeared in this distance of twenty miles,—the luggage had been passed on and we were ready to enter the train. Barfleur had purchased a number of papers, *Figaro*, *Gil Blas*, and others in order to indicate the difference between the national lives of the two countries which I was now to contrast. I never saw a man so eager to see what effect a new country would have on another. He wanted me to see the difference between the English and the French papers at once; and although I was thoroughly familiar with it already, I carefully examined these latest productions of the French presses. The same delicious nudities that have been flourishing in the French papers for years were there, the same subtle Gallic penchant for the absurd and the ridiculous. I marveled anew at the sprightliness of these figures, which never cross the Atlantic into American papers. We do not know how to draw them because we are not accustomed to them in our lives. As a matter of fact the American papers and magazines adhere rigorously to the English standard. We have varied some in presentation, but have not broadened the least in treatment. As a matter of fact I believe that the American weekly and monthly are even more conservative than the British paper of the same standard. We think we are different, but we are not. We have not even anything in common with the Germans, from whom we are supposed to have drawn so much of our national personality.

However,—the train started after a few moments and soon we were speeding through that low flat country which lies between Calais and Paris. It was a five-hour run direct, but we were going to stop off at Amiens to see the great cathedral there. I was struck at once by the difference between the English and the French landscape. Here the trees were far fewer, and what there were of them were not tinged with that rich green mold which is characteristic of every tree in England. The towns, too, as they flashed past—for this was an express—were radically different in their appearance. I noted the superabundance of conical red roofs swimming in a silvery light, and hard white walls that you could see for miles. No trees intervened to break the view, and now and then a silvery thread of a river appeared.

It was on this trip that I gathered my first impressions of a French railway as contrasted with those of England and America. The French rails were laid to the standard gage, I noticed, and the cars were after the American not the English style: large, clean, commodious, with this improvement over the American car that they were of the corridor and compartment style as contrasted with our one room, open-space style. After my taste of the compartment car in England I was fairly satisfied to part forever with the American plan of one long open room in which every one can see every one else, interesting as that spectacle may be to some. The idea of some privacy appealed to me more. The American Pullman has always seemed a criminal arrangement to me, anyhow, and at Manchester I had met a charming society woman who in passing had told me that the first time she was compelled to undress in an American sleeping car she cried. Her personal sense of privacy was so outrageously invaded. Our large magnates having their own private cars or being able to charter a whole train on occasion need not worry about this small matter of delicacy in others (it would probably never concern them personally anyhow) and so the mass and the unsuspecting stranger is made to endure what he bitterly resents and what they never feel. I trust time and a growing sense of chivalry in the men at the top as well as a sense of privilege and necessity in the mass at the bottom will alter all this. America is a changing country. In due time, after all the hogs are fed or otherwise disposed of, a sense of government of the people for the people will probably appear. It has made only the barest beginning as yet. There are some things that the rank and file are entitled to, however—even the rank and file—and these they will eventually get.

I was charmed with the very medieval air of Amiens, when we reached there, a bare, gray, cobble-stony city which, however, appeared to be solid and prosperous. Here, as in the rest of France, I found that the conical-roofed tower, the high-peaked roof, the solid gray or white wall, and the thick red tile, fluted or flat, combined to produce what may be looked upon as the national touch. The houses here varied considerably from the English standard in being in many cases very narrow and quite high for their width—four and five stories. They are crowded together, too, in a seemingly defensive way, and seem to lack light and air. The solid white or gray shutters, the thick fluted rain-pipe, and the severe, simple thickness of the walls produced an atmosphere which I came to look upon after a time as supremely Gallic, lingering on from a time when France was a very different country from what it is to-day.

Amiens was all of this. It would have seemed hard and cold and bare and dry except for these little quirks of roofs, and the lightness of the spirit of the people. We wandered through high-walled, cobble-paved streets until suddenly we came on the cathedral, soaring upward out of a welter of the dreary and commonplace. I had thought Canterbury was wonderful—but now I knew that I had never seen anything in my life before so imposing as Amiens. Pure Gothic, like Canterbury, it was so much larger; a perfect maze of pinnacles, towers, arches, buttresses and flying buttresses; it soared into the sky—carven saint above carven saint, and gargoyles leering from every cranny. I could scarcely believe that the faith of man had ever reared so lovely a thing. What a power religion must have been in those days! Or what a grip this form of art must have taken on the imagination of some! To what perfection the art of architecture had attained! The loving care that has been exercised in designing, shaping and placing these stones is enough to stagger the brain. I did not wonder when I saw it that Ruskin and Morris had attained to a sort of frenzy over the Gothic. It is a thing for sighs and tears. Both Barfleur and I walked around it in reverent silence, and I knew that he was rejoicing to know that I was feeling what I ought to feel.

We went inside after a time because it was threatening dusk and we had to make our train for Paris. I shall never forget the vast space within those wondrous doors—the world of purple and gold and blue in the windows, the blaze of a hundred and more candles upon the great altar, the shrines with their votive offerings of flaming tapers, the fat waddling mothers in bunchy skirts, the heavy priests with shovel hats and pig-like faces, the order of attendant sisters in blue collars and flaring linen headgear, the worshipful figures scattered here and there upon the hard stone floor on their knees. The vast space was full of a delicious incense; faint shadows were already pooling themselves in the arches above to blend into a great darkness. Up rose the columns, giant redwoods of stone, supporting the far-off roof; the glory of pointed windows, the richness of foliated decorations, the worshipfulness of graven saints set in shrines whose details seemed the tendrils of spring. Whatever the flower, the fruit, the leaf, the branch, could contribute in the way of artistic suggestion had here been seized upon. Only the highest order of inspiration could have conceived or planned or executed this delicious dream in stone.

A guide, for a franc or two, took us high up into the organ-loft and out upon a narrow balustrade leading about the roof. Below, all France was spread out; the city of Amiens, its contour, was defined accurately. You could see some little stream, the Somme, coming into the city and leaving it. Wonderful figures of saints and devils were on every hand. We were shown a high tower in which a treaty between France and Spain had been signed. I looked down into the great well of the nave inside and saw the candles glowing like gold and the people moving like small bugs across the floor. It was a splendid confirmation of the majesty of man, the power of his ideals, the richness and extent of his imagination, the sheer ability of his hands. I would not give up my fleeting impression of Amiens for anything that I know.

* * * * *

As we came away from the cathedral in the dusk we walked along some branch or canal of the Somme, and I saw for the first time the peculiar kind of boat or punt used on French streams—a long affair, stub-pointed at either end. It was black and had somewhat the effect of a gondola. A Frenchman in baggy corduroy trousers and soft wool cap pulled over one ear was poling it along. It contained hay piled in a rude mass. It was warm here, in spite of the fact that it was the middle of January, and there was a feeling of spring in the air. Barfleur informed me that the worst of winter in Paris appeared between January fifteenth and the middle of March, that the spring did not really show itself until the first of April or a little later.

"You will be coming back by then," he said, "and you will see it in all its glory. We will go to Fontainebleau and ride." That sounded very promising to me.

I could not believe that these dull cobble-stone streets through which we were passing were part of a city of over ninety thousand, and that there was much manufacturing here. There were so few people in sight. It had a gray, shut-up appearance—none of the flow and spirit of the towns of the American Middle West. It occurred to me at once that, though I might like to travel here, I should never like to live here. Then we reached the railway station again.

CHAPTER XXI
PARIS!

THERE is something about the French nation which, in spite of its dreary-looking cities, exhibits an air of metropolitan up-to-dateness. I don't know where outside of America you will find the snap and intensity of emotion, ambition, and romance which you find everywhere in French streets. The station, when we returned to it, was alive with a crowd of bustling, hurrying people, buying books and papers at news-stands, looking after their luggage in the baggage-room, and chattering to the ticket-sellers through their windows. A train from Paris was just in and they were hurrying to catch that; and as I made my first French purchase—twenty centimes' worth of post-cards of Amiens—our train rolled in. It was from the North—such a long train as you frequently see in America, with cars labeled Milan, Trieste, Marseilles, Florence, and Rome. I could hardly believe it, and asked Barfleur as he bustled about seeing that the luggage was put in the proper carriage, where it came from. He thought that some of these cars started from St. Petersburg and others from Denmark and Holland. They had a long run ahead of them yet—over thirty hours to Rome, and Paris was just one point in their journey. We crowded into one car—stuffy with luggage, its windows damp with human breath, various nationalities occupying the section—and disposed of our grips, portmanteaus, rugs and so on, as best we could. I slipped the bustling old *facteur* a franc—not so much because he deserved it, but because he had such a gay and rakish air. His apron swung around his legs like a skirt, and his accordion-plaited cap was lolling gaily over one ear. He waved me a smiling farewell and said something in French which I wished I could understand. Then I realized for the first time what a pity it is not to understand the language of the country in which you are traveling.

As the train sped on through the dark to Paris I fell to speculating on the wonders I was to see. Barfleur was explaining to me that in order to make my entrance into Paris properly gay and interesting, we were to dine at the Café de Paris and then visit the Folies-Bergère and afterwards have supper at the Abbaye Thélème.

I should say here that of all people I know Barfleur is as capable of creating an atmosphere as any—perhaps more so. The man lives so heartily in his moods, he sets the stage for his actions long beforehand, and then walks on like a good actor and plays his part thoroughly. All the way over—from the very first day we met in New York, I think—he was either consciously or unconsciously building up for me the glamour of smart and artistic life in Europe. Now these things are absolutely according to your capacity to understand and appreciate them; they are, if you please, a figment of the brain, a frame of mind. If you love art, if you love history, if the romance of sex and beauty enthralls you, Europe in places presents tremendous possibilities. To reach these ethereal paradises of charm, you must skip and blink and dispense with many things. All the long lines of commonplaces through which you journey must be as nothing. You buy and prepare and travel and polish and finally you reach the center of this thing which is so wonderful; and then, when you get there, it is a figment of your own mind. Paris and the Riviera are great realities—there are houses and crowds and people and great institutions and the remembrance and flavor of great deeds; but the thing that you get out of all this for yourself is born of the attitude or mood which you take with you. Toward gambling, show, romance, a delicious scene, Barfleur carries a special mood. Life is only significant because of these things. His great struggle is to avoid the dingy and the dull, and to escape if possible the penalties of encroaching age. I think he looks back on the glitter of his youth with a pathetic eye, and I know he looks forward into the dark with stoic solemnity. Just one hour of beauty, is his private cry, one more day of delight. Let the future take care of itself. He realizes, too, with the keenness of a realist, that if youth is not most vivid in yourself, it can sometimes be achieved through the moods of others. I know he found in me a zest and a curiosity and a wonder which he was keen to satisfy. Now he would see this thing over as he had seen it years before. He would observe me thrill and marvel, and so he would be able to thrill and marvel himself once more. He clung to me with delicious enthusiasm, and every now and then would say, "Come now, what are you thinking? I want to know. I am enjoying this as much as you are." He had a delicious vivacity which acted on me like wine.

As we neared Paris he had built this city up so thoroughly in my mood that I am satisfied that I could not have seen it with a realistic eye if I had tried. It was something—I cannot tell you what—Napoleon, the Louvre, the art quarter,

Montmartre, the gay restaurants, the boulevards, Balzac, Hugo, the Seine and the soldiery, a score and a hundred things too numerous to mention and all greatly exaggerated. I hoped to see something which was perfect in its artistic appearance—exteriorly speaking. I expected, after reading George Moore and others, a wine-like atmosphere; a throbbing world of gay life; women of exceptional charm of face and dress; the bizarre, the unique, the emotional, the spirited. At Amiens I had seen enough women entering the trains to realize that the dreary commonplace of the English woman was gone. Instead the young married women that we saw were positively daring compared to what England could show—shapely, piquant, sensitive, their eyes showing a birdlike awareness of what this world has to offer. I fancied Paris would be like that, only more so; and as I look back on it now I can honestly say that I was not greatly disappointed. It was not all that I thought it would be, but it was enough. It is a gay, brilliant, beautiful city, with the spirit of New York and more than the distinction of London. It is like a brilliant, fragile child—not made for contests and brutal battles, but gay beyond reproach.

When the train rolled into the Gare du Nord it must have been about eight o'clock. Barfleur, as usual, was on the qui vive for precedence and advantage. He had industriously piled all the bags close to the door, and was hanging out of a window doing his best to signal a facteur. I was to stay in the car and hand all the packages down rapidly while he ran to secure a taxi and an inspector and in other ways to clear away the impediments to our progress. With great executive enthusiasm he told me that we must be at the Hotel Normandy by eight-fifteen or twenty and that by nine o'clock we must be ready to sit down in the Café de Paris to an excellent dinner which he had ordered by telegraph.

I recall my wonder in entering Paris—the lack of any long extended suburbs, the sudden flash of electric lights and electric cars. Mostly we seemed to be entering through a tunnel or gully, and then we were there. The noisy facteurs in their caps and blue jumpers were all around the cars. They ran and chattered and gesticulated—so unlike the porters in Paddington and Waterloo and Victoria and Euston. The one we finally secured, a husky little enthusiast, did his best to gather all our packages in one grand mass and shoulder them, stringing them on a single strap. The result of it was that the strap broke right over a small pool of water, and among other things the canvas bag containing my blanket and magnificent shoes fell into the water. "Oh, my God," exclaimed Barfleur, "my hat box!"

"The fool ass," I added, "I knew he would do just that—My blanket! My shoes!"

The excited facteur was fairly dancing in anguish, doing his best to get the packages strung together. Between us we relieved him of about half of them, and from about his waist he unwrapped another large strap and strung the remainder on that. Then we hurried on—for nothing would do but that we must hurry. A taxi was secured and all our luggage piled on it. It looked half suffocated under bundles as it swung out into the street, and we were off at a mad clip through crowded, electric-lighted streets. I pressed my nose to the window and took in as much as I could, while Barfleur between calculations as to how much time this would take, and that would take, and whether my trunk had arrived safely, expatiated laconically on French characteristics.

"You smell this air—it is all over Paris."

"The taxis always go like this." (We were going like mad.)

"There is an excellent type—look at her."

"Now you see the chairs out in front—they are that way all over Paris."

I was looking at the interesting restaurant life which never really seems to be interrupted anywhere in Paris. You can always find a dozen chairs somewhere, if not fifty or a hundred, out on the sidewalk under the open sky, or a glass roof—little stone-topped tables beside them, the crowd surging to and fro in front. Here you can sit and have your coffee, your liqueur, your sandwich. Everybody seems to do it—it is as common as walking in the streets.

We whirled through street after street partaking of this atmosphere, and finally swung up in front of a rather plain hotel which, I learned this same night, was close to the Avenue de l'Opéra, on the corner of the Rue St. Honoré and the Rue de l'Echelle. Our luggage was quickly distributed and I was shown into my room by a maid who could not speak English. I unlocked my belongings and was rapidly changing my clothes when Barfleur, breathing mightily, fully arrayed, appeared to say that I should await him at the door below where he would arrive with two guests. I did so, and in fifteen minutes he returned, the car spinning up out of a steady stream that was flowing by. I think my head was dizzy with the whirl of impressions which I was garnering, but I did my best to keep a sane view of things, and to get my impressions as sharp and clear as I could.

I am quite satisfied of one thing in this world, and that is that the commonest intelligence is very frequently confused or hypnotized or overpersuaded by certain situations, and that the weaker ones are ever full of the wildest forms of illusion. We talk about the sanity of life—I question whether it exists. Mostly it is a succession of confusing, disturbing impressions which are only rarely valid. This night I know I was moving in a sort of maze, and when I stepped into the car and was introduced to the two girls who were with Barfleur, I easily succumbed to what was obviously their great beauty.

The artist Greuze has painted the type that I saw before me over and over—soft, buxom, ruddy womanhood. I think the two may have been twenty-four and twenty-six. The elder was smaller than the younger—although both were of good size—and not so ruddy; but they were both perfectly plump, round-faced, dimpled, and with a wealth of brownish-black hair, even white teeth, smooth plump arms and necks and shoulders. Their chins were adorably rounded, their lips red, and their eyes laughing and gay. They began laughing and chattering the moment I entered, extending their soft white hands and saying things in French which I could not understand. Barfleur was smiling—beaming through his monocle in an amused, superior way. The older girl was arrayed in pearl-colored silk with a black mantilla spangled with silver, and the younger had a dress of peach-blow hue with a white lace mantilla also spangled, and they breathed a faint perfume. We were obviously in beautiful, if not moral, company.

I shall never forget the grand air with which this noble company entered the Café de Paris. Barfleur was in fine feather and the ladies radiated a charm and a flavor which immediately attracted attention. This brilliant café was aglow with lights and alive with people. It is not large in size—quite small in fact—and triangular in shape. The charm of it comes not so much from the luxury of the fittings, which are luxurious enough, but from their exceeding good taste, and the fame of the cuisine. One does not see a bill of fare here that indicates prices. You order what you like and are charged what is suitable. Champagne is not an essential wine as it is in some restaurants—you may drink what you like. There is a delicious sparkle and spirit to the place which can only spring from a high sense of individuality. Paris is supposed to provide nothing better than the Café de Paris, in so far as food is concerned. It is as good a place to go for dinner as the city provides.

It amuses me now when I think of how the managerial ability of Barfleur had been working through all this. As the program had been arranged in his mind, I was to take the elder of the two ladies as my partner and he had reserved the younger for himself. As a matter of fact they were really equally pretty and charming—and I was interested in both until, after a few parleys and when I had exchanged a few laughing signs with the younger, he informed me that she was really closely tied up with some one else and was not available. This I really did not believe; but it did not make any particular difference. I turned my attention to the elder who was quite as vivacious, if not quite so forceful as her younger sister. I never knew what it meant before to sit in a company of this kind, welcome as a friend, looked to for gaiety as a companion and admirer, and yet not able to say a word in the language of the occasion. There were certain words which could be quickly acquired on an occasion of this kind, such as "beautiful," "charming," "very delightful," and so on, for which Barfleur gave me the French equivalent, and then I could make complimentary remarks which he would translate for all, and the ladies would say things in reply which would come to me by the same medium. It went gaily enough—for the conversation would not have been of a high order if I had been able to speak French. Barfleur objected to being used constantly as an interpreter, and when he became stubborn and chattered gaily without stopping to explain, I was compelled to fall back on the resources of looks and smiles and gestures. It interested me to see how quick these women were to adapt themselves to the difficulties of the situation. They were constantly laughing and chaffing between themselves— looking at me and saying obviously flattering things, and then laughing at my discomfiture in not being able to understand. The elder explained what certain objects were by lifting them up and insisting on the French name. Barfleur was constantly telling me of the compliments they made and how sad they thought it was that I could not speak French. We departed finally for the Folies-Bergère where the newest sensation of Paris, Mistinguett, was playing. She proved to be a brilliant hoyden to look upon; a gay, slim, yellow-haired tomboy who seemed to fascinate the large audience by her boyish manners and her wayward air. There was a brilliant chorus in spangled silks and satins, and finally a beautiful maiden without any clothing at all who was cloaked by the soldiery of the stage before she had half crossed it. The vaudeville acts were about as good as they are anywhere. I did not think that the performance was any better than one might see in one or two places in New York, but of course the humor was much broader. Now and then one of their remarkable *bons mots* was translated for me by Barfleur just to give me an inkling of the character of the place. Back of the seats was a great lobby or promenade where a fragment of the demi-monde of Paris was congregated—beautiful creatures, in many instances, and as unconventional as you please. I was particularly struck with the smartness of their costumes and the cheerful character of their faces. The companion type in London and New York is somewhat colder-looking. Their eyes snapped with Gallic intelligence, and they walked as though the whole world held their point of view and no other.

From here at midnight we left for the Abbaye Thélème; and there I encountered the best that Paris has to show in the way of that gaiety and color and beauty and smartness for which it is famous. One really ought to say a great deal about the Abbaye Thélème, because it is the last word, the quintessence of midnight excitement and international *savoir faire*. The Russian and the Brazilian, the Frenchman, the American, the Englishman, the German and the Italian all meet here on common ground. I saw much of restaurant life in Paris while I was there, but nothing better than this. Like the Café de Paris it was small—very small—when compared to restaurants of similar repute in New York and London. I fancy it was not more than sixty feet square—only it was not square but pentagonal, almost circular. The tables, to begin with, went round the walls, with seats which had the wall for a back; and then, as the guests poured in, the interior space was filled up with tables which were brought in for the purpose; and, later in the morning, when the guests began to leave, these tables were taken out again, and the space devoted to dancing and entertainers.

As in the Café de Paris I noticed that it was not so much the quality of the furnishings as the spirit of the place which was important. This latter was compounded of various elements—success, perfection of service, absolute distinction of cooking, and lastly the subtlety and magnetism of sex which is capitalized and used in Paris as it is nowhere else in the world. I never actually realized until I stepped into this restaurant what it is that draws a certain moneyed element to Paris. The Tomb of Napoleon and the Panthéon and the Louvre are not the significant attractions of that important city. Those things have their value—they constitute an historical and artistic element that is appealing, romantic and forceful. But over and above that there is something else—and that is sex. I did not learn what I am going to say now until later, but it might as well be said here, for it illustrates the point exactly. A little experience and inquiry in Paris quickly taught me that the owners and managers of the more successful restaurants encourage and help to sustain a certain type of woman whose presence is desirable. She must be young, beautiful, or attractive, and above all things possessed of temperament. A woman can rise in the café and restaurant world of Paris quite as she can on the stage; and she can easily graduate from the Abbaye Thélème and Maxim's to the stage, though the path is villainous. On the other hand, the stage contributes freely to the atmosphere of Maxim's, the Abbaye Thélème, and other restaurants of their kind. A large number of the figures seen here and at the Folies-Bergère and other places of the same type, are interchangeable. They are in the restaurants when they are not on the stage, and they are on the stage when they are not in the restaurants. They rise or fall by a world of strange devices, and you can hear brilliant or ghastly stories illustrating either conclusion. Paris—this aspect of it—is a perfect maelstrom of sex; and it is sustained by the wealth and the curiosity of the stranger, as well as the Frenchman.

The Abbaye Thélème on this occasion presented a brilliant scene. The carpet, as I recall it, was a rich green velvet; the walls a lavender-white. From the ceiling six magnificently prismed electroliers were suspended—three glowing with a clear peach-blow hue and three with a brilliant white. Outside a small railing near the door several negro singers, a mandolin and a guitar-player, several stage dancers, and others were congregated. A perfect storm of people was pouring through the doors—all with their tables previously arranged for. Out in the lobby, where a January wind was blowing, you could hear a wild uproar of slamming taxi doors, and the calls of doormen and chauffeurs getting their vehicles in and out of the way. The company generally, as on all such occasions, was on the qui vive to see who else were present and what the general spirit of the occasion was to be. Instantly I detected a number of Americans; three amazingly beautiful English women, such as I never saw in England, and their escorts; a few Spaniards or South Americans; and, after that, a variety of individuals whom I took to be largely French, although it was impossible to tell. The English women interested me because, during all my stay in Europe, I never saw three other women quite so beautiful, and because, during all my stay in England, I scarcely saw a good-looking English woman. Barfleur suggested that they were of that high realm of fashion which rarely remains in London during the winter season—when I was there; that if I came again in May or June and went to the races I would see plenty of them. Their lovely hair was straw-colored and their cheeks and foreheads a faint pink and cream. Their arms and shoulders were delightfully bare, and they carried themselves with amazing hauteur. By one o'clock, when the majority of the guests had arrived, this room fairly shimmered with white silks and satins, white arms and shoulders, roses in black hair and blue and lavender ribbons fastened about coiffures of lighter complexion. There were jewels in plenty—opals and amethysts and turquoises and rubies—and there was a perfect artillery of champagne corks. Every table was attended by its silver bucket of ice; and the mandolins and guitars in their crowded angle were strumming mightily.

I speculated interestedly as we seated ourselves as to what drew all these people from all parts of the world to see this, to be here together. Barfleur was eager to come here first and to have me see this, without delay. I do not know where you could go, and for a hundred francs see more of really amazing feminine beauty. I do not know where for the same money you could buy the same atmosphere of lightness and gaiety and enthusiasm. This place was fairly vibrating with a wild desire to live. I fancy the majority of those who were here for the first time—particularly of the young—would tell you that they

would rather be here than in any other spot you could name. The place had a peculiar glitter of beauty which was compounded by the managers with great skill. The waiters were all of them deft, swift, suave, good-looking; the dancers who stepped out on the floor after a few moments were of an orchid-like Spanish type—ruddy, brown, full-bodied, black-haired, black-eyed. They had on dresses that were as close fitting as the scales of a fish and that glittered with the same radiance. They waved and rattled and clashed castanets and tambourines and danced wildly and sinuously to and fro among the tables. Some of them sang, or voices accompanied them from the raised platform devoted to music.

After a while red, blue, pink and green balloons were introduced, anchored to the champagne bottles, and allowed to float gaily in the air. Paper parcels of small paste balls of all colors, as light as feathers, were distributed for the guests to throw at one another. In ten minutes a wild artillery battle was raging. Young girls were up on their feet, their hands full of these colored weapons, pelting the male strangers of their selection. You would see tall Englishmen and Americans exchanging a perfect volley of colored spheres with girls of various nationalities, laughing, chattering, calling, screaming. The cocotte in all her dazzling radiance was here—exquisitely dressed, her white arms shimmering, perfectly willing to strike up an understanding with the admirer who was pelting her.

After a time, when the audience had worn itself through fever and frenzy to satisfaction or weariness, or both, a few of the tables were cleared away and the dancing began, occasional guests joining. There were charming dances in costume from Russia, from Scotland, from Hungary, and from Spain. I had the wonder of seeing an American girl rise from her table and dance with more skill and grace than the employed talent. A wine-enthused Englishman took the floor, a handsome youth of twenty-six or eight, and remained there gaily prancing about from table to table, dancing alone or with whomsoever would welcome him. What looked like a dangerous argument started at one time because some high-mettled Brazilian considered that he had been insulted. A cordon of waiters and the managers soon adjusted that. It was between three and four in the morning when we finally left; and I was very tired.

It was decided that we should meet for dinner; and since it was almost daylight I was glad when we had seen our ladies to their apartment and returned to the hotel.

CHAPTER XXII
A MORNING IN PARIS

I SHALL never forget my first morning in Paris—the morning that I woke up after about two hours' sleep or less, prepared to put in a hard day at sight-seeing because Barfleur had a program which must be adhered to, and because he could only be with me until Monday, when he had to return. It was a bright day, fortunately, a little hazy and chill, but agreeable. I looked out of the window of my very comfortable room on the fifth floor which gave out on a balcony overhanging the Rue St. Honoré, and watched the crowd of French people below coming to shop or to work. It would be hard to say what makes the difference between a crowd of Englishmen and a crowd of Frenchmen, but there is a difference. It struck me that these French men and women walked faster and that their every movement was more spirited than either that of the English or the Americans. They looked more like Americans, though, than like the English; and they were much more cheerful than either, chatting and talking as they came. I was interested to see whether I could make the maid understand that I wanted coffee and rolls without talking French, but the wants of American travelers are an old story to French maids; and no sooner did I say *café* and make the sign of drinking from a cup than she said, "Oh, oui, oui, oui—oh, oui, oui, oui!" and disappeared. Presently the coffee was brought me—and rolls and butter and hot milk; and I ate my breakfast as I dressed.

About nine o'clock Barfleur arrived with his program. I was to walk in the Tuileries—which is close at hand—while he got a shave. We were to go for a walk in the Rue de Rivoli as far as a certain bootmaker's, who was to make me a pair of shoes for the Riviera. Then we were to visit a haberdasher's or two; and after that go straight about the work of sight-seeing—visiting the old bookstalls on the Seine, the churches of St. Étienne-du-Mont, Notre-Dame, Sainte-Chapelle, stopping at Foyot's for lunch; and thereafter regulating our conduct by the wishes of several guests who were to appear—Miss N. and Mr. McG., two neo-impressionist artists, and a certain Mme. de B., who would not mind showing me around Paris if I cared for her company.

We started off quite briskly, and my first adventure in Paris led me straight to the gardens of the Tuileries, lying west of the

Louvre. If any one wanted a proper introduction to Paris, I should recommend this above all others. Such a noble piece of gardening as this is the best testimony France has to offer of its taste, discrimination, and sense of the magnificent. I should say, on mature thought, that we shall never have anything like it in America. We have not the same lightness of fancy. And, besides, the Tuileries represents a classic period. I recall walking in here and being struck at once with the magnificent proportions of it all—the breadth and stately lengths of its walks, the utter wonder and charm of its statuary—snow-white marble nudes standing out on the green grass and marking the circles, squares and paths of its entire length. No such charm and beauty could be attained in America because we would not permit the public use of the nude in this fashion. Only the fancy of a monarch could create a realm such as this; and the Tuileries and the Place du Carrousel and the Place de la Concorde and the whole stretch of lovely tree-lined walks and drives that lead to the Arc de Triomphe and give into the Bois de Boulogne speak loudly of a noble fancy untrammeled by the dictates of an inartistic public opinion. I was astonished to find how much of the heart of Paris is devoted to public usage in this manner. It corresponds, in theory at least, to the space devoted to Central Park in New York—but this is so much more beautiful, or at least it is so much more in accord with the spirit of Paris. These splendid walks, devoted solely to the idling pedestrian, and set with a hundred sculptural fancies in marble, show the gay, pleasure-loving character of the life which created them. The grand monarchs of France knew what beauty was, and they had the courage and the taste to fulfil their desires. I got just an inkling of it all in the fifteen minutes that I walked here in the morning sun, waiting for Barfleur to get his shave.

From here we went to a Paris florist's where Madame pinned bright *boutonnières* on our coats, and thence to the bootmaker's where Madame again assisted her husband in the conduct of his business. Everywhere I went in Paris I was struck by this charming unity in the conduct of business between husband and wife and son and daughter. We talk much about the economic independence of women in America. It seems to me that the French have solved it in the only way that it can be solved. Madame helps her husband in his business and they make a success of it together. Monsieur Galoyer took the measurements for my shoes, but Madame entered them in a book; and to me the shop was fifty times as charming for her presence. She was pleasingly dressed, and the shop looked as though it had experienced the tasteful touches of a woman's hand. It was clean and bright and smart, and smacked of good housekeeping; and this was equally true of bookstalls, haberdashers' shops, art-stores, coffee-rooms, and places of public sale generally. Wherever Madame was, and she looked nice, there was a nice store; and Monsieur looked as fat and contented as could reasonably be expected under the circumstances.

The French have made much of the Seine

From Galoyer's we struck forth to Paris proper, its most interesting features, and I recall now with delight how fresh and trig and spick it all seemed. Paris has an air, a presence, from the poorest quarter of the Charenton district to the perfections of the Bois and the region about the Arc de Triomphe. It chanced that the day was bright and I saw the Seine, as bright as new buttons glimmering over the stones of its shallow banks and racing madly. If not a majestic stream it is at least a gay and dashing one—quick-tempered, rapid-flowing, artistically walled, crossed by a score of handsome bridges, and ornamented in every possible way. How much the French have made of so little in the way of a river! It is not very wide—about one-half as wide as the Thames at Blackfriars Bridge and not so wide as the Harlem River which makes Manhattan an island. I followed it from city wall to city wall one day, from Charenton to Issy, and found every inch of it delightful. I was never tired of looking at the wine barges near Charenton; the little bathing pavilions and passenger boats in the vicinity of the Louvre; the brick-barges, hay-barges, coal-barges and Heaven knows what else plying between the city's heart and points downstream past Issy. It gave me the impression of being one of the brightest, cleanest rivers in the world—a river on a holiday. I saw it once at Issy at what is known in Paris as the "green hour"—which is five o'clock—when the sun was going down and a deep palpable fragrance wafted from a vast manufactory of perfume filled the air. Men were poling boats of hay and laborers in their great wide-bottomed corduroy trousers, blue shirts and inimitable French caps, were trudging homewards, and I felt as though the world had nothing to offer Paris which it did not already have—even the joy of simple labor amid great beauty. I could have settled in a small house in Issy and worked as a laborer in a perfume factory, carrying my dinner pail with me every morning, with a right good-will—or such was the mood of the moment.

This morning, on our way to St.-Étienne-du-Mont and the cathedral, we examined the bookstalls along the Seine and tried to recall off-hand the interesting comment that had been made on them by great authors and travelers. My poor wit brought back only the references of Balzac; but Barfleur was livelier with thoughts from Rousseau to George Moore. They have a magnificent literary history; but it is only because they are on the banks of the Seine, in the center of this whirling pageant of life, that they are so delighted. To enjoy them one has to be in an idle mood and love out-of-doors; for they consist of a dusty row of four-legged boxes with lids coming quite to your chest in height, and reminding one of those high-legged counting-tables at which clerks sit on tall stools making entries in their ledgers. These boxes are old and paintless and weather-beaten; and at night the very dusty-looking keepers, who from early morning until dark have had their shabby-backed wares spread out where dust and sunlight and wind and rain can attack them, pack them in the body of the box on which they are lying and close the lid. You can always see an idler or two here—perhaps many idlers—between the Quai d'Orsay and the Quai Voltaire.

We made our way through the Rue Mazarin and Rue de l'Ancienne Comédie into that region which surrounds the École de Medecin and the Luxembourg. In his enthusiastic way Barfleur tried to indicate to me that I was in the most historic section of the left bank of the Seine, where were St.-Étienne-du-Mont, the Panthéon, the Sorbonne, the Luxembourg, the École des Beaux-Arts and the Latin Quarter. We came for a little way into the Boulevard St.-Michel, and there I saw my first artists in velvet suits, long hair, and broad-brimmed hats; but I was told that they were poseurs—the kind of artist who is so by profession, not by accomplishment. They were poetic-looking youths—the two that I saw swinging along together—with pale faces and slim hands. I was informed that the type had almost entirely disappeared and that the art student of to-day prefers to be distinctly inconspicuous. From what I saw of them later I can confirm this; for the schools which I visited revealed a type of boy and girl who, while being romantic enough, in all conscience, were nevertheless inconspicuously dressed and very simple and off-hand in their manner. I visited this region later with artists who had made a name for themselves in the radical world, and with students who were hoping to make a name for themselves—sitting in their cafés, examining their studios, and sensing the atmosphere of their streets and public amusements. There is an art atmosphere, strong and clear, compounded of romance, emotion, desire, love of beauty and determination of purpose, which is thrilling to experience—even vicariously.

Paris is as young in its mood as any city in the world. It is as wildly enthusiastic as a child. I noticed here, this morning, the strange fact of old battered-looking fellows singing to themselves, which I never noticed anywhere else in this world. Age sits lightly on the Parisian, I am sure; and youth is a mad fantasy, an exciting realm of romantic dreams. The Parisian—from the keeper of a market-stall to the prince of the money world, or of art—wants to live gaily, briskly, laughingly, and he will not let the necessity of earning his living deny him. I felt it in the churches, the depots, the department stores, the theaters, the restaurants, the streets—a wild, keen desire for life with the blood and the body to back it up. It must be in the soil and the air, for Paris sings. It is like poison in the veins, and I felt myself growing positively giddy with enthusiasm. I believe that for the first six months Paris would be a disease from which one would suffer greatly and recover slowly. After that you would settle down to live the life you found there in contentment and with delight; but you would not be in so much danger of wrecking your very mortal body and your uncertainly immortal soul.

I was interested in this neighborhood, as we hurried through and away from it to the Ile-de-la-Cité and Notre-Dame, as being not only a center for art strugglers of the Latin Quarter, but also for students of the Sorbonne. I was told that there were thousands upon thousands of them from various countries—eight thousand from Russia alone. How they live my informant did not seem to know, except that in the main they lived very badly. Baths, clean linen, and three meals a day, according to him, were not at all common; and in the majority of instances they starve their way through, going back to their native countries to take up the practice of law, medicine, politics and other professions. After Oxford and the American universities, this region and the Sorbonne itself, I found anything but attractive.

The church of St.-Étienne-du-Mont is as fine as possible, a type of the kind of architecture which is no type and ought to have a new name—modern would be as good as any. It has a creamish-gray effect, exceedingly ornate, with all the artificery of a jewel box.

The Panthéon seemed strangely bare to me, large and spacious but cold. The men who are not there as much as the men who are, made it seem somewhat unrepresentative to me as a national mausoleum. It is hard to make a national burying-ground that will appeal to all.

Notre-Dame after Canterbury and Amiens seems a little heavy but as contrasted with St. Paul's in London and anything existing in America, it seemed strangely wonderful. I could not help thinking of Hugo's novel and of St. Louis and Napoleon and the French Revolution in connection with it. It is so heavy and somber and so sadly great. The Hôtel Dieu, the Palais de Justice, Sainte-Chapelle and the Pont-Saint-Michel all in the same neighborhood interested me much, particularly Sainte-Chapelle—to me one of the most charming exteriors and interiors I saw in Paris. It is exquisite—this chapel which was once the scene of the private prayers of a king. This whole neighborhood somehow—from the bookstalls to Sainte-

Chapelle suggested Balzac and Hugo and the flavor of this world as they presented it, was in my mind.

And now there was luncheon at Foyot's, a little restaurant near the Luxembourg and the Musée de Cluny, where the wise in the matter of food love to dine and where, as usual, Barfleur was at his best. The French, while discarding show in many instances entirely, and allowing their restaurant chambers to look as though they had been put together with an effort, nevertheless attain a perfection of atmosphere which is astonishing. For the life of me I could not tell why this little restaurant seemed so bright, for there was nothing smart about it when you examined it in detail; and so I was compelled to attribute this impression to the probably all-pervading temperament of the owner. Always, in these cases, there is a man (or a woman) quite remarkable for his point of view. Otherwise you could not take such simple appointments and make them into anything so pleasing and so individual. A luncheon which had been ordered by telephone was now served; and at the beginning of its gastronomic wonders Mr. McG. and Miss N. arrived.

I shall not soon forget the interesting temperaments of these two; for even more than great institutions, persons who come reasonably close to you make up the atmosphere of a city. Mr. McG. was a solid, sandy, steady-eyed Scotchman who looked as though, had he not been an artist, he might have been a kilted soldier, swinging along with the enviable Scotch stride. Miss N. was a delightfully Parisianized American, without the slightest affectation, however, so far as I could make out, of either speech or manner. She was pleasingly good-looking, with black hair, a healthy, rounded face and figure, and a cheerful, good-natured air. There was no sense of either that aggressiveness or superiority which so often characterizes the female artist. We launched at once upon a discussion of Paris, London and New York and upon the delights of Paris and the progress of the neo-impressionist cult. I could see plainly that these two did not care to force their connection with that art development on my attention; but I was interested to know of it. There was something so solid and self-reliant about Mr. McG. that before the meal was over I had taken a fancy to him. He had the least suggestion of a Scotch burr in his voice which might have said "awaw" instead of away and "doon" instead of down; but it resulted in nothing so broad as that. They immediately gave me lists of restaurants that I must see in the Latin Quarter and asked me to come with them to the Café d'Harcourt and to Bullier's to dance and to some of the brasseries to see what they were like. Between two and three Mr. McG. left because of an errand, and Barfleur and I accompanied Miss N. to her studio close by the gardens of the Luxembourg. This public garden which, not unlike the Tuileries on the other side of the Seine, was set with charming statues, embellished by a magnificent fountain, and alive with French nursemaids and their charges, idling Parisians in cutaways and derbies, and a smart world of pedestrians generally impressed me greatly. It was lovely. The wonder of Paris, as I was discovering, was that, walk where you would, it was hard to escape the sense of breadth, space, art, history, romance and a lovely sense of lightness and enthusiasm for life.

Miss N.'s studio is in the Rue Deñfert-Rochereau. In calling here I had my first taste of the Paris concierge, the janitress who has an eye on all those who come and go and to whom all not having keys must apply. In many cases, as I learned, keys are not given to the outer gate or door. One must ring and be admitted. This gives this person a complete espionage over the affairs of all the tenants, mail, groceries, guests, purchases, messages—anything and everything. If you have a charming concierge, it is well and good; if not, not. The thought of anything so offensive as a spying concierge irritated me greatly and I found myself running forward in my mind picking fights with some possible concierge who might at some remote date possibly trouble me. Of such is the contentious disposition.

The studio of Mr. McG., in the Boulevard Raspail, overlooks a lovely garden—a heavenly place set with trees and flowers and reminiscent of an older day in the bits of broken stonework lying about, and suggesting the architecture of a bygone period. His windows, reaching from floor to ceiling and supplemented by exterior balconies, were overhung by trees. In both studios were scores of canvases done in the neo-impressionistic style which interested me profoundly.

It is one thing to see neo-impressionism hung upon the walls of a gallery in London, or disputed over in a West End residence. It is quite another to come upon it fresh from the easel in the studio of the artist, or still in process of production, defended by every thought and principle of which the artist is capable. In Miss N.'s studio were a series of decorative canvases intended for the walls of a great department store in America which were done in the raw reds, yellows, blues and greens of the neo-impressionist cult—flowers which stood out with the coarse distinctness of hollyhocks and sunflowers; architectural outlines which were as sharp as those of rough buildings, and men and women whose details of dress and feature were characterized by colors which by the uncultivated eye would be pronounced unnatural.

For me they had an immense appeal if for nothing more than that they represented a development and an individual point of view. It is so hard to break tradition.

It was the same in the studio of Mr. McG. to which we journeyed after some three-quarters of an hour. Of the two painters, the man seemed to me the more forceful. Miss N. worked in a softer mood, with more of what might be called an emotional attitude towards life.

During all this, Barfleur was in the heyday of his Parisian glory, and appropriately cheerful. We took a taxi through singing streets lighted by a springtime sun and came finally to the Restaurant Prunier where it was necessary for him to secure a table and order dinner in advance; and thence to the Théâtre des Capucines in the Rue des Capucines, where tickets for a farce had to be secured, and thence to a bar near the Avenue de l'Opéra where we were to meet the previously mentioned Mme. de B. who, out of the goodness of her heart, was to help entertain me while I was in the city.

This remarkable woman who by her beauty, simplicity, utter frankness, and moody immorality would shock the average woman into a deadly fear of life and make a horror of what seems a gaudy pleasure world to some, quite instantly took my fancy. Yet I think it was more a matter of Mme. de B.'s attitude, than it was the things which she did, which made it so terrible. But that is a long story.

One of the thousands upon thousands of cafés on the boulevards of Paris

We came to her out of the whirl of the "green hour," when the Paris boulevards in this vicinity were fairly swarming with people—the gayest world I have ever seen. We have enormous crowds in New York, but they seem to be going somewhere very much more definitely than in Paris. With us there is an eager, strident, almost objectionable effort to get home or to the theater or to the restaurant which one can easily resent—it is so inconsiderate and indifferent. In London you do not feel that there are any crowds that are going to the theaters or the restaurants; and if they are, they are not very cheerful about it; they are enduring life; they have none of the lightness of the Parisian world. I think it is all explained by the fact that Parisians feel keenly that they are living now and that they wish to enjoy themselves as they go. The American and the Englishman—the Englishman much more than the American—have decided that they are going to live in the future. Only the American is a little angry about his decision and the Englishman a little meek or patient. They both feel that life is intensely grim. But the Parisian, while he may feel or believe it, decides wilfully to cast it off. He lives by the way, out of books, restaurants, theaters, boulevards, and the spectacle of life generally. The Parisians move briskly, and they come out where they can see each other—out into the great widesidewalked boulevards and the thousands upon thousands of cafés; and make themselves comfortable and talkative and gay on the streets. It is so obvious that everybody is having a good time—not trying to have it; that they are enjoying the wine-like air, the cordials and *apéritifs* of the *brasseries*, the net-like movements of the cabs, the dancing lights of the roadways, and the flare of the shops. It may be chill or drizzling in Paris, but you scarcely feel it. Rain can scarcely drive the people off the streets. Literally it does not. There are crowds whether it rains or not, and they are not despondent. This particular hour that brought us to G.'s Bar was essentially thrilling, and I was interested to see what Mme. de B. was like.

CHAPTER XXIII
THREE GUIDES

IT was only by intuition, and by asking many questions, that at times I could extract the significance of certain places from Barfleur as quickly as I wished. He was always reticent or a little cryptic in his allusions. In this instance I gathered rapidly however that this bar was a very extraordinary little restaurant presided over by a woman of a most pleasant and practical type. She could not have been much over forty—buxom, good-looking, self-reliant, efficient. She moved about the two rooms which constituted her restaurant, in so far as the average diner was concerned, with an air of considerable social importance. Her dresses, as I noticed on my several subsequent visits, were always sober, but in excellent taste. About this time of day the two rooms were a little dark, the electric lights being reserved for the more crowded hours. Yet there were always a few people here. This evening when we entered I noticed a half-dozen men and three or four young women lounging here in a preliminary way, consuming *apéritifs* and chatting sociably. I made out by degrees that the mistress of this place had a following of a kind, in the Parisian scheme of things—that certain men and women came here for reasons of good-fellowship; and that she would take a certain type of struggling maiden, if she were good-looking and ambitious and smart, under her wing. The girl would have to know how to dress well, to be able to carry herself with an air; and when money was being spent very freely by an admirer it might as well be spent at this bar on occasion as anywhere else. There was obviously an *entente cordiale* between Madame G. and all the young women who came in here. They seemed so much at home that it was quite like a family party. Everybody appeared to be genial, cheerful, and to know everybody else. To enter here was to feel as though you had lived in Paris for years.

While we are sitting at a table sipping a brandy and soda, enter Mme. de B., the brisk, genial, sympathetic French personage whose voice on the instant gave me a delightful impression of her. It was the loveliest voice I have ever heard, soft and musical, a colorful voice touched with both gaiety and sadness. Her eyes were light blue, her hair brown and her manner sinuous and insinuating. She seemed to have the spirit of a delightfully friendly collie dog or child and all the gaiety and alertness that goes with either.

After I had been introduced, she laughed, and putting aside her muff and stole, shook herself into a comfortable position in a corner and accepted a brandy and soda. She was so interested for the moment, exchanging whys and wherefores with Barfleur, that I had a chance to observe her keenly. In a moment she turned to me and wanted to know whether I knew either of two American authors whom she knew—men of considerable repute. Knowing them both very well, it surprised me to think that she knew them. She seemed, from the way she spoke, to have been on the friendliest terms with both of them; and any one by looking at her could have understood why they should have taken such an interest in her.

"Now, you know, that Mistaire N., he is very nice. I was very fond of him. And Mistaire R., he is clever, don't you think?"

I admitted at once that they were both very able men and that I was glad that she knew them. She informed me that she had known Mr. R. and Mr. N. in London and that she had there perfected her English, which was very good indeed. Barfleur explained in full who I was and how long I would be in Paris and that he had written her from America because he wanted her to show me some attention during my stay in Paris.

If Mme. de B. had been of a somewhat more calculating type I fancy that, with her intense charm of face and manner and her intellect and voice, she would have been very successful. I gained the impression that she had been on the stage in some small capacity; but she had been too diffident—not really brazen enough—for the grim world in which the French actress rises. I soon found that Mme. de B. was a charming blend of emotion, desire, and refinement which had strayed into the wrong field. She would have done better in literature or music or art; and she seemed fitted by her moods and her understanding to be a light in any one of them or all. Some temperaments are so—missing by a fraction what they would give all the world to have. It is the little things that do it—the fractions, the bits, the capacity for taking pains in little things that make, as so many have said, the difference between success and failure and it is true.

I shall never forget how she looked at me, quite in the spirit of a gay uncertain child, and how quickly she made me feel that we would get along very well together. "Why, yes," she said quite easily in her soft voice, "I will go about with you, although I would not know what is best to see. But I shall be here, and if you want to come for me we can see things together." Suddenly she reached over and took my hand and squeezed it genially, as though to seal the bargain. We had more drinks to celebrate this rather festive occasion; and then Mme. de B., promising to join us at the theater, went away. It was high time then to dress for dinner; and so we returned to the hotel. We ate a companionable meal, watching the Parisian and his lady love (or his wife) arrive in droves and dine with that gusto and enthusiasm which is so characteristic of the French.

When we came out of this theater at half after eleven, Mme. de B. was anxious to return to her apartment, and Barfleur was anxious to give me an extra taste of the varied café life of Paris in order that I might be able to contrast and compare intelligently. "If you know where they are and see whether you like them, you can tell whether you want to see any more of them—which I hope you won't," said he wisely, leading the way through a swirling crowd that was for all the world like a rushing tide of the sea.

There are no traffic laws in Paris, so far as I could make out; vehicles certainly have the right-of-way and they go like mad. I have read of the Parisian authorities having imported a London policeman to teach Paris police the art of traffic regulation, but if so, the instruction has been wasted. This night was a bedlam of vehicles and people. A Paris guide, one of the tribe that conducts the morbid stranger through scenes that are supposedly evil, and that I know from observation to be utterly vain, approached us in the Boulevard des Capucines with the suggestion that he be allowed to conduct us through a realm of filthy sights, some of which he catalogued. I could give a list of them if I thought any human organization would ever print them, or that any individual would ever care to read them— which I don't. I have indicated before that Barfleur is essentially clean-minded. He is really interested in the art of the demi-mondaine, and the spectacle which their showy and, to a certain extent, artistic lives present; but no one in this world ever saw more clearly through the shallow make-believe of this realm than he does. He contents himself with admiring the art and the tragedy and the pathos of it. This world of women interests him as a phase of the struggle for existence, and for the artistic pretense which it sometimes compels. To him the vast majority of these women in Paris were artistic—whatever one might say for their morals, their honesty, their brutality and the other qualities which they possess or lack; and whatever they were, life made them so—conditions over which their temperaments, understandings and wills had little or no control. He is an amazingly tolerant man—one of the most tolerant I have ever known, and kindly in his manner and intention.

Nevertheless, he has an innate horror of the purely physical when it descends to inartistic brutality. There is much of that in Paris; and these guides advertise it; but it is filth especially arranged for the stranger. I fancy the average Parisian knows nothing about it; and if he does, he has a profound contempt for it. So has the well-intentioned stranger, but there is always an audience for this sort of thing. So when this guide approached us with the proposition to show us a selected line of vice, Barfleur took him genially in hand. "Stop a moment, now," he said, with his high hat on the back of his head, his fur coat expansively open, and his monocled eye fixing the intruder with an inquiring gaze, "tell me one thing—have you a mother?"

The small Jew who was the industrious salesman for this particular type of ware looked his astonishment.

They are used to all sorts of set-backs—these particular guides—for they encounter all sorts of people, severely moral and the reverse; and I fancy on occasion they would be soundly trounced if it were not for the police who stand in with them and receive a modicum for their protection. They certainly learn to understand something of the type of man who will listen to their proposition; for I have never seen them more than ignored and I have frequently seen them talked to in an off-hand way, though I was pleased to note that their customers were few.

This particular little Jew had a quizzical, screwed-up expression on his face, and did not care to answer the question at first; but resumed his announcement of his various delights and the price it would all cost.

"Wait, wait, wait," insisted Barfleur, "answer my question. Have you a mother?"

"What has that got to do with it?" asked the guide. "Of course I have a mother."

"Where is she?" demanded Barfleur authoritatively.

"She's at home," replied the guide, with an air of mingled astonishment, irritation and a desire not to lose a customer.

"Does she know that you are out here on the streets of Paris doing what you are doing to-night?" he continued with a very noble air.

The man swore under his breath.

"Answer me," persisted Barfleur, still fixing him solemnly through his monocle. "Does she?"

"Why, no, of course she doesn't," replied the Jew sheepishly.

"Would you want her to know?" This in sepulchral tones.

"No, I don't think so."

"Have you a sister?"

"Yes."

"Would you want her to know?"

"I don't know," replied the guide defiantly. "She might know anyhow."

"Tell me truly, if she did not know, would you want her to know?"

The poor vender looked as if he had got into some silly, inexplicable mess from which he would be glad to free himself; but he did not seem to have sense enough to walk briskly away and leave us. Perhaps he did not care to admit defeat so easily.

"No, I suppose not," replied the interrogated vainly.

"There you have it," exclaimed Barfleur triumphantly. "You have a mother—you would not want her to know. You have a sister—you would not want her to know. And yet you solicit me here on the street to see things which I do not want to see or know. Think of your poor gray-headed mother," he exclaimed grandiloquently, and with a mock air of shame and sorrow. "Once, no doubt, you prayed at her knee, an innocent boy yourself."

The man looked at him in dull suspicion.

"No doubt if she saw you here to-night, selling your manhood for a small sum of money, pandering to the lowest and most vicious elements in life, she would weep bitter tears. And your sister—don't you think now you had better give up this evil life? Don't you think you had better accept any sort of position and earn an honest living rather than do what you are doing?"

"Well, I don't know," said the man. "This living is as good as any other living. I've worked hard to get my knowledge."

"Good God, do you call this knowledge?" inquired Barfleur solemnly.

"Yes, I do," replied the man. "I've worked hard to get it."

These places were crowded with a gay and festive throng

"My poor friend," replied Barfleur, "I pity you. From the bottom of my heart I pity you. You are degrading your life and ruining your soul. Come now, to-morrow is Sunday. The church bells will be ringing. Go to church. Reform your life. Make a new start—do. You will never regret it. Your old mother will be so glad—and your sister."

"Oh, say," said the man, walking off, "you don't want a guide. You want a church." And he did not even look back.

"It is the only way I have of getting rid of them," commented Barfleur. "They always stop when I begin to talk to them about their mother. They can't stand the thought of their mother."

"Very true," I said. "Cut it out now, and come on. You have preached enough. Let us see the worst that Paris has to show." And off we went, arm in arm.

Thereafter we visited restaurant after restaurant,—high, low, smart, dull,-and I can say truly that the strange impression which this world made on me lingers even now. Obviously, when we arrived at Fysher's at twelve o'clock, the fun was just getting under way. Some of these places, like this Bar Fysher, were no larger than a fair-sized room in an apartment, but crowded with a gay and festive throng—Americans, South Americans, English and others. One of the tricks in Paris to make a restaurant successful is to keep it small so that it has an air of overflow and activity. Here at Fysher's Bar, after allowing room for the red-jacketed orchestra, the piano and the waiters, there was scarcely space for the forty or fifty guests who were present. Champagne was twenty francs the bottle and champagne was all they served. It was necessary here, as at all the restaurants, to contribute to the support of the musicians; and if a strange young woman should sit at your table for a moment and share either the wine or the fruit which would be quickly offered, you would have to pay for that. Peaches were three francs each, and grapes five francs the bunch. It was plain that all these things were offered in order that the house might thrive and prosper. It was so at each and all of them.

CHAPTER XXIV
"THE POISON FLOWER"

IT was after this night that Barfleur took his departure for London for two weeks, where business affairs were calling him during which time I was to make myself as idle and gay as I might alone or with the individuals to whom he had introduced me or to whom I had introductions direct. There was so much that I wished to see and that he did not care to see over again with me, having seen it all before—the Musée de Cluny, for instance, the Louvre, the Luxembourg and so on.

The next afternoon after a more or less rambling day I saw him off for London and then I plunged into this treasure world alone.

One of the things that seriously impressed me was the never-failing singing air of the city which was everywhere; and another the peculiarly moody atmosphere of the cemetery of Père-Lachaise—that wonderful world of celebrated dead—who crowd each other like the residents of a narrow city and who make a veritable fanfare of names. What a world! One whole day I idled here over the tombs of Balzac, Daudet, De Musset, Chopin, Rachel, Abélard and Héloise—a long, long list of celebrities. My brain fairly reeled with the futility of life—and finally I came away immensely sad. Another day I visited Versailles and all its splendor with one of the most interesting and amusing Americans I met abroad, a publisher by the name of H——, who regaled me with his own naïve experiences. I fairly choked at times over his quaint, slangy, amusing comments on things as when at Versailles, in the chambers of Marie Antoinette, he discovered a small secret stair only to remark, "There's where Louis XVI took a sneak often enough no doubt," or on one of the towers of Notre Dame when to a third person who was present he commented, "There's your gargoyles, old sox!" Think of the artistic irreverence of it! Concerning a group of buildings which related to the Beaux-Arts I believe he inquired, "What's the bunch of stuff to the right?" and so it went. But the beauty of Versailles—its stately artificiality!—how it all comes back.

After two weeks in which I enjoyed myself as much as I ever hope to, studying out the charm and color of Paris for myself, Barfleur returned fresh, interested, ready for the Riviera, ready for more of Paris, ready indeed for anything, I said to myself once more, when I saw him—and I was very glad to see him indeed.

The personality of Barfleur supplies a homey quality of comfortable companionship. He is so full of a youthful zest to live, and so keen after the shows and customs of the world. I have never pondered why he is so popular with women, or that his friends in different walks of life constitute so great a company. He seems to have known thousands of all sorts, and to be at home under all conditions. That persistent, unchanging atmosphere of "All is well with me," to maintain which is as much a duty as a tradition with him, makes his presence a constant delight.

We were soon joined by a small party of friends thereafter: Sir Scorp, who was bound for an extended stay on the Riviera, a sociologist, who was abroad on an important scientific investigation, and the representative of an American publishing house, who was coming to Paris to waylay Mr. Morgan Shuster, late of Persia, and secure his book. This goodly company descended upon the Hotel Normandy late one Friday afternoon; and it was planned that a party of the whole was to be organized the following night to dine at the Café de Paris and then to make a round of the lesser known and more picturesque of Parisian resorts.

Before this grand pilgrimage to the temples of vice and excitement, however, Barfleur and I spent a remarkable evening wandering from one restaurant to another in an effort to locate a certain Mlle. Rillette, a girl who, he had informed me when we first came to Paris, had been one of the most interesting figures of the Folies stage. Four or five years before she had held at the Folies-Bergère much the same position now recently attained by Mistinguett who was just then enthralling Paris—in other words, she was the sensation of that stormy world of art and romance of which these restaurants are a part. She was more than that. She had a wonderful mezzo-soprano voice of great color and richness and a spirit for dancing that was Greek in its quality. Barfleur was most anxious that I should get at least a glimpse of this exceptional Parisian type— the real spirit of this fast world, your true artistic poison flower, your lovely hooded cobra—before she should be too old, or too wretched, to be interesting.

We started out to visit G.'s Bar, the Bar Fysher, the Rat Mort, Palmyr's Bar, the Grelot, the Rabelais, in fact the whole list of restaurants and show-places where on occasion she might be expected to be seen. On the way Barfleur recounted bits of her interesting history, her marriages, divorces, vices, drug-habits, a strange category of tendencies that sometimes affect the most vigorous and eager of human temperaments.

At one café, on this expedition, quite by accident apparently, we encountered Miss X., whom I had not seen since we left Fishguard, and who was here in Paris doing her best to outvie the women of the gay restaurants in the matter of her dresses, her hats, and her beauty. I must say she presented a ravishing spectacle—quite as wonderful as any of the other women who were to be seen here; but she lacked, as I was to note, the natural vivacity of the French. We Americans, in spite of our high spirits and our healthy enthusiasm for life, are nevertheless a blend of the English, the German, and some of the sedate nations of the north; and we are inclined to a physical and mental passivity which is not common to the Latins. This Miss X., vivid creature that she was, did not have the spiritual vibration which accompanies the French women. So far as spirit was concerned, she seemed superior to most of the foreign types present—but the French women are naturally gayer, their eyes brighter, their motions lighter. She gave us at once an account of her adventures since I had seen her—where she had been living, what places she had visited, and what a good time she was having. I could not help marveling at the disposition which set above everything else in the world the privilege of moving in this peculiar realm which fascinated her so much. From a conventional point of view, much of what she did was, to say the least of it, unusual, but she did not trouble about this. As she told me on the *Mauretania*, all she hoped for was to become a woman of Machiavellian finesse, and to have some money. If she had money and attained to real social wisdom, conventional society could go to the devil; for the adventuress, according to her, was welcome everywhere—that is, anywhere she would care to go. She did not expect to retain her beauty entirely; but she did expect to have some money, and meanwhile to live brilliantly as she deemed that she was now doing. Her love of amusement was quite as marked as ever, and her comments on the various women of her class as hard and accurate as they were brilliant. I remember her saying of one woman, with an easy sweep of her hand, "Like a willow, don't you think?"—and of another, "She glows like a ruby." It was true—fine character delineation.

At Maxim's, an hour later, she decided to go home, so we took her to her hotel and then resumed our pursuit of Mlle. Rillette. After much wandering we finally came upon her, about four in the morning, in one of those showy pleasure resorts that I have so frequently described.

"Ah, yes, there she is," Barfleur exclaimed. I looked to a distant table to see the figure he indicated—that of a young girl seemingly not more than twenty-four or twenty-five, a white silk neckerchief tied about her brown hair, her body clothed in a rather nondescript costume for a world so showy as this. Most of the women wore evening clothes. Rillette had on a skirt of light brown wool, a white shirtwaist open in the front and the collar turned down showing her pretty neck. Her skirt was short, and I noticed that she had pleasing ankles and pretty feet and her sleeves were short, showing a solid forearm. Before she noticed Barfleur we saw her take a slender girl in black for a partner and dance, with others, in the open space between the tables which circled the walls. I studied her with interest because of Barfleur's description, because of the fact that she had been married twice, and because the physical and spiritual ruin of a dozen girls was, falsely or not, laid at her door. Her face did not suggest the depravity which her career would indicate, although it was by no means ruddy; but she seemed to scorn rouge. Her eyes—eyes are always significant in a forceful personage—were large and vague and brown, set beneath a wide, full forehead—very wonderful eyes. She appeared, in her idle security and profound nonchalance, like a figure out of the Revolution or the Commune. She would have been magnificent in a riot—marching up a Parisian street, her white band about her brown hair, carrying a knife, a gun, or a flag. She would have had the courage, too; for it was so plain that life had lost much of its charm and she nearly all of her caring. She came over when her dance was done, having seen Barfleur, and extended an indifferent hand. He told me, after their light conversation in French, that he had chided her to the effect that her career was ruining her once lovely voice. "I shall find it again at the next corner," she said, and walked smartly away.

"Some one should write a novel about a woman like that," he explained urgently. "She ought to be painted. It is amazing the sufficiency of soul that goes with that type. There aren't many like her. She could be the sensation again of Paris if she wanted to—would try. But she won't. See what she said of her voice just now." He shook his head. I smiled approvingly, for obviously the appearance of the woman—her full, rich eyes—bore him out.

She was a figure of distinction in this restaurant world; for many knew her and kept track of her. I watched her from time to time talking with the guests of one table and another, and the chemical content which made her exceptional was as obvious as though she were a bottle and bore a label. To this day she stands out in my mind in her simple dress and indifferent manner as perhaps the one forceful, significant figure that I saw in all the cafés of Paris or elsewhere.

I looked to a distant table to see the figure he indicated

I should like to add here, before I part forever with this curious and feverish Parisian restaurant world, that my conclusion had been, after much and careful observation, that it was too utterly feverish, artificial and exotic not to be dangerous and grimly destructive if not merely touched upon at long intervals. This world of champagne drinkers was apparently interested in but two things—the flare and glow of the restaurants, which were always brightly lighted and packed with people—and women. In the last analysis women, the young women of easy virtue, were the glittering attraction; and truly one might say they were glittering. Fine feathers make fine birds, and nowhere more so than in Paris. But there were many birds who would have been fine in much less showy feathers. In many instances they craved and secured a demure simplicity which was even more destructive than the flaring costumes of the demi-monde. It was strange to see American innocence—the products of Petoskey, Michigan, and Hannibal, Missouri, cheek by jowl with the most daring and the most vicious women which the great metropolis could produce. I did not know until some time later how hard some of these women were, how schooled in vice, how weary of everything save this atmosphere of festivity and the privilege of wearing beautiful clothes.

Most people come here for a night or two, or a month or two, or once in a year or so; and then return to the comparatively dull world from which they emanated—which is fortunate. If they were here a little while this deceptive world of delight would lose all its glamour; but a very few days and you see through the dreary mechanism by which it is produced; the brow-beating of shabby waiters by greedy managers, the extortionate charges and tricks by which money is lured from the pockets of the unwary, the wretched hallrooms and garrets from which some of these butterflies emanate to wing here in seeming delight and then disappear. It was a scorching world, and it displayed vice as an upper and a nether millstone between which youth and beauty is ground or pressed quickly to a worthless mass. I would defy anybody to live in this atmosphere so long as five years and not exhibit strongly the tell-tale marks of decay. When the natural glow of youth has gone comes the powder and paint box for the face, belladonna for the eyes, rouge for the lips, palms, and the nails, and perfumes and ornament and the glister of good clothing; but underneath it all one reads the weariness of the eye, the sickening distaste for bargaining hour by hour and day by day, the cold mechanism of what was once natural, instinctive coquetry. You feel constantly that so many of these demi-mondaines would sell their souls for one last hour of delight and then gladly take poison, as so many of them do, to end it all. Consumption, cocaine and opium maintain their persistent toll. This is a furnace of desire—this Montmartre district—and it burns furiously with a hard, white-hot flame until there is nothing left save black cinders and white ashes. Those who can endure its consuming heat are welcome to its wonders until emotion and feeling and beauty are no more.

CHAPTER XXV
MONTE CARLO

ALL my life before going abroad I had been filled with a curiosity as to the character of the Riviera and Monte Carlo. I had never quite understood that Nice, Cannes, Mentone, San Remo in Italy and Monte Carlo were all in the same vicinity—a stone's throw apart, as it were; and that this world is as distinct from the spirit of the north of France as the south of England is from the north of England.

As Barfleur explained it, we went due south from Paris to Marseilles and then east along the coast of the Mediterranean until we came to the first stopping-place he had selected, Agay, where we would spend a few days in peace and quiet, far from the hurry and flare of the café life we had just left, and then journey on the hour or two more which it takes to reach Monte Carlo. He made this arrangement in order that we might have the journey through France by day, and proceed from Agay of a morning, which would give us, if we had luck—and such luck usually prevails on the Riviera—a sunlight view of the Mediterranean breaking in rich blue waves against a coast that is yellow and brown and gold and green by turns.

Coming south from Paris I had the same sensation of wonder that I had traveling from Calais to Paris—a wonder as to where the forty odd millions of the population of France kept itself. It was not visible from the windows of the flying train. All the way we traveled through an almost treeless country past little white lawns and vineyards; and I never realized before, although I must have known, that these same vineyards were composed of separate vines, set in rows like corn stalks and standing up for all the world like a gnarled T. Every now and then a simple, straight-running, silvery stream would appear, making its way through a perfectly level lane and set on either bank with tall single lines of feathery poplars. The French landscape painters have used these over and over; and they illustrate exactly the still, lonely character of the country. To me, outside of Paris, France has an atmosphere of silence and loneliness; although, considering the character of the French people I do not understand how that can be.

On the way south there was much badinage between Barfleur and Sir Scorp, who accompanied us, as to the character of this adventure. A certain young friend of Barfleur's daughter was then resident at Lyons; and it was Barfleur's humorously expressed hope, that his daughter's friend would bring him a basket of cold chicken, cake, fruit, and wine. It seems that he had urged Berenice to write her friend that he was passing through; and I was hourly amused at Scorp's biting reference to Barfleur's "parental ruse," which he vindictively hoped would come to nothing. It was as he hoped; for at Lyons the young lady and her parents appeared, but no basket. There were some minutes of animated conversation on the platform; and then we were off again at high speed through the same flat land, until we reached a lovely mountain range in the south of France—a region of huts and heavy ox-wains. It reminded me somewhat of the mountain regions of northern Kentucky. At Marseilles there was a long wait in the dark. A large number of passengers left the train here; and then we rode on for an hour or two more, arriving by moonlight at Agay, or at least the nearest railway station to it.

The character of the world in which Agay was located was delicious. After the raw and cold of our last few days in Paris this satin atmosphere of moonlight and perfume was wonderful. We stepped out of a train at the little beach station of this summer coast to find the trees in full leaf and great palms extending their wide fronds into the warm air. There was much chatter in French while the cabby struggled to get all our numerous bags into one vehicle; but when it was all accomplished and the top lowered so that we could see the night, we set forth along a long white road between houses which had anything but a French aspect, being a showy development of things Spanish and Moorish, and past bright whitewashed walls of stone, over which wide-leaved palms leaned. It was wonderful to see the moonlight on the water, the bluish black waves breaking in white ripples on sandy shores, and to feel the wind of the South. I could not believe that a ten-hour ride from Paris would make so great a change; but so it was. We clattered up finally to the Grand Hôtel d'Agay; and although it possessed so fine a name it was nothing much more than a country inn—comparatively new and solidly built, with a charming vine-covered balcony overlooking the sea, and a garden of palms in which one might walk. However, the food, Barfleur assured us, would be passable. It was only three stories high and quite primitive in its appointments. We were lighted to our rooms with candles, but the rooms were large and cool, and the windows, I discovered by throwing mine open, commanded a magnificent view of the bay. I stood by my window transfixed by the beauty of the night. Not in France outside this coast—nor in England—can you see anything like this in summer. The air was like a caress. Under the white moon you could see the main outlines of the coast and the white strip of sand at the bottom. Below us, anchored near the garden, were some boats, and to the right white houses sheltered in trees and commanding the wonders of the water. I went to bed breathing a sigh of relief and feeling as if I should sleep soundly—which I did.

The next morning revealed a world if anything more wonderful. Now all the whiteness and the brownness and the sharpness of the coast line were picked out by a brilliant sun. The bay glittered in the light, a rich indigo blue; and a fisherman putting forth to sea hoisted a golden sail. I was astonished to find now that the houses instead of being the drab and white of northern France were as like to be blue or yellow or green—and always there was a touch of color somewhere, blue window-sills ornamenting a white house, brown chimneys contrasting with a blue one, the charm of the Moorish arch and the Moorish lattice suggesting itself at different points—and always palms. I dressed and went below and out upon the balcony and through the garden to the water's edge, sitting in the warm sun and tossing pebbles into the water. Flowers were in bloom here—blue and yellow blossoms—and when Barfleur came down we took a delightful morning walk up a green valley which led inland between hills. No northern day in June could have rivaled in perfection the wonder of this day; and we talked of the stagey make-believe of Parisian night-life as contrasted with this, and the wonder of spring generally.

"I should think the whole world would want to live here in winter," I said.

"The fact is," replied Barfleur, "what are called the best people do not come here so much nowadays."

"Where do they go?" I asked.

"Oh, Switzerland is now the thing in winter—the Alps and all that relates to them. The new rich have overdone this, and it is becoming a little banal."

"They cannot alter the wonder of the climate," I replied.

We had a table put on the balcony at eleven and ate our morning fish and rolls and salad there. I can see Sir Scorp cheerfully trifling with the cat we found there, the morning sun and scenery having put him in a gay mood, calling, "*Chat, chat, chat!*" and asking, "How do you talk to a cat in French?" There was an open carriage which came for us at one into which we threw our fur coats and blankets; and then climbed by degrees mile after mile up an exquisite slope by the side of a valley that gradually became a cañon; and at the bottom of which tinkled and gurgled a mountain stream. This road led to more great trees at the top of a range overlooking what I thought at first was a great valley where a fog prevailed, but which a few steps further was revealed as the wondrous sea—white sails, a distant pavilion protruding like a fluted marble toy into the blue water, and here and there a pedestrian far below. We made our way to a delightful inn some half way down and back, where under soaring black pine trees we had tea at a little green table—strawberry jam, new bread, and cakes. I shall never forget the bitter assault I unthinkingly provoked by dipping my spoon into the jelly jar. All the vials of social wrath were poured upon my troubled head. "It serves him right," insisted Barfleur, treacherously. "I saw him do that once before. These people from the Middle West, what can you expect?"

That night a grand row developed at dinner between Scorp and Barfleur as to how long we were to remain in Agay and whether we were to stop in or out of Monte Carlo. Barfleur's plan was for remaining at least three days here, and then going to a hotel not directly in Monte Carlo but half way between Monte Carlo and Mentone—the Hôtel Bella Riva. I knew that Barfleur had come here at the present time largely to entertain me; and since I would rather have had his presence than the atmosphere of the best hotel in Monte Carlo, it really did not matter so much to me where we went, so long as it was comfortable. Scorp was greatly incensed, or pretended to be, to think I should be brought here to witness the wonders of this festive world, and then be pocketed in some side spot where half the delicious life would escape me. "Agay!" he kept commenting, "Agay! We come all the way to the south of France to stop at Agay!

Candles to light us to bed and French peasants for servants. And then we'll go to Monte Carlo and stop at some third-rate hotel! Well, you can go to the Bella Riva if you choose; I am going to the Palace Hotel where I can see something, and have a decent bed. I am not going to be packed off any ten miles out of Monte Carlo, and be compelled to use a street car that stops at twelve o'clock and spend thirty francs getting home in a carriage!"

This kept up until bedtime with Barfleur offering solemn explanations of why he had come here, why it would be advisable for us to refresh ourselves at the fountain of simple scenery after the fogs of London and the theatric flare of Paris. He had a fine argument for the Bella Riva as a dwelling-site: it was just half way between Monte Carlo and Mentone, it commanded all the bay on which Monte Carlo stood. Cap Martin, with the hotel of that name, here threw its sharp rocky point far out into the sea. A car-line passed the door. In a half-hour either way we could be in either Mentone or Monte Carlo.

"Who wants to be in Mentone?" demanded Sir Scorp. "I would rather be an hour away from it instead of half an hour. If I came to see Monte Carlo I would not be bothering about Mentone. I, for one, will not go."

It was not long before I learned that Scorp did much protesting but equally much following. The patient silence of Barfleur coupled with direct action at the decisive moment usually won. Scorp's arguments did result in one thing. The next morning, instead of idling in the sun and taking a carriage ride over the adjacent range, we gathered all our belongings and deposited them at the near-by station, while Barfleur and I climbed to the top of an adjacent hill where was an old water-pool, to have a last look at the lovely, high-colored, florescent bay of Agay. Then the long train, with drawing-room cars from all parts of Europe rolled in; and we were off again.

Barfleur called my attention as we went along to the first of the umbrella trees—of which I was to see so many later in Italy—coming into view in the occasional sheltered valleys which we were passing, and later those marvels of southern France and all Italy, the hill cities, towering like great cathedrals high in the air. I shall never forget the impression the first sight of one of these made on me. In America we have nothing save the illusion of clouds over distant landscapes to compare with it. I was astonished, transported—the reality was so much more wonderful than the drawings of which I had seen so many. Outside the car windows the sweeping fronds of the palms seemed almost to brush the train, hanging over white enclosures of stone. Green shutters and green lattices; red roofs and bright blue jardinières; the half-Italianized Frenchman with his swarthy face and burning eyes. Presently the train stopped at Cannes. I struck out to walk in the pretty garden which I saw was connected with the depot, Barfleur to send a telegram, Scorp to show how fussy and cantankerous he could be. Here were long trains that had come from St. Petersburg via Vilna and Vienna; and others from Munich, Berlin and Copenhagen with diners labeled "*Speisewagen*" and sleepers "*Schlafwagen.*" Those from Paris, Calais, Brussels, Cherbourg bore the imposing legend, "*Compagnie Internationale des Wagons-Lits et des Grands Express Européens.*" There was a long black train rumbling in from the south with cars marked Tripoli, Roma, Firenze and Milano. You had a sense, from merely looking at the stations, that the idleness and the luxury of all the world was pouring in here at will.

In ten minutes we were off again—Barfleur expatiating solemnly on the fact that in England a homely girl was left to her own devices with no one to make anything of her, she being plain and that being the end of it; while here in France something was done with the poorest specimens.

"Now those two young ladies," he said, waving his hand dramatically in the direction of two departing travelers,—"they are not much—but look at them. See how smartly they are gotten up. Somebody will marry them. They have been encouraged to buck up,—to believe that there is always hope." And he adjusted his monocle cheerfully.

Our train was pulling into the station at Monte Carlo. I had the usual vague idea of a much-talked-of but never-seen place.

"I can hear the boys calling 'Ascenseur,'" exclaimed Barfleur to Scorp prophetically, when we were still a little way out. He was as keen for the adventure as a child—much more so than I was. I could see how he set store by the pleasure-providing details of the life here; and Scorp, for all his lofty superiority, was equally keen. They indicated to me the great masses of baggage which occupied the platforms—all bright and new and mostly of good leather. I was interested to see the crowds of people—for there was a train departing in another direction—and to hear the cries of "Ascenseur" as predicted—the elevators lifting to the terrace in front of the Casino, where the tracks enter along a shelf of a declivity considerably above the level of the sea. It is a tight little place—all that I had expected in point of showiness—gay rococo houses, white and cream, with red roofs climbing up the sides of the bare brown hill which rises to La Turbie above. We did not stop, but went on to Mentone where we were to lunch. It was charming to see striped awnings—pink and white and blue and green—gay sunshades of various colors and ladies in fresh linens and silks and men in white flannels and an atmosphere of outing generally. I think a sort of summer madness seizes on people under such circumstances and dull care is thrown to the winds, and you plan gay adventures and dream dreams and take yourself to be a singularly important person. And to think that this atmosphere should always be here, and that it can always be reached out of the snows of Russia and the bitter storms of New York and the dreary gray fogs of London, and the biting winds of Berlin and Paris!

We lunched at the Admiralty—one of those *restaurants celebrés* where the *haute cuisine* of France was to be found in its perfection, where balconies of flowers commanded the *côte d'azure*.

CHAPTER XXVI
THE LURE OF GOLD!

BEFORE I go a step further in this narrative I must really animadvert to the subject of restaurants and the *haute cuisine* of France generally, for in this matter Barfleur was as keen as the greatest connoisseurs are in the matter of pictures. He loved and remembered the quality of dishes and the method of their preparation and the character of the men who prepared them and the atmosphere in which they were prepared and in fact everything which relates to the culinary and gastronomic arts and the history of the gourmet generally.

In Paris and London Barfleur was constantly talking of the restaurants of importance and contrasting the borrowed French atmosphere of the best English restaurants with the glories of the parent kitchens in France. He literally schooled me in the distinction which was to be drawn between the Café Anglais, Voisin's and Paillard's, and those smart after-supper restaurants of the Montmartre district where the cuisine of France had been degraded by the addition of negroes, tinsel, dancers, and music. Nevertheless he was willing to admit that their cuisine was not bad. As I remember it now, I was advised to breakfast at Henry's, to dine at the Ritz, and to sup at Durand's; but if I chose to substitute the Café de Paris for the Ritz at dinner I was not going far wrong. He knew that M. Braquesec, the younger, was now in charge of Voisin's and that Paul was the *maître d'hôtel* and that during the Commune Voisin's had once served *consommé d'éléphant, le chameau roti à l'Anglais*, and *le chat planqué de rats*. He thought it must have been quite excellent because M. Braquesec, the elder, supervised it all and because the wines served with it were from twenty to forty years of age.

When it came to the Riviera he was well aware of all that region had to promise from Cannes to Mentone; and he could nicely differentiate the advantages of the Café de Paris; the grand dining-room of the Hôtel de Paris which was across the street; the Hermitage, which he insisted had quite the most beautiful dining-room in Monte Carlo; the Princess which one of the great stars of the opera had very regularly patronized some years before; the restaurant of the Grand Hotel which he considered very exceptional indeed; and the restaurant at the terminus of the La Turbie mountain railway—which he emphatically approved and which commanded a magnificent view of the coast and the sea. I was drilled to understand that if I had *mostelle à l'Anglais* at the Hôtel de Paris I was having a very excellent fish of the country, served in the very best manner, which is truly worth knowing. If we went to the Princess, the *maître d'hôtel*, whom he knew from an older day, would serve us midgeon in some marvelous manner which would be something for me to remember. At the Café de Paris we were to have soupe Monègasque which had a reminiscence, so he insisted, of Bouillabaisse and was very excellent. The soupions were octopi, but delicate little ones—not the kind that would be thrust upon one in Rome. I was lost among discourses regarding the value of the Regents at Nice; the art of M. Fleury, now the manager of the Hôtel de Paris; and what a certain head-master could do for one in the way of providing a little local color, as Barfleur termed it, in the food. To all of this, not being a gourmet, I paid as strict attention as I could; though I fear me much, that a large proportion of the exquisite significance of it all was lost on me. I can only say, however, that in spite of Scorp's jeering, which was constant, the only time we had a really wonderful repast was when Barfleur ordered it.

The first luncheon at the Admiralty was an excellent case in point. Barfleur being on the Riviera and being host to several, was in the most stupendous of artistic moods. He made up a menu of the most delicious of hors d'œuvre—which he insisted should never have been allowed to take the place of soup, but which, alas, the custom of the time sanctioned and the caviare of which in this case was gray, a point which he wished me particularly to note—sole walewski; roast lamb; salad nicois; and Genoese asparagus in order to give our meal the flavor of the land. We had coffee on the balcony afterwards, and I heard much concerning the wonders of this region and of the time when the Winter Palace was the place to lunch. A grand duke was a part of the day's ensemble, and two famous English authors before whom we paraded with dignity.

After lunch we made our way to the Hôtel Bella Riva, which Barfleur in spite of Scorp's complaints had finally selected. It stood on a splendid rise between Mentone and Monte Carlo; and here, after some slight bargaining we were assigned to three rooms *en suite* with bath. I was given the corner room with two balconies and a flood of sunshine and such a view as I have never seen from any window before or since. Straight before me lay the length of Cap Martin, a grove of thousands of olive trees reflecting from its burnished leaves the rays of the sun and crowding it completely, and beyond it the delicious sweep of the Mediterranean. To the right lay the bay of Monte Carlo, the heights of La Turbie, and all the glittering world which is Monte Carlo proper. To the left lay Mentone and the green and snow-capped mountains of Ventimiglia and San Remo faintly visible in the distance. Never an hour but the waters of the sea were a lighter or a darker shade of blue and never an hour but a lonely sail was crossing in the foreground. High above the inn at La Turbie, faintly visible in the distance, rose a ruined column of Augustus—a broken memory of the time when imperial Rome was dominant here, and when the Roman legions passed this way to Spain. At different hours I could hear the bugle of some frontier garrison sounding reveille, guard-mount, and the sun-set call. Oh, those wonderful mornings when I was waked by the clear note of a horn flying up the valleys of the mountains and sounding over the sea!

Immediately after our arrival it was settled that once we had made a swift toilet we would start for Monte Carlo. We were ready to bring back tremendous winnings—and eager to see this showy world, the like of which, Scorp insisted, was not to be found elsewhere.

"Oh, yes," he said, "I have been to Biarritz and to Ostend and Aix-les-Bains—but they are not like this. We really should live at the Palace where we could walk on the terrace in the morning and watch the pigeon-shooting." He told a significant story of how once having a toothache he came out of the card-rooms of the Casino into the grand lobby and attempted to pour a little laudanum out of a thin vial, with which to ease the pain. "I stepped behind a column," he explained, "so that I might not be seen; but just as I uncorked the vial four guards seized me and hurried me out of the place. They thought I was taking poison. I had to make plain my identity to the management before they would let me back."

We arrived at the edge of the corporation which is Monte Carlo and walked in, surveying the character of the place. It was as gaudy and rococoesque as one might well expect this world to be. It reminded me in part of that Parisian world which one finds about the Arc de Triomphe, rich and comfortable, only there are no carriages in Monte Carlo to speak of. The distances are too slight and the grades too steep. When we reached the square of the Casino, it did not strike me as having any especial charm. It was small and sloping, and laid off in square beds of reddish flowers with greensward about and gravel paths going down either side. At the foot lay the Casino, ornate and cream-white, with a glass and iron canopy over the door and a swarm of people moving to and fro—not an idling throng but rather having an air of considerable industry about it, quite as one might expect to find in a business world. People were bustling along as we were to get to the Casino or to go away from it on some errand and get back. We hurried down the short length of the sward, checking our coats, after waiting a lengthy time for our turn in line, and then entering the chambers where credentials are examined and cards of admission sold. There was quite some formality about this, letters being examined, our personal signature and home address taken and then we were ready to enter.

While Barfleur presented our credentials, Sir Scorp and I strolled about in the lobby observing the inpouring and outpouring throng. He showed me the exact pillar where he had attempted to ease his tooth. This was an interesting world of forceful people. The German, the Italian, the American, the Englishman and the Russian were easily recognizable. Sir Scorp was convinced that the faces of the winners and the losers could be distinguished, but I am afraid I was not enough of a physiognomist to do this. If there were any who had just lost their last dollar I did not detect them. On the contrary it seemed to me that the majority were abnormally cheerful and were having the best time in the world. A large bar at the end of the room opposite the general entrance to the card-rooms had a peculiarly American appearance. The one thing that was evident was that all here were healthy and vigorous, with a love of life in their veins, eager to be entertained, and having the means in a large majority of cases to accomplish this end. It struck me here as it has in so many other places where great pleasure-loving throngs congregate, that the difference between the person who has something and the person who has nothing is one of intense desire, and what, for a better phrase, I will call a capacity to live.

The inner chambers of the Casino were divided into two groups, the outer being somewhat less ornately decorated and housing those who for reasons of economy prefer to be less exclusive, and the inner more elaborate in decoration and having of an evening, it was said, a more gorgeously dressed throng. Just why one should choose less expensive rooms when gambling, unless low in funds, I could not guess. Those in both sets of rooms seemed to have enough money to gamble. I could not see, after some experience, that there was very much difference. The players seemed to wander rather indiscriminately through both sets of rooms. Certainly we did. An extra charge of five louis was made for the season's privilege of entering the inner group or *"Cirque privé"* as it was called.

I shall never forget my first sight of the famous gaming-tables in the outer rooms—for we were not venturing into the inner at present. Aside from the glamour of the crowd—which was as impressive as an opera first night—and the decorative quality of the room which was unduly rich and brilliant, I was most vividly impressed by the vast quantities of money scattered so freely over the tables, small piles of gold louis, stacks of eight, ten, fifteen and even twenty-five franc pieces, layers of pale crisp bank-notes whose value was anywhere from one hundred to one thousand francs. It was like looking through the cashier's window of an immense bank. The mechanism and manipulation of the roulette wheel I did not understand at first nor the exact duties of the many croupiers seated at each table. Their cry of "Rien ne *va plus*!" and the subsequent scraping together of the shining coin with the little rakes or the throwing back of silver, gold and notes to the lucky winner gripped my attention like a vise. "Great God!" I thought, "supposing I was to win a thousand pounds with my fifteen. I should stay in Europe an entire year."

Like all beginners I watched the process with large eyes and then seeing Barfleur get back five gold louis for one placed on a certain number I ventured one of my own. Result: three louis. I tried again on another number and won two more. I saw myself (in fancy) the happy possessor of a thousand pounds. My next adventure cost me two louis, whereupon I began to wonder whether I was such a fortunate player after all.

"Come with me," Barfleur said, coming around to where I

stood adventuring my small sums with indescribable excitement and taking my arm genially. "I want to send some money to my mother for luck. I've just won fifteen pounds."

"Talk about superstition," I replied, coming away from the table, "I didn't believe it of you."

"I'm discovered!" he smiled philosophically; "besides I want to send some sweets to the children."

We strolled out into the bright afternoon sun finding the terrace comparatively empty, for the Casino draws most of the crowd during the middle and late afternoon. It was strange to leave these shaded, artificially lighted rooms with their swarms of well-dressed men and women sitting about or bending over tables all riveted on the one thrilling thing—the drop of the little white ball in a certain pocket—and come out into the glittering white world with its blazing sun, its visible blue sea, its cream-colored buildings and its waving palms. We went to several shops—one for sweets and one for flowers, *haut parisiennes* in their atmosphere—and duly dispatched our purchases. Then we went to the post-office, plastered with instructions in various languages, and saw that the money was sent to Barfleur's mother. Then we returned to the Casino and Barfleur went his way, while I wandered from board to board studying the crowd, risking an occasional louis, and finally managing to lose three pounds more than I had won. In despair I went to see what Scorp was doing. He had three or four stacks of gold coin in front of him at a certain table, all of five hundred dollars. He was risking these in small stacks of ten and fifteen louis and made no sign when he won or lost. On several occasions I thought he was certain to win a great sum, so lavishly were gold louis thrown him by the croupier, but on others I felt equally sure he was to be disposed of, so freely were his gold pieces scraped away from him.

"How are you making out?" I asked.

"I think I've lost eight hundred francs. If I should win this though, I'll risk a bee-a."

"What's a bee-a?"

"A thousand franc note."

My poor little three louis seemed suddenly insignificant. A lady sitting next to him, a woman of perhaps fifty, with a cool, calculating face had perhaps as much as two thousand dollars in gold and notes piled up before her. All around the table were these piles of gold, silver and notes. It was a fascinating scene.

"There, that ends me," observed Scorp, all at once, his stock of gold on certain numbers disappearing with the rake of the croupier. "Now I'm done. We might walk out in the lobby and watch the crowd." All his good gold so quietly raked in by the croupier was lingering painfully in my memory. I was beginning to see plainly that I would not make a good gambler. Such a loss distressed me.

"How much did you lose?" I inquired.

"Oh, a thousand francs," he replied.

We strolled up and down, Scorp commenting sarcastically on one type and another and yet with a genial tolerance which was amusing.

I remember a charming-looking cocotte, a radiant type of brunette, with finely chiseled features, slim, delicate fingers, a dainty little foot, who, clad in a fetching costume of black and white silk which fitted her with all the airy grace of a bon-bon ribbon about its box, stood looking uncertainly about as if she expected to meet some one.

"Look at her," Scorp commented with that biting little ha! ha! of his, which involved the greatest depths of critical sarcasm imaginable. "There she is. She's lost her last louis and she's looking for some one to pay for her dinner!"

I had to smile to myself at the man's croaking indifference to the lady's beauty. Her obvious charms had not the slightest interest for him.

Of another lovely creature who went by with her head held high and her lips parted in a fetching, coaxing way he observed, "She practises that in front of her mirror!" and finding nothing else to attack, finally turned to me. "I say, it's a wonder you don't take a cocktail. There's your American bar."

"It's the wrong time, Scorp," I replied. "You don't understand the art of cocktail drinking."

"I should hope not!" he returned morosely.

Finally after much more criticism of the same sort Barfleur arrived, having lost ten louis, and we adjourned for tea. As usual an interesting argument arose now not only as to where we were to dine, but how we were to live our very lives in Monte Carlo.

"Now I should think," said Barfleur, "it would be nice if we were to dine at the Princess. You can get sole and *canard à la presse* there and their wines are excellent. Besides we can't drive to the Bella Riva every evening."

"Just as I thought!" commented Scorp bitterly. "Just as I thought. Now that we are staying at Bella Riva, a half hour or so away, we will dine in Monte Carlo. I knew it. We will do no such thing. We will go back to the Bella Riva, change our clothes, dine simply and inexpensively [this from the man who had just lost a thousand francs] come back here, buy our tickets for the *Cirque privé* and gamble inside. First we go to Agay and spend a doleful time among a lot of peasants and now we hang around the outer rooms of the Casino. We can't live at the Hôtel de Paris or enter the *Cirque privé* but we can dine at the Princess. Ha! ha! Well, we will do no such thing. Besides, a little fasting will not do you any harm. You need not waste all your money on your stomach."

The man had a gay acidity which delighted me.

Barfleur merely contemplated the ceiling of the lobby where we were gathered while Sir Scorp rattled on in this fashion.

"I expected to get tickets for the *Cirque privé*—" he soothed and added suggestively, "It will cost at least twenty francs to drive over to the Bella Riva."

"Exactly!" replied Scorp. "As I predicted. We can't live in Monte Carlo but we can pay twenty francs to get over to Cap Martin. Thank Heaven there are still street cars. I do not need to spend all my money on shabby carriages, riding out in the cold!" (It was a heavenly night.)

"I think we'd better dine at the Princess and go home early," pleaded Barfleur. "We're all tired. To-morrow I suggest that we go up to La Turbie for lunch. That will prove a nice diversion and after that we'll come down and get our tickets for the *Cirque privé*. Come now. Do be reasonable. Dreiser ought to see something of the restaurant life of Monte Carlo."

As usual Barfleur won. We *did* go to the Café Princess. We *did* have *sole Normande*. We *did* have *canard à la presse*. We *did* have some excellent wine and Barfleur was in his glory.

CHAPTER XXVII
WE GO TO EZE

THE charms of Monte Carlo are many. Our first morning there, to the sound of a horn blowing reveille in the distance, I was up betimes enjoying the wonderful spectacles from my balcony. The sun was just peeping up over the surface of an indigo sea, shooting sharp golden glances in every direction. Up on the mountains, which rise sharp and clear like great unornamented cathedrals back of the jeweled villages of this coast, it was picking out shepherd's hut and fallen mementoes of the glory that was Rome. A sailboat or two was already making its way out to sea, and below me on that long point of land which is Cap Martin, stretching like a thin green spear into the sea, was the splendid olive orchard which I noted the day before, its gleaming leaves showing a different shade of green from what it had then. I did not know it until the subject came up that olive trees live to be a thousand years old and that they do as well here on this little strip of coast, protected by the high mountains at their back, as they do anywhere in Italy. In fact, as I think of it, this lovely projection of land, no wider than to permit of a few small villages and cities crowding between the sea and the mountains, is a true projection of Italy itself, its palms, olive trees, cypresses, umbrella trees and its peasants and architecture. I understand that a bastard French—half French, half Italian—is spoken here and that only here are the hill cities truly the same as they are in Italy.

While I was gazing at the morning sun and the blue sea and marveling how quickly the comfortable Riviera Express had whirled us out of the cold winds of Paris into this sun-kissed land, Barfleur must have been up and shaving, for presently he appeared, pink and clean in his brown dressing-gown, to sit out on my lovely balcony with me.

"You know," he said, after he had commented on the wonder of the morning and the delicious soothing quality of the cool air, "Scorp is certainly an old fuss-button. There he lies in there now, ready to pounce on us. Of course he isn't very strong physically and that makes him irritable. He does so love to be contrary."

"I think he is a good running-mate for you," I observed. "If he leans to asceticism in the matter of food, you certainly run to the other extreme. Sybaritic is a mild expression for your character."

"You don't mean it?"

"I certainly do."

"In what way have I shown myself sybaritic?"

I charged him with various crimes. My amicable lecture was interrupted by the arrival of rolls and coffee and we decided to take breakfast in the company of Scorp. We knocked at his door.

"*Entrez!*"

There he was, propped up in bed, his ascetic face crowned by his brownish black hair and set with those burning dark eyes—a figure of almost classic significance.

"Ah!" he exclaimed grimly, "here he comes. The gourmet's guide to Europe!"

"Now, do be cheerful this morning, Scorp, do be," cooed Barfleur. "Remember it is a lovely morning. You are on the Riviera. We are going to have a charming time."

"You are, anyway!" commented Scorp.

"I am the most sacrificial of men, I assure you," commented Barfleur. "I would do anything to make you happy. We will go up to La Turbie to-day, if you say, and order a charming lunch. After that we will go to Eze, if you say, and on to Nice for dinner, if you think fit. We will go into the Casino there for a little while and then return. Isn't that a simple and satisfactory program? Dreiser and I will walk up to La Turbie. You can join us at one for lunch. You think he ought to see Eze, don't you?"

"Yes, if there isn't some Café de Paris hidden away up there somewhere where you can gormandize again. If we can just manage to get you past the restaurants!"

So it was agreed: Barfleur and I would walk; Sir Scorp was to follow by train. As the day was balmy and perfect, all those special articles of adornment purchased in London for this trip were extracted from our luggage and duly put on—light weight suits, straw hats and ties of delicate tints; and then we set forth. The road lay in easy swinging S's, up and up past terraced vineyards and garden patches and old stone cottages and ambling muleteers with their patient little donkeys heavily burdened. Automobiles, I noticed, even at this height came grumbling up or tearing down—and always the cypress tree with its whispering black-green needles and the graceful umbrella tree made artistic architectural frames for the vistas of the sea.

Here and now I should like to pay my tribute to the cypress tree. I saw it later in all its perfection at Pisa, Rome, Florence, Spello, Assisi and elsewhere in Italy, but here at Monte Carlo, or rather outside of it, I saw it first. I never saw it connected with anything tawdry or commonplace and wherever it grows there is dignity and beauty. It is not to be seen anywhere in immediate contact with this feverish Casino world of Monte Carlo. It is as proud as beauty itself, as haughty as achievement. By old ruins, in sacred burial grounds, by worn gates and forgotten palaces it sways and sighs. It is as mournful as death—as somber in its mien as great age and experience—a tree of the elders. Where Rome grew it grew, and to Greek and Roman temples in their prime and pride it added its sacred company.

Plant a cypress tree near my grave when I am dead. To think of its tall spearlike body towering like a stately monument over me would be all that I could artistically ask. If some of this illusory substance which seems to be that which is I, physically, here on this earth, should mingle with its fretted roots and be builded into the noble shaft of its body I should be glad. It would be a graceful and artistic way to disappear into the unknown.

Our climb to La Turbie was in every respect delightful. We stopped often to comment on the cathedral-like character of the peaks, to speculate as to the age of the stone huts.

About half way up we came to a little inn called the Corniche, which really hangs on the cornice of this great range, commanding the wide, blue sweep of the Mediterranean below; and here, under the shade of umbrella trees and cypresses and with the mimosa in full bloom and with some blossom which Barfleur called "cherry-pie" blowing everywhere, we took seats at a little green table to have a pot of tea. It is an American inn—this Corniche—with an American flag fluttering high on a white pole, and an American atmosphere not unlike that of a country farmhouse in Indiana. There were some chickens scratching about the door; and at least three canaries in separate bright brass cages hung in the branches of the surrounding trees. They sang with tremendous energy. With the passing of a muleteer, whose spotted cotton shirt and earth-colored trousers and dusty skin bespoke the lean, narrow life of the peasant, we discussed wealth and poverty, lavish expenditure and meager subsistence, the locust-like quality of the women of fashion and of pleasure, who eat and eat and gorge and glut themselves of the showy things of life without aim or even thought; the peasant on this mountainside, with perhaps no more than ten cents a day to set his beggar board, while below the idle company in the Casino, shining like a white temple from where we sat, were wasting thousands upon thousands of dollars hourly. Barfleur agreed most solemnly with it all. He was quite sympathetic. The tables there, he said, even while we looked, were glutted with gold, and the Prince of Monaco was building, with his surplus earnings, useless marine museums which no one visited.

I was constantly forgetting in our peregrinations about the neighborhood how small the Principality of Monaco is. I am sure it would fit nicely into ten city blocks. A large portion of Monte Carlo encroaches on French territory—only the Casino, the terrace, the heights of Monaco belong to the Principality. One-half of a well-known restaurant there, I believe, is in Monaco and the other half in France. La Turbie, on the heights here, the long road we had come, almost everything in fact, was in France. We went into the French post-office to mail cards and then on to the French restaurant commanding the heights. This particular restaurant commands a magnificent view. A circle about which the automobiles turned in front of its door was supported by a stone wall resting on the sharp slope of the mountain below. All the windows of its principal dining-room looked out over the sea, and of the wonderful view I was never weary. The room had an oriental touch, and the white tables and black-coated waiters accorded ill with this. Still it offered that smartness of service which only the French restaurants possess.

Barfleur was for waiting for Scorp who had not arrived. I was for eating, as I was hungry. Finally we sat down to luncheon and we were consuming the sweet when in he came. His brownish-black eyes burned with their usual critical fire. If Sir

Scorp had been born with a religious, reforming spirit instead of a penchant for art he would have been a St. Francis of Assisi. As it was, without anything to base it on, except Barfleur's gormandizing propensities, he had already established moral censorship over our actions.

"Ah, here you are, eating as usual," he observed with that touch of lofty sarcasm which at once amused and irritated me. "No excursion without a meal as its object."

"Sit down, El Greco," I commented, "and note the beautiful view. This should delight your esthetic soul."

"It might delight mine, but I am not so sure about yours. Barfleur would certainly see nothing in it if there were not a restaurant here—ha!"

"I found a waiter here who used to serve me in the Café Royal in London," observed Barfleur cheerfully.

"Now we can die content," sighed Scorp. "We have been recognized by a French waiter on the Riviera. Ha! Never happy," he added, turning to me, "unless he is being recognized by waiters somewhere—his one claim to glory."

We went out to see the ruined monument to Augustus Cæsar, crumbling on this high mountain and commanding the great blue sweep of the Mediterranean below. There were a number of things in connection with this monument which were exceedingly interesting. It illustrated so well the Roman method of construction: a vast core of rubble and brick, faced with marble. Barfleur informed me that only recently the French government had issued an order preventing the removal of any more of the marble, much of which had already been stolen, carted away or cut up here into other forms. Immense marble drums of pure white stone were still lying about, fallen from their places; and in the surrounding huts of the peasant residents of La Turbie could be seen parts of once noble pillars set into the fabric of their shabby doorways or used as corner-stones to support their pathetic little shelters. I recall seeing several of these immense drums of stone set at queer angles under the paper walls of the huts, the native peasants having built on them as a base, quite as a spider might attach its gossamer net to a substantial bush or stone. I reflected at length on the fate of greatness and how little the treasures of one age may be entrusted to another. Time and chance, dullness and wasteful ignorance, lie in wait for them all.

The village of La Turbie, although in France, gave me my first real taste of the Italian village. High up on this mountain above Monte Carlo, in touch really with the quintessence of showy expenditure—clothes, jewels, architecture, food—here it stood, quite as it must have been standing for the last three or four hundred years—its narrow streets clambering up and down between houses of gray stone or brick, covered with gray lichens. I thought of Benvenuto Cellini—how he always turned the corners of the dark, narrow streets of Rome in as wide a circle as possible in order to save himself from any lurking assassin—that he might draw his own knife quickly. Dirt and age and quaintness and romance: it was in these terms that La Turbie spoke to us. Although anxious to proceed to Eze, not so very far away, which they both assured me was so much more picturesque and characteristic, yet we lingered, looking lovingly up and down narrow passages where stairs clambered gracefully, where arches curved picturesquely over streets, and where plants bloomed bravely in spotted, crumbling windows. Age! age! And with it men, women and children of the usual poverty-stricken Italian type—not French, but Italians. Women with bunchy blue or purple skirts, white or colored kerchiefs, black hair, wrinkled, yellow or blackish-brown faces, glittering dark eyes and claw-like hands.

Not far from the center of this moldy scene, flourishing like a great lichen at the foot of Augustus, his magnificent column, was a public fountain, of what date I do not know. The housewives of the community were hard at their washing, piling the wet clothes in soapy masses on the stone rim of the basin. They were pattering and chattering, their skirts looped up at their hips, their heads wound about with cloths of various colors. It brought back to my mind, by way of contrast, the gloomy wash- and bath-house in Bethnal Green, which I have previously commented on. Despite poverty and ignorance, the scene here was so much more inviting—even inspiring. Under a blue sky, in the rays of a bright afternoon sun, beside a moldering but none the less lovely fountain, they seemed a very different kind of mortal—far more fortunate than those I had seen in Bethnal Green and Stepney. What can governments do toward supplying blue skies, broken fountains and humanly stirring and delightful atmosphere? Would Socialism provide these things?

With many backward glances, we departed, conveyed hence in an inadequate little vehicle drawn by one of the boniest horses it has ever been my lot to ride behind. The cheerful driver was as fat as his horse was lean, and as dusty as the road itself. We were wedged tightly in the single green cloth seat, Scorp on one side, I on the other, Barfleur in the middle, expatiating as usual on the charm of life and enduring cheerfully all the cares and difficulties of his exalted and self-constituted office of guide, mentor and friend.

Deep green valleys, dizzy precipices along which the narrow road skirted nervously, tall tops of hills that rose about you craggily or pastorally—so runs the road to Eze and we followed it jestingly, Sir Scorp so dizzy contemplating the depths that we had to hold him in. Barfleur was gay and ebullient. I never knew a man who could become so easily intoxicated with life.

"There you have it," said Sir Scorp, pointing far down a green slope to where a shepherd was watching his sheep, a cape coat over his arm, a crooked staff in his hand; "there is your pastoral, lineally descended from the ancient Greeks. Barfleur pretends to love nature, but that would not bring him out here. There is no *canard à la presse* attached to it—no *sole walewski*."

"And see the goose-girl!" I exclaimed, as a maiden in bare feet, her skirt falling half way below her knees, crossed the road.

"All provided, my dear boy," assured Barfleur, beaming on me through his monocle. "Everything as it should be for you. You see how I do. Goose-girls, shepherds, public fountains, old monuments to Cæsar, anything you like. I will show you Eze now. Nothing finer in Europe."

We were nearing Eze around the green edge of a mountain— its top—and there I saw it, my first hill-city. Not unlike La Turbie, it was old and gray, but with that spectacular dignity which anything set on a hill possesses. Barfleur carefully explained to me that in the olden days—some few hundred years before—the inhabitants of the seashore and plain were compelled to take to the hills to protect themselves against marauding pirates—that the hill-city dates from the earliest times in Italy and was common to the Latins before the dawn of history. Eze towered up, completely surrounded by a wall, the only road leading to it being the one on which we were traveling. By a bridge we crossed a narrow gully, dividing one mountain height from another, and then, discharging our fat cabman and his bony horse, mounted to the open gate or arched door, now quite unguarded. Some of the village children were selling the common flowers of the field, and a native in tight dusty trousers and soft hat was entering.

I think I devoured the strangeness and glamour of Eze as one very hungry would eat a meal. I examined all the peculiarities of this outer entrance and noted how like a hole in a snail shell it was, giving not directly into the old city, or village, but into a path that skirted the outer wall. Above were holes through which defenders could shower arrows and boiling oil upon those who might have penetrated this outer defense. There was a blind passage at one point, luring the invaders into a devilish pocket where their fate was sealed. If one gained this first gate and the second, which gave into a narrow, winding, upward-climbing street, the fighting would be hand to hand and always upward against men on a higher level. The citadel, as we found at last, was now a red and gray brick ruin, only some arches and angles of which were left, crowning the summit, from which the streets descended like the whorls of a snail-shell. Gray cobble-stone, and long narrow bricks set on their sides, form the streets or passages. The squat houses of brick and gray stone followed closely the convolutions of the street. It was a silent, sleepy little city. Few people were about. The small shops were guarded by old women or children. The men were sheep-herders, muleteers, gardeners and farmers on the slopes below. Anything that is sold in this high-placed city is brought up to it on the backs of slow-climbing, recalcitrant donkeys. One blessed thing, the sewage problem of these older Italian-French cities, because of their situation on the hillside, solves itself—otherwise, God help the cities. Barfleur insisted that there was leprosy hereabouts—a depressing thought.

Climbing up and around these various streets, peering in at the meager little windows where tobacco, fruit, cheese and modest staples were sold, we reached finally the summit of Eze, where for the first time in Italy—I count the Riviera Italian—the guide nuisance began. An old woman, in patois French, insisted on chanting about the ruins. Sir Scorp kept repeating,

"No, no, my good woman, go away," and I said in English, "Run, tell it to Barfleur. He is the bell-wether of this flock."

Barfleur clambered to safety up a cracked wall of the ruin and from his dizzy height eyed her calmly and bade her "Run along, now." But it was like King Canute bidding the sea to retreat, till she had successfully taken toll of us. Meanwhile we stared in delight at the Mediterranean, at the olive groves, the distant shepherds, at the lovely blue vistas and the pale threads of roads.

We were so anxious to get to Nice in time for dinner, and so opposed to making our way by the long dusty road which lay down the mountain, that we decided to make a short cut of it and go down the rocky side of the hill by a foot-wide path which was pointed out to us by the village priest, a haggard specimen of a man who, in thin cassock and beggarly shoes and hat, paraded before his crumbling little church door. We were a noble company, if somewhat out of the picture, as we piled down this narrow mountaineer's track—Barfleur in a brilliant checked suit and white hat, and Sir Scorp in very smart black. My best yellow shoes (ninety francs in Paris) lent a pleasing note to my otherwise inconspicuous attire, and gave me some concern, for the going was most rough and uncertain.

We passed shepherds tending sheep on sharp slopes, a donkey-driver making his way upward with three donkeys all heavily laden, an umbrella-tree sheltering a peasant so ancient that he must have endured from Grecian days, and olive groves whose shadows were as rich as that bronze which time has favored with its patina. It seemed impossible that half way between Monte Carlo and Nice—those twin worlds of spendthrift fashion and pampered vice—should endure a scene so idyllic. The Vale of Arcady is here; all that art could suggest or fancy desire, a world of simple things. Such scenes as this, remarked Sir Scorp, were favored by his great artistic admiration—Daubigny.

We found a railway station somewhere, and then we got to Nice for dinner. Once more a soul-stirring argument between Barfleur and Sir Scorp. We would take tea at Rumpelmeyer's—we would *not* take tea at Rumpelmeyer's. We would dine at The Regence; we would *not* dine at The Regence. We would pay I-forget-how-many louis and enter the baccarat chambers of the Casino; we would *not* do anything of the sort. It was desired by

Barfleur that I should see the wonders of the sea-walk with the waves spraying the protecting wall. It was desired by Scorp that I should look in all the jewelry shop windows with him and hear him instruct in the jeweler's art. How these matters were finally adjusted is lost in the haze of succeeding impressions. We *did* have tea at Rumpelmeyer's, however—a very commonplace but bright affair—and then we loitered in front of shop windows where Sir Scorp pointed out really astounding jewels offered to the public for fabulous sums. One great diamond he knew to have been in the possession of the Sultan of Turkey, and you may well trust his word and his understanding. A certain necklace here displayed had once been in his possession and was now offered at exactly ten times what he had originally sold it for. A certain cut steel brooch— very large and very handsome—was designed by himself, and was first given as a remembrance to a friend. Result—endless imitation by the best shops. He dallied over rubies and emeralds, suggesting charming uses for them. And then finally we came to the Casino—the Casino Municipale—with its baccarat chambers, its great dining-rooms, its public lounging-room with such a world of green wicker chairs and tables as I have never seen. The great piers at Atlantic City are not so large. Being the height of the season, it was of course filled to overflowing by a brilliant throng—cocottes and gamblers drawn here from all parts of Europe; and tourists of all nationalities.

Sir Scorp, as usual, in his gentle but decided way, raised an argument concerning what we should have for dinner. The mere suggestion that it should be *canard à la presse* and champagne threw him into a dyspeptic chill. "I will not pay for it. You can spend your money showing off if you choose; but I will eat a simple meal somewhere else."

"Oh, no," protested Barfleur. "We are here for a pleasant evening. I think it important that Dreiser should see this. It need not be *canard à la presse*. We can have sole and a light Burgundy."

So sole it was, and a light Burgundy, and a bottle of water for Sir Scorp.

CHAPTER XXVIII
NICE

NOT having as yet been in the *Cirque privé* at Monte Carlo, I was perhaps unduly impressed by the splendor of the rooms devoted to gambling in this amazingly large casino. There were eight hundred or a thousand people all in evening clothes, who had paid a heavy price for the mere privilege of entering, and were now gathered about handsome green-covered mahogany tables under glittering and ornate electroliers, playing a variety of carefully devised gambling games with a fervor that at times makes martyrs in other causes. To a humble-minded American person like myself, unused to the high world of fashion, this spectacle was, to say the least, an interesting one. Here were a dozen nationalities represented by men and women whose hands were manicured to perfection, whose toilets were all that a high social occasion might require, their faces showing in every instance a keen understanding of their world and how it works. Here in Nice, if you walk away from these centers of social perfection, where health and beauty and sophistication and money abound, the vast run of citizens are as poverty-stricken as any; but this collection of nobility and gentry, of millionaires, adventurers, intellectual prostitutes and savage beauties is recruited from all over the world. I hold that is something to see.

The tables were fairly swarming with a fascinating throng all very much alike in their attitude and their love of the game, but still individual and interesting. I venture to say that any one of the people I saw in this room, if you saw him in a crowd on the street, would take your attention. A native force and self-sufficiency went with each one. I wondered constantly where they all came from. It takes money to come to the Riviera; it takes money to buy your way into any gambling-room. It takes money to gamble; and what is more it takes a certain amount of self-assurance and individual selection to come here at all. By your mere presence you are putting yourself in contact and contrast with a notable standard of social achievement. Your intellectuality, your ability to take care of yourself, your breeding and your subtlety are at once challenged—not consciously, but unconsciously. Do you really belong here? the eyes of the attendants ask you as you pass. And the glitter and color and life and beauty of the room is a constant challenge.

It did not surprise me in the least that all these men and women in their health and attractiveness carried themselves with cynical, almost sneering hauteur. They might well do so—as the world judges these material things—for they are certainly far removed from the rank and file of the streets; and to see them extracting from their purses and their pockets handfuls of gold, unfolding layers of crisp notes that represented a thousand francs each, and with an almost indifferent air laying them on their favorite numbers or combinations was to my unaccustomed eye a gripping experience. Yet I was not interested in gambling—only in the people who played.

I know that to the denizens of this world who are fascinated by chance and find their amusement in such playing, this atmosphere is commonplace. It was not so to me. I watched the women—particularly the beautiful women—who strolled about the chambers with their escorts solely to show off their fine clothes. You see a certain type of youth here who seems to be experienced in this gay world that drifts from one resort to another, for you hear such phrases as "Oh, yes, I saw her at Aix-les-Bains," or, "She was at Karlsbad last summer." "Is that the same fellow she was with last year? I thought she was living with —" (this of a second individual). "My heaven, how well she keeps up!" or, "This must be her first season here—I have never seen her before." Two or three of these young bloods would follow a woman all around the rooms, watching her, admiring her beauty quite as a horseman might examine the fine points of a horse. And all the while you could see that she was keenly aware of the critical fire of these eyes.

"My heaven, how well she keeps up!"

At the tables was another type of woman whom I had first casually noticed at Monte Carlo, a not too good looking, rather practical, and perhaps disillusioned type of woman—usually inclined to stoutness, as is so often the case with women of indolent habits and no temperament—although, now that I think of it, I have the feeling that neither illusion nor disillusion have ever played much part in the lives of such as these. They looked to me like women who, from their youth up, had taken life with a grain of salt and who had never been carried away by anything much—neither love, nor fashion, nor children, nor ambition. Perhaps their keenest interest had always been money—the having and holding of it. And here they sat—not good-looking, not apparently magnetic—interested in chance, and very likely winning and losing by turns, their principal purpose being, I fancy, to avoid the dullness and monotony of an existence which they are not anxious to endure. I heard one or two derogatory comments on women of this type while I was abroad; but I cannot say that they did more than appeal to my sympathies. Supposing, to look at it from another point of view, you were a woman of forty-five or fifty. You have no family—nothing to hold you, perhaps, but a collection of dreary relatives, or the *ennui* of a conventional neighborhood with prejudices that are wearisome to your sense of liberty and freedom. If by any chance you have money, here on the Riviera is your resource. You can live in a wonderful climate of sun and blue water; you can see nature clad in her daintiest raiment the year round; you can see fashion and cosmopolitan types and exchange the gossip of all the world; you can go to really excellent restaurants—the best that Europe provides; and for leisure, from ten o'clock in the morning until four or five o'clock the next morning, you can gamble if you choose, gamble silently, indifferently, without hindrance as long as your means endure.

If you are of a mathematical or calculating turn of mind you can amuse yourself infinitely by attempting to solve the strange puzzle of chance—how numbers fall and why. It leads off at last, I know, into the abstrusities of chemistry and physics. The esoteric realms of the mystical are not more subtle than the strange abnormalities of psychology that are here indulged in. Certain people are supposed to have a chemical and physical attraction for numbers or cards. Dreams are of great importance. It is bad to sit by a losing person, good to sit by a winning one. Every conceivable eccentricity of thought in relation to personality is here indulged in; and when all is said and done, in spite of the wonders of their cobwebby calculations, it comes to about the same old thing—they win and lose, win and lose, win and lose.

Now and then some interesting personality—stranger, youth, celebrity, or other—wins heavily or loses heavily; in which case, if he plunges fiercely on, his table will be surrounded by a curious throng, their heads craning over each other's shoulders, while he piles his gold on his combinations. Such a man or woman for the time being becomes an intensely dramatic figure. He is aware of the audacity of the thing he is doing, and he moves with conscious gestures—the manner of a grand seigneur. I saw one such later—in the *Cirque privé* at Monte Carlo—a red-bearded man of fifty—tall, intense, graceful. It was rumored that he was a prince out of Russia—almost any one can be a prince out of Russia at Monte Carlo! He had stacks of gold and he distributed it with a lavish hand. He piled it in little golden towers over a score of numbers; and when his numbers fell wrong his towers fell with them, and the croupier raked great masses of metal into his basket. There was not the slightest indication on his pale impassive face that the loss or the gain was of the slightest interest to him. He handed crisp bills to the clerk in charge of the bank and received more gold to play his numbers. When he wearied, after a dozen failures—a breathing throng watching him with moist lips and damp, eager eyes—he rose and strolled forth to another chamber, rolling a cigarette as he went. He had lost thousands and thousands.

The next morning it was lovely and sunshiny again. Sitting out on my balcony high over the surrounding land, commanding as it did all of Monte Carlo, the bay of Mentone and Cap Martin, I made many solemn resolutions. This gay life here was meretricious and artificial, I decided. Gambling was a vice, in spite of Sir Scorp's lofty predilection for it; it drew to and around it the allied viciousness of the world, gormandizing, harlotry, wastefulness, vain-glory. I resolved here in the cool morning that I would reform. I would see something of the surrounding country and then leave for Italy where I would forget all this.

I started out with Barfleur about ten to see the Oceanographical Museum and to lunch at the Princess, but the day did not work out exactly as we planned. We visited the Oceanographical Museum; but I found it amazingly dull—the sort of a thing a prince making his money out of gambling would endow. It may have vast scientific ramifications, but I doubt it. A meager collection of insects and dried specimens quickly gave me a headache. The only case that really interested me was the one containing a half-dozen octopi of large size. I stood transfixed before their bulbous centers and dull, muddy, bronze-green arms, studded with suckers. I can imagine nothing so horrible as to be seized upon by one of these things, and I fairly shivered as I stood in front of the case. Barfleur contemplated solemnly the possibility of his being attacked by one of them, monocle and all. He foresaw a swift end to his career.

We came out into the sunlight and viewed with relief, by contrast with the dull museum, the very new and commonplace cathedral—oh, exceedingly poorly executed— and the castle or palace or residence of His Highness, the Prince of Monaco. I cannot imagine why Europe tolerates this man with his fine gambling privileges unless it is that the different governments look with opposition on the thought of any other government having so fine a source of wealth. France should have it by rights; and it would be suitable that the French temperament should conduct such an institution. The palace of the Prince of Monaco was as dull as his church and his museum; and the Monacoan Army drawn up in front of his residence for their morning exercise looked like a company of third-rate French policemen.

However I secured as fine an impression of the beauty of Monaco and the whole coast from this height, as I received at any time during my stay; for it is like the jewel of a ring projecting out of the sea. You climb up to the Oceanographical Museum and the palace by a series of stairways and walks that from time to time bring you out to the sheer edge of the cliff overlooking the blue waters below. There is expensive gardening done here, everywhere; for you find vines and flowers and benches underneath the shade of palms and umbrella trees where you can sit and look out over the sea. Lovely panoramas confront you in every direction; and below, perhaps as far down as three and four hundred feet, you can see and hear the waves breaking and the foam eddying about the rocks. The visitor to Monte Carlo, I fancy, is not greatly disturbed about scenery, however. Such walks as these are empty and still while the Casino is packed to the doors. The gaming-tables are the great center; and to these we ourselves invariably returned.

CHAPTER XXIX
A FIRST GLIMPSE OF ITALY

MY days in Monte Carlo after this were only four, exactly. In spite of my solemn resolutions of the morning the spirit of this gem-like world got into my bones by three o'clock; and at four, when we were having tea at the Riviera Palace Hotel high above the Casino, I was satisfied that I should like to stay here for months. Barfleur, as usual, was full of plans for enjoyment; and he insisted that I had not half exhausted the charms of the place. We should go to some old monastery at Laghet where miracles of healing were performed, and to Cannes and Beaulieu in order to see the social life there.

A part of one of these days we spent viewing a performance in Mentone. Another day Barfleur and I went to Laghet and Nice, beginning with a luncheon at the Riviera Palace and winding up at the Hôtel des Fleurs. The last day we were in the Casino, gambling cheerfully for a little while, and then on the terrace viewing the pigeon shooting, which Barfleur persistently refused to contemplate. This (to me) brutal sport was evidently fascinating to many, for the popping of guns was constant. It is so curious how radically our views differ in this world as to what constitutes evil and good. To Scorp this was a legitimate sport. The birds were ultimately destined for pies anyhow; why not kill them here in this manner? To me the crippling of the perfect winged things was a crime. I would never be one to hold a gun in such a sport.

It was this last day in the Café de Paris that Barfleur and I encountered Marcelle and Mme. Y., our companions of that first dinner in Paris. Barfleur was leaving for London, Scorp was to stay on at Monte Carlo, and for the first time I faced the prospect of traveling alone. Acting on impulse I turned to Marcelle and said: "Come with me as far as Ventimiglia," never thinking for a moment that she would. "*Oui*," she replied, "*oui, oui*," and seemed very cheerful over the prospect.

Marcelle arrived some fifteen minutes before my train was due, but she was not to speak to me until we were on the train. It took some manœuvering to avoid the suspicions of Scorp.

Barfleur left for the north at four-thirty, assuring me that we would meet in Paris in April and ride at Fontainebleau, and that we would take a walking tour in England. After he was gone, Scorp and I walked to and fro and then it was that Marcelle appeared. I had to smile as I walked with Scorp, thinking how wrathful he would have been if he had known that every so often we were passing Marcelle, who gazed demurely the other way. The platforms, as usual, were alive with passengers with huge piles of baggage. My train was a half hour late and it was getting dark. Some other train which was not bound for Rome entered, and Marcelle signaled to know whether she was to get into that. I shook my head and hunted up the Cook's tourist agent, always to be found on these foreign platforms, and explained to him that he was to go to the young lady in the blue suit and white walking-shoes and tell her that the train was a half hour late and ask her if she cared to wait. With quite an American *sang-froid* he took in the situation at once, and wanted to know how far she was going. I told him Ventimiglia and he advised that she get off at Garaban in order to catch the first train back. He departed, and presently returned, cutting me out from the company of Sir Scorp by a very wise look of the eye, and informed me that the lady would wait and would go. I promptly gave him a franc for his trouble. My pocket was bulging with Italian silver lire and paper five- and ten-lire pieces which I had secured the day before. Finally my train rolled in and I took one last look at the sea in the fading light and entered. Sir Scorp gave me parting instructions as to simple restaurants that I would find at different places in Italy—not the showy and expensive cafés, beloved of Barfleur. He wanted me to save money on food and have my portrait painted by Mancini, which I could have done, he assured me, with a letter from him. He looked wisely around the platform to see that there was no suspicious lady anywhere in the foreground and said he suspected one might be going with me.

"Oh, Scorp," I said, "how could you? Besides, I am very poor now."

"The ruling passion—strong in poverty," he commented, and waved me a farewell.

I walked forward through the train looking for my belongings and encountered Marcelle. She was eager to explain by signs that the Cook's man had told her to get off at Garaban.

"*M'sieur Thomas Cook, il m'a dit—il faut que je descends à Garaban—pas Ventimiglia—Garaban.*" She understood well enough that if she wanted to get back to Monte Carlo early in the evening she would have to make this train, as the next was not before ten o'clock.

I led the way to a table in the dining-car still vacant, and we talked as only people can talk who have no common language. By the most astonishing efforts Marcelle made it known that she would not stay at Monte Carlo very long now, and that if I wanted her to come to Florence when I got there she would. Also she kept talking about Fontainebleau and horseback riding in April. She imitated a smart rider holding the reins with one hand and clucking to the horse with her lips. She folded her hands expressively to show how heavenly it would be. Then she put her right hand over her eyes and waved her left hand to indicate that there were lovely vistas which we could contemplate. Finally she extracted all her bills from the Hôtel de Paris—and they were astonishing—to show me how expensive her life was at Monte Carlo; but I refused to be impressed. It did not make the least difference, however, in her attitude or her mood. She was just as cheerful as ever, and repeated "Avril—Fontainebleau," as the train stopped and she stepped off. She reached up and gave me an affectionate farewell kiss. The last I saw of her she was standing, her arms akimbo, her head thrown smartly back, looking after the train.

* * * * *

It was due to a railroad wreck about twenty miles beyond Ventimiglia that I owe my acquaintance with one of the most interesting men I have met in years, a man who was very charming to me afterwards in Rome, but before that I should like to relate how I first really entered Italy. One afternoon, several days before, Barfleur and I paid a flying visit to Ventimiglia, some twenty miles over the border, a hill city and the agreed customs entry city between France and Italy. No train leaving France in this region, so I learned, stopped before it reached Ventimiglia, and none leaving Ventimiglia stopped before it entered France, and once there customs inspectors seized upon one and examined one's baggage. If you have no baggage you are almost an object of suspicion in Italy.

On the first visit we came to scale the walls of this old city which was much like Eze and commanded the sea from a great eminence. But after Eze it was not Ventimiglia that interested me so much as the fact that Italy was so different from France. In landing at Fishguard I had felt the astonishing difference between England and the United States. In landing at Calais the atmosphere of England had fallen from me like a cloak and France—its high color and enthusiasm—had succeeded to it. Here this day, stepping off the train at Ventimiglia only a few miles from Monte Carlo, I was once more astonished at the sharp change that had come over the spirit of man. Here were Italians, not French, dark, vivid, interesting little men who, it seemed to me, were so much more inclined to strut and stare than the French that they appeared to be vain. They were keen, temperamental, avid, like the French but strange to say not so gay, so light-hearted, so devil-may-care.

Italy, it seemed to me at once, was much poorer than France and Barfleur was very quick to point it out. "A different people," he commented, "not like the French, much darker and more mysterious. See the cars—how poor they are. You will note that everywhere. And the buildings, the trains—the rolling stock is not so good. Look at the houses. The life here is more poverty-stricken. Italy is poor—very. I like it and I don't. Some things are splendid. My mother adores Rome. I crave the French temperament. It is so much more light-hearted." So he rambled on.

It was all true—accurate and keenly observed. I could not feel that I was anywhere save in a land that was seeking to rehabilitate itself but that had a long way to go. The men—the officials and soldiery of whom there were a legion clad in remarkable and even astonishing uniforms, appealed to my eye, but the souls of them to begin with, did not take my fancy. I felt them to be suspicious and greedy. Here for the first time I saw the uniform of the Italian *bersaglieri*: smart-looking in long capes, round hats of shiny leather with glossy green rooster feathers, and carrying short swords.

This night as I crossed the border after leaving Garaban I thought of all I had seen the day I came with Barfleur. When we reached Ventimiglia it was pitch dark and being alone and speaking no Italian whatsoever, I was confused by the thought of approaching difficulties.

Presently a customs inspector descended on me—a large, bearded individual who by signs made me understand that I had to go to the baggage car and open my trunk. I went. Torches supplied the only light: I felt as though I were in a bandit's cave. Yet I came through well enough. Nothing contraband was found. I went back and sat down, plunging into a Baedeker for Italian wisdom and wishing gloomily that I had read more history than I had.

Somewhere beyond Ventimiglia the train came to a dead stop in the dark, and the next morning we were still stalled in the same place. I had risen early, under the impression that I was to get out quickly, but was waved back by the porter who repeated over and over, "*Beaucoup de retard!*" I understood that much but I did not understand what caused it, or that I would not arrive in Pisa until two in the afternoon. I went into the dining-car and there encountered one of the most obstreperous English women that I have ever met. She was obviously of the highly intellectual class, but so haughty in her manner and so loud-spoken in her opinions that she was really offensive. She was having her morning fruit and rolls and some chops and was explaining to a lady, who was with her, much of the character of Italy as she knew it. She was of the type that never accepts an opinion from any one, but invariably gives her own or corrects any that may be volunteered. At one time I think she must have been attractive, for she was moderately tall and graceful, but her face had become waxy and sallow, and a little thin—I will not say hard, although it was anything but ingratiating. My one wish was that she would stop talking and leave the dining-car, she talked so loud; but she stayed on until her friend and her husband arrived. I took him to be her husband by the way she contradicted him.

He was a very pleasing, intellectual person—the type of man, I thought, who would complacently endure such a woman. He was certainly not above the medium in height, quite well filled out, and decidedly phlegmatic. I should have said from my first glance that he never took any exercise of any kind; and his face had that interesting pallor which comes from much brooding over the midnight oil. He had large, soft, lustrous gray eyes and a mop of gray hair which hung low over a very high white forehead. I must repeat here that I am the poorest judge of people whom I am going to like of any human being. Now and then I take to a person instantly, and my feeling endures for years. On the other hand I have taken the most groundless oppositions based on nothing at all to people of whom subsequently I have become very fond. Perhaps my groundless opposition in this case was due to the fact that the gentleman was plainly submissive and overborne by his loud-talking wife. Anyhow I gave him a single glance and dismissed him from my thoughts. I was far more interested in a stern, official-looking Englishman with white hair who ordered his bottle of Perrier in a low, rusty voice and cut his orange up into small bits with a knife.

Presently I heard a German explaining to his wife about a wreck ahead. We were just starting now, perhaps twenty-five or thirty miles from Ventimiglia, and were dashing in and out of rocky tunnels and momentarily bursting into wonderful views of walled caves and sunlit sweeps of sea. The hill-town, the striped basilica with its square, many-arched campanile was coming into view. I was delighted to see open plains bordered in the distance by snow-capped mountains, and dotted sparsely with little huts of stone and brick—how old, Heaven only knows. "Here once the Tuscan shepherds strayed." As Barfleur said, Italy was much poorer than France. The cars and stations seemed shabbier, the dress of the inhabitants much poorer. I saw natives, staring idly at the cars as we flashed past, or taking freight away from the platforms in rude carts drawn by oxen. Many of the vehicles appeared to be rattle-trap, dusty, unpainted; and some miles this side of Genoa—our first stop—we ran into a region where it had been snowing and the ground was covered with a wet slushy snowfall. After Monte Carlo, with its lemon and orange trees and its lovely palms, this was a sad comedown; and I could scarcely realize that we were not so much as a hundred miles away and going southward toward Rome at that. I often saw, however, distant hills crowned with a stronghold or a campanile in high browns and yellows, which made up for the otherwise poor foreground. Often we dashed through a cave, protected by high surrounding walls of rock, where the palm came into view again and where one could see how plainly these high walls of stone made for a tropic atmosphere. I heard the loud-voiced English woman saying, "It is such a delight to see the high colors again. England is so dreary. I never feel it so much as when we come down through here."

We were passing through a small Italian town, rich in whites, pinks, browns and blues, a world of clothes-lines showing between rows of buildings, and the crowds, pure Italian in type, plodding to and fro along the streets. It was nice to see windows open here and the sunshine pouring down and making dark shadows. I saw one Italian woman, in a pink-dotted dress partly covered by a bright yellow apron, looking out of a window; and then it was that I first got the tang of Italy—the thing that I felt afterwards in Rome and Florence and Assisi and Perugia—that wonderful love of color that is not rampant but just deliciously selective, giving the eye something to feed on when it least expects it. That is Italy!

When nearly all the diners had left the car the English lady left also and her husband remained to smoke. He was not so very far removed from me, but he came a little nearer, and said: "The Italians must have their striped churches and their wash lines or they wouldn't be happy."

It was some time before he volunteered another suggestion, which was that the Italians along this part of the coast had a poor region to farm. I got up and left presently because I did not want to have anything to do with his wife. I was afraid that I might have to talk to her, which seemed to me a ghastly prospect.

I sat in my berth and read the history of art as it related to Florence, Genoa, and Pisa, interrupting my paragraphs with glances at every interesting scene. The value of the prospect changed first from one side of the train to the other, and I went out into the corridor to open a window and look out. We passed through a valley where it looked as though grapes were flourishing splendidly, and my Englishman came out and told me the name of the place, saying that it was good wine that was made there. He was determined to talk to me whether I would or no, and so I decided to make the best of it. It just occurred to me that he might be the least bit lonely, and, seeing that I was very curious about the country through which we were passing, that he might know something about Italy. The moment it dawned upon me that he might be helpful to me in this respect I began to ask him questions, and I found his knowledge to be delightfully wide. He knew Italy thoroughly. As we proceeded he described how the country was divided into virtually three valleys, separated by two mountain ranges, and what the lines of its early, almost prehistoric, development, had been. He knew where it was that Shelley had come to spend his summers, and spots that had been preferred by Browning and other famous Englishmen. He talked of the cities that lie in a row down the center of Italy—Perugia, Florence, Bologna, Modena, Piacenza and Milan—of the fact that Italy had no educational system whatsoever and that the priests were bitterly opposed to it. He was sorry that I was not going to stop at Spezia, because at Spezia the climate was very mild and the gulf very beautiful. He was delighted to think that I was going to stop at Pisa and see the cathedral and the Baptistery. He commented on the charms of Genoa—commercialized as it had been these later years—saying that there was a very beautiful Campo Santo and that some of the palaces of the quarreling Guelphs and Ghibellines still remaining were well worth seeing. When we passed the quarries of Carrara he told me of their age and of how endless the quantity of marble still was. He was going to Rome with his wife and he wanted to know if I would not look him up, giving me the name of a hotel where he lived by the season. I caught a note of remarkable erudition; for we fell to discussing religion and priestcraft and the significance of government generally, and he astonished me by the breadth of his knowledge. We passed to the subject of metaphysics from which all religions spring; and then I saw how truly philosophic and esoteric he was. His mind knew no country, his knowledge no school. He led off by easy stages into vague speculations as to the transcendental character of race impulses; and I knew I had chanced upon a profound scholar as well as a very genial person. I was very sorry now that I had been so rude to him. By the time we reached Pisa we were fast friends, and he told me that he had a distinguished friend, now a resident of Assisi, and that he would give me a letter to him which would bring me charming intellectual companionship for a day or two. I promised to seek him out at his hotel; and as we passed the Leaning Tower and the Baptistery, not so very distant from the railroad track as we entered Pisa, he gave me his card. I recognized the name as connected with some intellectual labors of a most distinguished character and I said so. He accepted the recognition gracefully and asked me to be sure and come. He would show me around Rome.

I gathered my bags and stepped out upon the platform at Pisa, eager to see what I could in the few hours that I wished to remain.

CHAPTER XXX
A STOP AT PISA

BAEDEKER says that Pisa has a population of twenty-seven thousand two hundred people and that it is a quiet town. It is. I caught the spell of a score of places like this as I walked out into the open square facing the depot. The most amazing botch of a monument I ever saw in my life I saw here—a puffing, swelling, strutting representation of Umberto I, legs apart, whiskers rampant, an amazing cockade, all the details of a gaudy uniform, a breast like a pouter-pigeon—outrageous! It was about twelve or thirteen times as large as an ordinary man and not more than twelve or fifteen feet from the ground! He looked like a gorgon, a monster to eat babies, ready to leap upon you with loud cries. I thought, "In Heaven's name! is this what Italy is coming to! How can it brook such an atrocity?"

With the spirit of adventure strong within me I decided to find the campanile and the cathedral for myself. I had seen it up the railroad track, and, ignoring appealing guides with urgent, melancholy eyes, I struck up walled streets of brown and gray and green with solid, tight-closed, wooden shutters, cobble pavements and noiseless, empty sidewalks. They were not exactly narrow, which astonished me a little, for I had not learned that only the older portions of growing Italian cities have narrow streets. All the newer sections which surround such modern things as depots are wide and supposedly up to date. There was a handsome trolley-car just leaving as I came out, a wide-windowed shiny thing which illustrated just how fine trolley-cars can be, even in Italy. I had learned from my Baedeker that Pisa was on the Arno. I wanted to see the Arno because of Florence and Dante. Coming from Ventimiglia I had read the short history of Pisa given in Baedeker—its wars with Genoa, the building of its cathedral. It was interesting to learn that the Pisans had expelled the Saracens from Sardinia in 1025, and destroyed their fleet in 1063 near Palermo, that once they were the most powerful adherents of the Ghibellines, and how terribly they were defeated by the Genoese near Leghorn in 1284. I pumped up a vast desire to read endless volumes concerning the history of Italy, now that I was here on the ground, and when it could not be done on the instant. My book told me that the great cathedral was erected after the naval victory of the Pisans at Palermo and that the ancient bronze gates were very wonderful. I knew of the Campo Santo with its sacred earth brought from Palestine, and of the residence here of Niccolò Pisano. His famous hexagonal pulpit in the Baptistery is a commonplace—almost as much so as the Leaning Tower. I did not know that Galileo had availed himself of the oblique position of the tower to make his experiments regarding the laws of gravitation until I read it in my precious Baedeker, but it was a fact none the less delightful for encountering it there.

Let me here and now, once and for all, sing my praises of Baedeker and his books. When I first went abroad it was with a lofty air that I considered Barfleur's references to the fact that Baedeker on occasion would be of use to me. He wanted me to go through Europe getting my impressions quite fresh and not disturbed by too much erudition such as could be gathered from books. He might have trusted me. My longing for erudition was constantly great, but my willingness to burn the midnight oil in order to get it was exceedingly small. It was only at the last moment, when I was confronted with some utterly magnificent object, that I thumbed feverishly through my one source of supply—the ever-to-be-praised and blessed Karl Baedeker—his books. I think the German temperament is at its best when it is gathering all the data about anything and putting it in apple-pie order before you. I defy the most sneering and supercilious scholars and savants to look at these marvelous volumes and not declare them wonderful. There is no color in Baedeker anywhere, no joke, no emotion, no artistic enthusiasm. It is a plain statement of delightful fact— fact so pointless without the object before you, so invaluable when you are standing open-mouthed wondering what it is all about! Trust the industrious, the laborious, the stupendous, the painstaking Baedeker to put his finger on the exact fact and tell you not what you might, but what you must, know to really enjoy it. Take this little gem from page 430 of his volume on northern Italy. It concerns the famous Baptistery which I was so eagerly seeking.

The interior (visitors knock at the principal entrance; adm. free) rests on eight columns and four piers, above which there is a single triforium. In the center is a marble octagonal *Font* by Guido Bigarelli of Como (1246) and near it the famous hexagonal *PULPIT* borne by seven columns, by Niccolò

Pisano, 1260. The reliefs (comp. p.p. XXXIX, 432) on the pulpit are: (1) Annunciation and Nativity; (2) Adoration of the Magi; (3) Presentation in the Temple; (4) Crucifixion; (5) Last Judgment; in the spandrels, Prophets and Evangelists; above the columns, the Virtues.—Fine echo.

Dry as dried potatoes, say you. Exactly. But go to Italy without a Baedeker in your hand or precious knowledge stored up from other sources and see what happens. Karl Baedeker is one of the greatest geniuses Germany has ever produced. He knows how to give you what you want, and has spread the fame of German thoroughness broadcast. I count him a great human benefactor; and his native city ought to erect a monument to him. Its base ought to be a bronze library stand full of bronze Baedekers; and to this good purpose I will contribute freely and liberally according to my means.

When I reached the Arno, as I did by following this dull vacant street, I was delighted to stop and look at its simple stone bridges, its muddy yellow water not unlike that of the New River in West Virginia, the plain, still, yellow houses lining its banks as far as I could see. The one jarring note was the steel railroad bridge which the moderns have built over it. It was a little consoling to look at an old moss-covered fortress now occupied as a division headquarters by the Italian army, and at a charming old gate which was part of a fortified palace left over from Pisa's warring days. The potential force of Italy was overcoming me by leaps and bounds, and my mind was full of the old and powerful Italian families of which the Middle Ages are so redolent. I could not help thinking of the fact that the Renaissance had, in a way, its beginning here in the personality of Niccolò Pisano, and of how wonderful the future of Italy may yet be. There was an air of fallow sufficiency about it that caused me to feel that, although it might be a dull, unworked field this year or this century, another might see it radiant with power and magnificence. It is a lordly and artistic land—and I felt it here at Pisa.

Wandering along the banks of the Arno, I came to a spot whence I could see the collection of sacred buildings, far more sacred to art than to religion. They were amazingly impressive, even from this distance, towering above the low houses. A little nearer, standing on a space of level grass, the boxing of yellow and brown and blue Italian houses about them like a frame, they set my mouth agape with wonder and delight. I walked into Pisa thinking it was too bad that any place so dignified should have fallen so low as to be a dull, poverty-stricken city; but I remained to think that if the Italians are wise (and they *are* wise and new-born also) they will once more have their tremendous cities and their great artistic inheritances in the bargain. I think now that perhaps of all the lovely things I saw abroad the cathedral and tower and baptistery and campo santo of Pisa grouped as they are in one lovely, spacious, green-sodded area, are the loveliest and most perfect of all. It does not matter to me that the cathedral at Pisa is not a true Gothic cathedral, as some have pointed out. It is better than that—it is Italian Gothic; with those amazing artistic conceptions, a bell-tower and a baptistery and a campo santo thrown in. Trust the Italians to do anything that they do grandly, with a princely lavishness.

As I stepped first into this open square with these exquisite jewels of cream-colored stone pulsating under the rays of an evening sun, it was a spectacle that evoked a rare thrill of emotion, such as great art must always evoke. There they stood—fretted, fluted, colonnaded, crowded with lovely traceries, studded with lovely marbles, and showing in every line and detail all that loving enthusiasm which is the first and greatest characteristic of artistic genius. I can see those noble old first citizens who wanted Pisa to be great, calling to their aid the genius of such men as Pisano and Bonannus of Pisa and William of Innsbruck and Diotisalvi and all the noble company of talent that followed to plan, to carve, to color and to decorate. To me it is a far more impressive and artistic thing than St. Peter's in Rome. It has a reserve and an artistic subtlety which exceeds the finest Gothic cathedral in the world. Canterbury, Amiens and Rouen are bursts of imagination and emotion; but the collection of buildings at Pisa is the reserved, subtle, princely calculation of a great architect and a great artist. It does not matter if it represents the handiwork, the judgment and the taste of a hundred men of genius. It may be without the wildfire of a cathedral like that at Cologne, but it approximates the high classic reserve of a temple of Pallas Athene. It is Greek in its dignity and beauty, not Christian and Gothic in its fire and zeal. As I think of it, I would not give it for anything I have seen; I would not have missed it if I had been compelled to sacrifice almost everything else; and the Italian Government has done well to take it and all similar achievements under its protection and to declare that however religion may wax or wane this thing shall not be disturbed. It is a great, a noble, a beautiful thing; and as such should be preserved forever.

The interior of the basilica was to me a soothing dream of beauty. There are few interiors anywhere in this world that truly satisfy, but this is one of them. White marble turned yellow by age is gloriously satisfying. This interior, one hundred feet in diameter and one hundred and seventy-nine feet high, has all the smooth perfection of a blown bubble. Its curve recedes upward and inward so gracefully that the eye has no quarrel with any point. My mind was fascinated by the eight columns and four piers which seemingly support it all and by the graceful open gallery or arcade in the wall resting above the arches below. The octagonal baptismal font, so wide and so beautiful, and the graceful pulpit by Pisano, with its seven columns and three friendly-looking lions, is utterly charming. While I stood and stroked the heads of these amiable-looking beasts, a guide who had seen me enter came in, and without remark of any kind began slowly and clearly to articulate the scale, in order that I might hear the "fine echo" mentioned by Baedeker. Long practice had made him perfect, for by giving each note sufficient space to swell and redouble and quadruple itself he finally managed to fill the great chamber with a charming harmony, rich and full, not unlike that of a wind-harp.

If I fell instantly in love with the Baptistery, I was equally moved by the Leaning Tower—a perfect thing. If man is wise and thoughtful he can keep the wonders of great beauty by renewing them as they wear; but will he remain wise and thoughtful? So little is thought of true beauty. Think of the guns thundering on the Parthenon and of Napoleon carrying away the horses of St. Mark's! I mounted the steps of the tower (one hundred and seventy-nine feet, the same height as the Baptistery), walking out on and around each of its six balustrades and surveying the surrounding landscape rich in lovely mountains showing across a plain. The tower tilts fourteen feet out of plumb, and as I walked its circular arcades at different heights I had the feeling that I might topple over and come floundering down to the grass below. As I rose higher the view increased in loveliness; and at the top I found an old bell-man who called my attention by signs to the fact that the heaviest of the seven bells was placed on the side opposite the overhanging wall of the tower to balance it. He also pointed in the different directions which presented lovely views, indicating to the west and southwest the mouth of the Arno, the Mediterranean, Leghorn and the Tuscan Islands, to the north the Alps and Mount Pisani where the Carrara quarries are, and to the south, Rome. Some Italian soldiers from the neighboring barracks came up as I went down and entered the cathedral, which interiorly was as beautiful as any which I saw abroad. The Italian Gothic is so much more perfectly spaced on the interior than the Northern Gothic and the great flat roof, coffered in gold, is so much richer and more soothing in its aspect. The whole church is of pure marble yellowed by age, relieved, however, by black and colored bands.

I came away after a time and entered the Campo Santo, the loveliest thing of its kind that I saw in Europe. I never knew, strange to relate, that graveyards were made, or could be made, into anything so impressively artistic. This particular ground was nothing more than an oblong piece of grass, set with several cypress trees and surrounded with a marble arcade, below the floor and against the walls of which are placed the marbles, tombs and sarcophagi. The outer walls are solid, windowless and decorated on the inside with those naïve, light-colored frescoes of the pupils of Giotto. The inner wall is full of arched, pierced windows with many delicate columns through which you look to the green grass and the cypress trees and the perfectly smooth, ornamented dome at one end. I have paid my tribute to the cypress trees, so I will only say that here, as always, wherever I saw them—one or many—I thrilled with delight. They are as fine artistically as any of the monuments or bronze doors or carved pulpits or perfect baptismal fonts. They belong where the great artistic impulse of Italy has always put them—side by side with perfect things. For me they added the one final, necessary touch to this realm of romantic memory. I see them now and I hear them sigh.

I walked back to my train through highly colored, winding, sidewalkless, quaint-angled streets crowded with houses, the façades of which we in America to-day attempt to imitate on our Fifth Avenues and Michigan Avenues and Rittenhouse Squares. The medieval Italians knew so well what to do with the door and the window and the cornice and the wall space.

The size of their window is what they choose to make it, and the door is instinctively put where it will give the last touch of elegance. How often have I mentally applauded that selective artistic discrimination and reserve which will use one panel of colored stone or one niche or one lamp or one window, and no more. There is space—lots of it—unbroken until you have had just enough; and then it will be relieved just enough by a marble plaque framed in the walls, a coat-of-arms, a window, a niche. I would like to run on in my enthusiasm and describe that gem of a palace that is now the Palazzo Communale at Perugia, but I will refrain. Only these streets in Pisa were rich with angles and arcades and wonderful doorways and solid plain fronts which were at once substantial and elegant. Trust the Italian of an older day to do well whatever he did at all; and I for one do not think that this instinct is lost. It will burst into flame again in the future; or save greatly what it already possesses.

CHAPTER XXXI
FIRST IMPRESSIONS OF ROME

AS we approached Rome in the darkness I was on the qui vive for my first glimpse of it; and impatient with wonder as to what the morning would reveal. I was bound for the Hotel Continental—the abode, for the winter at least, of Barfleur's mother, the widow of an Oxford don. I expected to encounter a severe and conservative lady of great erudition who would eye the foibles of Paris and Monte Carlo with severity.

"My mother," Barfleur said, "is a very conservative person. She is greatly concerned about me. When you see her, try to cheer her up, and give her a good report of me. I don't doubt you will find her very interesting; and it is just possible that she will take a fancy to you. She is subject to violent likes and dislikes."

I fancied Mrs. Barfleur as a rather large woman with a smooth placid countenance, a severe intellectual eye that would see through all my shams and make-believes on the instant.

It was midnight before the train arrived. It was raining; and as I pressed my nose to the window-pane viewing the beginning lamps, I saw streets and houses come into view—apartment houses, if you please, and street cars and electric arc-lights, and asphalt-paved streets, and a general atmosphere of modernity. We might have been entering Cleveland for any particular variation it presented. But just when I was commenting to myself on the strangeness of entering ancient Rome in a modern compartment car and of seeing box cars and engines, coal cars and flat cars loaded with heavy material, gathered on a score of parallel tracks, a touch of the ancient Rome came into view for an instant and was gone again in the dark and rain. It was an immense, desolate tomb, its arches flung heavenward in great curves, its rounded dome rent and jagged by time. Nothing but ancient Rome could have produced so imposing a ruin and it came over me in an instant, fresh and clear like an electric shock, like a dash of cold water, that this was truly all that was left of the might and glory of an older day. I recall now with delight the richness of that sensation. Rome that could build the walls and the baths in far Manchester and London, Rome that could occupy the Ile-St.-Louis in Paris as an outpost, that could erect the immense column to Augustus on the heights above Monte Carlo, Rome that could reach to the uppermost waters of the Nile and the banks of the Tigris and Euphrates and rule, was around me. Here it was—the city to which St. Paul had been brought, where St. Peter had sat as the first father of the Church, where the first Latins had set up their shrine to Romulus and Remus, and worshiped the she-wolf that had nourished them. Yes, this was Rome, truly enough, in spite of the apartment houses and the street cars and the electric lights. I came into the great station at five minutes after twelve amid a clamor of Italian porters and a crowd of disembarking passengers. I made my way to the baggage-room, looking for a Cook's guide to inquire my way to the Continental, when I was seized upon by one.

"Are you Mr. Dreiser?" he said.

I replied that I was.

"Mrs. Barfleur told me to say that she was waiting for you and that you should come right over and inquire for her."

I hurried away, followed by a laboring porter, and found her waiting for me in the hotel lobby,—not the large, severe person I had imagined, but a small, enthusiastic, gracious little lady. She told me that my room was all ready and that the bath that I had demanded was connected with it, and that she had ordered some coffee sent up, but that I could have anything else that I chose. She began with a flood of questions—how was her poor dear son, and her daughter in London? And had we lost much money at Monte Carlo? And had we been very nice and quiet in Paris? And had I had a pleasant trip? And was it very cold in Paris? And would I like to go with her here and there for a few days, particularly until I was acclimated and able to find my own way about? I answered her freely and rapidly, for I took a real liking to her and decided at once that I was going to have a very nice time—she was so motherly and friendly. It struck me as delightful that she should wait up for me, and see that I was welcomed and comfortably housed; I can see her now with a loving memory in her charming gray silk dress and black lace shawl.

The first morning I arose in Rome it was raining; but to my joy, in an hour or two the sun came out and I saw a very peculiar city. Rome has about the climate of Monte Carlo, except that it is a little more changeable, and in the mornings and evenings quite chill. Around noon every day it was very warm—almost invariably bright, deliciously bright; but dark and cool where the buildings or the trees cast a shadow. I was awakened by huzzaing which I learned afterwards was for some officer who had lately returned from Morocco.

Like the English, the Italians are not yet intimately acquainted with the bathroom, and this particular hotel reminded me of the one in Manchester with its bath chambers as large as ordinary living-rooms. My room looked out into an inner court, which was superimposed upon the lobby of the hotel, and was set with palms and flowers which flourished mightily. I looked out through an opening in this court to some brown buildings over the way—brown as only the Italians know how to paint them, and bustling with Italian life.

Mrs. Barfleur had kindly volunteered to show me about this first day, and I was to meet her promptly at ten in the lobby. She wanted me to take a street car to begin with, because there was one that went direct to St. Peter's along the Via Nazionale, and because there were so many things she could show me that way. We went out into the public square which adjoined the hotel and there it was that she pointed out the Museo delle Terme, located in the ancient baths of Diocletian, and assured me that the fragments of wall that I saw jutting out from between buildings in one or two places dated from the Roman Empire. The fragment of the wall of Servius Tullius which we encountered in the Via Nazionale dates from 578 B. C., and the baths of Diocletian, so close to the hotel, from 303 A. D. The large ruin that I had seen the night before on entering the city was a temple to Minerva Medica, dating from about 250 A. D. I shall never forget my sensation on seeing modern stores—drug stores, tobacco stores, book stores, all with bright clean windows, adjoining these very ancient ruins. It was something for the first time to see a fresh, well-dressed modern throng going about its morning's business amid these rude suggestions of a very ancient life.

Nearly all the traces of ancient Rome, however, were apparently obliterated, and you saw only busy, up-to-date thoroughfares, with street cars, shops, and a gay metropolitan life generally. I have to smile when I think that I mistook a section of the old wall of Servius Tullius for the remnants of a warehouse which had recently been removed. All the time in Rome I kept suffering this impression—that I was looking at something which had only recently been torn down, when as a matter of fact I was looking at the earlier or later walls of the ancient city or the remnants of famous temples and baths. This particular street car line on which we were riding was a revelation in its way, for it was full of black-frocked priests in shovel hats, monks in brown cowls and sandals, and Americans and English old maids in spectacles who carried their Baedekers with severe primness and who were, like ourselves, bound for the Vatican. The conductors, it struck me, were a trifle more civil than the American brand, but not much; and the native passengers were a better type of Italian than we usually see in America. I sighted the Italian policeman at different points along the way—not unlike the Parisian gendarme in his high cap and short cape. The most striking characteristic, however, was the great number of priests and soldiers who were much more numerous than policemen and taxi drivers in New York. It seemed to me that on this very first morning I saw bands of priests going to and fro in all directions, but, for the rest of it, Rome was not unlike Monte Carlo and Paris combined, only that its streets were comparatively narrow and its colors high.

Mrs. Barfleur was most kindly and industrious in her explanations. She told me that in riding down this Via Nazionale we were passing between those ancient hills, the Quirinale and the Viminale, by the Forum of Trajan, the Gallery of Modern Art, the palaces of the Aldobrandini and Rospigliosi, and a score of other things which I have forgotten. When we reached the open square which faces St. Peter's, I expected to be vastly impressed by my first glimpse of the first Roman Church of the world; but in a way I was very much disappointed. To me it was not in the least beautiful, as Canterbury was beautiful, as Amiens was beautiful, and as Pisa was beautiful. I was not at all enthusiastic over the semicircular arcade in front with its immense columns. I knew that I ought to think it was wonderful, but I could not. I think in a way that the location and arrangement of the building does not do it justice, and it has neither the somber gray of Amiens nor the delicate creamy hue of the buildings of Pisa. It is brownish and gray by turns. As I drove nearer I realized that it was very large—astonishingly large—and that by some hocus-pocus of perspective and arrangement this was not easily realizable. I was eager to see its interior, however, and waived all exterior consideration until later.

As we were first going up the steps of St. Peter's and across the immense stone platform that leads to the door, a small Italian wedding-party arrived, without any design of being married there, however; merely to visit the various shrines and altars. The gentleman was somewhat self-conscious in a long black frock coat and high hat—a little, brown, mustached, dapper man whose patent leather shoes sparkled in the sun. The lady was a rosy Italian girl, very much belaced and besilked, with a pert, practical air; a little velvet-clad page carried her train. There were a number of friends—the parents on both sides, I took it—and some immediate relatives who fell solemnly in behind, two by two; and together this little ant-like band crossed the immense threshold. Mrs. Barfleur and I followed eagerly after—or at least I did, for I fancied they were to be married here and I wanted to see how it was to be done at St. Peter's. I was disappointed, however; for they merely went from altar to altar and shrine to shrine, genuflecting, and finally entered the sacred crypt, below which the bones of St. Peter are supposed to be buried. It was a fine religious beginning to what I trust has proved a happy union.

St. Peter's, if I may be permitted to continue a little on that curious theme, is certainly the most amazing church in the world. It is not beautiful—I am satisfied that no true artist would grant that; but after you have been all over Europe and have seen the various edifices of importance, it still sticks in your mind as astounding, perhaps the most astounding of all. While I was in Rome I learned by consulting guide-books, attending lectures and visiting the place myself, that it is nothing more than a hodge-podge of the vagaries and enthusiasms of a long line of able pontiffs. To me the Catholic Church has such a long and messy history of intrigue and chicanery that I for one cannot contemplate its central religious pretensions with any peace of mind. I am not going into the history of the papacy, nor the internecine and fratricidal struggles of medieval Italy; but what veriest tyro does not grasp the significance of what I mean? Julius II, flanking a Greek-cross basilica with a hexastyle portico to replace the Constantinian basilica, which itself had replaced the oratory of St. Anacletus on this spot, and that largely to make room for his famous tomb which was to be the finest thing in it; Urban VIII melting down the copper roof of the Panthéon portico in order to erect the showy baldachino! I do not now recall what ancient temples were looted for marble nor what popes did the looting, but that it was plentifully done I am satisfied and Van Ranke will bear me out. It was Julius II and Leo X who resorted to the sale of indulgences, which aided in bringing about the Reformation, for the purpose of paying the enormous expenses connected with the building of this lavish structure. Think of how the plans of Bramante and Michelangelo and Raphael and Carlo Maderna were tossed about between the Latin cross and the Greek cross and between a portico of one form and a portico of another form! Wars, heartaches, struggles, contentions—these are they of which St. Peter's is a memorial. As I looked at the amazing length—six hundred and fifteen feet—and the height of the nave—one hundred and fifty-two feet—and the height of the dome from the pavement in the interior to the roof—four hundred and five feet—and saw that the church actually contained forty-six immense altars and read that it contained seven hundred and forty-eight columns of marble, stone or bronze, three hundred and eighty-six statues and two hundred and ninety windows, I began to realize how astounding the whole thing was. It was really so large, and so tangled historically, and so complicated in the history of its architectural development, that it was useless for me to attempt to synchronize its significance in my mind. I merely stared, staggered by the great beauty and value of the immense windows, the showy and astounding altars. I came back again and again; but I got nothing save an unutterable impression of overwhelming grandeur. It is far too rich in its composition for mortal conception. No one, I am satisfied, truly completely realizes how *grand* it is. It answers to that word exactly. Browning's poem, "The Bishop Orders His Tomb at St. Praxed's," gives a faint suggestion of what any least bit of it is like. Any single tomb of any single pope—of which it seemed to me there were no end—might have had this poem written about it. Each one appears to have desired a finer tomb than the other; and I can understand the eager enthusiasm of Sixtus V (1588), who kept eight hundred men working night and day on the dome in order to see how it was going to look. And well he might. Murray tells the story of how on one occasion, being in want of another receptacle for water, the masons tossed the body of Urban VI out of his sarcophagus, put aside his bones in a corner, and gave the ring on his finger to the architect. The pope's remains were out of their receptacle for fifteen years or more before they were finally restored.

The Vatican sculptural and art museums were equally astonishing. I had always heard of its eleven hundred rooms and its priceless collections; but it was thrilling and delightful to see them face to face, all the long line of Greek and Roman and medieval perfections, chiseled or painted, transported from ruins or dug from the earth—such wonders as the porphyry vase and Laocoon, taken from the silent underground rooms of Nero's house, where they had stood for centuries, unheeded, in all their perfection; and the river god, representative of the Tiber. I was especially interested to see the vast number of portrait busts of Roman personalities—known and unknown—which gave me a face-to-face understanding of that astounding people. They came back now or arose vital before me—Claudius, Nerva, Hadrian, Faustina the elder, wife of Antoninus Pius, Pertinax, whose birthplace was near Monte Carlo, Julius Cæsar, Cicero, Antoninus Pius, Tiberius, Mark Antony, Aurelius Lepidus, and a score of others. It was amazing to me to see how like the modern English and Americans they were, and how practical and present-day-like they appeared. It swept away the space of two thousand years as having no significance whatever, and left you face to face with the far older problem of humanity. I could not help thinking that the duplicates of these men are on our streets to-day in New York and Chicago and London—urgent, calculating, thinking figures—and that they are doing to-day much as these forerunners did two thousand years before. I cannot see the slightest difference between an emperor like Hadrian and a banker like Morgan. And the head of a man like Lord Salisbury is to be found duplicated in a score of sculptures in various museums throughout the Holy City. I realized, too, that any one of hundreds of these splendid marbles, if separated from their populous surroundings and given to a separate city, meager in artistic possessions, would prove a great public attraction. To him that hath shall be given, however; and to those that have not shall be taken away even the little that they have. And so it is that Rome fairly suffocates with its endless variety of artistic perfection—one glory almost dimming the other—while the rest of the world yearns for a crust of artistic beauty and has nothing. It is like the Milky Way for jewels as contrasted with those vast starless spaces that give no evidence of sidereal life.

I wandered in this region of wonders attended by my motherly friend until it was late in the afternoon, and then we went for lunch. Being new to Rome, I was not satisfied with what I had seen, but struck forth again—coming next into the region of Santa Maria Maggiore and up an old stairway that had formed a part of a Medici palace now dismantled—only to find myself shortly thereafter and quite by accident in the vicinity of the Colosseum. I really had not known that I was coming to it, for I was not looking for it. I was following idly the lines of an old wall that lay in the vicinity of San Pietro in Vincoli when suddenly it appeared, lying in a hollow at the foot of a hill—the Esquiline. I was rejoicing in having discovered an old well that I knew must be of very ancient date, and a group of cypresses that showed over an ancient wall, when I looked—and there it was. It was exactly as the pictures have represented it—oval, many-arched, a thoroughly ponderous ruin. I really did not gain a suggestion of the astonishing size of it until I came down the hill, past tin cans that were lying on the grass—a sign of the modernity that possesses Rome—and entered through one of the many arches. Then it came on me—the amazing thickness of the walls, the imposing size and weight of the fragments, the vast dignity of the uprising flights of seats, and the great space now properly cleared, devoted to the arena. All that I ever knew or heard of it came back as I sat on the cool stones and looked about me while other tourists walked leisurely about, their Baedekers in their hands. It was a splendid afternoon. The sun was shining down in here; and it was as warm as though it were May in Indiana. Small patches of grass and moss were detectable everywhere, growing soft and green between the stones. The five thousand wild beasts slaughtered in the arena at its dedication, which remained as a thought from my high-school days, were all with me. I read up as much as I could, watching several workmen lowering themselves by ropes from the top of the walls, the while they picked out little tufts of grass and weeds beginning to flourish in the earthy niches. Its amazing transformations from being a quarry for greedy popes by whom most of its magnificent marbles were removed, to its narrow escape from becoming a woolen-mill operated by Sixtus V, were all brooded over here. It was impossible not to be impressed by the thought of the emperors sitting on their especial balcony; the thousands upon thousands of Romans intent upon some gladiatorial feat; the guards outside the endless doors, the numbers of which can still be seen, giving entrance to separate sections and tiers of seats; and the vast array of civic life which must have surged about. I wondered whether there were venders who sold sweets or food and what their cries were in Latin. One could think of the endless procession that wound its way here on gala days. Time works melancholy changes.

I left as the sun was going down, tremendously impressed with the wonder of a life that is utterly gone. It was like finding the glistening shell of an extinct beetle or the suggestion in rocks of a prehistoric world. As I returned to my hotel along the thoroughly modern streets with their five- and six-story tenement and apartment buildings, their street cars and customary vehicles, their newspaper, flower and cigar stands, I tried to restore and keep in my mind a suggestion of the magnificence that Gibbon makes so significant. It was hard; for be one's imagination what it will, it is difficult to live outside of one's own day and hour. The lights already beginning to flourish in the smart shops, distracted my mood.

CHAPTER XXXII
MRS. Q. AND THE BORGIA FAMILY

"I AM going to introduce you to such a nice woman," Mrs. Barfleur told me the second morning I was in Rome, in her very enthusiastic way. "She is charming. I am sure you will like her. She comes from America somewhere—New York, I think. Her husband is an author, I believe. I heard so." She chattered on in her genial, talk-making way. "I don't understand these American women; they go traveling about Europe without their husbands in such a strange way. Now, you know in England we would not think of doing anything of that kind."

Mrs. Barfleur was decidedly conservative in her views and English in manner and speech, but she had the saving proclivity of being intensely interested in life, and realized that all is not gold that glitters. She preferred to be among people who know and maintain good form, who are interested in maintaining the social virtues as they stand accepted and who, if they do not actually observe all of the laws and tenets of society, at least maintain a deceiving pretense. She had a little coterie of friends in the hotel, as I found, and friends outside, such as artists, newspaper correspondents and officials connected with the Italian court and the papal court. I never knew a more industrious social mentor in the shape of a woman, though among men her son outstripped her. She was apparently here, there and everywhere about the hotel, in the breakfast-room, in the dining-room, in the card-room, in the writing-room, greeting her friends, planning games, planning engagements, planning sightseeing trips. She was pleasant, too; delightful; for she knew what to do and when to do it, and if she was not impelled by a large constructive motive of any kind, nevertheless she had a sincere and discriminating love of the beautiful which caused her to excuse much for the sake of art. I found her well-disposed, kindly, sympathetic and very anxious to make the best of this sometimes dull existence, not only for herself, but for every one else. I liked her very much.

Mrs. Q. I found on introduction, to be a beautiful woman of perhaps thirty-three or four, with two of the healthiest, prettiest, best-behaved children I have ever seen. I found her to be an intellectual and brilliant woman with an overwhelming interest in the psychology of history and current human action.

"I trust I see an unalienated American," I observed as Mrs. Barfleur brought her forward, encouraged by her brisk, quizzical smile.

"You do, you do," she replied smartly, "as yet. Nothing has happened to my Americanism except Italy, and that's only a second love."

She had a hoarse little laugh which was nevertheless agreeable. I felt the impact of a strong, vital temperament, self-willed, self-controlled, intensely eager and ambitious. I soon discovered she was genuinely interested in history, which is one of my great failings and delights. She liked vital, unillusioned biography such as that of Jean Jacques Rousseau's Confessions, Cellini's Diary, and the personal reminiscences of various court favorites in different lands. She was interested in some plays, but cared little for fiction, which I take to be commendable. Her great passion at the moment, she told me, was the tracing out in all its ramifications of the history and mental attitude of the Borgia family especially Cæsar and Lucrezia—which I look upon as a remarkable passion for a woman. It takes a strong, healthy, clear-thinking temperament to enjoy the mental vagaries of the Borgias—father, son and daughter. She had conceived a sincere admiration for the courage, audacity, passion and directness of action of Cæsar, to say nothing of the lymphatic pliability and lure of Lucrezia, and the strange philosophic anarchism and despotic individualism of their father, Alexander VI.

I wonder how much the average reader knows of the secret history of the Borgias. It is as modern as desire, as strange as the strangest vagaries of which the mind is capable. I am going to give here the outline of the Borgia family history as Mrs. Q. crisply related it to me, on almost the first evening we met, for I, like so many Americans, while knowing something of these curious details in times past had but the haziest recollection then. To be told it in Rome itself by a breezy American who used the vernacular and who simply could not suppress her Yankee sense of humor, was as refreshing an experience as occurred in my whole trip. Let me say first that Mrs. Q. admired beyond words the Italian subtlety, craft, artistic insight, political and social wisdom, governing ability, and as much as anything their money-getting and money-keeping capacities. The raw practicality of this Italian family thrilled her.

You will remember that Rodrigo Lanzol, a Spaniard who afterwards assumed the name of Rodrigo Borgia, because his maternal uncle of that name was fortunate enough to succeed to the papacy as Calixtus III, and could do him many good turns afterwards, himself succeeded to the papacy by bribery and other outrages under the title of Alexander VI. That was August 10, 1442. Before that, however, as nephew to Calixtus III, he had been made bishop, cardinal, and vice-chancellor of the Church solely because he was a relative and favored by his uncle; and all this before he was thirty-five. He had proceeded to Rome, established himself with many mistresses at his call in a magnificent palace, and at the age of thirty-seven, his uncle Calixtus III having died, was reprimanded by Pius II, the new pope, for his riotous and adulterous life. By 1470, when he was forty-nine he took to himself, as his favorite, Vanozza dei Cattani, the former wife of three different husbands. By Vanozza, who was very charming, he had four children, all of whom he prized highly—Giovanni, afterwards Duke of Gandia, born 1474; Cæsar, 1476; Lucrezia, 1480; Geoffreddo or Giuffré, born 1481 or 1482. There were other children—Girolamo, Isabella and Pier Luigi, whose parentage on the mother's side is uncertain; and still another child, Laura, whom he acquired via Giulia Farnese, the daughter of the famous family of that name, who was his mistress after he tired, some years later, of Vanozza. Meanwhile his children had grown up or were fairly well-grown when he became pope, which opened the most astonishing chapter of the history of this strange family.

Alexander was a curious compound of paternal affection, love of gold, love of women, vanity, and other things. He certainly was fond of his children or he would not have torn Italy with dissension in order to advantage them in their fortunes. His career is the most ruthless and weird of any that I know.

He was no sooner pope (about April, 1493) than he proposed to carve out careers for his family—his favored children by his favorite mistress. In 1492, the same year he was made pope, he created Cæsar, his sixteen-year-old son, studying at Pisa, a cardinal, showing the state of the papacy in those days. He proposed to marry his daughter Lucrezia well, and having the year before, when she was only eleven, betrothed her to one Don Cherubin de Centelles, a Spaniard, he broke this arrangement and had Lucrezia married by proxy to Don

Gasparo de Procida, son of the Count of Aversa, a man of much more importance, who, he thought, could better advance her fortune.

Italy, however, was in a very divided and disorganized state. There was a King of Naples, a Duke of Venice, a Duke of Milan, a separate state life at Pisa, Genoa, Florence and elsewhere. In order to build himself up and become very powerful, and to give preferment to each of his sons, some of these states had to be conquered and controlled; and so the old gentleman, without conscience and without mercy except as suited his whim, was for playing politics, making war, exercising treachery, murdering, poisoning, persuading, bribing—anything and everything to obtain his ends. He must have been well thought of as a man of his word, for when he had made a deal with Charles VIII of France to assist him in invading and conquering Naples, the king demanded and obtained Cæsar, Alexander's son, aged twenty-one, as a hostage for faithful performance of agreement. He had not taken him very far, however, before the young devil escaped and returned to Rome, where subsequently his father, finding it beneficial to turn against the King of France, did so.

But to continue. While his father was politicking and trafficking in this way for the benefit of himself and his dear family, young Cæsar was beginning to develop a few thoughts and tendencies of his own. Alexander VI was planning to create fiefs or dukedoms out of the papal states and out of the Kingdom of Naples and give them to his eldest son, Giovanni, and his youngest, Giuffré. Cæsar would have none of this. He saw himself as a young cardinal being left out in the cold. Besides, there was a cause of friction between him and his brother Giovanni over the affections of their youngest brother Giuffré's wife, Sancha. They were both sharing the latter's favors, and so one day, in order to clear matters up and teach his father (whose favorite he was) where to bestow his benefits and so that he might have Sancha all to himself—he murdered his brother Giovanni. The latter's body, after a sudden and strange absence, was found in the Tiber, knife-marked, and all was local uproar until the young cardinal was suspected, when matters quieted down and nothing more was thought of it. There was also thought to be some rivalry between Cæsar and Giovanni over the affections of their sister Lucrezia.

After this magnificent evidence of ability, the way was clear for Cæsar. He was at once (July, 1497) sent as papal legate to Naples to crown Frederick of Aragon; and it was while there that he met Carlotta, the daughter of the king, and wanted to marry her. She would have none of him. "What, marry that priest, that bastard of a priest!" she is alleged to have said; and that settled the matter. This may have had something to do with Cæsar's desire to get out of Holy Orders and return to civil life, for the next year (1498) he asked leave of the papal consistory not to be a cardinal any longer and was granted this privilege "for the good of his soul." He then undertook the pleasant task, as papal legate, of carrying to Louis XII of France the pope's bull annulling the marriage of Louis with Jeanne of France in order that he might marry Anne of Brittany. On this journey he met Charlotte d'Albret, sister of the King of Navarre, whom he married. He was given the duchy of Valentinois for his gracious service to Louis XII and, loaded with honors, returned to Rome in order to further his personal fortunes with his father's aid.

In the meanwhile there were a number of small principalities in Romagna, a territory near Milan, which his father Alexander VI was viewing with a covetous eye. One of these was controlled by Giovanni Sforza, Lord of Pesaro, whom Alexander, at a time when he wanted to pit the strength of Milan against the subtle machinations of the King of Naples—caused Lucrezia his daughter, then only thirteen years of age, to marry, her union with the Count of Aversa having by this time been severed. Alexander having won the friendship of the King of Naples, he decided to proceed against the princelings of Romagna and confiscated their property. Cæsar was tolled off as general to accomplish this for himself, being provided men and means. Young Sforza, who had married Lucrezia, found himself in a treacherous position,—his own brother-in-law, with the assistance of his father-in-law, plotting against his life,—and fled with his wife, the fair Lucrezia, aged fifteen, to Pesaro. There he was fought by Cæsar who, however, not having sufficient troops was checked for the time being and returned to Rome. A year or so later, Pope Alexander being in a gentler frame of mind—it was Christmas and he desired all his children about him—invited them all home, including Lucrezia and her husband. Then followed a series of magnificent fêtes and exhibitions in honor of all this at Rome, and the family, including the uncertain son-in-law, husband of Lucrezia, seemed to be fairly well united in bonds of peace.

Unfortunately, however, a little later (1497) the pope's mood changed again. He was now, after some intermediate quarrels, once more friendly with the King of Naples and decided that Sforza was no longer a fit husband for Lucrezia. Then came the annulment of this marriage and the remarriage of Lucrezia to Alphonso of Aragon, Duke of Bisceglie, a relative and favorite of the King of Naples, aged eighteen and handsome. But, alas! no sooner is this fairly begun than new complications arise. The pope thinks he sees an opportunity to destroy the power of Naples as a rival with the aid of the King of France, Louis XII. He lends assistance to the latter, who comes to invade Naples, and young Bisceglie, now fearing for his life at the hands of his treacherous father-in-law, deserts Rome and Lucrezia and flees. Louis XII proceeds against Naples. Spoleto falls and Lucrezia, Bisceglie's wife, as representative of the pope (aged eighteen) is sent to receive the homage of Spoleto!

But the plot merely thickens. There comes a nice point in here on which historians comment variously. Incest is the basis. It was one time assumed that Alexander, the father, during all these various shifts treated his daughter as his mistress. Her brother Cæsar also bore the same relation to her. Father and son were rivals, then, for the affections and favors of the daughter-sister. To offset the affections of the son the father has the daughter lure her husband, Bisceglie, back to Rome. From all accounts he was very much in love with his wife who was beautiful but dangerous because of her charms and the manner in which she was coveted by others. In 1499, when he was twenty and Cæsar twenty-three, he was lured back and the next year, because of Cæsar's jealousy of his monopoly of his own wife (Cæsar being perhaps denied his usual freedom) Bisceglie was stabbed while going up the steps of the papal palace by Cæsar Borgia, his brother-in-law, and that in the presence of his father-in-law, Alexander VI, the pope of Rome. According to one account, on sight of Cæsar, jumping out from behind a column, Alphonso sought refuge behind Alexander, the pope, who spread out his purple robe to protect him, through which Cæsar drove his knife into the bosom of his brother-in-law. The dear old father and father-in-law was severely shocked. He was quite depressed, in fact. He shook his head dismally. The wound was not fatal, however. Bisceglie was removed to the house of a cardinal near-by, where he was attended by his wife, Lucrezia, and his sister-in-law, Sancha, wife of Giuffré, both of whom he apparently feared a little, for they were compelled first to partake of all food presented in order to prove that it was not poisoned. In this house—in this sick-chamber doorway—suddenly and unexpectedly one day there appears the figure of Cæsar. The ensuing scene (Lucrezia and Sancha present) is not given. Bisceglie is stabbed in his bed and this time dies. Is the crime avenged? Not at all. This is Papa Alexander's own dominion. This is a family affair, and father is very fond of Cæsar, so the matter is hushed up.

Witness the interesting final chapters. Cæsar goes off, October, 1500, to fight the princes in Romagna once more, among whom are Giovanni, and Sforza, one of Lucrezia's ex-husbands. July, 1501, Alexander leaves the papal palace in Rome to fight the Colonna, one of the two powerful families of Rome, with the assistance of the other powerful family, the Orsini. In his absence Lucrezia, his beloved, is acting-pope! January first (or thereabouts), 1501, Lucrezia is betrothed to Alphonso, son and heir to Ercole d'Este, whose famous villa near Rome is still to be seen. Neither Alphonso nor his father was anxious for this union, but Papa Alexander, Pope of Rome, has set his heart on it. By bribes and threats he brings about a proxy marriage—Alphonso not being present—celebrated with great pomp at St. Peter's. January, 1502, Lucrezia arrives in the presence of her new husband who falls seriously in love with her. Her fate is now to settle down, and no further tragedies befall on account of her, except one. A certain Ercole Strozzi, an Italian noble, appears on the scene and falls violently in love with her. She is only twenty-three or four even now. Alphonso d'Este, her new husband, becomes violently jealous and murders Ercole. Result: further peace until her death in 1511 in her thirty-ninth year, during which period she had four children by Alphonso—three boys and one girl.

As for brother Cæsar he was, unfortunately, leading a more checkered career. On December 21, 1502, when he was only twenty-six, as a general fighting the allied minor princes in Romagna, he caused to be strangled in his headquarters at Senigallia, Vitellozzo Viletti and Oliveralto da Fermo, two princelings who with others had conspired against him some time before at Perugia. Awed by his growing power, they had been so foolish as to endeavor to placate him by capturing Senigallia for him from their allies and presenting it to him and allowing themselves to be lured to his house by protestations of friendship. Result: strangulation.

August 18, 1503, Father Borgia, Pope Alexander VI, charming society figure, polished gentleman, lover of the chase, patron of the arts, for whom Raphael, Michelangelo and Brabante had worked, breathes his last. He and Cæsar had fallen desperately sick at the same time of a fever. When Cæsar recovers sufficiently to attend to his affairs, things are already in a bad way. The cardinals are plotting to seat a pope unfriendly to the Borgias. The Spanish cardinals on whom he has relied do not prove friendly and he loses his control. The funds which Papa Borgia was wont to supply for his campaigns are no longer forthcoming. Pope Julius II succeeding to the throne, takes away from Cæsar the territories assigned to him by his father "for the honor of recovering what our predecessors have wrongfully alienated." In May, 1504, having gone to Naples on a safe conduct for the Spanish governor of that city, he is arrested and sent to Spain, where he is thrown into prison. At the end of two years he manages to escape and flees to the court of his brother-in-law, the King of Navarre, who permits him to aid in besieging the castle of a refractory subject. Here, March 12, 1507, while Lucrezia elsewhere is peacefully residing with her spouse, he is killed.

I have given but a feeble outline of this charming Renaissance idyl. Mixed in with it are constant murders or poisonings of wealthy cardinals and the confiscation of their estates whenever cash for the prosecution of Cæsar's wars or the protection of papal properties are needed. The uxorious and child-loving old pope was exceedingly nonchalant about these little matters of human life. When he died there was a fight over his coffin between priests of different factions and mercenaries belonging to Cæsar Borgia. The coffin being too short, his body was jammed down in it, minus his miter, and finally upset. Think of so much ambition coming to such a shameful end! He achieved his desire, however. He wrote his name large, if not in fame, at least in infamy. He lived in astonishing grandeur and splendor. By his picturesque iniquities he really helped to bring about the Reformation. He had a curious affection for his children and he died immensely rich—and, pope. The fair Lucrezia stands out as a strange chemical magnet of disaster. To love her was fear, disappointment, or death. And it was she and her brother Cæsar, who particularly interested Mrs. Q., although the aged Alexander amused her.

During her vigorous recital I forgot the corner drug store and modern street cars of Rome, enthralled by the glamour of the ancient city. It was a delight to find that we had an intellectual affinity in the study of the vagaries of this strange phantasmagoria called human life, in which to be dull is to be a bond-slave, and to be wise is to be a mad philosopher, knowing neither right from wrong nor black from white.

Together Mrs. Q. and I visited the Borghese and Barberini Palaces, the Villa Doria, the Villa Umberto, the Villa d'Este and the Appian Way. We paid a return visit to the Colosseum and idled together in the gardens of the Pincian, the paths of the Gianicolo, the gardens of the Vatican and along the Tiber. It was a pleasure to step into some old court of a palace where the walls were encrusted with fragments of monuments, inscriptions, portions of sarcophagi and the like, found on the place or in excavating, and set into the walls to preserve them—and to listen to this clever, wholesome woman comment on the way the spirit of life builds shells and casts them off. She was not in the least morbid. The horror and cruelties of lust and ambition held no terrors for her. She liked life as a spectacle.

CHAPTER XXXIII
THE ART OF SIGNOR TANNI

THE first Sunday I was in Rome I began my local career with a visit to the church of Santa Maria Maggiore, that faces the Via Cavour not far from the Continental Hotel where I was stopping, and afterwards San Prassede close beside it. After Canterbury, Amiens, Pisa and St. Peter's, I confess churches needed to be of great distinction to interest me much; but this church, not so divinely harmonious, exteriorly speaking, left me breathless with its incrustations of marbles, bronzes, carvings, and gold and silver inlay. There is a kind of beauty, or charm, or at least physical excitation, in contemplating sheer gorgeousness which I cannot withstand, even when my sense of proportion and my reason are offended, and this church had that. Many of the churches in Rome have just this and nothing more. At least, what else they may have I am blind to. It did not help me any to learn as I did from Mrs. Barfleur, that it was very old, dating from 352 A. D., and that the blessed Virgin herself had indicated just where this basilica in her honor was to be built by having a small, private fall of snow which covered or outlined the exact dimensions of which the church was to be. I was interested to learn that they had here five boards of the original manger at Bethlehem inclosed in an urn of silver and crystal which is exposed in the sacristy on Christmas Eve and placed over the high altar on Christmas Day, and that here were the tombs and chapels of Sixtus V and Paul V and Clement VIII of the Borghese family and, too, a chapel of the Sforza family. Nevertheless the hodge-podge of history, wealth, illusion and contention, to say nothing of religious and social discovery, which go to make up a church of this kind, is a little wearisome, not to say brain-achey, when contemplated en masse. These churches! Unless you are especially interested in a pope or a saint or a miracle or a picture or a monument or an artist—they are nothing save intricate jewel-boxes; nothing more.

For the first five or six days thereafter I went about with a certain Signor Tanni who was delivering peripatetic lectures at the principal places of interest in Rome. This is a curious development of the modern city, for so numerous are the travelers and so great their interest in the history of Rome that they gladly pay the three to twelve lire each, which is charged by the various lecturers for their discussions and near-by trips. There was a Nashville, Tennessee, chicken-and-egg merchant who, with his wife, was staying at our hotel and who was making the matter of seeing Rome quite as much of a business as that of chickens and eggs in Tennessee. He was a man of medium height, dark, pale, neat, and possessed of that innate courtesy, reserve, large-minded fairness and lively appreciation—within set convictions—which is so characteristic of the native, reasonably successful American. We are such innocent, pure-minded Greeks—most of us Americans. In the face of such tawdry vulgarity and vileness as comprises the underworld café life of Paris, or before such a spectacle of accentuated craft, lust, brutality, and greed as that presented by the Borgias, a man such as my chicken-merchant friend, or any other American of his type, of whom there are millions, would find himself utterly nonplused. It would be so much beyond his ken, or intention, that I question whether he would see or understand it at all if it were taking place before his very eyes. There is something so childlike and pure about the attitude of many strong, able Americans that I marvel sometimes that they do as well as they do. Perhaps their very innocence is their salvation. I could not have told this chicken-merchant and his wife, for instance, anything of the subtleties of the underworld of Paris and Monte Carlo as I encountered them; and if I had he would not have believed me, he would have recoiled from it all as a burned child would recoil from fire. He was as simple and interesting and practical as a man could be, and yet so thoroughly efficient that at the age of forty-five he had laid by a competence and was off on a three years' tour of the world.

Mrs. Chicken Merchant was a large woman—very stout, very fair, very cautious of her thoughts and her conduct, thoroughly sympathetic and well-meaning. Before leaving her native town, she told me, she had inaugurated a small library, the funds for which she had helped collect. Occasionally she was buying engravings of famous historic buildings, such as the Colosseum and the Temple of Vesta, which would eventually grace the walls of the library. She and her husband felt that they were educating themselves; and that they would return better citizens, more useful to their country, for this exploration of the ancient world. They had been going each day, morning and afternoon, to some lecture or ancient ruin; and after I came they would seek me out of an evening and tell me what they had seen. I took great satisfaction in this, because I really liked them for their naïve point of view and their thoroughly kindly and whole-hearted interest in life. It flattered me to think that I was so acceptable to them and that we should get along so well together. Frequently they invited me to their table to dinner. On these occasions my friend would open a bottle of wine, concerning which he had learned something since he had come abroad.

It was Mr. and Mrs. Chicken Merchant who gave me a full description of the different Roman lecturers, their respective merits, their prices, and what they had to show. They had already been to the Forum, the Palatine, the Colosseum and the House of Nero, St. Peter's, the Castle of St. Angelo, the Appian Way, the Catacombs and the Villa Frascati. They were just going to the Villa d'Este and to Ostia, the old seaport at the mouth of the Tiber. They were at great pains to get me to join the companies of Signor Tanni who, they were convinced, was the best of them all. "He tells you something. He makes you see it just as it was. By George! when we were in the Colosseum you could just fairly see the lions marching out of those doors; and that House of Nero, as he tells about it, is one of the most wonderful things in the world."

I decided to join Signor Tanni's classes at once, and persuaded Mrs. Barfleur and Mrs. Q. to accompany me at different times. I must say that in spite of the commonplaceness of the idea my mornings and afternoons with Signor Tanni and his company of sightseers proved as delightful as anything else that befell me in Rome. He was a most interesting person, born and brought up, as I learned, at Tivoli near the Villa d'Este, where his father controlled a small inn and livery stable. He was very stocky, very dark, very ruddy, and very active. Whenever we came to the appointed rendezvous where his lecture was to begin, he invariably arrived, swinging his coat-tails, glancing smartly around with his big black eyes, rubbing and striking his hands in a friendly manner, and giving every evidence of taking a keen interest in his work. He was always polite and courteous without being officious, and never for a moment either dull or ponderous. He knew his subject thoroughly of course; but what was much better, he had an eye for the dramatic and the spectacular. I shall never forget how in the center of the Forum Romanum he lifted the cap from the ancient manhole that opens into the Cloaca Maxima and allowed us to look in upon the walls of that great sewer that remains as it was built before the dawn of Roman history. Then he exclaimed dramatically: "The water that Cæsar and the emperors took their baths in no doubt flowed through here just as the water of Roman bath-tubs does to-day!"

On the Palatine, when we were looking at the site of the Palace of Elagabalus, he told how that weird worthy had a certain well, paved at the bottom with beautiful mosaic, in order that he might leap down upon it and thus commit suicide, but how he afterwards changed his mind—which won a humorous smile from some of those present and from others a blank look of astonishment. In the House of Nero, in one of those dark underhill chambers, which was once out in the clear sunlight, but now, because of the lapse of time and the crumbling of other structures reared above it, is deep under ground, he told how once, according to an idle legend, Nero had invited some of his friends to dine and when they were well along in their feast, and somewhat intoxicated, no doubt, it began to rain rose leaves from the ceiling. Nothing but delighted cries of approval was heard for this artistic thought until the rose leaves became an inch thick on the floor and then two and three, and four and five inches thick, when the guests tried the doors. They were locked and sealed. Then the shower continued until the rose leaves were a foot deep, two feet deep, three feet deep, and the tables were covered. Later the guests had to climb on tables and chairs to save themselves from their rosy bath; but when they had climbed this high they could climb no higher, for the walls were smooth and the room was thirty feet deep. By the time the leaves were ten feet deep the guests were completely covered; but the shower continued until the smothering weight of them ended all life.—An ingenious but improbable story.

No one of Signor Tanni's wide-mouthed company seemed to question whether this was plausible or not; and one American standing next to me exclaimed, "Well, I'll be switched!" My doubting mind set to work to figure out how I could have overcome this difficulty if I had been in the room; and in my mind I had all the associated guests busy tramping down rose leaves in order to make the quantity required as large as possible. My idea was that I could tire Nero out on this rose-leaf proposition. The picture of these noble Romans feverishly trampling down the fall of rose leaves cheered me greatly.

After my first excursion with Signor Tanni I decided to take his whole course; and followed dutifully along behind him, listening to his interesting and good-natured disquisitions, during many delightful mornings and afternoons in the Forum, on the Palatine, in the Catacombs, on the Appian Way and in the Villas at Frascati and Tivoli! I shall never forget how clearly and succinctly the crude early beginnings and characteristics of Christianity came home to me as I walked in the Catacombs and saw the wretched little graves hidden away in order that they might not be desecrated, and the underground churches where converts might worship free from molestation and persecution.

On the Palatine the fact that almost endless palaces were built one on top of the other, the old palace leveled by means of the sledge and the crowbar and the new one erected upon the smoothed-over space, is easily demonstrated. They find the remains of different ruins in different layers as they dig down, coming eventually to the early sanctuaries of the kings and the federated tribes. It is far more interesting to walk through these old ruins and underground chambers accompanied by some one who loves them, and who is interested in them, and who by fees to the state servitors has smoothed the way, so that the ancient forgotten chambers are properly lighted for you, than it is to go alone. And to have a friendly human voice expatiating on the probable arrangement of the ancient culinary department and how it was all furnished, is worth while. I know that the wonder and interest of the series of immense, dark rooms which were once the palace of Nero, and formerly were exposed to the light of day, before the dust and incrustation of centuries had been heaped upon them, but which now underlie a hill covered by trees and grass, came upon me with great force because of these human explanations; and the room in which, in loneliness and darkness for centuries stood the magnificent group of Laocoon and the porphyry vase now in the Vatican, until some adventuring students happened to put a foot through a hole, thrilled me as though I had come upon them myself. Until one goes in this way day by day to the site of the Circus Maximus, the Baths of Caracalla, the ruins of Hadrian's Villa, the Castle of St. Angelo, the Forum, the Palatine and the Colosseum, one can have no true conception of that ancient world. When you realize, by standing on the ground and contemplating these ancient ruins and their present fragments, that the rumored immensity of them in their heyday and youth is really true, you undergo an ecstasy of wonder; or if you are of a morbid turn you indulge in sad speculations as to the drift of life. I cannot tell you how the mosaics from the palace of Germanicus on the Palatine affected me, or how strange I felt when the intricacies of the houses of Caligula and Tiberius were made clear. To walk through the narrow halls which they trod, to know truly that they ruled in terror and with the force of murder, that Caligula waylaid and assaulted and killed, for his personal entertainment, in these narrow alleys which were then the only streets, and where torches borne by hand furnished the only light, is something. A vision of the hugeness and audacity of Hadrian's villa which now stretches apparently, one would say, for miles, the vast majority of its rooms still unexcavated and containing what treasures Heaven only knows, is one of the strangest of human experiences. I marveled at this vast series of rooms, envying the power, the subtlety and the genius which could command it. Truly it is unbelievable—one of those things which stagger the imagination. One can hardly conceive how even an emperor of Rome would build so beautifully and so vastly. Rome is so vast in its suggestion that it is really useless to apostrophize. That vast empire that stretched from India to the Arctic was surely fittingly represented here; and while we may rival the force and subtlety and genius and imagination of these men in our day, we will not truly outstrip them. Mind was theirs—vast, ardent imagination; and if they achieved crudely it was because the world was still young and the implements and materials of life were less understood. They were the great ones—the Romans. We must still learn from them.

CHAPTER XXXIV
AN AUDIENCE AT THE VATICAN

THE remainder of my days in Rome were only three or four. I had seen much of it that has been in no way indicated here. True to my promise I had looked up at his hotel my traveling acquaintance, the able and distinguished Mr. H., and had walked about some of the older sections of the city hearing him translate Greek and Latin inscriptions of ancient date with the ease with which I put my ordinary thought into English. Together we visited the Farnese Palace, the Mamertine Prison, the Temple of Vesta, Santa Maria in Cosmedin and other churches too numerous and too pointless to mention. It was interesting to me to note the facility of his learning and the depth of his philosophy. In spite of the fact that life, in the light of his truly immense knowledge of history and his examination of human motives, seemed a hodge-podge of contrarieties and of ethical contradictions, nevertheless he believed that through all the false witness and pretense and subtlety of the ages, through the dominating and apparently guiding impulses of lust and appetite and vanity, seemingly untrammeled by mercy, tenderness or any human consideration, there still runs a constructive, amplifying, art-enlarging, life-developing tendency which is comforting, dignifying, and purifying, making for larger and happier days for each and all. It did not matter to him that the spectacle as we read it historically is always one of the strong dominating the weak, of the strong battling with the strong, of greed, hypocrisy and lying. Even so, the world was moving on—to what he could not say,—we were coming into an ethical understanding of things. The mass was becoming more intelligent and better treated. Opportunity, of all sorts, was being more widely diffused, even if grudgingly so. We would never again have a Nero or a Caligula he thought—not on this planet. He called my attention to that very interesting agreement between leading families of the Achæan League in lower Greece in which it was stipulated that the "ruling class should be honored like gods" and that the subject class should be "held in subservience like beasts." He wanted to know if even a suspicion of such an attitude to-day would not cause turmoil. I tried out his philosophy by denying it, but he was firm. Life was better to him, not merely different as some might take it to be.

I gave a dinner at my hotel one evening in order to pay my respects to those who had been so courteous to me and put it in charge of Mrs. Barfleur, who was desirous of nothing better. She was fond of managing. Mrs. Q. sat at my left and Mrs. H. at my right and we made a gay hour out of history, philosophy, Rome, current character and travel. The literary executor of Oscar Wilde was present, Mr. Oscar Browning, and my Greek traveler and merchant, Mr. Bouris. An American publisher and his wife, then in Rome, had come, and we were as gay as philosophers and historians and antiquaries can be. Mr. H. drew a laugh by announcing that he never read a book under 1500 years of age any more, and the literary executor of Oscar Wilde told a story of the latter to the effect that the more he contemplated his own achievements, the more he came to admire himself, and the less use he had for other people's writings. One of the most delightful stories I have heard in years was told by H. who stated that an Italian thief, being accused of stealing three rings from the hands of a statue of the Virgin that was constantly working miracles, had declared that, as he was kneeling before her in solemn prayer, the Virgin had suddenly removed the rings from her finger and handed them to him. But the priests who were accusing him (servitors of the Church) and the judge who was trying him, all firm believers, would not accept this latest development of the miraculous tendencies of the image and he was sent to jail. Alas! that true wit should be so poorly rewarded.

One of the last things I did in Rome was to see the Pope. When I came there, Lent was approaching, and I was told that at this time the matter was rather difficult. None of my friends seemed to have the necessary influence, and I had about decided to give it up, when one day I met the English representative of several London dailies who told me that sometimes, under favorable conditions, he introduced his friends, but that recently he had overworked his privilege and could not be sure. On the Friday before leaving, however, I had a telephone message from his wife, saying that she was taking her cousin and would I come. I raced into my evening clothes though it was early morning and was off to her apartment in the Via Angelo Brunetti, from which we were to start.

Presentation to the Pope is one of those dull formalities made interesting by the enthusiasm of the faithful and the curiosity of the influential who are frequently non-catholic, but magnetized by the amazing history of the Papacy and the scope and influence of the Church. All the while that I was in Rome I could not help feeling the power and scope of this organization—much as I condemn its intellectual stagnation and pharisaism. Personally I was raised in the Catholic Church, but outgrew it at an early age. My father died a rapt believer in it and I often smile when I think how impossible it would have been to force upon him the true history of the Papacy and the Catholic hierarchy. His subjugation to priestly influence was truly a case of the blind leading the blind. To him the Pope was truly infallible. There could be no wrong in any Catholic priest, and so on and so forth. The lives of Alexander VI and Boniface VIII would have taught him nothing.

In a way, blind adherence to principles is justifiable, for we have not as yet solved the riddle of the universe and one may well agree with St. Augustine that the vileness of the human agent does not invalidate the curative or corrective power of a great principle. An evil doctor cannot destroy the value of medicine; a corrupt lawyer or judge cannot invalidate pure law. Pure religion and undefiled continues, whether there are evil priests or no, and the rise and fall of the Roman Catholic hierarchy has nothing to do with what is true in the teachings of Christ.

It was interesting to me as I walked about Rome to see the indications or suggestions of the wide-spread influence of the Catholic Church—priests from England, Ireland, Spain, Egypt and monks from Palestine, the Philippines, Arabia, and Africa. I was standing in the fair in the Campo dei Fiori, where every morning a vegetable-market is held and every Wednesday a fair where antiquities and curiosities of various lands are for sale, when an English priest, seeing my difficulties in connection with a piece of jewelry, offered to translate for me and a little later a French priest inquired in French whether I spoke his language. In the Colosseum I fell in with a German priest from Baldwinsville, Kentucky, who invited me to come and see a certain group of Catacombs on a morning when he intended to say mass there, which interested me but I was prevented by another engagement; and at the Continental there were stopping two priests from Buenos Ayres; and so it went. The car lines which led down the Via Nazionale to St. Peter's and the Vatican was always heavily patronized by priests, monks, and nuns; and I never went anywhere that I did not encounter groups of student-priests coming to and from their studies.

This morning that we drove to the papal palace at eleven was as usual bright and warm. My English correspondent and his wife, both extremely intelligent, had been telling of the steady changes in Rome, its rapid modernization, the influence of the then Jewish mayor in its civic improvement and the waning influence of the Catholics in the matter of local affairs. "All Rome is probably Catholic," he said, "or nearly so; but it isn't the kind of Catholicism that cares for papal influence in political affairs. Why, here not long ago, in a public speech the mayor charged that the papacy was the cause of Rome's being delayed at least a hundred years in its progress and there was lots of applause. The national parliament which meets here is full of Catholics but it is not interested in papal influence. It's all the other way about. They seem to be willing to let the Pope have his say in spiritual matters but he can't leave the Vatican and priests can't mix in political affairs very much."

I thought, what a change from the days of Gregory VII and even the popes of the eighteenth century!

The rooms of the Vatican devoted to the Pope—at least those to which the public is admitted at times of audience seemed to me merely large and gaudy without being impressive. One of the greatest follies of architecture, it seems to me, is the persistent thought that mere size without great beauty of form has any charm whatever. The Houses of Parliament in England are large but they are also shapely. As much might be said for the Palais Royal in Paris though not for the Louvre and almost not for Versailles. The Vatican is another great splurge of nothing—mere size without a vestige of charm as to detail.

All I remember of my visit was that arriving at the palace entrance we were permitted by papal guards to ascend immense flights of steps, that we went through one large red room after another where great chandeliers swung from the center and occasional decorations or over-elaborate objects of art appeared on tables or pedestals. There were crowds of people in each room, all in evening dress, the ladies with black lace shawls over their heads, the men in conventional evening clothes. Over-elaborately uniformed guards stood about, and prelates of various degrees of influence moved to and fro. We took our station in a room adjoining the Pope's private chambers where we waited patiently while various personages of influence and importance were privately presented.

It was dreary business waiting. Loud talking was not to be thought of, and the whispering on all sides as the company increased was oppressive. There was a group of ladies from Venice who were obviously friends of the Holy Father's family. There were two brown monks, barefooted and with long gray beards, patriarchal types, who stationed themselves by one wall near the door. There were three nuns and a mother superior from somewhere who looked as if they were lost in prayer. This was a great occasion to them. Next to me was a very official person in a uniform of some kind who constantly adjusted his neck-band and smoothed his gloved hands. Some American ladies, quite severe and anti-papistical if I am not mistaken, looked as if they were determined not to believe anything they saw, and two Italian women of charming manners had in tow an obstreperous small boy of say five or six years of age in lovely black velvet, who was determined to be as bad and noisy as he could. He beat his feet and asked questions in a loud whisper and decided that he wished to change his place of abode every three seconds; all of which was accompanied by many "sh-sh-es" from his elders and whisperings in his ear, severe frowns from the American ladies and general indications of disapproval, with here and there a sardonic smile of amusement.

Every now and then a thrill of expectation would go over the company. The Pope was coming! Papal guards and prelates would pass through the room with speedy movements and it looked as though we would shortly be in the presence of the vicar of Christ. I was told that it was necessary to rest on one knee at least, which I did, waiting patiently the while I surveyed the curious company. The two brown monks were appropriately solemn, their heads bent. The sisters were praying. The Italian ladies were soothing their restive charge. I told my correspondent-friend of the suicide of a certain journalist, whom he and his wife knew, on the day that I left New York—a very talented but adventurous man; and he exclaimed: "My God! don't tell that to my wife. She'll feel it terribly." We waited still longer and finally in sheer weariness began jesting foolishly; I said that it must be that the Pope and Merry del Val, the Pope's secretary, were inside playing jackstones with the papal jewels. This drew a convulsive laugh from my newspaper friend—I will call him W.—who began to choke behind his handkerchief. Mrs. W. whispered to me that if we did not behave we would be put out and I pictured myself and W. being unceremoniously hustled out by the forceful guards, which produced more laughter. The official beside me, who probably did not speak English, frowned solemnly. This produced a lull, and we waited a little while longer in silence. Finally the sixth or seventh thrill of expectation produced the Holy Father, the guards and several prelates making a sort of aisle of honor before the door. All whispering ceased. There was a rustle of garments as each one settled into a final sanctimonious attitude. He came in, a very tired-looking old man in white wool cassock and white skull cap, a great necklace of white beads about his neck and red shoes on his feet. He was stout, close knit, with small shrewd eyes, a low forehead, a high crown, a small, shapely chin. He had soft, slightly wrinkled hands, the left one graced by the papal ring. As he came in he uttered something in Italian and then starting on the far side opposite the door he had entered came about to each one, proffering the hand which some merely kissed and some seized on and cried over, as if it were the solution of a great woe or the realization of a too great happiness. The mother superior did this and one of the Italian ladies from Venice. The brown monks laid their foreheads on it and the official next to me touched it as though it were an object of great value.

I was interested to see how the Supreme Pontiff—the Pontifex Maximus of all the monuments—viewed all this. He looked benignly but rather wearily down on each one, though occasionally he turned his head away, or, slightly interested, said something. To the woman whose tears fell on his hands he said nothing. With one of the women from Venice he exchanged a few words. Now and then he murmured something. I could not tell whether he was interested but very tired, or whether he was slightly bored. Beyond him lay room after room crowded with pilgrims in which this performance had to be repeated. Acquainted with my newspaper correspondent he gave no sign. At me he scarcely looked at all, realizing no doubt my critical unworthiness. At the prim, severe American woman he looked quizzically. Then he stood in the center of the room and having uttered a long, soft prayer, which my friend W. informed me was very beautiful, departed. The crowd arose. We had to wait until all the other chambers were visited by him and until he returned guarded on all sides by his soldiers and disappeared. There was much conversation, approval, and smiling satisfaction. I saw him once more, passing quickly between two long lines of inquisitive, reverential people, his head up, his glance straight ahead and then he was gone.

We made our way out and somehow I was very glad I had come. I had thought all along that it really did not make any difference whether I saw him or not and that I did not care, but after seeing the attitude of the pilgrims and his own peculiar mood I thought it worth while. Pontifex Maximus! The Vicar of Christ! What a long way from the Catacomb-worshiping Christians who had no Pope at all, who gathered together "to sing responsively a hymn to Christ as to a God" and who bound themselves by a sacramental oath to commit no thefts, nor robberies, nor adulteries, nor break their word, nor deny a deposit when called upon, and who for nearly three hundred years had neither priest nor altar, nor bishop nor Pope, but just the rumored gospels of Christ.

CHAPTER XXXV
THE CITY OF ST. FRANCIS

THE Italian hill-cities are such a strange novelty to the American of the Middle West—used only to the flat reaches of the prairie, and the city or town gathered primarily about the railway-station. One sees a whole series of them ranged along the eastern ridge of the Apennines as one travels northward from Rome. All the way up this valley I had been noting examples on either hand but when I got off the train at Assisi I saw what appeared to be a great fortress on a distant hill—the sheer walls of the church and monastery of St. Francis. It all came back to me, the fact that St. Francis had been born here of a well-to-do father, that he had led a gay life in his youth, had had his "vision"—his change of heart—which caused him to embrace poverty, the care of the poor and needy and to follow precisely that idealistic dictum which says: "Lay not up for yourselves treasures upon earth,... but lay up for yourselves treasures in heaven,... for where your treasure is there will your heart be also." I had found in one of the little books I had with me, "Umbrian Towns," a copy of the prayer that he devised for his Order which reads:

Poverty was in the crib and like a faithful squire she kept herself armed in the great combat Thou didst wage for our redemption. During Thy passion she alone did not forsake Thee. Mary, Thy Mother, stopped at the foot of the cross, but poverty mounted it with Thee and clasped Thee in her embrace unto the end; and when Thou wast dying of thirst as a watchful spouse she prepared for Thee the gall. Thou didst expire in the ardor of her embraces, nor did she leave Thee when dead, O Lord Jesus, for she allowed not Thy body to rest elsewhere than in a borrowed grave. O poorest Jesus, the grace I beg of Thee is to bestow on me the treasure of the highest poverty. Grant that the distinctive mark of our Order may be never to possess anything as its own under the sun for the glory of Thy name and to have no other patrimony than begging.

I wonder if there is any one who can read this without a thrill of response. This world sets such store by wealth and comfort. We all batten on luxury so far as our means will permit,—many of us wallow in it; and the thought of a man who could write such a prayer as that, and live it, made my hair tingle to the roots. I can understand Pope Innocent III's saying that the rule offered by St. Francis and his disciples to ordinary mortals was too severe, but I can also conceive the poetic enthusiasm of a St. Francis. I found myself on the instant in the deepest accord with him, understanding how it was that he wanted his followers not to wear a habit, and to work in the fields as day-laborers, begging only when they could not earn their way. The fact that he and his disciples had lived in reed huts on the site of Santa Maria degli Angeli, the great church which stands in the valley near the station, far down from the town, and had practised the utmost austerity, came upon me as a bit of imaginative poetry of the highest sort. Before the rumbling bus arrived, which conveyed me and several others to the little hotel, I was thrilling with enthusiasm for this religious fact, and anything that concerned him interested me.

In some ways Assisi was a disappointment because I expected something more than bare picturesqueness; it is very old and I fancy, as modern Italy goes, very poor. The walls of the houses are for the most part built of dull gray stone. The streets climbed up hill and down dale, hard, winding, narrow, stony affairs, lined right to the roadway by these bare, inhospitable-looking houses. No yards, no gardens—at least none visible from the streets, but, between walls, and down street stairways, and between odd angles of buildings the loveliest vistas of the valley below, where were spread great orchards of olive trees, occasional small groups of houses, distant churches and the mountains on the other side of the valley. Quite suited to the self-abnegating spirit of St. Francis, I thought,—and I wondered if the town had changed greatly since his day—1182!

As I came up in the bus, looking after my very un-St. Francis-like luggage, and my precious fur overcoat, I encountered a pale, ascetic-looking French priest,—"L'Abbé Guillmant, Vicar General, Arras (Pas-de-Calais), France;" he wrote out his address for me,—who, looking at me over his French Baedeker every now and then, finally asked in his own tongue, "Do you Speak French?" I shook my head deprecatingly and smiled regretfully. "Italiano?" Again I had to shake my head. "C'est triste!" he said, and went on reading. He was clad in a black cassock that reached to his feet, the buttons ranging nicely down his chest, and carried only a small portmanteau and an umbrella. We reached the hotel and I found that he was stopping there. Once on the way up he waved his hand out of the window and said something. I think he was indicating that we could see Perugia further up the valley. In the dining-room where I found him after being assigned to my room he offered me his bill-of-fare and indicated that a certain Italian dish was the best.

This hotel to which we had come was a bare little affair. It was new enough—one of Cook's offerings,—to which all the tourists traveling under the direction of that agency are sent. The walls were quite white and clean. The ceilings of the rooms were high, over high latticed windows and doors. My room, I found, gave upon a balcony which commanded the wonderful sweep of plain below.

The dining-room contained six or seven other travelers bound either southward towards Rome or northward towards Perugia and Florence. It was a rather hazy day, not cold and not warm, but cheerless. I can still hear the clink of the knives and forks as the few guests ate in silence or conversed in low tones. Travelers in this world seem almost innately fearsome of each other, particularly when they are few in number and meet in some such out-of-the-way place as this. My Catholic Abbé was longing to be sociable with me, I could feel it; but this lack of a common tongue prevented him, or seemed to. As I was leaving I asked the proprietor to say to him that I was sorry that I did not speak French, that if I did I would be glad to accompany him; and he immediately reported that the Abbé said, Would I not come along, anyhow? "He haav ask," said the proprietor, a small, stout, dark man, "weel you not come halong hanyhow?"

"Certainly," I replied. And so the Abbé Guillmant and I, apparently not understanding a word of each other's language, started out sightseeing together—I had almost said arm-in-arm.

I soon learned that while my French priest did not speak English, he read it after a fashion, and if he took plenty of time he could form an occasional sentence. It took time, however. He began,—in no vivid or enthusiastic fashion, to be sure,—to indicate what the different things were as we went along.

Now the sights of Assisi are not many. If you are in a hurry and do not fall in love with the quaint and picturesque character of it and its wonderful views you can do them all in a day,—an afternoon if you skimp. There is the church of St. Francis with its associated monastery (what an anachronism a monastery seems in connection with St. Francis, who thought only of huts of branches, or holes in the rocks!) with its sepulcher of the saint in the lower church, and the frescoed scenes from St. Francis's life by Giotto in the upper; the church of St. Clare (Santa Chiara) with its tomb and the body of that enthusiastic imitator of St. Francis; the Duomo, or cathedral, begun in 1134—a rather poor specimen of a cathedral after some others—and the church of St. Damiano, which was given—the chapel of it—to St. Francis by the Benedictine monks of Monte Subasio soon after he had begun his work of preaching the penitential life. There is also the hermitage of the Carceri, where, in small holes in the rocks the early Franciscans led a self-depriving life, and the new church raised on the site of the house belonging to Pietro Bernardone, the father of St. Francis, who was in the cloth business.

I cannot say that I followed with any too much enthusiasm the involved architectural, historical, artistic, and religious details of these churches and chapels. St. Francis, wonderful "jongleur of God" that he was, was not interested in churches and chapels so much as he was in the self-immolating life of Christ. He did not want his followers to have monasteries in the first place. "Carry neither gold nor silver nor money in your girdles, nor bag, nor two coats, nor sandals, nor staff, for the workman is worthy of his hire." I liked the church of St. Francis, however, for in spite of the fact that it is gray and bare as befits a Franciscan edifice, it is a double church—one below the other, and seemingly running at right angles; and they are both large Gothic churches, each complete with sacristy, choir nave, transepts and the like. The cloister is lovely, in the best Italian manner, and through the interstices of the walls wonderful views of the valley below may be secured. The lower church, gray and varied in its interior, is rich in frescoes by Cimabue and others dealing with the sacred vows of the Franciscans, the upper (the nave) decorated with frescoes by Giotto, illustrating the life of St. Francis. The latter interested me immensely because I knew by now that these were almost the beginning of Italian and Umbrian religious art and because Giotto, from the evidences his work affords, must have been such a naïve and pleasant old soul. I fairly laughed aloud as I stalked about this great nave of the upper church—the Abbé was still below—at some of the good old Italian's attempts at characterization and composition. It is no easy thing, if you are the founder of a whole line of great artists, called upon to teach them something entirely new in the way of life-expression, to get all the wonderful things you see and feel into a certain picture or series of pictures, but Giotto tried it and he succeeded very well, too. The decorations are not great, but they are quaint and lovely, even if you have to admit at times that an apprentice of to-day could draw and compose better. He couldn't "intend" better, however, nor convey more human tenderness and feeling in gay, light coloring,—and therein lies the whole secret!

There are some twenty-eight of these frescoes ranged along the lower walls on either side—St. Francis stepping on the cloak of the poor man who, recognizing him as a saint, spread it down before him; St. Francis giving his cloak to the poor nobleman; St. Francis seeing the vision of the palace which was to be reared for him and his followers; St. Francis in the car of fire; St. Francis driving the devils away from Arezzo; St. Francis before the Sultan; St. Francis preaching to the birds; and so on. It was very charming. I could not help thinking what a severe blow has been given to religious legend since those days however; nowadays, except in the minds of the ignorant, saints and devils and angels and stigmata and holy visions have all but disappeared. The grand phantasmagoria of religious notions as they relate to the life of Christ have all but vanished, for the time being anyhow, even in the brains of the masses, and we are having an invasion of rationalism or something approximating it, even at the bottom. The laissez-faire opportunism which has characterized the men at the top in all ages is seeping down to the bottom. Via the newspaper and the magazine, even in Italy—in Assisi—something of astronomy, botany, politics and mechanics, scientifically demonstrated, is creeping in. The inflow seems very meager as yet, a mere trickle, but it has begun. Even in Assisi I saw newspapers and a weekly in a local barber-shop. The natives—the aged ones—very thin, shabby and pale, run into the churches at all hours of the day to prostrate themselves before helpless saints; but nevertheless the newspapers are in the barber-shops. Old Cosimo Medici's truism that governments are not managed by paternosters is slowly seeping down. We have scores of men in the world to-day as able as old Cosimo Medici and as ruthless. We will have hundreds and thousands after a while, only they will be much more circumspect in their ruthlessness and they will work hard for the State. Perhaps there won't be so much useless praying before useless images when that time comes. The thought of divinity *in the individual* needs to be more fully developed.

While I was wandering thus and ruminating I was interested at the same time in the faithful enthusiasm my Abbé was manifesting in the details of the art of this great church. He followed me about for a time in my idle wanderings as I studied the architectural details of this one of the earliest of Gothic churches and then he went away by himself, returning every so often to find in my guide-book certain passages which he wanted me to read, pointing to certain frescoes and exclaiming, "Giotto!" "Cimabue!" "Andrea da Bologna!" Finally he said in plain English, but very slowly: "Did—you—ever—read—a—life—of St. Francis?"

I must confess that my knowledge of the intricacies of Italian art, aside from the lines of its general development, is slim. Alas, dabbling in Italian art, and in art in general, is like trifling with some soothing drug—the more you know the more you want to know.

We continued our way and finally we found a Franciscan monk who spoke both English and French—a peculiar-looking man, tall, and athletic, who appeared to be very widely experienced in the world, indeed. He explained more of the frescoes, the history of the church, the present state of the Franciscans here, and so on.

The other places Franciscan, as I have said, did not interest me so much, though I accompanied my friend, the Abbé, wherever he was impelled to go. He inquired about New York, looking up and waving his hand upward as indicating great height, great buildings, and I knew he was thinking of our skyscrapers. "American bar!" he said, twittering to himself like a bird, "American stim-eat [steam heat]; American 'otel."

I had to smile.

Side by side we proceeded through the church of St. Clare, the Duomo, the new church raised on the site of the house that belonged to Pietro Bernardone, the father of the saint; and finally to the Church of San Damiano, where after St. Francis had seen the vision of the new life, he went to pray. After it was given him by the Benedictines he set about the work of repairing it and when once it was in charge of the poor Clares, after resigning the command of his order, he returned thither to rest and compose the "Canticle of the Law." I never knew until I came to Assisi what a business this thing of religion is in Italy—how valuable the shrines and churches of an earlier day are to its communities. Thousands of travelers must pass this way each year. They support the only good hotels. Travelers from all nations come, English, French, German, American, Russian, and Japanese. The attendants at the shrines reap a small livelihood from the tips of visitors and they are always there, lively and almost obstreperous in their attentions. The oldest and most faded of all the guides and attendants throng about the churches and shrines of Assisi, so old and faded that they seemed almost epics of poverty. My good priest was for praying before every shrine. He would get down on his knees and cross himself, praying four or five minutes while I stood irreligiously in the background, looking at him and wondering how long he would be. He prayed before the tomb of St. Francis in the Franciscan church; before the body of St. Clare (clothed in a black habit and shown behind a glass case), in the church of St. Clare; before the altar in the chapel of Saint Damiano, where St. Francis had first prayed; and so on. Finally when we were all through, and it was getting late evening, he wanted to go down into the valley, near the railroad station, to the church of Santa Maria degli Angeli, where the cell in which St. Francis died, is located. He thought I might want to leave him now, but I refused. We started out, inquiring our way of the monks at Saint Damiano and found that we had to go back through the town. One of the monks, a fat, bare-footed man, signaled me to put on my hat, which I was carrying because I wanted to enjoy the freshness of the evening wind. It had cleared off now, the sun had come out and we were enjoying one of those lovely Italian spring evenings which bring a sense of childhood to the heart. The good monk thought I was holding my hat out of reverence to his calling. I put it on.

We went back through the town and then I realized how lovely the life of a small Italian town is, in spring. Assisi has about five thousand population. It was cool and pleasant. Many doorways were now open, showing evening fires within the shadows of the rooms. Some children were in the roadways. Carts and wains were already clattering up from the fields below and church-bells—the sweetest echoes from churches here and there in the valley and from those here in Assisi— exchanged melodies. We walked fast because it was late and when we reached the station it was already dusk. The moon had risen, however, and lighted up this great edifice, standing among a ruck of tiny homes. A number of Italian men and women were grouped around a pump outside—those same dark, ear-ringed Italians with whom we are now so familiar in America. The church was locked, but my Abbé went about to the cloister gate which stood at one side of the main entrance, and rang a bell. A brown-cowled monk appeared and they exchanged a few words. Finally with many smiles we were admitted into a moonlit garden, where cypress trees and box and ilex showed their lovely forms, and through a long court that had an odor of malt, as if beer were brewed here, and so finally by a circuitous route into the main body of the church and the chapel containing the cell of St. Francis. It was so dark by now that only the heaviest objects appeared distinctly, the moonlight falling faintly through several of the windows. The voices of the monks sounded strange and sonorous, even though they talked in low tones. We walked about looking at the great altars, the windows, and the high, flat ceiling. We went into the chapel, lined on either side by wooden benches, occupied by kneeling monks, and lighted by one low, swinging lamp which hung before the cell in which St. Francis died. There was much whispering of prayers here and the good Abbé was on his knees in a moment praying solemnly.

St. Francis certainly never contemplated that his beggarly cell would ever be surrounded by the rich marbles and bronze work against which his life was a protest. He never imagined, I am sure, that in spite of his prayer for poverty, his Order would become rich and influential and that this, the site of his abstinence, would be occupied by one of the most ornate churches in Italy. It is curious how barnacle-wise the spirit of materiality invariably encrusts the ideal! Christ died on the cross for the privilege of worshiping God "in spirit and in truth" after he had preached the sermon on the mount,—and then you have the gold-incrusted, power-seeking, wealth-loving Papacy, with women and villas and wars of aggrandizement and bastardy among the principal concomitants. And following Francis, imitating the self-immolation of the Nazarene, you have another great Order whose churches and convents in Italy are among the richest and most beautiful. And everywhere you find that lust for riches and show and gormandizing and a love of seeming what they are not, so that they may satisfy a faint scratching of the spirit which is so thickly coated over that it is almost extinguished.

Or it may be that the ideal is always such an excellent device wherewith to trap the unwary and the unsophisticated. "Feed them with a fine-seeming and then put a tax on their humble credulity" seems to be the logic of materialism in regard to the mass. Anything to obtain power and authority! Anything to rule! And so you have an Alexander VI, Vicar of Christ, poisoning cardinals and seizing on estates that did not belong to him: leading a life of almost insane luxury; and a Medicean pope interested in worldly fine art and the development of a pagan ideal.

CHAPTER XXXVI
PERUGIA

WE returned at between seven and eight that night. After a bath I sat out on the large balcony, or veranda, commanding the valley, and enjoyed the moonlight. The burnished surface of the olive trees, and brown fields already being plowed with white oxen and wooden shares, gave back a soft glow that was somehow like the patina on bronze. There was a faint odor of flowers in the wind and here and there lights gleaming. From some street in the town I heard singing and the sound of a mandolin. I slept soundly.

At breakfast,—coffee, honey, rolls and butter,—my Abbé gave me his card. He was going to Florence. He asked the hotel man to say to me that he had had a charming time and would I not come to France and visit him? "When I learn to speak French," I replied, smiling at him. He smiled and nodded. We shook hands and parted.

After breakfast I called a little open carriage such as they use in Paris and Monte Carlo and was off for Spello; and he took an early omnibus and caught his train.

On this trip which Barfleur had recommended as offering a splendid view of cypresses I was not disappointed: about some villa there was an imposing architectural arrangement of them and an old Roman amphitheater nearby—the ruins of it—bespoke the prosperous Roman life which had long since disappeared. Spello, like Assisi, and beyond it Perugia, (all these towns in this central valley in fact) was set on top of a high ridge, and on some peak of it at that. As seen from the valley below it was most impressive. Close at hand, in its narrow winding streets it was simply strange, outre, almost bizarre, and yet a lovely little place after its kind. Like Assisi it was very poor—only more so. A little shrine to some old Greek divinity was preserved here and at the very top of all, on the extreme upper round of the hill was a Franciscan monastery which I invaded without a by your leave and walked in its idyllic garden. There and then I decided that if ever fortune should permit I would surely return to Spello and write a book, and that this garden and monastery should be my home. It was so eerie here—so sweet. The atmosphere was so wine-like. I wandered about under green trees and beside well-kept flower beds enjoying the spectacle until suddenly peering over a wall I beheld a small garden on a slightly lower terrace and a brown-cowled monk gathering vegetables. He had a basket on his arm, his hood back over his shoulders—a busy and silent anchorite. After a time as I gazed he looked and smiled, apparently not startled by my presence and then went on with his work. "When I come again," I said, "I shall surely live here and I'll get him to cook for me." Lovely thought! I leaned over other walls and saw in the narrow, winding streets below natives bringing home bundles of fagots on the backs of long-eared donkeys, and women carrying water. Very soon, I suppose, a car line will be built and the uniformed Italian conductors will call "Assisi!" "Perugia!" and even "The Tomb of St. Francis!"

* * * * *

Of all the hill-cities I saw in Italy certainly Perugia was the most remarkable, the most sparkling, the most forward in all things commercial. It stands high, very high, above the plain as you come in at the depot and a wide-windowed trolley-car carries you up to the principal square, the Piazza Vittorio Emanuele, stopping in front of the modern hotels which command the wide sea-like views which the valley presents below. Never was a city so beautifully located. Wonderful ridges of mountains fade into amazing lavenders, purples, scarlets, and blues, as the evening falls or the dawn brightens. If I were trying to explain where some of the painters of the Umbrian school, particularly Perugino, secured their wonderful sky touches, their dawn and evening effects, I should say that they had once lived at Perugia. Perugino did. It seemed to me as I wandered about it the two days that I was there that it was the most human and industrious little city I had ever walked into. Every living being seemed to have so much to do. You could hear, as you went up and down the streets—streets that ascend and descend in long, winding stairways, step by step, for blocks—pianos playing, anvils ringing, machinery humming, saws droning, and, near the great abattoir where cattle were evidently slaughtered all day long, the piercing squeals of pigs in their death throes. There was a busy market-place crowded from dawn until noon with the good citizens of Perugia buying everything from cabbages and dress-goods to picture post-cards and hardware. Long rows of fat Perugian old ladies, sitting with baskets of wares in front of them, all gossiped genially as they awaited purchasers. In the public square facing the great hotels, nightly between seven and ten, the whole spirited city seemed to be walking, a whole world of gay, enthusiastic life that would remind you of an American manufacturing town on a Saturday night—only this happens every night in Perugia.

When I arrived there I went directly to my hotel, which faces the Piazza Vittorio Emanuele. It was excellent, charmingly built, beautifully located, with a wide view of the Umbrian plain which is so wonderful in its array of distant mountains and so rich in orchards, monasteries, convents and churches. I think I never saw a place with so much variety of scenery, such curious twists of streets and lanes, such heights and depths of levels and platforms on which houses, the five- and six-story tenement of the older order of life in Italy, are built. The streets are all narrow, in some places not more than ten or fifteen feet wide, arched completely over for considerable distances, and twisting and turning, ascending or descending as they go, but they give into such adorable squares and open places, such magnificent views at every turn!

I do not know whether what I am going to say will have the force and significance that I wish to convey, but a city like Perugia, taken as a whole, all its gates, all its towers, all its upward-sweeping details, is like a cathedral in itself, a Gothic cathedral. You would have to think of the ridge on which it stands as providing the nave and the transepts and the apse and then the quaint little winding streets of the town itself with their climbing houses and towers would suggest the pinnacles, spandrels, flying buttresses, airy statues and crosses of a cathedral like Amiens. I know of no other simile that quite suggests Perugia,—that is really so true to it.

No one save an historical zealot could extract much pleasure from the complicated political and religious history of this city. However once upon a time there was a guild of money-changers and bankers which built a hall, called the Hall of the Cambio, which is very charming; and at another time (or nearly the same time) there was a dominant Guelph party which, in conjunction with some wealthy townsmen known as the "Raspanti," built what is now known as the Palazzo Publico or Palazzo Communale, in what is now known as the Piazza del Municipio, which I think is perfect. It is not a fortress like the Bargello or the Palazzo Vecchio at Florence, but it is a perfect architectural thing, the charm of which remains with me fresh and keen. It is a beautiful structure—one that serves charmingly the uses to which it is put—that of a public center for officials and a picture-gallery. It was in one of these rooms, devoted to a collection of Umbrian art, that I found a pretentious collection of the work of Perugino, the one really important painter who ever lived or worked in Perugia—and the little city now makes much of him.

If I felt like ignoring the long-winded art discussions of comparatively trivial things, the charm and variety of the town and its present-day life was in no wise lost upon me.

The unheralded things, the things which the guide-books do not talk about, are sometimes so charming. I found it entrancing to descend of a morning by lovely, cool, stone passages from the Piazza of Vittorio Emanuele to the Piazza of the Army, and watch the soldiers, principally cavalry, drill. Their ground was a space about five acres in extent, as flat as a table, set high above the plain, with deep ravines descending on either hand, and the quaint houses and public institutions of Perugia looking down from above. To the left, as you looked out over the plain, across the intervening ravine, was another spur of the town, built also on a flat ridge with the graceful church of St. Peter and its beautiful Italian-Gothic tower, and the whole road that swept along the edge of the cliff, making a delightful way for carriages and automobiles. I took delight in seeing how wonderfully the deep green ravines separate one section of the town from another, and in watching the soldiers, Italy then being at war with Tripoli.

You could stand, your arms resting upon some old brownish-green wall, and look out over intervening fields to distant ranges of mountains, or tower-like Assisi and Spoleto. The variety of the coloring of the plain below was never wearying.

This Italian valley was so beautiful that I should like to say one more word about the skies and the wonderful landscape effects. North of here, in Florence, Venice and Milan, they do not occur so persistently and with such glorious warmth at this season of the year. At this height the nights were not cold, but cool, and the mornings burst with such a blaze of color as to defy the art of all save the greatest painters. They were not so much lurid as richly spiritualized, being shot through with a strange electric radiance. This did not mean, as it would so often in America, that a cloudy day was to follow. Rather the radiance slowly gave place to a glittering field of light that brought out every slope and olive orchard and distant cypress and pine with amazing clearness. The bells of the churches in Perugia and in the valley below were like muezzins calling to each other from their praying-towers. As the day closed the features of the landscape seemed to be set in crystal, and the greens and browns and grays to have at times a metallic quality. Outside the walls in the distance were churches, shrines, and monasteries, always with a cypress or two, sometimes with many, which stood out with great distinctness, and from distant hillsides you would hear laborers singing in the bright sun. Well might they sing, for I know of no place where life would present to them a fairer aspect.

CHAPTER XXXVII
THE MAKERS OF FLORENCE

WITH all the treasures of my historic reading in mind from the lives of the Medici and Savonarola to that of Michelangelo and the Florentine school of artists, I was keen to see what Florence would be like. Mrs. Q. had described it as the most individual of all the Italian cities that she had seen. She had raved over its narrow, dark, cornice-shaded streets, its fortress-like palaces, its highly individual churches and cloisters, the way the drivers of the little open vehicles plied everywhere cracking their whips, until, she said, it sounded like a Fourth of July in Janesville. I was keen to see how large the dome of the cathedral would look and whether it would really tower conspicuously over the remaining buildings of the city, and whether the Arno would look as picturesque as it did in all the photographs. The air was so soft and the sun so bright, although sinking low in the west, as the train entered the city, that I was pleased to accept, instead of the ancient atmosphere which I had anticipated, the wide streets and rows of four- and six-family apartment houses which characterize all the newer sections. They have the rich browns and creams of the earlier portion of Florence; but they are very different in their suggestion of modernity. The distant hills, as I could see from the car windows, were dotted with houses and villas occupying delightful positions above the town. Suddenly I saw the Duomo; and although I knew it only from photographs I recognized it in an instant. It spoke for itself in a large, dignified way. Over the housetops it soared like a great bubble; and some pigeons flying in the air gave it the last touch of beauty. We wound around the city in a circle—I could tell this by the shifting position of the sun—through great yards of railway-tracks with scores of engines and lines of small box-cars; and then I saw a small stream and a bridge,—nothing like the Arno, of course,—a canal; and the next thing we were rolling into a long crowded railway-station, the guards calling Firenze. I got up, gathered my overcoat and bags into my arms, signaled a *facino* and gave them to him; and then I sought a vehicle that would convey me to the hotel for which I was bound—the Hotel de Ville on the Arno. I sat behind a fat driver while he cracked his whip endlessly above the back of a lazy horse, passing the while the showy façade of Santa Maria Novella, striped with strange bands of white and bluish gray or drab,—

a pleasing effect for a church. I could see at once that the Florence of the Middle Ages was a much more condensed affair than that which now sprawls out in various directions from the Loggia dei Lanzi and the place of the cathedral.

The narrow streets were alive with people; and the drivers of vehicles everywhere seemed to drive as if their lives depended on it. Suddenly we turned into a *piazza* very modern and very different from that of Santa Maria Novella; and then we were at the hotel door. It was a nice-looking square, as I thought, not very large,—clean and gracious. To my delight I found that my room opened directly upon a balcony which overlooked the Arno, and that from it, sitting in a chair, I could command all of that remarkable prospect of high-piled medieval houses hanging over the water's edge. It was beautiful. The angelus bells were ringing; there was a bright glow in the west where the sun was going down; the water of the stream was turquoise blue, and the walls of all the houses seemingly brown. I stood and gazed, thinking of the peculiarly efficient German manager I had encountered, the German servants who were in charge of this hotel, and the fact that Florence had long since radically changed from what it was. A German porter came and brought my bags; a German maid brought hot water; a German clerk took my full name and address for the register, and possibly for the police; and then I was at liberty to unpack and dress for dinner. Instead I took a stroll out along the stream-banks to study the world of jewelry shops which I saw there, and the stands for flowers, and the idling crowd.

I dare not imagine what the interest of Florence would be to any one who did not know her strange and variegated history, but I should think, outside of the surrounding scenic beauty, it would be little or nothing. Unless one had a fondness for mere quaintness and gloom and solidity, it would in a way be repulsive, or at best dreary. But lighted by the romance, the tragedy, the lust, the zealotry, the brutality and the artistic idealism that surrounds such figures as Dante, the Medici, Savonarola, Donatello, Michelangelo, Brunelleschi, and the whole world of art, politics, trade, war, it takes on a strange luster to me, that of midnight waters lighted by the fitful gleams of distant fires. I never think of it without seeing in my mind's eye the Piazza della Signoria as it must have looked on that day in 1494 when that famous fiasco, in regard to "the test by fire," entered into between Savonarola and the Franciscan monks, took place,—those long, ridiculous processions of Dominicans and Franciscans, Savonarola bearing the chalice aloft; or that other day when Charles VIII of France at the instance of Savonarola paraded the street in black helmet with mantle of gold brocade, his lance leveled before him, his retainers gathered about him, and then disappointed the people by getting off his horse and showing himself to be the insignificant little man that he was, almost deformed and with an idiotic expression of countenance. Neither can I forget the day that Savonarola was beheaded and burnt for his religious zealotry in this same Piazza della Signoria; nor all the rivals of the Medici hung from the windows of the Palazzo Vecchio or beheaded in the Bargello. Think of the tonsured friars and grave citizens of this medieval city, under Savonarola's fiery incitement, their heads garlanded with flowers, mingling with the overwrought children called to help in purifying the city, dancing like David before the ark and shouting "Long live Christ and the Virgin, our rulers"; of the days when Alessandro Medici and his boon companion and cousin, Lorenzo, rode about the city on a mule together, defiling the virtue of innocent girls, roistering in houses of ill repute, and drinking and stabbing to their hearts' content; of Fra Girolamo preaching to excited crowds in the Duomo and of his vision of a black cross over Rome, a red one over Jerusalem; of Machiavelli writing his brochure "The Prince"; and of Michelangelo defending the city walls as an engineer. Can any other city match this spectacular, artistic, melodramatic progress in so short a space of time, or present the galaxy of artists, the rank company of material masters such as the Medici, the Pazzi, the Strozzi, plotting and counter-plotting to the accompaniment of lusts and murders? Other cities have had their amazing hours, all of them, from Rome to London. But Florence! It has always seemed to me that the literary possibilities of Florence, in spite of the vast body of literature concerning it, have scarcely been touched.

The art section alone is so vast and so brilliant that one of the art merchants told me while I was there that at least forty thousand of the city's one hundred and seventy thousand population is foreign (principally English and American), drawn to it by its art merits, and that the tide of travel from April to October is amazing. I can believe it. You will hear German and English freely spoken in all the principal thoroughfares.

Because of a gray day and dull, following the warmth and color and light of Perugia and Rome, Florence seemed especially dark and somber to me at first; but I recovered. Its charm and beauty grew on me by degrees so that by the time I had done inspecting Santa Maria Novella, Santa Croce, San Marco, the Cathedral group and the Bargello, I was really desperately in love with the art of it all, and after I had investigated the galleries, the Pitti, Uffizi, Belle Arti, and the Cloisters, I was satisfied that I could find it in my heart to live here and work, a feeling I had in many other places in Europe.

Truly, however, there is no other city in Europe just like Florence; it has all the distinction of great individuality. My mood changed about, at times, as I thought of the different periods of its history, the splendor of its ambitions or the brutality of its methods; but when I was in the presence of some of its perfect works of art, such as Botticelli's "Spring" in the Belle Arti, or Michelangelo's "Tombs of the Medici" in San Lorenzo, or Titian's "Magdalen," or Raphael's "Leo X" in the Pitti, or Benozzo Gozzoli's fresco (the journey of the three kings to Bethlehem) in the old Medici Palace, then I was ready to believe that nothing could be finer than Florence. I realized now that of all the cities in Europe that I saw Florence was possessed of the most intense art atmosphere,—something that creeps over your soul in a grim realistic way and causes you to repeat over and over: "Amazing men worked here—amazing men!"

It was so strange to find driven home to me,—even more here than in Rome, that illimitable gulf that divides ideality of thought and illusion from reality. Men painted the illusions of Christianity concerning the saints and the miracles at this time better than ever before or since, and they believed something else. A Cosimo Medici who could patronize the Papacy with one hand and make a cardinal into a pope, could murder a rival with the other; and Andrea del Castagno, who was seeking to shine as a painter of religious art—madonnas, transfigurations, and the like—could murder a Domenico Veneziano in order to have no rival in what he considered to be a permanent secret of how to paint in oils. The same munificence that could commission Michelangelo to design and execute a magnificent façade for San Lorenzo (it was never done, of course) could suborn the elective franchise of the people and organize a school on the lines of Plato's Academy. In other words, in

Florence as in the Court of Alexander VI at Rome, we find life stripped of all sham in action, in so far as an individual and his conscience were concerned, and filled with the utmost subtlety in so far as the individual and the public were concerned. Cosimo and Lorenzo de' Medici, Andrea del Castagno, Machiavelli, the Pazzi, the Strozzi,—in fact, the whole "kit and kaboodle" of the individuals comprising the illustrious life that foregathered here, were cut from the same piece of cloth. They were, one and all, as we know, outside of a few artistic figures, shrewd, calculating, relentless and ruthless seekers after power and position; lust, murder, gormandizing, panoplizing, were the order of the day. Religion,—it was to be laughed at; weakness,—it was to be scorned. Poverty was to be misused. Innocence was to be seized upon and converted. Laughing at virtue and satisfying themselves always, they went their way, building their grim, dark, almost windowless palaces; preparing their dungeons and erecting their gibbets for their enemies. No wonder Savonarola saw "a black cross over Rome." They struck swiftly and surely and smiled blandly and apparently mercifully; they had the Asiatic notion of morality,—charity, virtue, and the like, combined with a ruthless indifference to them. Power was the thing they craved—power and magnificence; and these were the things they had. But, oh, Florence! Florence! how you taught the nothingness of life itself; its shams; its falsehoods; its atrocities; its uselessness. It has never been any wonder to me that the saddest, darkest, most pathetic figure in all art, Michelangelo Buonarroti, should have appeared and loved and dreamed and labored and died at this time. His melancholy was a fit commentary on his age, on life, and on all art. Oh, Buonarroti, loneliest of figures: I think I understand how it was with you.

Bear with me while I lay a flower on this great grave. I cannot think of another instance in art in which indomitable will and almost superhuman energy have been at once so frustrated and so successful.

I never think of the great tomb for which the Moses in San Pietro in Vincoli—large, grave, thoughtful; the man who could walk with God—and the slaves in the Louvre were intended without being filled with a vast astonishment and grief to think that life should not have permitted this design to come to fulfilment. To think that a pope so powerful as Julius should have planned a tomb so magnificent, with Michelangelo to scheme it out and actually to begin it, and then never permit it to reach completion. All the way northward through Italy this idea of a parallelogram with forty figures on it and covered with reliefs and other ornaments haunted me. At Florence, in the Belle Arti, I saw more of the figures (casts), designed for this tomb—strange, unfolding thoughts half-hewn out of the rock, which suggest the source from which Rodin has drawn his inspiration,—and my astonishment grew. Before I was out of Italy, this man and his genius, the mere dreams of the things he hoped to do, enthralled me so that to me he has become the one great art figure of the world. Colossal is the word for Michelangelo,—so vast that life was too short for him to suggest even a tithe of what he felt. But even the things that he did, how truly monumental they are.

I am sure I am not mistaken when I say that there is a profound sadness, too, running through all that he ever did. His works are large, Gargantuan, and profoundly melancholy; witness the Moses that I have been talking of, to say nothing of the statues on the tombs of the Medici in San Lorenzo at Florence. I saw them in Berlin, reproduced there in plaster in the Kaiser-Friederich-Museum, and once more I was filled with the same sense of profound, meditative melancholy. It is present in its most significant form here in Florence, in San Lorenzo, the façade of which he once prepared to make magnificent, but here he was again frustrated. I saw the originals of these deep, sad figures that impressed me as no other sculptural figures ever have done. "Dawn and Dusk"; "Day and Night." How they dwell with me constantly. I was never able to look at any of his later work—the Sistine Chapel frescoes, the figures of slaves in the Louvre, the Moses in San Pietro in Vincoli, or these figures here in Florence, without thinking how true it was that this great will had rarely had its way and how, throughout all his days, his energy was so unfortunately compelled to war with circumstance. Life plays this trick on the truly great if they are not ruthless and of material and executive leanings. Art is a pale flower that blooms only in sheltered places and to drag it forth and force it to contend with the rough usages of the world is to destroy its perfectness. It was so in this man's case who at times, because of unlucky conjunctions, was compelled to fly for his life, or to sue for the means which life should have been honored to bestow upon him, or else to abandon great purposes.

Out of such a mist of sorrow, and only so, however, have come these figures that now dream here year after year in their gray chapel, while travelers come and go, draining their cup of wonder,—rising ever and anon to the level of the beauty they contemplate. I can see Browning speculating upon the spirit of these figures. "Night" with her heavy lids, lost in great weariness; and "Day" with his clear eyes. I can see Rodin gathering substance for his "Thinker," and Shelley marveling at the suggestions which arise from these mighty figures. There is none so great as this man who, in his medieval gloom and mysticism, inherited the art of Greece.

CHAPTER XXXVIII
A NIGHT RAMBLE IN FLORENCE

WHATEVER the medieval atmosphere of Florence may have been, and when I was there the exterior appearance of the central heart was obviously somewhat akin to its fourteenth- and fifteenth-century predecessor, to-day its prevailing spirit is thoroughly modern. If you walk in the Piazza della Signoria or the Piazza del Duomo or the Via dei Calzaioli, the principal thoroughfare, you will encounter most of the ancient landmarks—a goodly number of them, but they will look out of place, as in the case of the palaces with their windowless ground floors, built so for purposes of defense, their corner lanterns, barricaded windows, and single great entrances easily guarded. To-day these regions have, if not the open spacing of the modern city, at least the commercial sprightliness and matter-of-fact business display and energy which is characteristic of commerce everywhere.

I came to the Piazza della Signoria, the most famous square of the city, quite by accident, the first night following a dark, heavily corniced street from my hotel and at once recognized the Palazzo Vecchio, with its thin angular tower; the Loggia dei Lanzi, where in older times public performances were given in the open; and the equestrian statue of Cosimo I. I idled long here, examining the bronze slab which marks the site of the stake at which Savonarola and two other Dominicans were burned in 1498, the fountain designed by Bartolommeo Ammanati; the two lions at the step of the Loggia and Benvenuto Cellini's statue of "Perseus" with the head of Medusa. A strange genius, that. This figure is as brilliant and thrilling as it is ghastly.

It was a lovely night. The moon came up after a time as it had at Perugia and Assisi and I wandered about these old streets, feeling the rough brown walls, looking in at the open shop windows, most of them dark and lighted by street lamps, and studying always the wide, overhanging cornices. All really interesting cities are so delightfully different. London was so low, gray, foggy, heavy, drab, and commonplace; Paris was so smart, swift, wide-spaced, rococo, ultra-artistic, and fashionable; Monte Carlo was so semi-Parisian and semi-Algerian or Moorish, with sunlight and palms; Rome was so higgledy-piggledy, of various periods, with a strange mingling of modernity and antiquity, and over all blazing sunlight and throughout all cypresses; and now in Florence I found the compact, dark atmosphere, suggestive of what Paris once was, centuries before, with this distinctive feature, that the wide cornice is here an essential characteristic. It is so wide! It protrudes outward from the building line at least three or four feet and it may be much more, six or seven. One thing is certain, as I found to my utter delight on a rainy afternoon, you can take shelter under its wide reach and keep comparatively dry. Great art has been developed in making it truly ornamental and it gives the long narrow streets a most individual and, in my judgment, distinguished appearance.

It was quite by accident, also, on this same evening that I came upon the Piazza del Duomo where the street cars are. I did not know where I was going until suddenly turning a corner there I saw it—the Campanile at last and a portion of the Cathedral standing out soft and fair in the moonlight! I shall always be glad that I saw it so, for the strange stripe and arabesque of its stone work,—slabs of white or cream-colored stone interwoven in lovely designs with slabs of slate-colored granite, had an almost eerie effect. It might have been something borrowed from Morocco or Arabia or the Far East. The dome, too, as I drew nearer, and the Baptistery soared upwards in a magnificent way and, although afterwards I was sorry that the municipality has never had sense enough to tear out the ruck of buildings surrounding it and leave these three monuments—the Cathedral, the Campanile, and the Baptistery—standing free and clear, as at Pisa, on a great stone platform or square,—nevertheless, cramped as I think they are, they are surely beautiful.

I was not so much impressed by the interior of the cathedral. Its beauty is largely on the outside.

I ascended the Campanile still another day and from its height viewed all Florence, the windings of the Arno, San Miniato, Fiesole, but, try as I might, I could not think of it in modern terms. It was too reminiscent of the Italy of the Medici, of the Borgias, Julius II, Michelangelo and all the glittering company who were their contemporaries. One thing that was strongly impressed upon me there was that every city should have a great cathedral. Not so much as a symbol or theory of religion as an object of art, something which would indicate the perfection of the religious ideal taken from an artistic point of view. Here you can stand and admire the exquisite double windows with twisted columns, the infinite variety of the inlaid marble work, and the quaint architecture of the niches supported by columns. It was after midnight and the moon was high in the heavens shining down with a rich springlike effect before I finally returned from the Duomo Square, following the banks of the Arno and admiring the shadows cast by the cornices and so finally reached my hotel and my bed.

The Uffizi and Pitti collections of paintings are absolutely the most amazing I saw abroad. There are other wonderful collections, the Louvre being absolutely unbelievable for size; but here the art is so uniformly relative to Italy, so identified with the Renaissance, so suggestive of the influence and the patronage which gave it birth. The influence of religion, the wealth of the Catholic Church, the power of individual families such as the Medici and the Dukes of Venice are all clearly indicated. Botticelli's "Adoration of the Magi" in the Uffizi, showing the proud Medici children, the head of Cosimo Pater Patriae, and the company of men of letters and statesmen of the time, all worked in as figures about the Christ child, tell the whole story. Art was flattering to the nobility of the day. It was dependent for its place and position upon religion, upon the patronage of the Church, and so you have endless "Annunciations," "Adorations," "Flights into Egypt," "Crucifixions," "Descents from the Cross," "Entombments," "Resurrections," and the like. The sensuous "Magdalena," painted for her form and the beauty of suggestion, you will encounter over and over again. All the saints in the calendar, the proud Popes and Cardinals of a dozen families, the several members of the Medici family—they are all there. Now and then you will encounter a Rubens, a Van Dyck, a Rembrandt, or a Frans Hals from the Netherlands, but they are rare. Florence, Rome, Venice, Pisa, and Milan, are best represented by their own sculptors, painters and architects and it is the local men largely in whom you rejoice. The bits from other lands are few and far between.

Rome for sculptures, frescoes, jewel-box churches, ancient ruins, but Florence for paintings and the best collections of medieval artistic craftsmanship.

In the Uffizi, the Pitti, and the Belle Arti I browsed among the vast collections of paintings sharpening my understanding of the growth of Italian art. I never knew until I reached Florence how easy it is to trace the rise of Christian art, to see how one painter influenced another, how one school borrowed from another. It is all very plain. If by the least effort you fix the representatives of the different Italian schools in mind, you can judge for yourself.

I returned three times to look at Botticelli's "Spring" in the Belle Arti, that marvelous picture which I think in many respects is the loveliest picture in the world, so delicate, so poetically composed, so utterly suggestive of the art and refinement of the painter and of life at its best. The "Three Graces," so lightly clad in transparent raiment, are so much the soul of joy and freshness, the utter significance of spring. The ruder figures to the left do so portray the cold and blue of March, the warmer April, and the flower-clad May! I could never tire of the artistry which could have March blowing on April's mouth from which flowers fall into the lap of May. Nor could I weary of the spirit that could select green, sprouting things for the hem of April's garment; or above Spring's head place a wingèd and blindfolded baby shooting a fiery arrow at the Three Graces. To me Botticelli is the nearest return to the Greek spirit of beauty, grace and lightness of soul, combined with later delicacy and romance that the modern world has known. It is so beautiful that for me it is sad—full of the sadness that only perfect beauty can inspire.

I sated myself on the house fronts or backs below the Ponte Vecchio

I think now, of all the places I saw in Italy, perhaps Florence really preserves in spite of its changes most of the atmosphere of the past, but that is surely not for long, either; for it is growing and the Germans are arriving. They were in complete charge of my hotel here and of other places, as I shortly saw, and I fancy that the future of northern Italy is to be in the hands of the Germans.

As I walked about this city, lingering in its doorways, brooding over its pictures, reconstructing for myself the life of the Middle Ages, I could not help thinking how soon it must all go. No doubt the churches, palaces, and museums will be retained in their present form for hundreds of years, and they should be, but soon will come wider streets and newer houses even in the older section (the heart of the city) and then farewell to the medieval atmosphere. In all likelihood the wide cornices, now such a noticeable feature of the city, will be abandoned and then there will be scarcely anything to indicate the Florence of the past. Already the street cars were clang-clanging their way through certain sections.

The Arno here is so different from the Tiber at Rome; and yet so much like it, for it has in the main the same unprepossessing look, running as it does through the city between solid walls of stone but lacking the spectacles of the castle of St. Angelo, Saint Peter's, the hills and the gardens of the Aventine and the Janiculum. There are no ancient ruins on the Arno,—only the suggestive architecture of the Middle Ages, the wonderful Ponte Vecchio and the houses adjacent to it.

Indeed the river here is nothing more than a dammed stream— shallow before it reaches the city, shallow after it leaves it, but held in check here by great stone dams which give it a peculiarly still mass and depth. The spirit of the people was not the same as that of those in Rome or other cities; the spirit of the crowd was different. A darker, richer, more phlegmatic populace, I thought. The people were slow, leisurely, short and comfortable. I sated myself on the house fronts or backs below the Ponte Vecchio and on the little jewelry shops of which there seemed to be an endless variety; and then feeling that I had had a taste of the city, I returned to larger things. The Duomo, the palaces of the Medici, the Pitti Palace, and that world which concerned the Council of Florence, and the dignified goings to and fro of old Cosimo Pater and his descendants were the things that I wished to see and realize for myself if I could.

I think we make a mistake when we assume that the manners, customs, details, conversation, interests and excitements of people anywhere were ever very much different from what they are now. In three or four hundred years from now people in quite similar situations to our own will be wondering how we took our daily lives; quite the same as our ancestors, I should say, and no differently from our descendants. Life works about the same in all times. Only exterior aspects change. In the particular period in which Florence, and all Italy for that matter, was so remarkable, Italy was alive with ambitious men—strong, remarkable, capable characters. *They* made the wonder of the life, it was not the architecture that did it and not the routine movements of the people. Florence has much the same architecture to-day, better in fact; but not the men. Great men make great times—and only struggling, ambitious, vainglorious men make the existence of the artist possible, however much he may despise them. They are the only ones who in their vainglory and power can readily call upon him to do great things and supply the means. Witness Raphael and Michelangelo in Italy, Rubens in Holland, and Velasquez in Spain.

CHAPTER XXXIX
FLORENCE OF TO-DAY

IT was while I was in Florence that a light was thrown on an industry of which I had previously known little and which impressed me much.

Brooding over the almost endless treasures of the city, I ambled into the Strozzi Palace one afternoon, that perfect example of Florentine palatial architecture, then occupied by an exposition of objects of art, reproductions and originals purporting to be the work of an association of Italian artists. After I had seen, cursorily, most of the treasures in the Palazzo Strozzi, I encountered a thing which I had long heard of but never seen,—an organization for the reproduction, the reduplication, of all the wonders of art, and cheaply, too. The place was full of marbles of the loveliest character, replicas of famous statues in the Vatican, the Louvre, the Uffizi, and elsewhere; and in many instances, also, copies of the great pictures. There was beautiful furniture imitated, even as to age, from many of the Italian palaces, the Riccardi, Albizzi, Pazzi, Pitti, Strozzi, and others; and as for garden-fittings—fountains, fauns, cupids, benches, metal gateways, pergolas, and the like, they were all present. They were marvelous reproductions from some of the villas, with the patina of age upon them, and I thought at first that they were original. I was soon undeceived, for I had not been there long, strolling about, when an attendant brought and introduced to me a certain Prof. Ernesto Jesuram, a small, dark, wiry man with clear, black, crowlike eyes who made clear the whole situation.

The markets of the world, according to Mr. Jesuram, a Jew, were being flooded with cheap imitations of every truly worthy object of art, from Italian stone benches to landscapes by Corot or portraits by Frans Hals—masquerading as originals; and it had been resolved by this Association of Italian Artists that this was unfair, not only to the buyer and the art-loving public generally, but also to the honest craftsman who could make an excellent living reproducing, frankly, copies of ancient works of merit at a nominal price, if only they were permitted to copy them. Most, in fact all of them, could make interesting originals but in many cases they would lack that trait of personality which makes all the difference between success and failure; whereas they could perfectly reproduce the masterpieces of others and that, too, for prices with which no foreigner could compete. So they had banded themselves together, determined to do better work, and sell more cheaply than the fly-by-night rascals who were confounding and degrading all good art and to say frankly to each and all: "Here is a perfect reproduction of a very lovely thing. Do you want it at a very low cost?" or, "We will make for you an exact copy of anything that you see and admire and wish to have and we will make it so cheaply that you cannot afford to dicker with doubtful dealers who sell you imitations *as originals* and charge you outrageous prices."

I have knocked about sufficiently in my time in the showy chambers of American dealers and elsewhere to know that there is entirely too much in what was told me.

The wonder of Florence grew a little under the Professor's quiet commercial analysis, for after exhausting this matter of reproducing so cheaply, we proceeded to a discussion of the present conditions of the city.

"It's very different commercially from anything in America or the north of Europe," he said, "or even the north of Italy, for as yet we have scarcely anything in the way of commerce here. We still build in the fashion they used five hundred years ago—narrow streets and big cornices in order to keep up the atmosphere of the city, for we are not strong enough commercially yet to go it alone, and besides I don't think the Italians will ever be different. They are an easy-going race. They don't need the American "two dollars a day" to live on. Fifty centimes will do. For one thousand dollars (five thousand lire) you can rent a palace here for a year and I can show you whole floors overlooking gardens that you can rent for seventeen dollars a month. We have a garden farther out that we use as a workshop here in Florence, in the heart of the city, which we rent for four hundred dollars a year."

"What about the Italian's idea of progress? Isn't he naturally constructive?" I asked Mr. Jesuram.

"Rarely the Italian. Not at this date. We have many Jews and Germans here who are doing well, and foreign capital is building street-railways. I think the Italians will have to be fused with another nation to experience a new birth. The Germans are mixing with them. If they ever get as far south as Sicily, Italy will be made over; the Germans themselves will be made over. I notice that the Italians and Germans get along well together."

I thought of the age-long wars between the Teutons and the Italians from the fifth to the twelfth century, but those days are over. They can apparently mingle in peace now, as I saw here and farther north.

It was also while I was in Florence that I first became definitely and in an irritated way conscious of a certain aspect of travel which no doubt thousands of other travelers have noted for themselves but of which, nevertheless, I feel called upon to speak.

I could never come in to the breakfast table either there, or at Rome, or in Venice, or Milan, without encountering a large company of that peculiarly American brand of sightseers, not enormously rich, of no great dignity, but comfortable and above all enormously pleased with themselves. I could never look at any of this tribe, comfortably clothed, very pursy and fussy, without thinking what a far cry it is from the temperament which makes for art or great originality to the temperament which makes for normality—the great, so-called sane, conservative mass. God spare me! I'll admit that for general purposes, the value of breeding, trading, rearing of children in comfort, producing the living atmosphere of life in which we "find" ourselves and from which art, by the grace of great public occasions may rise, people of this type are essential. But seen individually, dissociated from great background masses, they are—but let me not go wild. Viewed from the artistic angle, the stress of great occasions, great emotion, great necessities, they fall into such pigmy weaknesses, almost ridiculous. Here abroad they come so regularly, Pa and Ma. Pa infrequently, and a little vague-looking from overwork and limited vision of soul; Ma not infrequently, a little superior, vain, stuffy, envious, dull and hard. I never see such a woman as that but my gorge rises a little. The one idea of a pair like this, particularly of the mother, is the getting her children (if there be any) properly married, the girls particularly, and in this phase of family politics Pa has obviously little to say. Their appearance abroad, accompanied by Henry and

George, Junior, and Mary and Anabel, is for—I scarcely know what. It is so plain on the face of it that no single one of them has the least inkling of what he is seeing. I sat in a carriage with two of them in Rome, viewing the ruins of the Via Appia, and when we reached the tomb of Cæcilia Metella I heard:

"Oh, yes. There it is. What was *she*, anyhow? He was a Roman general, I think, and *she* was his wife. His house was next door and he built this tomb here so she would be near him. Isn't it wonderful? Such a nice idea!"

So far as I could make out from watching this throng the principal idea was to be able to say that they had been abroad. Poor old Florence! Its beauty and its social significance passed unrecognized. Art, so far as I could judge from the really unmoved spectators present, was for crazy people. The artist was some weird, spindling, unfortunate fool, a little daft perhaps, but tolerable for a strange furore he seemed to have created. Great men made and used him. He was, after his fashion, a servant. The objectionable feature of a picture like Botticelli's "Spring" would be the nudity of the figures! From a Rubens or a nude Raphael we lead brash, unctuous, self-conscious Mary away in silence. If we encounter, perchance, quite unexpectedly a "Leda" by Michelangelo or a too nude "Assumption" by Bronzino, we turn away in disgust. Art must be limited to conventional theories and when so limited is not worth much anyhow.

It was amazing to see them strutting in and out, their good clothes rustling, an automobile in waiting, noisily puffing the while they gather aimless "impressions" wherewith to browbeat their neighbors. George and Henry and Mary and Anabel, protesting half the time or in open rebellion, are duly led to see the things which have been the most enthusiastically recommended, be they palaces or restaurants.

I often wondered what it was—the best—which these people got out of their trip abroad. The heavy Germans I saw I always suspected of having solid Teutonic understanding and appreciation of everything; the English were uniformly polite, reserved, intelligent, apparently discriminating. But these Americans! If you told them the true story of Antinous, whose head I saw them occasionally admiring; or forced upon them the true details of the Borgias, the Sforzas, the Medici, or even the historical development of Art, they would fly in horror. They have no room in their little crania for anything save their own notions,—the standards of the Methodist Church at Keokuk. I think, sometimes, perhaps it is because we are all growing to a different standard, trying to make life something different from what it has always been, or appeared to be, that all the trouble comes about. Time will remedy that. Life,—its heavy, interminable processes,—will break any theory. I conceive of life as a blind goddess, pouring from separate jars, one of which she holds in each hand, simultaneously, the streams of good and evil, which mingling, make this troubled existence, flowing ever onward to the sea.

It was also while I was at Florence that I finally decided to change my plan and visit Venice. "It is a city without a disappointment," a publisher-friend of mine had one time assured me, with the greatest confidence. And so, here at Florence, on this first morning, I altered my plans; I changed my ticket at Thomas Cook's and crowded Venice in between Florence and Milan. I gave myself a stay of four days, deciding to lengthen it if I chose.

I really think that every traveler of to-day owes a debt of gratitude to Thomas Cook & Sons. I never knew, until I went abroad what an accommodation the offices of this concern are. Your mail is always courteously received and cared for; your routes and tickets are changed and altered at your slightest whim; your local bank is their cash-desk and the only advisers you have, if you are alone and without the native tongue at your convenience, are their clerks and agents at the train. It does not make any difference to me that that is their business and that they make a profit. In a foreign city where you are quite alone you would grant them twice the profit for this courtesy. And it was my experience, in the slight use I made of their service, that their orders and letters of advice were carefully respected and that when you came conducted by Thomas Cook, whether you took the best or the worst, you were politely and assiduously looked after.

One of the most amusing letters that I received while abroad was from this same publisher-friend who wanted me to go to Venice. Not so long before I left Rome, he had arrived with his wife, daughter, and a young girl friend of his daughter whose first trip abroad they were sponsoring. At a luncheon they had given me, the matter of seeing the Pope had come up and I mentioned that I had been so fortunate as to find some one who could introduce me, and that it was just possible, if they wished it, that my friend would extend his courtesy to them. The young girls in particular were eager, but I was not sure. I left Rome immediately afterward, writing to my British correspondent, bespeaking his interest in their behalf, and at the same time to my publisher-friend that I was doing so. As an analysis of girlhood vagaries, keen and clever, read his letter:

My Dear Dreiser:

The young woman who thinks she wants to see the Pope goes under the name of Margaret,—but I wouldn't try very hard to bring it about, because if Margaret went, my daughter would want to go, and if Margaret and my daughter went, my wife would feel out in the cold. (The old man can stand it.)

Margaret's motives are simply childish curiosity, possibly combined with a slight desire to give pleasure to the Holy Father.

But don't try to get that Papal interview for Margaret unless you can get it for all the ladies. You will introduce a serpent into my paradise.

No serpent was introduced because I couldn't get the interview.

And the cells and cloister of San Marco,—shall I ever forget them? I went there on a spring morning (spring in Italy) when the gleaming light outside filled the cloister with a cool brightness, and studied the frescoes of Fra Angelico and loitered between the columns of the arches in the cloister proper, meditating upon the beauty of the things here gathered. Really, Italy is too beautiful. One should be a poet in soul, insatiable as to art, and he should linger here forever. Each poorest cell here has a small fresco by Fra Angelico, and the refectory, the chapter house, and the foresteria are filled with large compositions, all rich in that symbolism which is only wonderful because of the art-feeling of the master. I lingered in the cells, the small chambers once occupied by Savonarola, and meditated on the great zealot's imaginings. In a way his dream of the destruction of the Papacy came true.

Even as he preached, the Reformation was at hand, only he did not know it. Martin Luther was coming. The black cross was over Rome! And also true was his thought that the end of the old order in Italy had come. It surely had. Never afterwards was it quite the same and never would it be so again. And equally true was his vision of the red cross over Jerusalem, for never was the simple humanism of Jesus so firmly based in the minds of men as it is to-day, though all creeds and religious theories totter wearily to their ruin. Savonarola was destroyed, but not his visions or his pleas. They are as fresh and powerful to-day, as magnetic and gripping, as are any that have been made in history.

It was the same with the Bargello, the tombs of the Medici, San Miniato and the basilica and monastery at Fiesole. That last, with the wind singing in the cypresses, a faint mist blowing down the valley of the Arno, all Florence lying below and the lights of evening beginning to appear, stands fixed and clear in my mind. I saw it for the last time the evening before I left. I sat on a stone bench overlooking a wonderful prospect, rejoicing in the artistic spirit of Italy which has kept fresh and clean these wonders of art, when I was approached by a brown Dominican, his feet and head bare, his body stout and comfortable. He asked for alms! I gave him a lira for the sake of Savonarola who belonged to his order and—because of the spirit of Italy, that in the midst of a changing, commercializing world still ministers to these shrines of beauty and keeps them intact and altogether lovely.

One last word and I am done. I strolled out from Santa Croce one evening a little confused by the charm of all I had seen and wondering how I could best bestow my time for the remaining hours of light. I tried first to find the house of Michelangelo which I fancied was somewhere in the vicinity, but not finding it, came finally to the Arno which I followed upstream. The evening was very pleasant, quite a sense of spring in the air and of new-made gardens, and I overcame my disappointment at having failed to accomplish my original plan. I passed new streets, wider than the old ones in the heart of the city, with street lamps, arc-lights, modern awnings and a trolley-car running in the distance. Presently I came to a portion of the Arno lovelier than any I had yet seen. Of course the walls through which it flows in the city had disappeared and in their place came grass-covered banks with those tall thin poplars I had so much admired in France. The waters were a "Nile green" at this hour and the houses, collected in small groups, were brown, yellow, or white, with red or brown roofs and brown or green shutters. The old idea of arches with columns and large projecting roofs still persisted in these newer, outlying houses and made me wonder whether Florence might not, after all, always keep this characteristic.

As I went farther out the houses grew less frequent and lovely bluish-black hills appeared. There was a smoke-stack in the distance, just to show that Florence was not dead to the idea of manufacturing, and beyond in a somewhat different direction the dome of the cathedral,—that really impressive dome.

Some men were fishing in the stream from the bank, apparently catching nothing. I noticed the lovely cypresses of the South in the distance, the large villas on the hills, and here and there clumps of those tall, slender trees of France, not conspicuous elsewhere on my journey.

In one place I noticed the largest display of washing I have ever seen, quite the largest,—a whole field of linen, no less, hung out to dry; and in another place some slow-moving men cutting wood.

It was very warm, very pleasant, slightly suggestive of rain, with the smoke going up straight, and after a while when the evening church-bells were beginning to ring, calling to each other from vale and hill, my sense of springtime and pleasant rural and suburban sweetness was complete.

Laughter carried I noticed, in some peculiar, echoing way. The music of the bells was essentially quieting. I had no sense of Florence, old or new, but just spring, hope, new birth. And as I turned back after a time I knew I had acquired a different and very precious memory of Florence—something that would last me years and years. I should always think of the Arno as it looked this evening—how safe and gracious and still. I should always hear the voices in laughter, and the bells; I should always see the children playing on the green banks, quite as I used to play on the Wabash and the Tippecanoe; and their voices in Italian were no less sweet than our childish voices. I had a feeling that somehow the spirit of Italy was like that of America, and that somehow there is close kinship between us and Italy, and that it was not for nothing that an Italian discovered America or that Americans, of all people, have apparently loved Italy most and rivaled it most closely in their periods of greatest achievement.

CHAPTER XL
MARIA BASTIDA

IN studying out my itinerary at Florence I came upon the homely advice in Baedeker that in Venice "care should be taken in embarking and disembarking, especially when the tide is low, exposing the slimy lower steps." That, as much as anything I had ever read, visualized this wonder city to me. These Italian cities, not being large, end so quickly that before you can say Jack Robinson you are out of them and away, far into the country. It was early evening as we pulled out of Florence; and for a while the country was much the same as it had been in the south—hill-towns, medieval bridges and strongholds, the prevailing solid browns, pinks, grays and blues of the architecture, the white oxen, pigs and shabby carts, but gradually, as we neared Bologna, things seemed to take on a very modern air of factories, wide streets, thoroughly modern suburbs and the like. It grew dark shortly after that and the country was only favored by the rich radiance of the moon which made it more picturesque and romantic, but less definite and distinguishable.

In the compartment with me were two women, one a comfortable-looking matron traveling from Florence to Bologna, the other a young girl of twenty or twenty-one, of the large languorous type, and decidedly good looking. She was very plainly dressed and evidently belonged to the middle class.

The married Italian lady was small and good-looking and *bourgeoise*. Considerably before dinner-time, and as we were nearing Bologna, she opened a small basket which she carried and took from it a sandwich, an apple, and a bit of cheese, which she ate placidly. For some reason she occasionally smiled at me good-naturedly, but not speaking Italian, I was without the means of making a single observation. At Bologna I assisted her with her parcels and received a smiling backward glance and then I settled myself in my seat wondering what the remainder of the evening would bring forth. I was not so very long in discovering.

Once the married lady of Bologna had disappeared, my young companion took on new life. She rose, smoothed down her dress and reclined comfortably in her seat, her cheek laid close against the velvet-covered arm, and looked at me occasionally out of half-closed eyes. She finally tried to make herself more comfortable by lying down and I offered her my fur overcoat as a pillow. She accepted it with a half-smile.

About this time the dining-car steward came through to take a memorandum of those who wished to reserve places for dinner. He looked at the young lady but she shook her head negatively. I made a sudden decision. "Reserve two places," I said. The servitor bowed politely and went away. I scarcely knew why I had said this, for I was under the impression my young lady companion spoke only Italian, but I was trusting much to my intuition at the moment.

A little later, when it was drawing near the meal time, I said, "Do you speak English?"

"*Non*," she replied, shaking her head.

"*Sprechen Sie Deutsch?*"

"*Ein wenig*," she replied, with an easy, babyish, half-German, half-Italian smile.

"*Sie sind doch Italianisch*," I suggested.

"*Oh, oui!*" she replied, and put her head down comfortably on my coat.

"*Reisen Sie nach Venedig?*" I inquired.

"*Oui*," she nodded. She half smiled again.

I had a real thrill of satisfaction out of all this, for although I speak abominable German, just sufficient to make myself understood by a really clever person, yet I knew, by the exercise of a little tact I should have a companion to dinner.

"You will take dinner with me, won't you?" I stammered in my best German. "I do not understand German very well, but perhaps we can make ourselves understood. I have two places."

She hesitated, and said—"*Ich bin nicht hungerich.*"

"But for company's sake," I replied.

"*Mais, oui*," she replied indifferently.

I then asked her whether she was going to any particular hotel in Venice—I was bound for the Royal Danieli—and she replied that her home was in Venice.

Maria Bastida was a most interesting type. She was a Diana for size, pallid, with a full rounded body. Her hair was almost flaxen and her hands large but not unshapely. She seemed to be strangely world-weary and yet strangely passionate—the kind of mind and body that does and does not, care; a kind of dull, smoldering fire burning within her and yet she seemed indifferent into the bargain. She asked me an occasional question about New York as we dined, and though wine was proffered she drank little and, true to her statement that she was not hungry, ate little. She confided to me in soft, difficult German that she was trying not to get too stout, that her mother was German and her father Italian and that she had been visiting an uncle in Florence who was in the grocery business. I wondered how she came to be traveling first class.

The time passed. Dinner was over and in several hours more we would be in Venice. We returned to our compartment and because the moon was shining magnificently we stood in the corridor and watched its radiance on clustered cypresses, villa-crowned hills, great stretches of flat prairie or marsh land, all barren of trees, and occasionally on little towns all white and brown, glistening in the clear light.

"It will be a fine night to see Venice for the first time," I suggested.

"*Oh, oui! Herrlich! Prachtvoll!*" she replied in her queer mixture of French and German.

I liked her command of sounding German words.

She told me the names of stations at which we stopped, and finally she exclaimed quite gaily, "Now we are here! The Lagoon!"

I looked out and we were speeding over a wide body of water. It was beautifully silvery and in the distance I could see the faint outlines of a city. Very shortly we were in a car yard, as at Rome and Florence, and then under a large train shed, and then, conveyed by an enthusiastic Italian porter, we came out on the wide stone platform that faces the Grand Canal. Before me were the white walls of marble buildings and intervening in long, waving lines a great street of water; the gondolas, black, shapely, a great company of them, nudging each other on its rippling bosom, green-stained stone steps, sharply illuminated by electric lights leading down to them, a great crowd of gesticulating porters and passengers. I startled Maria by grabbing her by the arm, exclaiming in German, "Wonderful! Wonderful!"

"*Est ist herrlich*" (It is splendid), she replied.

We stepped into a gondola, our bags being loaded in afterwards. It was a singularly romantic situation, when you come to think of it: entering Venice by moonlight and gliding off in a gondola in company with an unknown and charming Italian girl who smiled and sighed by turns and fairly glowed with delight and pride at my evident enslavement to the beauty of it all.

She was directing the gondolier where to leave her when I exclaimed, "Don't leave me—please! Let's do Venice together!"

She was not offended. She shook her head, a bit regretfully I like to think, and smiled most charmingly. "Venice has gone to your head. To-morrow you'll forget me!"

And there my adventure ended!

It is a year, as I write, since I last saw the flaxen-haired Maria, and I find she remains quite as firmly fixed in my memory as Venice itself, which is perhaps as it should be.

*   *   *   *   *

But the five or six days I spent in Venice—how they linger. How shall one ever paint water and light and air in words. I had wild thoughts as I went about of a splendid panegyric on Venice—a poem, no less—but finally gave it up, contenting myself with humble notes made on the spot which at some time I hoped to weave into something better. Here they are—a portion of them—the task unfinished.

What a city! To think that man driven by the hand of circumstance—the dread of destruction—should have sought out these mucky sea islands and eventually reared as splendid a thing as this. "The Veneti driven by the Lombards," reads my Baedeker, "sought the marshy islands of the sea." Even so. Then came hard toil, fishing, trading, the wonders of the wealth of the East. Then came the Doges, the cathedral, these splendid semi-Byzantine palaces. Then came the painters, religion, romance, history. To-day here it stands, a splendid shell, reminiscent of its former glory. Oh, Venice! Venice!

* * * * *

The Grand Canal under a glittering moon. The clocks striking twelve. A horde of black gondolas. Lovely cries. The rest is silence. Moon picking out the ripples in silver and black. Think of these old stone steps, white marble stained green, laved by the waters of the sea these hundreds of years. A long, narrow street of water. A silent boat passing. And this is a city of a hundred and sixty thousand!

* * * * *

Wonderful painted arch doorways and windows. Trefoil and quadrifoil decorations. An old iron gate with some statues behind it. A balcony with flowers. The Bridge of Sighs! Nothing could be so perfect as a city of water.

* * * * *

The Lagoon at midnight under a full moon. Now I think I know what Venice is at its best. Distant lights, distant voices. Some one singing. There are pianos in this sea-isle city, playing at midnight. Just now a man silhouetted blackly, under a dark arch. Our gondola takes us into the very hallway of the Royal-Danieli.

* * * * *

Water! Water! The music of all earthly elements. The lap of water! The sigh of water! The flow of water! In Venice you have it everywhere. It sings at the base of your doorstep; it purrs softly under your window; it suggests the eternal rhythm and the eternal flow at every angle. Time is running away; life is running away, and here in Venice, at every angle (under your window) is its symbol. I know of no city which at once suggests the lapse of time hourly, momentarily, and yet soothes the heart because of it. For all its movement or because of it, it is gay, light-hearted, without being enthusiastic. The peace that passes all understanding is here, soft, rhythmic, artistic. Venice is as gay as a song, as lovely as a jewel (an opal or an emerald), as rich as marble and as great as verse. There can only be one Venice in all the world!

* * * * *

No horses, no wagons, no clanging of cars. Just the patter of human feet. You listen here and the very language is musical. The voices are soft. Why should they be loud? They have nothing to contend with. I am wild about this place. There is a sweetness in the hush of things which woos, and yet it is not the hush of silence. All is life here, all movement—a sweet, musical gaiety. I wonder if murder and robbery can flourish in any of these sweet streets. The life here is like that of children playing. I swear in all my life I have never had such ravishing sensations of exquisite art-joy, of pure, delicious enthusiasm for the physical, exterior aspect of a city. It is as mild and sweet as moonlight itself.

* * * * *

This hotel, Royal Danieli, is a delicious old palace, laved on one side by a canal. My room commands the whole of the Lagoon. George Sand and Alfred de Musset occupied a room here somewhere. Perhaps I have it.

* * * * *

Venice is so markedly different from Florence. There all is heavy, somber, defensive, serious. Here all is light, airy, graceful, delicate. There could be no greater variation. Italy is such a wonderful country. It has Florence, Venice, Rome and Naples, to say nothing of Milan and the Riviera, which should really belong to it. No cornices here in Venice. They are all left behind in Florence.

* * * * *

What shall I say of St. Mark's and the Ducal Palace—mosaics of history, utterly exquisite. The least fragment of St. Mark's I consider of the utmost value. The Ducal Palace should be guarded as one of the great treasures of the world. It is perfect.

* * * * *

There can only be one Venice

Fortunately I saw St. Mark's in the morning, in clear, refreshing, springlike sunlight. Neither Venice nor Florence have the hard glitter of the South—only a rich brightness. The domes are almost gold in effect. The nine frescoes of the façade, gold, red and blue. The walls, cream and gray. Before it is the oblique quadrangle which necessitates your getting far to one side to see the church squarely—a perfect and magnificently individual jewel. All the great churches are that, I notice. Overhead a sky of blue. Before you a great, smooth pavement, crowded with people, the Campanile (just recompleted) soaring heavenward in perfect lines. What a square! What a treasure for a city to have! Momentarily this space is swept over by great clouds of pigeons. The new reproduction of the old Campanile glows with a radiance all its own. Above all, the gilded crosses of the church. To the right the lovely arcaded façade of the library. To the right of the church, facing the square, the fretted beauty of the Doge's Palace—a portion of it. As I was admiring it a warship in the harbor fired a great gun—twelve o'clock. Up went all my pigeons, thousands it seemed, sweeping in great restless circles while church bells began to chime and whistles to blow. Where are the manufactories of Venice?

*   *   *   *   *

At first you do not realize it, but suddenly it occurs to you—a city of one hundred and sixty thousand without a wagon, or horse, without a long, wide street, anywhere, without trucks, funeral processions, street cars. All the shops doing a brisk business, citizens at work everywhere, material pouring in and out, but no wagons—only small barges and gondolas. No noise save the welcome clatter of human feet; no sights save those which have a strange, artistic pleasantness. You can hear people talking sociably, their voices echoed by the strange cool walls. You can hear birds singing high up in pretty windows where flowers trail downward; you can hear the soft lap of waters on old steps at times, the softest, sweetest music of all.

*   *   *   *   *

I find boxes, papers, straw, vegetable waste, all cast indifferently into the water and all borne swiftly out to sea. People open windows and cast out packages as if this were the only way. I walked into the Banca di Napoli this afternoon, facing the Grand Canal. It was only a few moments after the regular closing hour. I came upon it from some narrow lane—some "dry street." It was quite open, the ground floor. There was a fine, dark-columned hall opening out upon the water. Where were the clerks, I wondered? There were none. Where that ultimate hurry and sense of life that characterizes the average bank at this hour? Nowhere. It was lovely, open, dark,—as silent as a ruin. When did the bank do business, I asked myself. No answer. I watched the waters from its steps and then went away.

*   *   *   *   *

One of the little tricks of the architects here is to place a dainty little Gothic balcony above a door, perhaps the only one on the façade, and that hung with vines.

* * * * *

Venice is mad about campaniles. It has a dozen, I think, some of them leaning, like the tower at Pisa.

* * * * *

I must not forget the old rose of the clouds in the west.

* * * * *

A gondolier selling vegetables and crying his wares is pure music. At my feet white steps laved by whitish-blue water. Tall, cool, damp walls, ten feet apart. Cool, wet, red brick pavements. The sun shining above makes one realize how lovely and cool it is here; and birds singing everywhere.

* * * * *

Gondolas doing everything, carrying casks, coal, lumber, lime, stone, flour, bricks, and boxed supplies generally, and others carrying vegetables, fruit, kindling and flowers. Only now I saw a boat slipping by crowded with red geraniums.

* * * * *

Lovely pointed windows and doors; houses, with colonnades, trefoils, quadrifoils, and exquisite fluted cornices to match, making every house that strictly adheres to them a jewel. It is Gothic, crossed with Moorish and Byzantine fancy. Some of them take on the black and white of London smoke, though why I have no idea. Others being colored richly at first are weathered by time into lovely half-colors or tones.

* * * * *

These little canals are heavenly! They wind like scattered ribbons, flung broadcast, and the wind touches them only in spots, making the faintest ripples. Mostly they are as still as death. They have exquisite bridges crossing in delightful arches and wonderful doors and steps open into them, steps gray or yellow or black with age, steps that have green and brown moss on them and that are alternately revealed or hidden by a high or low tide. Here comes a gondolier now, peddling oranges. The music of his voice!

* * * * *

Latticework is everywhere, and it so obviously *belongs* here. Latticework in the churches, the houses, the public buildings. Venice loves it. It is oriental and truly beautiful.

*   *   *   *   *

I find myself at a branch station of the water street-car service. There are gondolas here, too,—a score for hire. This man hails me genially, his brown hands and face, and small, old, soft roll hat a picture in the sun. I feel as if I were dreaming or as if this were some exquisite holiday of my childhood. One could talk for years of these passages in which, amidst the shadow and sunlight of cool, gray walls a gleam of color has shown itself. You look down narrow courts to lovely windows or doors or bridges or niches with a virgin or a saint in them. Now it is a black-shawled housewife or a fat, phlegmatic man that turns a corner; now a girl in a white skirt and pale green shawl, or a red skirt and a black shawl. Unexpected doorways, dark and deep with pleasant industries going on inside, bakeries with a wealth of new, warm bread; butcheries with red meat and brass scales; small restaurants, where appetizing roasts and meat-pies are displayed. Unexpected bridges, unexpected squares, unexpected streams of people moving in the sun, unexpected terraces, unexpected boats, unexpected voices, unexpected songs. That is Venice.

*   *   *   *   *

To-day I took a boat on the Grand Canal to the Giardino which is at the eastern extreme of the city. It was evening. I found a lovely island just adjoining the gardens—a Piazza d'Arena. Rich green grass and a line of small trees along three sides. Silvery water. A second leaning tower and more islands in the distance. Cool and pleasant, with that lovely sense of evening in the air which comes only in spring. They said it would be cold in Venice, but it isn't. Birds twittering, the waters of the bay waveless, the red, white and brown colors of the city showing in rich patches. I think if there is a heaven on earth, it is Venice in spring.

*   *   *   *   *

Just now the sun came out and I witnessed a Turner effect. First this lovely bay was suffused with a silvery-gold light—its very surface. Then the clouds in the west broke into ragged masses. The sails, the islands, the low buildings in the distance began to stand out brilliantly. Even the Campanile, San Giorgio Maggiore and the Salute took on an added glory. I was witnessing a great sky-and-water song, a poem, a picture—something to identify Venice with my life. Three ducks went by, high in the air, honking as they went. A long black flotilla of thin-prowed coal barges passed in the foreground. The engines of a passing steamer beat rhythmically and I breathed deep and joyously to think I had witnessed all.

*   *   *   *   *

Bells over the water, the lap of waves, the smell of seaweed. How soft and elevated and ethereal voices sound at this time. An Italian sailor, sitting on the grass looking out over it all, has his arms about his girl.

*   *   *   *   *

It would be easy to give an order for ten thousand lovely views of Venice, and get them.

*   *   *   *   *

CHAPTER XLI
VENICE

ASIDE from the cathedral of St. Mark's, the Doge's Palace and the Academy or Venetian gallery of old masters, I could find little of artistic significance in Venice—little aside from the wonderful spectacle of the city as a whole. As a spectacle, viewed across the open space of water, known as the Lagoon, the churches of San Giorgio Maggiore and Santa Maria della Salute with their domes and campaniles strangely transfigured by light and air, are beautiful. Close at hand, for me, they lost much romance which distance gave them, though the mere space of their interiors was impressive. The art, according to my judgment, was bad and in the main I noticed that my guide books agreed with me—spiritless religious representations which, after the Sistine Chapel in Rome and such pictures as those of Michelangelo's "Holy Family" and Botticelli's "Adoration of the Magi" in the Uffizi at Florence, were without import. I preferred to speculate on the fear of the plague which had produced the Salute and the discovery of the body of St. Stephen, the martyr, which had given rise to San Giorgio, for it was interesting to think, with these facts before me, how art and spectacle in life so often take their rise from silly, almost pointless causes and a plain lie is more often the foundation of a great institution than a truth. Santa Maria didn't save the citizens of Venice from the plague in 1630, and in 1110 the Doge Ordelafo Faliero did not bring back the true body of St. Stephen from Palestine, although he may have thought he did,—at least there are other "true bodies." But the old, silly progress of illusion, vanity, politics and the like has produced these and other institutions throughout the world and will continue to do so, no doubt, until time shall be no more. It was interesting to me to see the once large and really beautiful Dominican monastery surrounding San Giorgio turned into barracks and offices for government officials. I do not see why these churches should not be turned into libraries or galleries. Their religious import is quite gone.

In Venice it was, I think, that I got a little sick of churches and second- and third-rate art. The city itself is so beautiful, exteriorly speaking, that only the greatest art could be tolerated here, yet aside from the Academy, which is crowded with canvases by Bellini, Tintoretto, Titian, Veronese and others of the Venetian school, and the Ducal Palace, largely decorated by Tintoretto and Veronese, there is nothing, save of course St. Mark's. Outside of that and the churches of the Salute and San Giorgio,—both bad, artistically, I think,—there are thirty-three or thirty-four other churches all with bits of something which gets them into the catalogues, a Titian, a Tintoretto, a Giorgione or a Paolo Veronese, until the soul wearies and you say to yourself—"Well, I've had about enough of this—what is the use?"

There is no use. Unless you are tracing the rise of religious art, or trying to visit the tombs of semi-celebrated persons, or following out the work of some one man or group of men to the last fragment you might as well desist. There is nothing in it. I sought church after church, entering dark, pleasant, but not often imposing, interiors only to find a single religious representation of one kind or another hardly worth the trouble. In the Frari I found Titian's famous Madonna of the Pescaro family and a pretentious mausoleum commemorating Canova, and in Santa Maria Formosa Palma Vecchio's St. Barbara and four other saints, which appealed to me very much, but in the main I was disappointed and made dreary. After St. Peter's, the Vatican, St. Paul's Without the Walls in Rome, the cathedrals at Pisa and elsewhere, and the great galleries of Florence, Venice seemed to me artistically dull. I preferred always to get out into the streets again to see the small shops, to encounter the winding canals, to cross the little bridges and to feel that here was something new and different, far different and more artistic than anything which any church or museum could show.

One of the strangest things about Venice to me was the curious manner in which you could always track a great public square or market place of some kind by following some thin trickling of people you would find making their way in a given direction. Suddenly in some quite silent residence section, with all its lovely waterways about you, you would encounter a small thin stream of people going somewhere, perhaps five or six in a row, over bridges, up narrow alleys, over more bridges, through squares or triangles past churches or small stores and constantly swelling in volume until you found yourself in the midst of a small throng turning now right, now left, when suddenly you came out on the great open market place or piazza to which they were all tending. They always struck me as a sheep-like company, these Venetians, very mild, very soft, pattering here and there with vague, almost sad eyes. Here in Venice I saw no newspapers displayed at all, nor ever heard any called, nor saw any read. There was none of that morning vigor which characterizes an American city. It was always more like a quiet village scene to me than any aspect of a fair-sized city. Yet because I was comfortable in Venice and because all the while I was there it was so radiantly beautiful, I left it with real sorrow. To me it was perfect.

*   *   *   *   *

The one remaining city of Italy that I was yet to see, Milan, because already I had seen so much of Italy and because I was eager to get into Switzerland and Germany, was of small interest to me. It was a long, tedious ride to Milan, and I spent my one day there rambling about without enthusiasm. Outside of a half-dozen early Christian basilicas, which I sedulously avoided (I employed a guide), there was only the cathedral, the now dismantled palace and fortress of the Sforzas masquerading as a museum and the local art gallery, an imposing affair crowded with that same religious art work of the Renaissance which, one might almost say in the language of the Milwaukee brewer, had made Italy famous. I was, however, about fed up on art. As a cathedral that of Milan seemed as imposing as any, great and wonderful. I was properly impressed with its immense stained-glass windows, said to be the largest in the world, its fifty-two columns supporting its great roof, its ninety-eight pinnacles and two thousand statues. Of a splendid edifice such as this there is really nothing to say—it is like Amiens, Rouen, and Canterbury—simply astounding. It would be useless to attempt to describe the emotions it provoked, as useless as to indicate the feelings some of the pictures in the local gallery aroused in me. It would be Amiens all over again, or some of the pictures in the Uffizi. It seemed to me the newest of all the Gothic cathedrals I saw, absolutely preserved in all its details and as recently erected as yesterday, yet it was begun in 1386.

The wonder of this and of every other cathedral like it that I saw, to me, was never their religious but their artistic significance. Some one with a splendid imagination must always have been behind each one—and I can never understand the character or the temper of an age or a people that will let anything happen to them.

But if I found little of thrilling artistic significance after Rome and the south I was strangely impressed with the modernity of Milan. Europe, to me, is not so old in its texture anywhere as one would suppose. Most European cities of large size are of recent growth, just as American cities are. So many of the great buildings that we think of as time-worn, such as the Ducal Palace at Venice, and elsewhere, are in an excellent state of preservation—quite new looking. Venice has many new buildings in the old style. Rome is largely composed of modern tenements and apartment houses. There are elevators in Perugia, and when you reach Milan you find it newer than St. Louis or Cleveland. If there is any medieval spirit anywhere remaining in Milan I could not find it. The shops are bright and attractive. There are large department stores, and the honk-honk of the automobile is quite as common here as anywhere. It has only five hundred thousand population, but, even so, it evidences great commercial force. If you ride out in the suburbs, as I did, you see new houses, new factories, new streets, new everything. Unlike the inhabitants of southern Italy, the people are large physically and I did not understand this until I learned that they are freely mingled with the Germans. The Germans are here in force, in control of the silk mills, the leather manufactories, the restaurants, the hotels, the book stores and printing establishments. It is a wonder to me that they are not in control of the Opera House and the musical activities, and I have no doubt that they influence it greatly. The director of La Scala ought to be a German, if he is not. I got a first suggestion of Paris in the tables set before the cafés in the Arcade of Vittorio Emanuele and had my first taste of Germany in the purely German beer-halls with their orchestras of men or women, where for a few cents expended for beer you can sit by the hour and listen to the music. In the hotel where I stopped the German precision of regulation was as marked as anywhere in Germany. It caused me to wonder whether the Germans would eventually sweep down and possess Italy and, if they did, what they would make of it or what Italy would make of them.

CHAPTER XLII
LUCERNE

I ENTERED Switzerland at Chiasso, a little way from Lake Como in Italy, and left it at Basle near the German frontier, and all I saw was mountains—mountains—mountains—some capped with snow and some without, tall, sharp, craggy peaks, and rough, sharp declivities, with here and there a patch of grass, here and there a deep valley, here and there a lonely, wide-roofed, slab-built house with those immense projecting eaves first made familiar to me by the shabby adaptations which constitute our "L" stations in New York. The landscape hardens perceptibly a little way out of Milan. High slopes and deep lakes appear. At Chiasso, the first stop in Switzerland, I handed the guard a half-dozen letters I had written in Milan and stamped with Italian stamps. I did not know until I did this that we were out of Italy, had already changed guards and that a new crew—Swiss—was in charge of the train. "Monsieur," he said, tapping the stamp significantly, "vous êtes en Suisse." I do not understand French, but I did comprehend that, and I perceived also that I was talking to a Swiss. All the people on the platform were "Schweitzers" as the Germans call them, fair, chunky, stolid-looking souls without a touch of that fire or darkness so generally present a few miles south. Why should a distance of ten miles, five miles, make such an astonishing change? It is one of the strangest experiences of travel, to cross an imaginary boundary-line and find everything different; people, dress, architecture, landscape, often soil and foliage. It proves that countries are not merely soil and climatic conditions but that there is something more—a race stock which is not absolutely a product of the soil and which refuses to yield entirely to climate. Races like animals have an origin above soil and do hold their own in spite of changed or changing climatic conditions. Cross any boundary you like from one country into another and judge for yourself.

Now that I was started, really out of Italy, I was ready for any change, the more marked the better; and here was one. Switzerland is about as much like Italy as a rock is like a bouquet of flowers—a sharp-edged rock and a rich colorful, odorous bouquet. And yet, in spite of all its chill, bare bleakness, its high ridges and small shut-in valleys, it has beauty, cold but real. As the train sped on toward Lucerne I kept my face glued to the window-pane on one side or the other, standing most of the time in the corridor, and was rewarded constantly by a magnificent panorama. Such bleak, sharp crags as stood always above us, such cold, white fields of snow! Sometimes the latter stretched down toward us in long deep cañons or ravines until they disappeared as thin white streaks at the bottom. I saw no birds of any kind flying; no gardens nor patches of flowers anywhere, only brown or gray or white châlets with heavy overhanging eaves and an occasional stocky, pale-skinned citizen in a short jacket, knee trousers, small round hat and flamboyant waistcoat. I wondered whether I was really seeing the national costume. I was. I saw more of it at Lucerne, that most hotelly of cities, and in the mountains and valleys of the territory beyond it—toward Basle. Somebody once said of God that he might love all the creatures he had made but he certainly couldn't admire them. I will reverse that for Switzerland. I might always admire its wonders but I could never love them.

And yet after hours and hours of just this twisting and turning up slope and down valley, when I reached Lucerne I thought it was utterly beautiful. Long before we reached there the lake appeared and we followed its shores, whirling in and out of tunnels and along splendid slopes. Arrived at Lucerne, I came out into the piazza which spreads before the station to the very edge of the lake. I was instantly glad that I had included Lucerne in my itinerary. It was evening and the lamps in the village (it is not a large city) were already sparkling and the water of the lake not only reflected the glow of the lamps along its shores but the pale pinks and mauves over the tops of the peaks in the west. There was snow on the upper stretches of the mountains but down here in this narrow valley filled with quaint houses, hotels, churches and modern apartments, all was balmy and pleasant,—not at all cold. My belongings were bundled into the attendant 'bus and I was rattled off to one of the best hotels I saw abroad—the National—of the Ritz-Carlton system; very quiet, very ornate, and with all those conveniences and comforts which the American has learned to expect, plus a European standard of service and politeness of which we can as yet know nothing in America.

I am afraid I have an insatiable appetite for natural beauty. I am entertained by character, thrilled by art, but of all the enlarging spiritual influences the natural panorama is to me the most important. This night, after my first day of rambling about Lucerne, I sat out on my hotel balcony, overlooking the lake and studied the dim moonlit outlines of the peaks crowding about it, the star-shine reflected in the water, the still distances and the moon sinking over the peaks to the west of the quaint city. Art has no method of including, or suggesting even, these vast sidereal spaces. The wonder of the night and moonlight is scarcely for the painter's brush. It belongs in verse, the drama, great literary pageants such as those of Balzac, Turgenieff and Flaubert, but not in pictures. The human eye can see so much and the human heart responds so swiftly that it is only by suggestion that anything is achieved in art. Art cannot give you the night in all its fullness save as, by suggestion, it brings back the wonder of the reality which you have already felt and seen.

I think perhaps of the two impressions that I retained most distinctly of Lucerne, that of the evening and of the morning, the morning was best. I came out on my balcony at dawn, the first morning after I arrived, when the lake was lying below me in glassy, olive-black stillness. Up the bank to my left were trees, granite slopes, a small châlet built out over the water, its spiles standing in the still lake in a soothing, restful way. To my right, at the foot of the lake, lay Lucerne, its quaint outlines but vaguely apparent in the shadow. Across the lake only a little space were small boats, a dock, a church, and beyond them, in a circle, gray-black peaks. At their extreme summits along a rough, horny skyline were the suggestions of an electric dawn, a pale, steely gray brightening from dark into light.

It was not cold at Lucerne, though it was as yet only early March. The air was as soft and balmy as at Venice. As I sat there the mountain skyline brightened first to a faint pink, the snow on the ridges took on a lavender and bluish hue as at evening, the green of the lower slopes became softly visible and the water began to reflect the light of the sky, the shadow of the banks, the little boats, and even some wild ducks flying over its surface,—ducks coming from what bleak, drear spaces I could only guess. Presently I saw a man come out from a hotel, enter a small canoe and paddle away in the direction of the upper lake. No other living thing appeared until the sky had changed from pink to blue, the water to a rich silvery gray, the green to a translucent green and the rays of the sun came finally glistering over the peaks. Then the rough notches and gaps of the mountains—gray where blown clear of snow, or white where filled with it—took on a sharp, brilliant roughness. You could see the cold peaks outlined clearly in the water, and the little steeples of the churches. My wild ducks were still paddling briskly about. I noticed that a particular pair found great difficulty in finding the exact spot to suit them. With a restless quank, quank, quank, they would rise and fly a space only to light with a soft splatter and quack cheerfully. When they saw the lone rower returning they followed him, coming up close to the hotel dock and paddling smartly in his vicinity. I watched him fasten his boat and contemplate the ducks. After he had gone away I wondered if they were pets of his. Then the day having clearly come, I went inside.

By ten o'clock all Lucerne seemed to have come out to promenade along the smooth walks that border the shore. Pretty church-bells in severe, conical towers began to ring and students in small, dark, tambourine-like hats, jackets, tight trousers, and carrying little canes about the size of batons, began to walk smartly up and down. There were a few travelers present, wintering here, no doubt,—English and Americans presenting their usual severe, intellectual, inquiring and self-protective dispositions. They stood out in sharp contrast to the native Swiss,—a fair, stolid, quiescent people. The town itself by day I found to be as clean, spruce and orderly as a private pine forest. I never saw a more spick and span place, not even in ge-washed and ge-brushed Germany.

This being Sunday and wonderfully fair, I decided to take the trip up the lake on one of the two small steamers that I saw anchored at apparently rival docks. They may have served boats plying on different arms of the lake. On this trip I fell in with a certain "Major Y. Myata, M.D., Surgeon, Imperial Japanese Army" as his card read, who, I soon learned, was doing Europe much as I was, only entirely alone. I first saw him as he bought his ticket on board the steamer at Lucerne,— a small, quiet, wiry man, very keen and observant, who addressed the purser in English first and later in German. He came on the top deck into the first-class section, a fair-sized camera slung over his shoulder, a notebook sticking out of the pocket, and finding a seat, very carefully dusted his small feet with the extreme corners of his military overcoat, and rubbed his thin, horse-hairy mustache with a small, claw-like hand. He looked about in a quiet way and began after the boat started to take pictures and make copious notes. He had small, piercing, bird-like eyes and a strangely unconscious-seeming manner which was in reality anything but unconscious. We fell to talking of Switzerland, Germany and Italy, where he had been, and by degrees I learned the route of his trip, or what he chose to tell me of it, and his opinions concerning Europe and the Far East—as much as he chose to communicate.

It appeared that before coming to Europe this time he had made but one other trip out of Japan, namely to California, where he had spent a year. He had left Japan in October, sailed direct for London and reached it in November; had already been through Holland and Belgium, France, Germany, Italy, and was bound for Munich and Hungary and, not strange to relate, Russia. He was coming to America—New York particularly, and was eager to know of a good hotel. I mentioned twenty. He spoke English, French, Italian and German, although he had never before been anywhere except to California. I knew he spoke German, for I talked to him in that language and after finding that he could speak it better than I could I took his word for the rest. We lunched together. I mentioned the little I knew of the Japanese in New York. He brightened considerably. We compared travel notes—Italy, France, England. "I do not like the Italians," he observed in one place. "I think they are tricky. They do not tell the truth."

"They probably held up your baggage at the station."

"They did more than that to me. I could never depend on them."

"How do you like the Germans?" I asked him.

"A very wonderful people. Very civil I thought. The Rhine is beautiful."

I had to smile when I learned that he had done the night cafés of Paris, had contrasted English and French farce as represented by the Empire and the Folies-Bergère, and knew all about the Post Impressionists and the Futurists or Cubists. The latter he did not understand. "It is possible," he said in his strange, sing-songy way, "that they represent some motives of constructive subconscious mind with which we are not any of us familiar yet. Electricity came to man in some such way as that. I do not know. I do not pretend to understand it."

At the extreme upper end of Lucerne where the boat stopped, we decided to get out and take the train back. He was curious to see the shrine or tomb of William Tell which was listed as being near here, but when he learned that it was two or three miles and that we would miss a fast train, he was willing to give it up. With a strange, old-world wisdom he commented on the political organization of Switzerland, saying that it struck him as strange that these Alpine fastnesses should ever have achieved an identity of their own. "They have always been separate communities until quite recently," he said, "and I think that perhaps only railroads, tunnels, telegraph and telephone have made their complete union satisfactory now."

I marveled at the wisdom of this Oriental as I do at so many of them. They are so intensely matter-of-fact and practical. Their industry is uncanny. This man talked to me of Alpine botany as contrasted with that of some of the mountain regions of Japan and then we talked of Lincoln, Grant, Washington, Li Hung Chang and Richard Wagner. He suggested quite simply that it was probable that Germany's only artistic outlet was music.

I was glad to have the company of Major Myata for dinner that same evening, for nothing could have been duller than the very charming Louis Quinze dining-room filled with utterly conventional American and English visitors. Small, soldierly, erect, he made quite an impression as he entered with me. The Major had been in two battles of the Russian-Japanese War and had witnessed an attack somewhere one night after midnight in a snowstorm. Here at table as he proceeded to explain in his quiet way, by means of knives and forks, the arrangement of the lines and means of caring for the wounded, I saw the various diners studying him. He was a very forceful-looking person. Very. He told me of the manner in which the sanitary and surgical equipment and control of the Japanese army had been completely revolutionized since the date of the Japanese-Russian War and that now all the present equipment was new. "The great things in our army to-day," he observed very quietly at one point, "are artillery and sanitation." A fine combination! He left me at midnight, after several hours in various cafés.

CHAPTER XLIII
ENTERING GERMANY

IF a preliminary glance at Switzerland suggested to me a high individuality, primarily Teutonic but secondarily national and distinctive, all I saw afterwards in Germany and Holland with which I contrasted it, confirmed my first impression. I believe that the Swiss, for all that they speak the German language and have an architecture that certainly has much in common with that of medieval Germany, are yet of markedly diverging character. They struck me in the main as colder, more taciturn, more introspective and less flamboyant than the Germans. The rank and file, in so far as I could see, were extremely sparing, saving, reserved. They reminded me more of such Austrians and Tyrolians as I have known, than of Germans. They were thinner, livelier in their actions, not so lusty nor yet so aggressive.

The new architecture which I saw between Lucerne and the German frontier reminded me of much of that which one sees in northern Ohio and Indiana and southern Michigan. There are still traces of the over-elaborate curlicue type of structure and decoration so interesting as being representative of medieval Teutonic life, but not much. The new manufacturing towns were very clean and spruce with modern factory buildings of the latest almost-all-glass type; and churches and public buildings, obviously an improvement or an attempt at improvement on older Swiss and Teutonic ideals, were everywhere apparent. Lucerne itself is divided into an old section, honored and preserved for its historic and commercial value, as being attractive to travelers; a new section, crowded with stores, tenements and apartments of the latest German and American type; and a hotel section, filled with large Anglicized and Parisianized structures, esplanades, small lounging squares and the like. I never bothered to look at Thorwaldsen's famous lion. One look at a photograph years ago alienated me forever.

I had an interesting final talk on the morning of my departure from Lucerne with the resident manager of the hotel who was only one of many employees of a company that controlled, so he told me, hotels in Berlin, Frankfort, Paris, Rome and London. He had formerly been resident manager of a hotel in Frankfort, the one to which I was going, and said that he might be transferred any time to some other one. He was the man, as I learned, whom I had seen rowing on the lake the first morning I sat out on my balcony—the one whom the wild ducks followed.

"I saw you," I said as I paid my bill, "out rowing on the lake the other morning. I should say that was pleasant exercise."

"I always do it," he said very cheerfully. He was a tall, pale, meditative man with a smooth, longish, waxen countenance and very dark hair. He was the last word as to toilet and courtesy. "I am glad to have the chance. I love nature."

"Are those wild ducks I see on the lake flying about?"

"Oh, yes. We have lots of them. They are not allowed to be shot. That's why they come here. We have gulls, too. There is a whole flock of gulls that comes here every winter. I feed them right out here at the dock every day."

"Why, where can they come from?" I asked. "This is a long way from the sea."

"I know it," he replied. "It is strange. They come over the Alps from the Mediterranean I suppose. You will see them on the Rhine, too, if you go there. I don't know. They come though. Sometimes they leave for four or five days or a week, but they always come back. The captain of the steamer tells me he thinks they go to some other lake. They know me though. When they come back in the fall and I go out to feed them they make a great fuss."

"They are the same gulls, then?"

"The very same."

I had to smile.

"Those two ducks are great friends of mine, too," he went on, referring to the two I had seen following him. "They always come up to the dock when I come out and when I come back from my row they come again. Oh, they make a great clatter."

He looked at me and smiled in a pleased way.

* * * * *

The train which I boarded at Lucerne was a through express from Milan to Frankfort with special cars for Paris and Berlin. It was crowded with Germans of a ruddy, solid variety, radiating health, warmth, assurance, defiance. I never saw a more marked contrast than existed between these travelers on the train and the local Swiss outside. The latter seemed much paler and less forceful by contrast, though not less intellectual and certainly more refined.

One stout, German lady, with something like eighteen packages, had made a veritable express room of her second-class compartment. The average traveler, entitled to a seat beside her, would take one look at her defenses and pass on. She was barricaded beyond any hope of successful attack.

I watched interestedly to see how the character of the people, soil and climate would change as we crossed the frontier into Germany. Every other country I had entered had presented a great contrast to the last. After passing fifteen or twenty Swiss towns and small cities, perhaps more, we finally reached Basle and there the crew was changed. I did not know it, being busy thinking of other things, until an immense, rotund, guttural-voiced conductor appeared at the door and wanted to know if I was bound for Frankfort. I looked out. It was just as I expected: another world and another atmosphere had been substituted for that of Switzerland. Already the cars and depot platforms were different, heavier I thought, more pretentious. Heavy German porters (packträger) were in evidence. The cars, the vast majority of them here, bore the label of Imperial Germany—the wide-winged, black eagle with the crown above it, painted against a pinkish-white background, with the inscription "Kaiserlicher Deutsche Post." A station-master, erect as a soldier, very large, with splendiferous parted whiskers, arrayed in a blue uniform and cap, regulated the departure of trains. The "Uscita" and "Entrata" of Italy here became "Eingang" and "Ausgang," and the "Bagaglia" of every Italian station was here "Gepäck." The endless German "Verboten," and "Es ist untersagt" also came into evidence. We rolled out into a wide, open, flat, mountainless plain with only the thin poplars of France in evidence and no waterways of any kind, and then I knew that Switzerland was truly no more.

If you want to see how the lesser Teutonic countries vary from this greater one, the dominant German Empire, pass this way from Switzerland into Germany, or from Germany into Holland. At Basle, as I have said, we left the mountains for once and for all. I saw but few frozen peaks after Lucerne. As we approached Basle they seemed to grow less and less and beyond that we entered a flat plain, as flat as Kansas and as arable as the Mississippi Valley, which stretched unbroken from Basle to Frankfort and from Frankfort to Berlin. Judging from what I saw the major part of Germany is a vast prairie, as flat as a pancake and as thickly strewn with orderly, new, bright forceful towns as England is with quaint ones.

However, now that I was here, I observed that it was just these qualities which make Germany powerful and the others weak. Such thoroughness, such force, such universal superintendence! Truly it is amazing. Once you are across the border, if you are at all sensitive to national or individual personalities you can feel it, vital, glowing, entirely superior and more ominous than that of Switzerland, or Italy, and often less pleasant. It is very much like the heat and glow of a furnace. Germany is a great forge or workshop. It resounds with the industry of a busy nation; it has all the daring and assurance of a successful man; it struts, commands, defies, asserts itself at every turn. You would not want to witness greater variety of character than you could by passing from England through France into Germany. After the stolidity and civility of the English, and the lightness and spirit of France, the blazing force and defiance of the Germans comes upon you as almost the most amazing of all.

In spite of the fact that my father was German and that I have known more or less of Germans all my life, I cannot say that I admired the personnel of the German Empire, the little that I saw of it, half so much as I admired some of the things they had apparently achieved. All the stations that I saw in Germany were in apple-pie order, new, bright, well-ordered. Big blue-lettered signs indicated just the things you wanted to know. The station platforms were exceedingly well built of red tile and white stone; the tracks looked as though they were laid on solid hardwood ties; the train ran as smoothly as if there were no flaws in it anywhere and it ran swiftly. I had to smile as occasionally on a platform—the train speeding swiftly—a straight, upstanding German officer or official, his uniform looking like new, his boots polished, his gold epaulets and buckles shining as brightly as gold can shine, his blond whiskers, red cap, glistening glasses or bright monocle, and above all his sharp, clear eyes looking directly at you, making an almost amazing combination of energy, vitality and superiority, came into view and disappeared again. It gave you a startling impression of the whole of Germany. "Are they all like that?" I asked myself. "Is the army really so dashing and forceful?"

As I traveled first to Frankfort, then to Mayence, Coblenz and Cologne and again from Cologne to Frankfort and Berlin, and thence out of the country via Holland, the wonder grew. I should say now that if Germany has any number of defects of temperament, and it truly has from almost any American point of view, it has virtues and capacities so noteworthy, admirable and advantageous that the whole world may well sit up and take notice. The one thing that came home to me with great force was that Germany is in no way loose jointed or idle but, on the contrary, strong, red-blooded, avid, imaginative. Germany is a terrific nation, hopeful, courageous, enthusiastic, orderly, self-disciplining, at present anyhow, and if it can keep its pace without engaging in some vast, self-destroying conflict, it can become internally so powerful that it will almost stand irresistible. I should say that any nation that to-day chose to pick a quarrel with Germany on her home ground would be foolish in the extreme. It is the beau ideal of the aggressive, militant, orderly spirit and, if it were properly captained and the gods were kind, it would be everywhere invincible.

* * * * *

When I entered Germany it was with just two definite things in mind. One was to seek out my father's birthplace, a little hamlet, as I understood it, called Mayen, located somewhere between the Moselle and the Rhine at Coblenz,—the region where the Moselle wines come from. The other was to visit Berlin and see what Germany's foremost city was really like and to get a look at the Kaiser if possible. In both of these I was quickly successful, though after I reached Frankfort some other things transpired which were not on the program.

Frankfort was a disappointment to me at first. It was a city of over four hundred thousand population, clean, vigorous, effective; but I saw it in a rain, to begin with, and I did not like it. It was too squat in appearance—too unvarying in its lines; it seemed to have no focal point such as one finds in all medieval cities. What has come over the spirit of city governments, directing architects, and individual enterprise? Is there no one who wants really to do the very exceptional thing? No German city I saw had a central heart worthy of the name—no Piazza del Campidoglio such as Rome has; no Piazza della Signoria such as Florence has; no Piazza San Marco such as Venice has; not even a cathedral center, lovely thing that it is, such as Milan has. Paris with its Gardens of the Tuileries, its Champs-de-Mars, its Esplanades des Invalides, and its Arc de Triomphe and Place de l'Opéra, does so much better in this matter than any German city has dreamed of doing. Even London has its splendid focal point about the Houses of Parliament, St. Paul's and the Embankment, which are worth something. But German cities! Yet they are worthy cities, every one of them, and far more vital than those of Italy.

I should like to relate first, however, the story of the vanishing birthplace. Ever since I was three or four years old and dandled on my father's knee in our Indiana homestead, I had heard more or less of Mayen, Coblenz, and the region on the Rhine from which my father came. As we all know, the Germans are a sentimental, fatherland-loving race and my father, honest German Catholic that he was, was no exception. He used to tell me what a lovely place Mayen was, how the hills rose about it, how grape-growing was its principal industry, how there were castles there and grafs and rich burghers, and how there was a wall about the city which in his day constituted it an armed fortress, and how often as a little child he had been taken out through some one of its great gates seated on the saddle of some kindly minded cavalryman and galloped about the drill-ground. He seems to have become, by the early death of his mother and second marriage of his father, a rather unwelcome stepchild and, early, to escape being draughted for the Prussian army which had seized this town—which only a few years before had belonged to France, though German enough in character—he had secretly decamped to the border with three others and so made his way to Paris. Later he came to America, made his way by degrees to Indiana, established a woolen-mill on the banks of the Wabash at Terre Haute and there, after marrying in Ohio, raised his large family. His first love was his home town, however, and Prussia, which he admired; and to his dying day he never ceased talking about it. On more than one occasion he told me he would like to go back, just to see how things were, but the Prussian regulations concerning deserters or those who avoided service were so drastic and the likelihood of his being recognized so great that he was afraid of being seized and at least thrown into prison if not shot, so he never ventured it. I fancy this danger of arrest and his feeling that he could not return cast an additional glamour over the place and the region which he could never revisit. Anyhow I was anxious to see Mayen and to discover if the family name still persisted there.

When I consulted with the Cook's agent at Rome he had promptly announced, "There isn't any such place as Mayen. You're thinking of Mayence, near Frankfort, on the Rhine."

"No," I said, "I'm not. I'm thinking of Mayen—M-a-y-e-n. Now you look and see."

"There isn't any such place, I tell you," he replied courteously. "It's Mayence, not very far from Frankfort."

"Let me see," I argued, looking at his map. "It's near the junction of the Rhine and the Moselle."

"Mayence is the place. See, here it is. Here's the Moselle and here's Mayence."

I looked, and sure enough they seemed reasonably close together. "All right," I said, "give me a ticket to Berlin via Mayence."

"I'll book you to Frankfort. That's only thirty minutes away. There's nothing of interest at Mayence—not even a good hotel."

Arrived at Frankfort, I decided not to send my trunks to the hotel as yet but to take one light bag, leaving the remainder "*im Gepäck*" and see what I could at Mayence. I might want to stay all night, wandering about my father's old haunts, and I might want to go down the Rhine a little way—I was not sure.

The Mayence to which I was going was not the Mayen that I wanted, but I did not know that. You have heard of people weeping over the wrong tombstones. This was a case in point. Fortunately I was going in the direction of the real Mayen, though I did not know that either. I ran through a country which reminded me very much of the region in which Terre Haute is located and I said to myself quite wisely: "Now I can see why my father and so many other Germans from this region settled in southern Indiana. It is like their old home. The wide, flat fields are the same."

When we reached Mayence and I had deposited my kit-bag, for the time being I strolled out into the principal streets wondering whether I should get the least impression of the city or town as it was when my father was here as a boy. It is curious and amusing how we can delude ourselves at times. Mayence I really knew, if I had stopped to consider, could not be the Mayen, where my father was born. The former was the city of that Bishop-Elector Albert of Brandenburg who in need of a large sum of money to pay Rome for the privilege of assuming the archbishopric, when he already held two other sees, made an arrangement with Pope Leo X—the Medici pope who was then trying to raise money to rebuild or enlarge St. Peter's—to superintend the sale of indulgences in Germany (taking half the proceeds in reward for his services) and thus by arousing the ire of Luther helped to bring about the Reformation in Germany. This was the city also of that amiable Dominican Prior, John Tetzel, who, once appealing for ready purchasers for his sacerdotal wares declared:

"Do you not hear your dead parents crying out 'Have mercy on us? We are in sore pain and you can set us free for a mere pittance. We have borne you, we have trained and educated you, we have left you all our property, and you are so hardhearted and cruel that you leave us to roast in the flames when you could so easily release us.'"

I shall always remember Mayence by that ingenious advertisement. My father had described to me a small, walled town with frowning castles set down in a valley among hills. He had said over and over that it was located at the junction of the Rhine and the Moselle. I recalled afterward that he told me that the city of Coblenz was very near by, but in my brisk effort to find this place quickly I had forgotten that. Here I was in a region which contained not a glimpse of any hills from within the city, the Moselle was all of a hundred miles away, and no walls of any medieval stronghold were visible anywhere and yet I was reasonably satisfied that this was the place.

"Dear me," I thought, "how Mayence has grown. My father wouldn't know it." (Baedeker gave its population at one hundred and ten thousand). "How Germany has grown in the sixty-five years since he was here. It used to be a town of three or four thousand. Now it is a large city." I read about it assiduously in Baedeker and looked at the rather thriving streets of the business heart, trying to visualize it as it should have been in 1843. Until midnight I was wandering about in the dark and bright streets of Mayence, satisfying myself with the thought that I was really seeing the city in which my father was born.

For a city of so much historic import Mayence was very dull. It was built after the theories of the fifteenth and sixteenth centuries with, however, many modern improvements. The Cathedral was a botch, ornamented with elaborate statues of stuffy bishops and electors. The houses were done in many places in that heavy scroll fashion common to medieval Germany. The streets were narrow and winding. I saw an awful imitation of our modern Coney Island in the shape of a moving circus which was camped on one of the public camping places. A dull heavy place, all told.

Coming into the breakfast-room of my hotel the next morning, I encountered a man who looked to me like a German traveling salesman. He had brought his grip down to the desk and was consuming his morning coffee and rolls with great gusto, the while he read his paper. I said to him, "Do you know of any place in this part of Germany that is called Mayen?—not Mayence." I wanted to make sure of my location.

"Mayen? Mayen?" he replied. "Why, yes. I think there is such a place near Coblenz. It isn't very large."

"Coblenz! That's it," I replied, recalling now what my father had told me of Coblenz. "To be sure. How far is that?"

"Oh, that is all of three hours from here. It is at the juncture of the Moselle."

"Do you know how the trains run?" I asked, getting up, a feeling of disgusted disappointment spreading over me.

"I think there is one around half-past nine or ten."

"Damn!" I said, realizing what a dunce I had been. I had just forty-five minutes in which to pay my bill and make the train. Three hours more! I could have gone on the night before.

I hurried out, secured my bag, paid my bill and was off. On the way I had myself driven to the old "Juden-Gasse," said to be full of picturesque medieval houses, for a look. I reached the depot in time to have a two-minute argument with my driver as to whether he was entitled to two marks or one—one being a fair reward—and then hurried into my train. In a half hour we were at Bingen-on-the-Rhine, and in three-quarters of an hour those lovely hills and ravines which make the Rhine so picturesque had begun, and they continued all the way to Coblenz and below that to Cologne.

CHAPTER XLIV
A MEDIEVAL TOWN

AFTER Italy and Switzerland the scenery of the Rhine seemed very mild and unpretentious to me, yet it was very beautiful. The Hudson from Albany to New York is far more imposing. A score of American rivers such as the Penobscot, the New in West Virginia, the James above Lynchburg, the Rio Grande, and others would make the Rhine seem simple by comparison; yet it has an individuality so distinct that it is unforgettable. I always marvel over this thing—personality. Nothing under the sun explains it. So, often you can say "this is finer," "that is more imposing," "by comparison this is nothing," but when you have said all this, the thing with personality rises up and triumphs. So it is with the Rhine. Like millions before me and millions yet to come, I watched its slopes, its castles, its islands, its pretty little German towns passing in review before the windows of this excellent train and decided that in its way nothing could be finer. It had personality. A snatch of old wall, with peach trees in blossom; a long thin side-wheel steamer, one smokestack fore and another aft, labeled "William Egan Gesellschaft"; a dismantled castle tower, with a flock of crows flying about it and hills laid out in ordered squares of vines gave it all the charm it needed.

When Coblenz was reached, I bustled out, ready to inspect Mayen at once. Another disappointment. Mayen was not at Coblenz but fifteen or eighteen miles away on a small branch road, the trains of which ran just four times a day, but I did not learn this until, as usual, I had done considerable investigating. According to my map Mayen appeared to be exactly at the junction of the Rhine and the Moselle, which was here, but when I asked a small boy dancing along a Coblenz street where the Moselle was, he informed me, "If you walk fast you will get there in half an hour!"

When I reached the actual juncture of the Rhine and the Moselle, however, I found I was mistaken; I was entertained at first by a fine view of the two rivers, darkly walled by hills and a very massive and, in a way, impressive equestrian statue of Emperor William I, armed in the most flamboyant and aggressive military manner and looking sternly down on the fast-traveling and uniting waters of the two rivers. Idling about the base of this monument, to catch sightseers, was a young picture-post-card seller with a box of views of the Rhine, Coblenz, Cologne and other cities, for sale. He was a very humble-looking youth,—a bit doleful,—who kept following me about until I bought some post-cards. "Where is Mayen?" I asked, as I began to select a few pictures of things I had and had not seen, for future reference.

"Mayence?" he asked doubtfully. "Mayence? Oh, that is a great way from here. Mayence is up the river near Frankfort."

"No, no," I replied irritably. (This matter was getting to be a sore point with me.) "I have just come from Mayence. I am looking for Mayen. Isn't it over there somewhere?" I pointed to the fields over the river.

He shook his head. "Mayen!" he said. "I don't think there is such a place."

"Good heavens!" I exclaimed, "what are you talking about? Here it is on the map. What is that? Do you live here in Coblenz?"

"Gewiss!" he replied. "I live here."

"Very good, then. Where is Mayen?"

"I have never heard of it," he replied.

"My God!" I exclaimed to myself, "perhaps it was destroyed in the Franco-Prussian War. Maybe there isn't any Mayen."

"You have lived here all your life," I said, turning to my informant, "and you have never heard of Mayen?"

"Mayen, no. Mayence, yes. It is up the river near Frankfort."

"Don't tell me that again!" I said peevishly, and walked off. The elusiveness of my father's birthplace was getting on my nerves. Finally I found a car-line which ended at the river and a landing wharf and hailed the conductor and motorman who were idling together for a moment.

"Where is Mayen?" I asked.

"Mayence?" they said, looking at me curiously.

"No, no. M-a-y-e-n, Mayen—not Mayence. It's a small town around here somewhere."

"Mayen! Mayen!" they repeated. "Mayen!" And then frowned.

"Oh, God!" I sighed. I got out my map. "Mayen—see?" I said.

"Oh, yes," one of them replied brightly, putting up a finger. "That is so. There *is* a place called Mayen! It is out that way. You must take the train."

"How many miles?" I asked.

"About fifteen. It will take you about an hour and a half."

I went back to the station and found I must wait another two hours before my train left. I had reached the point where I didn't care a picayune whether I ever got to my father's town or not. Only a dogged determination not to be beaten kept me at it.

It was at Coblenz, while waiting for my train, that I had my first real taste of the German army. Around a corner a full regiment suddenly came into view. They swung past me and crossed a bridge over the Rhine, their brass helmets glittering. Their trousers were gray and their jackets red, and they marched with a slap, slap, slap of their feet that was positively ominous. Every man's body was as erect as a poker; every man's gun was carried with almost loving grace over his shoulder. They were all big men, stolid and broad-chested. As they filed over the bridge, four abreast, they looked, at that distance, like a fine scarlet ribbon with a streak of gold in it. They eventually disappeared between the green hills on the other side.

In another part of the city I came upon a company of perhaps fifty, marching in loose formation and talking cheerfully to one another. Behind me, coming toward the soldiers, was an officer, one of those band-box gentlemen in the long gray, military coat of the Germans, the high-crowned, low-visored cap, and lacquered boots. I learned before I was out of Germany to listen for the clank of their swords. The moment the sergeant in charge of the men saw this officer in the distance, he gave vent to a low command which brought the men four by four instantly. In the next breath their guns, previously swinging loosely in their hands, were over their shoulders and as the officer drew alongside a sharp "*Vorwärts!*" produced that wonderful jack-knife motion "the goose-step"—each leg brought rigidly to a level with the abdomen as they went slap—slap—slapping by, until the officer was gone.

Then, at a word, they fell into their old easy formation again and were human beings once more.

It was to me a most vivid glimpse of extreme military efficiency. All the while I was in Germany I never saw a lounging soldier. The officers, all men of fine stature, were so showily tailored as to leave a sharp impression. They walked briskly, smartly, defiantly, with a tremendous air of assurance but not of vain-glory. They were so superior to anything else in Germany that for me they made it. But to continue.

At half-past two my train departed and I entered a fourth-class compartment—the only class one could book for on this branch road. They were hard, wooden-seated little cars, as stiff and heavy as cars could possibly be. My mind was full of my father's ancestral heath and the quaint type of life that must have been lived here a hundred years before. This was a French border country. My father, when he ran away, had escaped into Alsace, near by. He told me once of being whipped for stealing cherries, because his father's house adjoined the priest's yard and a cherry-tree belonging to that holy man had spread its branches, cherry-laden, over the walls, and he had secretly feasted upon the fruit at night. His stepmother, informed by the priest, whipped him. I wondered if I could find that stone wall.

The train was now running through a very typical section of old-time Germany. Solid, healthy men and buxom women got leisurely on and off at the various small but well-built stations. You could feel distinctly a strong note of commercial development here. Some small new factory buildings were visible at one place and another. An occasional real-estate sign, after the American fashion, was in evidence. The fields looked well and fully tilled. Hills were always in the distance somewhere.

As the train pulled into one small station, Metternich by name, I saw a tall, raw-boned yokel, lounging on the platform. He was a mere boy, nineteen or twenty, six feet tall, broad-shouldered, horny-handed, and with as vacuous a face as it is possible for an individual to possess. A cheap, wide-brimmed, soft hat, offensively new, and of a dusty mud color, sat low over one ear; and around it, to my astonishment, was twined a slim garland of flowers and leaves which, interwoven and chained, hung ridiculously down his back. He was all alone, gazing sheepishly about him and yet doing his best to wear his astounding honors with an air of bravado. I was looking at his collarless shirt, his big feet and hands and his bow legs, when I heard a German in the next seat remark to his neighbor, "He won't look like that long."

"Three months—he'll be fine."

They went on reading their papers and I fell to wondering what they could mean.

At the next station were five more yokels, all similarly crowned, and around them a bevy of rosy, healthy village girls. These five, constituting at once a crowd and a center of attention, were somewhat more assured—more swaggering—than the lone youth we had seen.

"What is that?" I asked the man over the seat. "What are they doing?"

"They've been drawn for the army," he replied. "All over Germany the young men are being drawn like this."

"Do they begin to serve at once?"

"At once."

I paused in amazement at this trick of statecraft which could make of the drawing for so difficult and compulsory a thing as service in the army a gala occasion. For scarcely any compensation—a few cents a day—these yokels and village men are seized upon and made to do almost heroic duty for two years, whether they will or no. I did not know then, quite, how intensely proud Germany is of her army, how perfectly willing the vast majority are to serve, how certain the great majority of Germans are that Germany is called of God to rule—*beherrschen* is their vigorous word—the world. Before I was out of Frankfort and Berlin, I could well realize how intensely proud the average boy is to be drawn. He is really a man then; he is permitted to wear a uniform and carry a gun; the citizens from then on, at least so long as he is in service, respect him as a soldier. By good fortune or ability he may become a petty officer. So they crown him with flowers, and the girls gather round him in admiring groups. What a clever custom thus to sugar-coat the compulsory pill. And, in a way, what a travesty.

The climax of my quest was reached when, after traveling all this distance and finally reaching the "Mayen" on the railroad, I didn't really reach it after all! It proved to be "West Mayen"—a new section of the old town—or rather a new rival of it—and from West Mayen I had to walk to Mayen proper, or what might now be called East Mayen—a distance of over a mile. I first shook my head in disgust, and then laughed. For there, in the valley below me, after I had walked a little way, I could actually see the town my father had described, a small walled city of now perhaps seven or eight thousand population, with an old Gothic church in the center containing a twisted spire, a true castle or *Schloss* of ancient date, on the high ground to the right, a towered gate or two, of that medieval conical aspect so beloved of the painters of romance, and a cluster or clutter of quaint, many-gabled, sharp-roofed and sharp-pointed houses which speak invariably of days and nations and emotions and tastes now almost entirely superseded. West Mayen was being built in modern style. Some coal mines had been discovered there and manufactories were coming in. At Mayen all was quite as my father left it. I am sure, some seventy years before.

*   *   *   *   *

Those who think this world would be best if we could have peace and quiet, should visit Mayen. Here is a town that has existed in a more or less peaceful state for all of six hundred years. The single Catholic church, the largest structure outside of the adjacent castle, was begun in the twelfth century. Frankish princes and Teuton lords have by turns occupied its site. But Mayen has remained quite peacefully a small, German, walled city, doing—in part at least—many of the things its ancestors did. Nowhere in Europe, not even in Italy, did I feel more keenly the seeming out-of-placeness of the modern implements of progress. When, after a pause at the local graveyard, in search of ancestral Dreisers, I wandered down into the town proper, crossed over the ancient stone bridge that gives into an easily defended, towered gate, and saw the presence of such things as the Singer Sewing Machine Company, a thoroughly up-to-date bookstore, an evening newspaper office and a moving-picture show, I shook my head in real despair. "Nothing is really old" I sighed, "nothing!"

Like all the places that were highly individual and different, Mayen made a deep impression on me. It was like entering the shell of some great mollusc that had long since died, to enter this walled town and find it occupied by another type of life from that which originally existed there. Because it was raining now and soon to grow dark, I sauntered into the first shelter I saw—a four-story, rather presentable brick inn, located outside the gate known as the Brückentor (bridge-gate) and took a room here for the night. It was a dull affair, run by as absurd a creature as I have ever encountered. He was a little man, sandy-haired, wool-witted, inquisitive, idle, in a silly way drunken, who was so astonished by the onslaught of a total stranger in this unexpected manner that he scarcely knew how to conduct himself.

"I want a room for the night," I suggested.

"A room?" he queried, in an astonished way, as if this were the most unheard-of thing imaginable.

"Certainly," I said. "A room. You rent rooms, don't you?"

"Oh, certainly, certainly. To be sure. A room. Certainly. Wait. I will call my wife."

He went into a back chamber, leaving me to face several curious natives who went over me from head to toe with their eyes.

"Mah-ree-ah!" I heard my landlord calling quite loudly in the rear portion of the house. "There is one here who wants a room. Have we a room ready?"

I heard no reply.

Presently he came back, however, and said in a high-flown, deliberate way, "Be seated. Are you from Frankfort?"

"Yes, and no. I come from America."

"O-o-oh! America. What part of America?"

"New York."

"O-o-oh—New York. That is a great place. I have a brother in America. Since six years now he is out there. I forget the place." He put his hand to his foolish, frizzled head and looked at the floor.

His wife now appeared, a stout, dull woman, one of the hard-working potato specimens of the race. A whispered conference between them followed, after which they announced my room would soon be ready.

"Let me leave my bag here," I said, anxious to escape, "and then I will come back later. I want to look around for awhile."

He accepted this valid excuse and I departed, glad to get out into the rain and the strange town, anxious to find a better-looking place to eat and to see what I could see.

My search for dead or living Dreisers, which I have purposely skipped in order to introduce the town, led me first, as I have said, to the local graveyard—the old "Kirchhof." It was lowering to a rain as I entered, and the clouds hung in rich black masses over the valley below. It was half-after four by my watch. I made up my mind that I would examine the inscription of every tombstone as quickly as possible, in order to locate all the dead Dreisers, and then get down into the town before the night and the rain fell, and locate the live ones—if any. With that idea in view I began at an upper row, near the church, to work down. Time was when the mere wandering in a graveyard after this fashion would have produced the profoundest melancholy in me. It was so in Paris; it made me morbidly weary and ineffably sad. I saw too many great names—Chopin, Balzac, Daudet, Rachel—solemnly chiseled in stone. And I hurried out, finally, quite agonized and unspeakably lonely.

Here in Mayen it was a simpler feeling that was gradually coming over me—an amused sentimental interest in the simple lives that had had, too often, their beginning and their end in this little village. It was a lovely afternoon for such a search. Spring was already here in South Germany, that faint, tentative suggestion of budding life; all the wind-blown leaves of the preceding fall were on the ground, but in between them new grass was springing and, one might readily suspect, windflowers and crocuses, the first faint green points of lilies and the pulsing tendrils of harebells. It was beginning to sprinkle, the faintest suggestion of a light rain; and in the west, over the roofs and towers of Mayen, a gleam of sunlight broke through the mass of heavy clouds and touched the valley with one last lingering ray.

"*Hier ruht im Gott*" (Here rests in God), or "*Hier sanft ruht*" (Here softly rests), was too often the beginning. I had made my way through the sixth or seventh row from the top, pushing away grass at times from in front of faded inscriptions, rubbing other lichen-covered letters clean with a stick and standing interested before recent tombstones. All smart with a very recently developed local idea of setting a black piece of glass into the gray of the marble and on that lettering the names of the departed in gold! It was to me a very thick-witted, truly Teutonic idea, dull and heavy in its mistakes but certainly it was no worse than the Italian idea of putting the photograph of the late beloved in the head of the slab, behind glass in a stone-cut frame and of further ornamenting the graves with ghastly iron-shafted lamps with globes of yellow, pink and green glass. That was the worst of all.

As I was meditating how, oysterlike, little villages reproduce themselves from generation to generation, a few coming and a few going but the majority leading a narrow simple round of existence. I came suddenly, so it seemed to me, upon one grave which gave me a real shock. It was a comparatively recent slab of gray granite with the modern plate of black glass set in it and a Gothic cross surmounting it all at the top. On the glass plate was lettered:

Here Rests
Theodor Dreiser,
Born 16—Feb—1820.
Died 28—Feb—1882.
R. I. P.

I think as clear a notion as I ever had of how my grave will look after I am gone and how utterly unimportant both life and death are, anyhow, came to me then. Something about this old graveyard, the suggestion of the new life of spring, a robin trilling its customary evening song on a near-by twig, the smoke curling upward from the chimneys in the old houses below, the spire of the medieval church and the walls of the medieval castle standing out in the softening light—one or all of them served to give me a sense of the long past that is back of every individual in the race of life and the long future that the race has before it, regardless of the individual. Religion offers no consolation to me. Psychic research and metaphysics, however meditated upon, are in vain. There is in my judgment no death; the universe is composed of life; but, nevertheless, I cannot see any continuous life for any individual. And it would be so unimportant if true. Imagine an eternity of life for a leaf, a fish-worm, an oyster! The best that can be said is that ideas of types survive somewhere in the creative consciousness. That is all. The rest is silence.

Besides this, there were the graves of my father's brother John, and some other Dreisers; but none of them dated earlier than 1800.

CHAPTER XLV
MY FATHER'S BIRTHPLACE

IT was quite dark when I finally came across a sort of tap-room "restaurant" whose quaint atmosphere charmed me. The usual pewter plates and tankards adorned the dull red and brown walls. A line of leather-covered seats followed the walls, in front of which were ranged long tables.

My arrival here with a quiet request for food put a sort of panic into the breast of my small but stout host, who, when I came in, was playing checkers with another middle-aged Mayener, but who, when I asked for food, gave over his pleasure for the time being and bustled out to find his wife. He looked not a little like a fat sparrow.

"Why, yes, yes," he remarked briskly, "what will you have?"

"What *can* I have?"

On the instant he put his little fat hand to his semi-bald pate and rubbed it ruminatively. "A steak, perhaps. Some veal? Some sausage?"

"I will have a steak, if you don't mind and a cup of black coffee."

He bustled out and when he came back I threw a new bomb into camp. "May I wash my hands?"

"Certainly, certainly," he replied, "in a minute." And he bounded upstairs. "Katrina! Katrina! Katrina!" I heard him call, "have Anna make the washroom ready. He wishes to wash his hands. Where are the towels? Where is the soap?"

There was much clattering of feet overhead. I heard a door being opened and things being moved. Presently I heard him call, "Katrina, in God's name, where is the soap!" More clattering of feet, and finally he came down, red and puffing. "Now, mein Herr, you can go up."

I went, concealing a secret grin, and found that I had dislocated a store-room, once a bath perhaps; that a baby-carriage had been removed from a table and on it pitcher, bowl, towel, and soap had been placed—a small piece of soap and cold water. Finally, after seeing me served properly, he sat down at his table again and sighed. The neighbor returned. Several more citizens dropped in to read and chat. The two youngest boys in the family came downstairs with their books to study. It was quite a typical German family scene.

It was here that I made my first effort to learn something about the Dreiser family. "Do you know any one by the name of Dreiser, hereabouts?" I asked cautiously, afraid to talk too much for fear of incriminating myself.

"Dreiser, Dreiser?" he said. "Is he in the furniture business?"

"I don't know. That is what I should like to find out. Do you know of any one by that name?"

"Is not that the man, Henry,"—he turned to one of his guests—"who failed here last year for fifty thousand marks?"

"The same," said this other, solemnly (I fancied rather feelingly).

"Goodness, gracious!" I thought. "This is the end. If he failed for fifty thousand marks in Germany he is in disgrace. To think a Dreiser should ever have had fifty thousand marks! Would that I had known him in his palmy days."

"There was a John Dreiser here," my host said to me, "who failed for fifty thousand marks. He is gone though, now I think. I don't know where he is."

It was not an auspicious beginning, and under the circumstances I thought it as well not to identify myself with this Dreiser too closely. I finished my meal and went out, wondering how, if at all, I was to secure any additional information. The rain had ceased and the sky was already clearing. It promised to be fine on the morrow. After more idle rambling through a world that was quite as old as Canterbury I came back finally to my hotel. My host was up and waiting for me. All but one guest had gone.

"So you are from America," he observed. "I would like very much to talk with you some more."

"Let me ask *you* something," I replied. "Do you know any one here in Mayen by the name of Dreiser?"

"Dreiser—Dreiser? It seems to me there was some one here. He failed for a lot of money. You could find out at the *Mayener Zeitung*. Mr. Schroeder ought to know."

I decided that I would appeal to Mr. Schroeder and his paper in the morning; and pretending to be very tired, in order to escape my host, who by now was a little tipsy. I went to the room assigned me, carrying a candle. That night I slept soundly, under an immense, stuffy feather-bed.

The next morning at dawn I arose and was rewarded with the only truly satisfying medieval prospect I have ever seen in my life. It was strange, remote, Teutonic, Burgundian. The "grafs" and "burghers" of an older world might well have been enacting their life under my very eyes. Below me in a valley was Mayen,—its quaint towers and housetops spread out in the faint morning light. It was beautiful. Under my window tumbled the little stream that had served as a moat in earlier days—a good and natural defense. Opposite me was the massive Brückentor. Further on was a heavy circular sweep of wall and a handsome watch-tower. Over the wall, rising up a slope, could be seen the peak-roofed, gabled houses, of solid brick and stone with slate and tile roofs. Never before in my life had I looked on a truly medieval city of the castellated, Teutonic order. Nothing that I had seen in either France, England, or Italy had the peculiar quality of this remote spot. I escaped the opportunities of my talkative host by a ruse, putting the two marks charged for the room in an envelope and leaving it on the dresser. I went out and followed the stream in the pleasant morning light. I mailed post-cards at the local post-office to all and sundry of my relatives, stating the local condition of the Dreisers, as so far learned, and then sought out the office of the *Mayener Zeitung*, where I encountered one Herr Schroeder, but he could tell me nothing of any Dreisers save of that unfortunate one who had failed in the furniture business. He advised me to seek the curator of the local museum, a man who had the history of Mayen at his finger-tips. He was a cabinet-maker by trade. I could not find him at home and finally, after looking in the small local directory published by Mr. Schroeder and finding no Dreisers listed, I decided to give up and go back to Frankfort; but not without one last look at the private yard attached to the priest's house and the cherry-tree which had been the cause of the trouncing, and lastly the local museum.

It is curious how the most innocent and idle of sentiments will lead a person on in this way. In the little Brückentor Museum, before leaving, I studied with the greatest interest—because it was my father's town—the ancient Celtic, Teutonic, Roman and Merovingian antiquities. It was here that I saw for the first time the much-talked-of wheat discovered in a Celtic funeral urn, which, although thousands of years have elapsed since it was harvested, is still—thanks to dryness, so the local savant assured me—fertile, and if planted would grow! Talk of suspended animation!

Below the town I lingered in the little valley of the Moselle, now laid out as a park, and reëxamined the gate through which my father had been wont to ride. I think I sentimentalized a little over the long distance that had separated my father from his old home and how he must have longed to see it at times, and then finally, after walking about the church and school where he had been forced to go, I left Mayen with a sorrowful backward glance. For in spite of the fact that there was now no one there to whom I could count myself related, still it was from here that my ancestors had come. I had found at least the church that my father had attended, the priest's house and garden where possibly the identical cherry-tree was still standing—there were several. I had seen the gate through which my father had ridden as a boy with the soldiers and from which he had walked finally, never to return any more. That was enough. I shall always be glad I went to Mayen.

CHAPTER XLVI
THE ARTISTIC TEMPERAMENT

BEFORE leaving Frankfort I hurried to Cook's office to look after my mail. I found awaiting me a special delivery letter from a friend of Barfleur's, a certain famous pianist, Madame A., whom I had met in London. She had told me then that she was giving a recital at Munich and Leipzig and that she was coming to Frankfort about this very time. She was scheduled to play on Wednesday, and this was Monday. She was anxious to see me. There was a long account of the town outside Berlin where she resided, her house, its management by a capable housekeeper, etc. Would I go there? I could have her room. If I did, would I wait until she could come back at the latter end of the month? It was a most hospitable letter, and, coming from such a busy woman, a most flattering one and evidently instigated by Barfleur. I debated whether to accept this charming invitation as I strolled about Frankfort.

At one corner of the shopping district I came upon a music store in the window of which were displayed a number of photographs of musical celebrities. A little to my surprise I noticed that the central place was occupied by a large photograph of Madame A. in her most attractive pose. A nearby bill-board contained full announcement of her coming. I meditated somewhat more mellowly after this and finally returned to Cook's to leave a telegram. I would wait, I said, here at Frankfort until Wednesday.

In due time Madame A. arrived and her recital, as such things go, was a brilliant success. So far as I could judge, she had an enthusiastic following in Frankfort, quite as significant, for instance, as a woman like Carreno would have in America. An institution known as the Saalbau, containing a large auditorium, was crowded, and there were flowers in plenty for Madame A. who opened and closed the program. The latter arrangement resulted in an ovation to her, men and women crowding about her feet below the platform and suggesting one composition and another that she might play—selections, obviously, that they had heard her render before.

She looked forceful, really brilliant, and tender in a lavender silk gown and wearing a spray of an enormous bouquet of lilacs that I had sent her.

This business of dancing attendance upon a national musical favorite was a bit strange for me, although once before in my life it fell to my lot, and tempestuous business it was, too. The artistic temperament! My hair rises! Madame A. I knew, after I saw her, was expecting me to do the unexpected—to give edge as it were to her presence in Frankfort. And so strolling out before dinner I sought a florist's, and espying a whole jardinière full of lilacs, I said to the woman florist, "How much for all those lilacs?"

"You mean all?" she asked.

"All," I said.

"Thirty marks," she replied.

"Isn't that rather high?" I said, assuming that it was wise to bargain a little anywhere.

"But this is very early spring," she said. "These are the very first we've had."

"Very good," I said, "but if I should take them all would you put a nice ribbon on them?"

"O-o-oh!" she hesitated, almost pouting, "ribbon is very dear, my good sir. Still—if you wish—it will make a wonderful bouquet."

"Here is my card," I said, "put that in it." And then I gave her the address and the hour. I wrote some little nonsense on the card, about tender melodies and spring-time, and then I went back to the hotel to attend Madame.

A more bustling, aggressive little artist you would not want to find. When I called at eight-thirty—the recital was at nine—I found several musical satellites dancing attendance upon her. There was one beautiful little girl from Mayence I noticed, of the Jewish type, who followed Madame A. with positively adoring glances. There was another woman of thirty who was also caught in the toils of this woman's personality and swept along by her quite as one planet dislocates the orbit of another and makes it into a satellite. She had come all the way from Berlin. "Oh, Madame A.," she confided to me upon introduction, "oh, wonderful! wonderful! Such playing! It is the most wonderful thing in the world to me."

This woman had an attractive face, sallow and hollow, with burning black eyes and rich black hair. Her body was long and thin, supple and graceful. She followed Madame A. too, with those strange, questioning eyes. Life is surely pathetic. It was interesting, though, to be in this atmosphere of intense artistic enthusiasm.

When the last touch had been added to Madame's coiffure, a sprig of blossom of some kind inserted in her corsage, a flowing opera cloak thrown about the shoulders, she was finally ready. So busy was she, suggesting this and that to one and another of her attendants, that she scarcely saw me. "Oh, there you are," she beamed finally. "Now, I am *quite* ready. Is the machine here, Marie? Oh, very good. And Herr Steiger! O-o-oh!" This last to a well-known violinist who had arrived.

It turned out that there were two machines—one for the satellites and Herr Steiger who was also to play this evening, and one for Madame A., her maid and myself. We finally debouched from the hall and elevator and fussy lobby, where German officers were strolling to and fro, into the machines and were away. Madame A. was lost in a haze of artistic contemplation with thoughts, no doubt, as to her program and her success. "Now maybe you will like my program better," she suggested after a while. "In London it was not so goot. I haf to feel my audience iss—how do you say?—vith me. In Berlin and here and Dresden and Leipzig they like me. In England they do not know me." She sighed and looked out of the window. "Are you happy to be with me?" she asked naïvely.

"Quite," I replied.

When we reached the auditorium we were ushered by winding passages into a very large green-room, a salon, as it were, where the various artists awaited their call to appear. It was already occupied by a half-dozen persons, or more, the friends of Madame A., the local manager, his hair brushed aloft like a cockatoo, several musicians, the violinist Herr Steiger, Godowsky the pianist, and one or two others. They all greeted Madame A. effusively.

There was some conversation in French here and there, and now and then in English. The room was fairly babbling with temperament. It is always amusing to hear a group of artists talk. They are so fickle, make-believe, innocently treacherous, jealous, vainglorious, flattering. "Oh, yes—how splendid he was. That aria in C Major—perfect! But you know I did not care so much for his rendering of the Pastoral Symphony—very weak in the *allegro ma non troppo*—very. He should not attempt that. It is not in his vein—not the thing he does best"—fingers lifted very suggestively and warningly in the air.

Some artist and his wife did not agree (very surprising); the gentleman was the weaker instrument in this case.

"Oh!"—it was Madame A. talking, "now that is too-oo ridiculous. She must go places and he must go along as manager! Herr Spink wrote me from Hamburg that he would not have him around. She has told him that he affects her playing. Still he goes! It is too-oo much. They will not live together long."

"Where is Herr Schochman?" (This being incident number three.) "Isn't he leading to-night? But they promised me! No, I will not play then! It is always the way. I know him well! I know why he does it! It is to annoy me. He doesn't like me and he disappoints me."

Great business of soothing the principal performer of the evening—the manager explaining volubly, friends offering soothing comment. More talk about other artists, their wives, flirtations, successes, failures.

In the midst of this, by some miscalculation (they were to have been delivered over the footlights after the end of Madame A.'s first number) in came my flowers. They looked like a fair-sized bush being introduced.

"Oh!" exclaimed Madame A. when the card was examined and they were offered to her, "how heavenly. Good heavens! it is a whole tree. Oh—wonderful, wonderful! And these be-yutiful words! O-o-oh!"

More coquettish glances and tender sighs. I could have choked with amusement. It was all such delicious by-play—quite the thing that artists expect and must have. She threw away the sprig of jasmine she wore and drawing out a few sprigs of the lilac wore those instead. "Now I can play," she exclaimed.

Deep breathings, sighs, ecstatic expressions.

Her turn came and, as I expected after hearing her in London, I heard delicious music. She had her following. They applauded her to the echo. Her two female satellites sat with me, and little

Miss Meyer of Mayence—as I will call her—fairly groaned with happiness at times. Truly Madame A. was good to look upon, quite queenly, very assured. At the end of it all a fifteen- or twenty-minute ovation. It was beautiful, truly.

While we were in the green-room talking between sections of the program and intermediate soloists, I said to her, "You are coming with me to supper, of course."

"Of course! What else did you expect?"

"Are there any other restaurants besides those of the Frankforter Hof?"

"I think not."

"How will you get rid of your friends after the performance?"

"Oh, I shall send them away. You take a table anywhere you like and I will come. Make it twelve o'clock."

We were bundled back to the hotel, flowers, wraps, maid, satellites, and I went to see about the supper. In fifteen minutes it was ready; and in twenty minutes more Madame A. came, quite rosy, all awake temperamentally, inquisitive, defensive, coquettish, eager. We are all greedy animals at best—the finer the greedier. The whole world is looking to see what life will give it to eat—from ideas, emotions, enthusiasms down to grass and potatoes. We are organized appetites, magnificent, dramatic, pathetic at times, but appetites just the same. The greater the appetite the more magnificent the spectacle. Satiety is deadly discouraging. The human stomach is the grand central organ—life in all its amazing, subtle, heavenly, pathetic ramifications has been built up around that. The most pathetic thing in life is a hungry man; the most stirringly disturbing thing, a triumphant, greedy one. Madame A. sat down to our cold chicken, salad, champagne, and coffee with beaming birdlike eyes.

"Oh, it is so good to see you again!" she declared; but her eyes were on the chicken. "I was so afraid when I wrote you from Munich that you would not get my letter. I can't tell you how you appeal to me; we have only met twice, yet you see we are quite old friends already!"

Just as her none too subtle flattery was beginning to work, she remarked casually, "Do you know Mr. Barfleur well?"

"Oh, fairly well. Yes, I know a little something about him."

"You like him, don't you?"

"I am very fond of him," I answered, my vanity deflating rapidly.

"He is so fond of you," she assured me. "Oh, he admires you so much. What you think must have considerable weight with him, eh? Where did you first meet him?" she asked.

"In New York."

"Now, between us: he is one of the few men in the world I deeply care for—but I don't think he cares for me."

"Good Lord!" I said to myself wearily, "why is it that all the charming ladies I meet either are or have been in love with Barfleur. It's getting monotonous!" But I had to smile.

"You will visit me in Berlin?" she was saying. "I will be back by the twenty-sixth. Can't you wait that long? Berlin is so interesting. When I come, we shall have such nice talks!"

"Yes—about Barfleur!" I thought to myself. Aloud I said vaguely, "It is charming of you; I will stop over to see you, if I possibly can." Then I said good night and left.

CHAPTER XLVII
BERLIN

BERLIN, when I reached it, first manifested itself in a driving rain. If I laugh at it forever and ever as a blunder-headed, vainglorious, self-appreciative city I shall always love it too. Paris has had its day, and will no doubt have others; London is content with an endless, conservative day; Berlin's is still to come and come brilliantly. The blood is there, and the hope, and the moody, lustful, Wagnerian temperament.

But first, before I reached it, I suffered a strange mental revolt at being in Germany at all. Why? I can scarcely say. Perhaps I was beginning to be depressed with what in my prejudice I called the dullness of Germany. A little while later I recognized that while there is an extreme conflict of temperament between the average German and myself, I could yet admire them without wishing to be anything like them. Of all the peoples I saw I should place the Germans first for sobriety, industry, thoroughness, a hearty intolerance of sham, a desire and a willingness to make the best of a very difficult earthly condition. In many respects they are not artistically appetizing, being gross physically, heartily passionate, vain, and cocksure; but those things after all are unimportant. They have, in spite of all their defects, great emotional, intellectual, and physical capacities, and these things *are* important. I think it is unquestionable that in the main they take life far too seriously. The belief in a hell, for instance, took a tremendous grip on the Teutonic mind and the Lutheran interpretation of Protestantism, as it finally worked out, was as dreary as anything could be—almost as dreary as Presbyterianism in Scotland. That is the sad German temperament. A great nationality, business success, public distinction is probably tending to make over or at least modify the Teutonic cast of thought which is gray; but in parts of Germany, for instance at Mayence, you see the older spirit almost in full force.

In the next place I was out of Italy and that land had taken such a strange hold on me. What a far cry from Italy to Germany! I thought. Gone; once and for all, the wonderful clarity of atmosphere that pervades almost the whole of Italy from the Alps to Rome and I presume Sicily. Gone the obvious *dolce far niente*, the lovely cities set on hills, the castles, the fortresses, the strange stone bridges, the hot, white roads winding like snowy ribbons in the distance. No olive trees, no cypresses, no umbrella trees or ilexes, no white, yellow, blue, brown and sea-green houses, no wooden plows, white oxen and ambling, bare-footed friars. In its place (the Alps and Switzerland between) this low rich land, its railroads threading it like steel bands, its citizens standing up as though at command, its houses in the smaller towns almost uniformly red, its architecture a twentieth century modification of an older order of many-gabled roofs—the order of Albrecht Dürer—with its fanciful decorations, conical roofs and pinnacles and quaint windows and doors that suggest the bird-boxes of our childhood. Germany appears in a way to have attempted to abandon the medieval architectural ideal that still may be seen in Mayence, Mayen, the heart of Frankfort, Nuremberg, Heidelberg and other places and to adapt its mood to the modern theory of how buildings ought to be constructed, but it has not quite done so. The German scroll-loving mind of the Middle Ages is still the German scroll-loving mind of to-day. Look and you will see it quaintly cropping out everywhere. Not in those wonderful details of intricacy, Teutonic fussiness, naïve, jester-like grotesqueness which makes the older sections of so many old German cities so wonderful, but in a slight suggestion of them here and there—a quirk of roof, an over-elaborateness of decoration, a too protuberant frieze or grape-viney, Bacchus-mooded, sex-ornamented panel, until you say to yourself quite wisely, "Ah, Teutons will be Teutons still." They are making a very different Germany from what the old Germany was—modern Germany dating from 1871—but it is not an entirely different Germany. Its citizens are still stocky, red-blooded, physically excited and excitable, emotional, mercurial, morbid, enthusiastic, women-loving and life-loving, and no doubt will be so, praise God, until German soil loses its inherent essentials, and German climate makes for some other variations not yet indicated in the race.

A German dance hall, Berlin

But to return to Berlin. I saw it first jogging down Unter den Linden from the Friedrichstrasse Bahnhof (station) to Cook's Berlin agency, seated comfortably in a closed cab behind as fat a horse and driver as one would wish to see. And from there, still farther along Unter den Linden and through the Wilhelmstrasse to Leipzigstrasse and the Potsdamer Bahnhof I saw more of it. Oh, the rich guttural value of the German "platzes" and "strasses" and "ufers" and "dams." They make up a considerable portion of your city atmosphere for you in Berlin. You just have to get used to them—just as you have to accept the "fabriks" and the "restaurations" and the "wein handlungs," and all the other "ichs," "lings," "bergs," "brückes," until you sigh for the French and Italian "-rics" and the English-American "-rys." However, among the first things that impressed me were these: all Berlin streets, seemingly, were wide with buildings rarely more than five stories high. Everything, literally *everything*, was American new—and newer—German new! And the cabbies were the largest, fattest, most broad-backed, most thick-through and *Deutschiest* looking creatures I have ever beheld. Oh, the marvel of those glazed German cabby hats with the little hard rubber decorations on the side. Nowhere else in Europe is there anything like these cabbies. They do not stand; they sit, heavily and spaciously—alone.

The faithful Baedeker has little to say for Berlin. Art? It is almost all in the Kaiser-Friedrich-Museum, in the vicinity of the Kupferdam. And as for public institutions, spots of great historic interest—they are a dreary and negligible list. But, nevertheless and notwithstanding, Berlin appealed to me instantly as one of the most interesting and forceful of all the cities, and that solely because it is new, crude, human, growing feverishly, unbelievably; and growing in a distinct and individual way. They have achieved and are achieving something totally distinct and worth while—a new place to go; and after a while, I haven't the slightest doubt, thousands and even hundreds of thousands of travelers will go there. But for many and many a day the sensitive and artistically inclined will not admire it.

My visit to Cook's brought me a mass of delayed mail which cheered me greatly. It was now raining pitchforks but my bovine driver, who looked somehow like a segment of a wall, managed to bestow my trunk and bags in such a fashion that they were kept dry, and off we went for the hotel. I had a preconceived notion that Unter den Linden was a magnificent avenue lined shadily with trees and crowded with palaces. Nothing could have been more erroneous. The trees are few and insignificant, the palaces entirely wanting. It is a very wide business street, lined with hotels, shops, restaurants, newspaper offices and filled with a parading throng in pleasant weather. At one end it gives into an area known as the Lustgarten crowded with palaces, art galleries, the Berlin Cathedral, the Imperial Opera House and what not; at the other end (it is only about a mile long) into the famous Berlin Thiergarten, formerly a part of the Imperial (Hohenzollern) hunting-forest. On the whole, the avenue was a disappointment.

For suggestions of character, individuality, innate Teutonic charm or the reverse—as these things strike one—growth, prosperity, promise, and the like, Berlin cannot be equaled in Europe. Quite readily I can see how it might irritate and repel the less aggressive denizens of less hopeful and determined realms. The German, when he is oppressed is terribly depressed; when he is in the saddle, nothing can equal his bump of I-am-ity. It becomes so balloon-like and astounding that the world may only gaze in astonishment or retreat in anger, dismay, or uproarious amusement. The present-day Germans do take themselves so seriously and from many points of view with good reason, too.

I don't know where in Europe, outside of Paris, if even there, you will see a better-kept city. It is so clean and spruce and fresh that it is a joy to walk there—anywhere. Mile after mile of straight, imposing streets greet your gaze. Berlin needs a great Pantheon, an avenue such as Unter den Linden lined with official palaces (not shops), and unquestionably a magnificent museum of art—I mean a better building. Its present public and imperial structures are most uninspired. They suggest the American-European architecture of 1860–1870. The public monuments of Berlin, and particularly their sculptural adornments are for the most part a crime against humanity.

I remember standing and looking one evening at that noble German effort known as the memorial statue of William I, in the Lustgarten, unquestionably the fiercest and most imposing of all the Berlin military sculptures. This statue speaks loudly for all Berlin and for all Germany and for just what the Teutonic disposition would like to be—namely, terrible, colossal, astounding, world-scarifying, and the like. It almost shouts "Ho! see what I am," but the sad part of it is that it does it badly, not with that reserve that somehow invariably indicates tremendous power so much better than mere bluster does. What the Germans seem not to have learned in their art at least is that "easy does it." Their art is anything but easy. It is almost invariably showy, truculent, vainglorious. But to continue: The whole neighborhood in which this statue occurs, and the other neighborhood at the other end of Unter den Linden, where stands the Reichstag and the like, all in the center of Berlin, as it were, is conceived, designed, and executed (in my judgment) in the same mistaken spirit. Truly, when you look about you at the cathedral (save the mark) or the Royal Palace in the Lustgarten, or at the Winged Victory before the Reichstag or at the Reichstag itself, and the statue of Bismarck in the Königs-Platz (the two great imperial centers), you sigh for the artistic spirit of Italy. But no words can do justice to the folly of spending three million dollars to erect such a thing as this Berlin *Dom* or cathedral. It is so bad that it hurts. And I am told that the Kaiser himself sanctioned some of the architectural designs. And it was only completed between 1894 and 1906. Shades of Brabante and Pisano!

But if I seem disgusted with this section of Berlin—its evidence of Empire, as it were—there was much more that truly charmed me. Wherever I wandered I could perceive through all the pulsing life of this busy city the thoroughgoing German temperament—its moody poverty, its phlegmatic middle-class prosperity, its aggressive commercial, financial, and, above all, its official and imperial life. Berlin is shot through with the constant suggestion of officialism and imperialism. The German policeman with his shining brass helmet and brass belt; the Berlin sentry in his long military gray overcoat, his musket over his shoulder, his high cap shading his eyes, his black-and-white striped sentry-box behind him, stationed apparently at every really important corner and before every official palace; the German military and imperial automobiles speeding their independent ways, all traffic cleared away before them, the small flag of officialdom or imperialism fluttering defiantly from the foot-rails as they flash at express speed past you;—these things suggest an individuality which no other European city that I saw quite equaled. It represented what I would call determination, self-sufficiency, pride. Berlin is new, green, vigorous, astounding—a city that for speed of growth puts Chicago entirely into the shade; that for appearance, cleanliness, order, for military precision and thoroughness has no counterpart anywhere. It suggests to you all the time, something very much greater to come which is the most interesting thing that can be said about any city, anywhere.

One panegyric I should like to write on Berlin concerns not so much its social organization as a city, though that is interesting enough, but specifically its traffic and travel arrangements. To be sure it is not yet such a city as either New York, London or Paris, but it has over three million people, a crowded business heart and a heavy, daily, to-and-fro-swinging tide of suburban traffic. There are a number of railway stations in the great German capital, the Potsdamer Bahnhof, the Friedrichstrasse Bahnhof, the Anhalter Bahnhof and so on, and coming from each in the early hours of the morning, or pouring toward them at evening are the same eager streams of people that one meets in New York at similar hours.

The Germans are amazingly like the Americans. Sometimes I think that we get the better portion of our progressive, constructive characteristics from them. Only, the Germans, I am convinced, are so much more thorough. They go us one better in economy, energy, endurance, and thoroughness. The American already is beginning to want to play too much. The Germans have not reached that stage.

The railway stations I found were excellent, with great switching-yards and enormous sheds arched with glass and steel, where the trains waited. In Berlin I admired the suburban train service as much as I did that of London, if not more. That in Paris was atrocious. Here the trains offered a choice of first, second, and third class, with the vast majority using the second and third. I saw little difference in the crowds occupying either class. The second-class compartments were upholstered in a greyish-brown corduroy. The third-class seats were of plain wood, varnished and scrupulously clean. I tried all three classes and finally fixed on the third as good enough for me.

I wish all Americans who at present suffer the indignities of the American street-railway and steam-railway suburban service could go to Berlin and see what that city has to teach them in this respect. Berlin is much larger than Chicago. It is certain soon to be a city of five or six millions of people—very soon. The plans for handling this mass of people comfortably and courteously are already in operation. The German public service is obviously not left to supposedly kindly minded business gentlemen—"Christian gentlemen,"—as Mr. Baer of the Reading once chose to put it, "in partnership with God." The populace may be underlings to an imperial Kaiser, subject to conscription and eternal inspection, but at least the money-making "Christian gentlemen" with their hearts and souls centered on their private purses and working, as Mr. Croker once said of himself, "for their own pockets all the time," are not allowed to "take it out of" the rank and file.

No doubt the German street-railways and steam-railways are making a reasonable sum of money and are eager to make more. I haven't the least doubt but that heavy, self-opinionated, vainglorious German directors of great wealth gather around mahogany tables in chambers devoted to meetings of directors and listen to ways and means of cutting down expenses and "improving" the service. Beyond the shadow of a doubt there are hard, hired managers, eager to win the confidence and support of their superiors and ready to feather their own nests at the expense of the masses, who would gladly cut down the service, "pack 'em in," introduce the "cutting out" system of car service and see that the "car ahead" idea was worked to the last maddening extreme; but in Germany, for some strange, amazing reason, they don't get a chance. What is the matter with Germany, anyhow? I should like to know. Really I would. Why isn't the "Christian gentleman" theory of business introduced there? The population of Germany, acre for acre and mile for mile, is much larger than that of America. They have sixty-five million people crowded into an area as big as Texas. Why don't they "pack 'em in"? Why don't they introduce the American "sardine" subway service? You don't find it anywhere in Germany, for some strange reason. Why? They have a subway service in Berlin. It serves vast masses of people, just as the subway does in New York; its platforms are crowded with people. But you can get a seat just the same. There is no vociferated "step lively" there. Overcrowding isn't a joke over there as it is here—something to be endured with a feeble smile until you are spiritually comparable to a door mat. There must be "Christian gentlemen" of wealth and refinement in Germany and Berlin. Why don't they "get on the job"? The thought arouses strange uncertain feelings in me.

Take, for instance, the simple matter of starting and stopping street-railway cars in the Berlin business heart. In so far as I could see, that area, mornings and evenings, was as crowded as any similar area in Paris, London, or New York. Street-cars have to be run through it, started, stopped; passengers let on and off—a vast tide carried in and out of the city. Now the way this matter is worked in New York is quite ingenious. We operate what might be described as a daily guessing contest intended to develop the wits, muscles, lungs, and tempers of the people. The scheme, in so far as the street railway companies are concerned, is (after running the roads as economically as possible) to see how thoroughly the people can be fooled in their efforts to discover when and where a car will stop. In Berlin, however, they have, for some reason, an entirely different idea. There the idea is not to fool the people at all but to get them in and out of the city as quickly as possible. So, as in Paris, London, Rome, and elsewhere, a plan of fixed stopping-places has been arranged. Signs actually indicate where the cars stop and there—marvel of marvels—

they all stop even in the so-called rush hours. No traffic policeman, apparently, can order them to go ahead without stopping. They must stop. And so the people do not run for the cars, the motorman has no joy in outwitting anybody. Perhaps that is why the Germans are neither so agile, quick-witted, or subtle as the Americans.

And then, take in addition—if you will bear with me another moment—this matter of the Berlin suburban service as illustrated by the lines to Potsdam and elsewhere. It is true the officers, and even the Emperor of Germany, living at Potsdam and serving the Imperial German Government there may occasionally use this line, but thousands upon thousands of intermediate and plebeian Germans use it also. You can *always* get a seat. Please notice this word *always*. There are three classes and you can *always* get a seat in any class—not the first or second classes only, but the third class and particularly the *third* class. There are "rush" hours in Berlin just as there are in New York, dear reader. People swarm into the Berlin railway stations and at Berlin street-railway corners and crowd on cars just as they do here. The lines fairly seethe with cars. On the tracks ranged in the Potsdamer Bahnhof, for instance, during the rush hours, you will see trains consisting of eleven, twelve, and thirteen cars, mostly third-class accommodation, waiting to receive you. And when one is gone, another and an equally large train is there on the adjoining track and it is going to leave in another minute or two also. And when that is gone there will be another, and so it goes.

There is not the slightest desire evident anywhere to "pack" anybody in. There isn't any evidence that anybody wants to make anything (dividends, for instance) out of straps. There *are* no straps. These poor, unliberated, Kaiser-ruled people would really object to straps and standing in the aisles, They would compel a decent service and there would be no loud cries on the part of "Christian gentlemen" operating large and profitable systems as to the "rights of property," the need of "conserving the constitution," the privilege of appealing to Federal judges, and the right of having every legal technicality invoked to the letter;—or, if there were, they would get scant attention. Germany just doesn't see public service in that light. It hasn't fought, bled, and died, perhaps, for "liberty." It hasn't had George Washington and Thomas Jefferson and Andrew Jackson and Abraham Lincoln. All it has had is Frederick the

Great and Emperor William I and Bismarck and Von Moltke. Strange, isn't it? Queer, how Imperialism apparently teaches people to be civil, while Democracy does the reverse. We ought to get a little "Imperialism" into our government, I should say. We ought to make American law and American government supreme, but over it there ought to be a "supremer" people who really know what their rights are, who respect liberties, decencies, and courtesies for themselves and others, and who demand and see that their government and their law and their servants, public and private, are responsive and responsible to them, rather than to the "Christian gentlemen" who want to "pack 'em in." If you don't believe it, go to Berlin and then see if you come home again cheerfully believing that this is still the land of the *free* and the home of the *brave*. Rather I think you will begin to feel that we are getting to be the land of the *dub* and the home of the *door-mat*. Nothing more and nothing less.

CHAPTER XLVIII
THE NIGHT-LIFE OF BERLIN

DURING the first ten days I saw considerable of German night-life, in company with Herr A., a stalwart Prussian who went out of his way to be nice to me. I cannot say that, after Paris and Monte Carlo, I was greatly impressed, although all that I saw in Berlin had this advantage, that it bore sharply the imprint of German nationality. The cafés were not especially noteworthy. I do not know what I can say about any of them which will indicate their individuality. "Piccadilly" was a great evening drinking-place near the Potsdamer Platz, which was all glass, gold, marble, glittering with lights and packed with the Germans, *en famille*, and young men and their girls.

"La Clou" was radically different. In a way it was an amazing place, catering to the moderately prosperous middle class. It seated, I should say, easily fifteen hundred people, if not more, on the ground floor; and every table, in the evening at least, was full. At either end of the great center aisle bisecting it was stationed a stringed orchestra and when one ceased the other immediately began, so that there was music without interruption. Father and mother and young Lena, the little Heine, and the two oldest girls or boys were all here. During the evening, up one aisle and down another, there walked a constant procession of boys and girls and young men and young women, making shy, conservative eyes at one another.

In Berlin every one drinks beer or the lighter wines—the children being present—and no harm seems to come from it. I presume drunkenness is not on the increase in Germany. And in Paris they sit at tables in front of cafés—men and women—and sip their liqueurs. It is a very pleasant way to enjoy your leisure. Outside of trade or the desire to be *president*, *vice-president*, or *secretary* of something, we in America have so often no real diversions.

In no sense could either of these restaurants be said to be smart. But Berlin, outside of one or two selected spots, does not run to smartness. The "Cabaret Linden" and the "Cabaret Arcadia" were, once more, of a different character. There was one woman at the Cabaret Linden who struck me as having real artistic talent of a strongly Teutonic variety. Claire Waldoff was her name, a hard, shock-headed tomboy of a girl, who sang in a harsh, guttural voice of soldiers, merchants, janitors, and policemen—a really brilliant presentation of local German characteristics. It is curious how these little touches of character drawn from everyday life invariably win thunders of applause. How the world loves the homely, the simple, the odd, the silly, the essentially true! Unlike the others at this place, there was not a suggestive thing about anything which this woman said or did; yet this noisy, driving audience could not get enough of her. She was truly an artist.

One night we went to the Palais de Danse, admittedly Berlin's greatest night-life achievement. For several days Herr A. had been saying: "Now to-morrow we must go to the Palais de Danse, then you will see something," but every evening when we started out, something else had intervened. I was a little skeptical of his enthusiastic praise of this institution as being better than anything else of its kind in Europe. You had to take Herr A.'s vigorous Teutonic estimate of Berlin with a grain of salt, though I did think that a city that had put itself together in this wonderful way in not much more than a half-century had certainly considerable reason to boast.

"But what about the Café de Paris at Monte Carlo?" I suggested, remembering vividly the beauty and glitter of the place.

"No, no, no!" he exclaimed, with great emphasis—he had a habit of unconsciously making a fist when he was emphatic—"not in Monte Carlo, not in Paris, not anywhere."

"Very good," I replied, "this must be very fine. Lead on."

So we went.

I think Herr A. was pleased to note how much of my skepticism melted after passing the sedate exterior of this astounding place.

"I want to tell you something," said Herr A. as we climbed out of our taxi—a good, solid, reasonably priced, Berlin taxi—"if you come with your wife, your daughter, or your sister you buy a ticket for yourself—four marks—and walk in. Nothing is charged for your female companions and no notice is taken of them. If you come here with a demi-mondaine, you pay four marks for yourself and four for her, and you cannot get in without. They know. They have men at the door who are experts in this matter. They want you to bring such women, but you have to pay. If such a woman comes alone, she goes in free. How's that?"

Once inside we surveyed a brilliant spectacle—far more ornate than the Café l'Abbaye or the Café Maxim, though by no means so enticing. Paris is Paris and Berlin is Berlin and the Germans cannot do as do the French. They haven't the air—the temperament. Everywhere in Germany you feel that—that strange solidity of soul which cannot be gay as the French are gay. Nevertheless the scene inside was brilliant. Brilliant was the word. I would not have believed, until I saw it, that the German temperament or the German sense of thrift would have permitted it and yet after seeing the marvelous German officer, why not?

The main chamber—very large—consisted of a small, central, highly polished dancing floor, canopied far above by a circular dome of colored glass, glittering white or peach-pink by turns, and surrounded on all sides by an elevated platform or floor, two or three feet above it, crowded with tables ranged in circles on ascending steps, so that all might see. Beyond the tables again was a wide, level, semi-circular promenade, flanked by ornate walls and divans and set with palms, marbles and intricate gilt curio cases. The general effect was one of intense light, pale, diaphanous silks of creams and lemon hues, white-and-gold walls, white tables,—a perfect glitter of glass mirrors, and picturesque paneling. Beyond the dancing-floor was a giant, gold-tinted, rococo organ, and within a recess in this, under the tinted pipes, a stringed orchestra. The place was crowded with women of the half-world, for the most part Germans—unusually slender, in the majority of cases delicately featured, as the best of these women are, and beautifully dressed. I say beautifully. Qualify it any way you want to. Put it dazzlingly, ravishingly, showily, outrageously—any way you choose. No respectable woman might come so garbed. Many of these women were unbelievably attractive, carried themselves with a grand air, pea-fowl wise, and lent an atmosphere of color and life of a very showy kind. The place was also crowded, I need not add, with young men in evening clothes. Only champagne was served to drink—champagne at twenty marks the bottle. Champagne at twenty marks the bottle in Berlin is high. You can get a fine suit of clothes for seventy or eighty marks.

The principal diversions here were dining, dancing, drinking. As at Monte Carlo and in Paris, you saw here that peculiarly suggestive dancing of the habitués and the more skilled performances of those especially hired for the occasion. The Spanish and Russian dancers, as in Paris, the Turkish and Tyrolese specimens, gathered from Heaven knows where, were here. There were a number of handsome young officers present who occasionally danced with the women they were escorting. When the dancing began the lights in the dome turned pink. When it ceased, the lights in the dome were a glittering white. The place is, I fancy, a rather quick development for Berlin. We drank champagne, waved away charmers, and finally left, at two or three o'clock, when the law apparently compelled the closing of this great central chamber; though after that hour all the patrons who desired might adjourn to an inner sanctum, quite as large, not so showy, but full of brilliant, strolling, dining, drinking life where, I was informed, one could stay till eight in the morning if one chose. There was some drunkenness here, but not much, and an air of heavy gaiety. I left thinking to myself, "Once is enough for a place like this."

I went one day to Potsdam and saw the Imperial Palace and grounds and the Royal Parade. The Emperor had just left for Venice. As a seat of royalty it did not interest me at all. It was a mere imitation of the grounds and palace at Versailles, but as a river valley it was excellent. Very dull, indeed, were the state apartments. I tried to be interested in the glass ballrooms, picture galleries, royal auditoriums and the like. But alas! The servitors, by the way, were just as anxious for tips as any American waiters. Potsdam did not impress me. From there I went to Grunewald and strolled in the wonderful forest for an enchanted three hours. That was worth while.

*　　　*　　　*　　　*　　　*

The rivers of every city have their individuality and to me the Spree and its canals seem eminently suited to Berlin. The water effects—and they are always artistically important and charming—are plentiful.

The most pleasing portions of Berlin to me were those which related to the branches of the Spree—its canals and the lakes about it. Always there were wild ducks flying over the housetops, over offices and factories; ducks passing from one bit of water to another, their long necks protruding before them, their metallic colors gleaming in the sun.

You see quaint things in Berlin, such as you will not see elsewhere—the Spreewald nurses, for instance, in the Thiergarten with their short, scarlet, balloon skirt emphasized by a white apron, their triangular white linen head-dress, very conspicuous. It was actually suggested to me one day as something interesting to do, to go to the Zoological Gardens and see the animals fed! I chanced to come there when they were feeding the owls, giving each one a mouse,—live or dead, I could not quite make out. That was enough for me. I despise flesh-eating birds anyhow. They are quite the most horrible of all evolved specimens. This particular collection—eagles, hawks, condors, owls of every known type and variety, and buzzards—all sat in their cages gorging themselves on raw meat or mice. The owls, to my disgust, fixed me with their relentless eyes, the while they tore at the entrails of their victims. As a realist, of course, I ought to accept all these delicate manifestations of the iron constitution of the universe as interesting, but I can't. Now and then, very frequently, in fact, life becomes too much for my hardy stomach. I withdraw, chilled and stupefied by the way strength survives and weakness goes under. And to think that as yet we have no method of discovering why the horrible appears and no reason for saying that it should not. Yet one can actually become surfeited with beauty and art and take refuge in the inartistic and the unlovely!

*   *   *   *   *

One of the Berliners' most wearying characteristics is their contentious attitude. To the few, barring the women, to whom I was introduced, I could scarcely talk. As a matter of fact, I was not expected to. *They* would talk to *me*. Argument was, in its way, obviously an insult. Anything that I might have to say or suggest was of small importance; anything they had to say was of the utmost importance commercially, socially, educationally, spiritually,—any way you chose,—and they emphasized so many of their remarks with a deep voice, a hard, guttural force, a frown, or a rap on the table with their fists that I was constantly overawed.

Take this series of incidents as typical of the Berlin spirit: One day as I walked along Unter den Linden I saw a minor officer standing in front of a sentry who was not far from his black-and-white striped sentry-box, his body as erect as a ramrod, his gun "presented" stiff before him, not an eyelash moving, not a breath stirring. This endured for possibly fifty seconds or longer. You would not get the importance of this if you did not realize how strict the German military regulations are. At the sound of an officer's horn or the observed approach of a superior officer there is a noticeable stiffening of the muscles of the various sentries in sight. In this instance the minor officer imagined that he had not been saluted properly, I presume, and suspected that the soldier was heavy with too much beer. Hence the rigid test that followed. After the officer was gone, the soldier looked for all the world like a self-conscious house-dog that has just escaped a good beating, sheepishly glancing out of the corners of his eyes and wondering, no doubt, if by any chance the officer was coming back. "If he had moved so much as an eyelid," said a citizen to me, emphatically and approvingly, "he would have been sent to the guard-house, and rightly. *Swine-hound!* He should tend to his duties!"

Coming from Milan to Lucerne, and again from Lucerne to Frankfort, and again from Frankfort to Berlin, I sat in the various dining-cars next to Germans who were obviously in trade and successful. Oh, the compact sufficiency of them! "Now, when you are in Italy," said one to another, "you see signs—'French spoken,' or 'English spoken'; not 'German spoken.' Fools! They really do not know where their business comes from."

On the train from Lucerne to Frankfort I overheard another sanguine and vigorous pair. Said one: "Where I was in Spain, near Barcelona, things were wretched. Poor houses, poor wagons, poor clothes, poor stores. And they carry English and American goods—these dunces! Proud and slow. You can scarcely tell them anything."

"We will change all that in ten years," replied the other. "We are going after that trade. They need up-to-date German methods."

In a café in Charlottenberg, near the Kaiser-Friedrich Gedächtnis-Kirche, I sat with three others. One was from Leipzig, in the fur business. The others were merchants of Berlin. I was not of their party, merely an accidental auditor.

"In Russia the conditions are terrible. They do not know what life is. Such villages!"

"Do the English buy there much?"

"A great deal."

"We shall have to settle this trade business with war yet. It will come. We shall have to fight."

"In eight days," said one of the Berliners, "we could put an army of one hundred and fifty thousand men in England with all supplies sufficient for eight weeks. Then what would they do?"

Do these things suggest the German sense of self-sufficiency and ability? They are the commonest of the commonplaces.

During the short time that I was in Berlin I was a frequent witness of quite human but purely Teutonic bursts of temper—that rapid, fiery mounting of choler which verges apparently on a physical explosion,—the bursting of a blood vessel. I was going home one night late, with Herr A., from the Potsdamer Bahnhof, when we were the witnesses of an absolutely magnificent and spectacular fight between two Germans—so Teutonic and temperamental as to be decidedly worth while. It occurred between a German escorting a lady and carrying a grip at the same time, and another German somewhat more slender and somewhat taller, wearing a high hat and carrying a walking-stick. This was on one of the most exclusive suburban lines operating out of Berlin.

Teutonic bursts of temper

It appears that the gentleman with the high hat and cane, in running to catch his train along with many others, severely jostled the gentleman with the lady and the portmanteau. On the instant, an absolutely terrific explosion! To my astonishment—and, for the moment, I can say my horror—I saw these two very fiercely attack each other, the one striking wildly with his large portmanteau, the other replying with lusty blows of his stick, a club-like affair which fell with hard whacks on his rival's head. Hats were knocked off, shirt-fronts marked and torn; blood began to flow where heads and faces were cut severely, and almost pandemonium broke loose in the surrounding crowd.

Fighting always produces an atmosphere of intensity in any nationality, but this German company seemed fairly to coruscate with anguish, wrath, rage, blood-thirsty excitement. The crowd surged to and fro as the combatants moved here and there. A large German officer, his brass helmet a welcome shield in such an affair, was brought from somewhere. Such noble German epithets as "Swine-hound!" "Hundsknochen!" (dog's bone), "Schafskopf!" (sheep's head), "Schafsgesicht!" (sheep-face), and even more untranslatable words filled the air. The station platform was fairly boiling with excitement. Husbands drove their wives back, wives pulled their husbands away, or tried to, and men immediately took sides as men will. Finally the magnificent representative of law and order, large and impregnable as Gibraltar, interposed his great bulk between the two. Comparative order was restored. Each contestant was led away in an opposite direction. Some names and addresses were taken by the policeman. In so far as I could see no arrests were made; and finally both combatants, cut and bleeding as they were, were allowed to enter separate cars and go their way. That was Berlin to the life. The air of the city, of Germany almost, was ever rife with contentious elements and emotions.

I should like to relate one more incident, and concerning quite another angle of Teutonism. This relates to German sentiment, which is as close to the German surface as German rage and vanity. It occurred in the outskirts of Berlin—one of those interesting regions where solid blocks of gold- and silver-balconied apartment houses march up to the edge of streetless, sewerless, lightless green fields and stop. Beyond lie endless areas of truck gardens or open common yet to be developed. Cityward lie miles on miles of electric-lighted, vacuum-cleaned, dumb-waitered and elevator-served apartments, and, of course, street cars.

I had been investigating a large section of land devoted to free (or practically free) municipal gardens for the poor, one of those socialistic experiments of Germany which, as is always the way, benefit the capable and leave the incapable just where they were before. As I emerged from a large area of such land divided into very small garden plots, I came across a little graveyard adjoining a small, neat, white concrete church where a German burial service was in progress. The burial ground was not significant or pretentious—a poor man's graveyard, that was plain. The little church was too small and too sectarian in its mood, standing out in the wind and rain of an open common, to be of any social significance. Lutheran, I fancied. As I came up a little group of pall-bearers, very black and very solemn, were carrying a white satin-covered coffin down a bare gravel path leading from the church door, the minister following, bareheaded, and after him the usual company of mourners in solemn high hats or thick black veils, the foremost—a mother and a remaining daughter I took them to be—sobbing bitterly. Just then six choristers in black frock coats and high hats, standing to one side of the gravel path like six blackbirds ranged on a fence, began to sing a German parting-song to the melody of "Home Sweet Home." The little white coffin, containing presumably the body of a young girl, was put down by the grave while the song was completed and the minister made a few consolatory remarks.

I have never been able, quite, to straighten out for myself the magic of what followed—its stirring effect. Into the hole of very yellow earth, cut through dead brown grass, the white coffin was lowered and then the minister stood by and held out first to the father and then to the mother and then to each of the others as they passed a small, white, ribbon-threaded basket containing broken bits of the yellow earth intermixed with masses of pink and red rose-leaves. As each sobbing person came forward he, or she, took a handful of earth and rose leaves and let them sift through his fingers to the coffin below. A lump rose in my throat and I hurried away.

CHAPTER XLIX
ON THE WAY TO HOLLAND

I CAME near finding myself in serious straights financially on leaving Berlin; for, owing to an oversight, and the fact that I was lost in pleasant entertainment up to quite the parting hour, on examining my cash in hand I found I had only fifteen marks all told. This was Saturday night and my train was leaving in just thirty minutes. My taxi fare would be two marks. I had my ticket, but excess baggage!—I saw that looming up largely. It could mean anything in Europe—ten, twenty, thirty marks. "Good Heavens!" I thought. "Who is there to cash a letter of credit for me on Saturday night?" I thought of porters, taxis, train hands at Amsterdam. "If I get there at all," I sighed, "I get there without a cent." For a minute I thought seriously of delaying my departure and seeking the aid of Herr A. However, I hurried on to the depot where I first had my trunk weighed and found that I should have to pay ten marks excess baggage. That was not so bad. My taxi chauffeur demanded two. My *Packträger* took one more, my parcel-room clerk, one mark in fees, leaving me exactly one mark and my letter of credit. "Good Heavens!" I sighed. "I can see the expectant customs officers at the border! Without money I shall have to open every one of my bags. I can see the conductor expecting four or five marks and getting nothing. I can see—oh, Lord!"

Still I did not propose to turn back, I did not have time. The clerk at the Amsterdam hotel would have to loan me money on my letter of credit. So I bustled ruminatively into the train. It was a long, dusty affair, coming from St. Petersburg and bound for Holland, Paris, and the boats for England. It was crowded with passengers but, thank Heaven, all of them safely bestowed in separate compartments or "drawing-rooms" after the European fashion. I drew my blinds, undressed swiftly and got into bed. Let all conductors rage, I thought. Porters be damned. Frontier inspectors could go to blazes. I am going to sleep, my one mark in my coat pocket.

I was just dozing off when the conductor called to ask if I did not want to surrender the keys to my baggage in order to avoid being waked in the morning at the frontier. This service merited a tip which, of course, I was in no position to give. "Let me explain to you," I said. "This is the way it is. I got on this train with just one mark." I tried to make it clear how it all happened, in my halting German.

He was a fine, tall, military, solid-chested fellow. He looked at me with grave, inquisitive eyes. "I will come in a little later," he grunted. Instead, he shook me rudely at five-thirty A. M., at some small place in Holland, and told me that I would have to go out and open my trunk. Short shrift for the man who cannot or will not tip!

Still I was not so downcast. For one thing we were in Holland, actually and truly,—quaint little Holland with its five million population crowded into cities so close together that you could get from one to another in a half-hour or a little over. To me, it was first and foremost the land of Frans Hals and Rembrandt van Ryn and that whole noble company of Dutch painters. All my life I had been more or less fascinated by those smooth surfaces, the spirited atmosphere, those radiant simplicities of the Dutch interiors, the village inns, windmills, canal scenes, housewives, fishwives, old topers, cattle, and nature scenes which are the basis and substance of Dutch art. I will admit, for argument's sake, that the Dutch costume with its snowy neck and head-piece and cuffs, the Dutch windmill, with its huge wind-bellied sails, the Dutch landscape so flat and grassy and the Dutch temperament, broad-faced and phlegmatic, have had much to do with my art attraction, but over and beyond those there has always been so much more than this— an indefinable something which, for want of a better phrase, I can only call the wonder of the Dutch soul, the most perfect expression of commonplace beauty that the world has yet seen. So easily life runs off into the mystical, the metaphysical, the emotional, the immoral, the passionate and the suggestive, that for those delicate flaws of perfection in which life is revealed static, quiescent, undisturbed, innocently gay, naïvely beautiful, how can we be grateful enough! For those lovely, idyllic minds that were content to paint the receipt of a letter, an evening school, dancing peasants, a gust of wind, skaters, wild ducks, milk-time, a market, playing at draughts, the fruiterer, a woman darning stockings, a woman scouring, the drunken roysterers, a cow stall, cat and kittens, the grocer's shop, the chemist's shop, the blacksmith's shop, feeding-time, and the like, my heart has only reverence. And it is not (again) this choice of subject alone, nor the favorable atmosphere of Holland in which these were found, so much as it is that delicate refinement of soul, of perception, of feeling—the miracle of temperament—through which these things were seen. *Life seen through a temperament! that is the miracle of art.*

Yet the worst illusion that can be entertained concerning art is that it is apt to appear at any time in any country, through a given personality or a group of individuals without any deep relation to much deeper mystical and metaphysical things. Some little suggestion of the artistry of life may present itself now and then through a personality, but art in the truest sense is the substance of an age, the significance of a country—a nationality. Even more than that, it is a time-spirit (the *Zeitgeist* of the Germans) that appears of occasion to glorify a land, to make great a nation. You would think that somewhere in the sightless substance of things—the chemistry back of the material evidence of life—there was a lovely, roseate milling of superior principle at times. Strange and lovely things come to the fore—the restoration in England, the Renaissance in Italy, Florence's golden period, Holland's classic art—all done in a century. "And the spirit of God moved upon the face of the waters," and there was that which we know as art.

I think it was years before those two towering figures—Rembrandt and Frans Hals (and of the two, Frans Hals is to me the greater)—appeared in my consciousness and emphasized the distinction of Holland for me, showing me that the loveliness of Dutch art,—the naïveté of Wouverman, the poetic realism of Nicolaes Maes, the ultimate artistry of Vermeer, de Hoogh, Ruysdael and all that sweet company of simple painters of simple things,—had finally come to mean *to me* all that *I* can really hope for in art—those last final reflections of halcyon days which are the best that life has to show.

Sometimes when I think of the homely splendors of Dutch art, which in its delicate commonplaceness has nothing to do with the more universal significance of both Hals and Rembrandt, I get a little wild artistically. Those smooth persuasive surfaces—pure enamel—and symphonies of blue light which are Vermeer; those genial household intimacies and candle-light romances which are Dou; those alleluiahs of light and water which are Vandervelde, Backhysen, Van Goyen; those merry-makings, perambulations, doorway chats, poultry intimacies, small trade affections and exchanges which are Terburg and Van Ostade! Truly, words fail me. I do not know how to suggest the poetry, the realism, the mood, the artistic craftsmanship that go with these things. They suggest a time, a country, an age, a mood, which is at once a philosophy, a system, a spirit of life. What more can art be? What more can it suggest? How, in that fortune of chance, which combines it with color-sense, temperament, craft, can it be exceeded? And all of this is what Dutch art—those seemingly minor phases, after Hals and Rembrandt—means to me.

But I was in Holland now, and not concerned so much for the moment with Dutch art as with my trunks. Still I felt here, at the frontier, that already I was in an entirely different world. Gone was that fever of the blood which is Germany. Gone the heavy, involute, enduring, Teutonic architecture. The upstanding German,—kaiserlich, self-opinionated, drastic, aggressive—was no longer about me. The men who were unlocking trunks and bags here exemplified a softer, milder, less military type. This mystery of national temperaments—was I never to get done with it? As I looked about me against a pleasant rising Sunday sun I could see and feel that not only the people but the landscape and the architecture had changed. The architecture was obviously so different, low, modest, one-story cottages standing out on a smooth, green level land, so smooth and so green and so level that anything projected against the skyline—it mattered not how modest—thereby became significant. And I saw my first Holland windmill turning its scarecrow arms in the distance. It was like coming out of a Russian steam bath into the cool marble precincts of the plunge, to be thus projected from Germany into Holland. If you will believe me I was glad that I had no money in order that I might be driven out to see all this.

*   *   *   *   *

I had no trouble with trunks and bags other than opening them and being compelled to look as though I thought it a crime to tip anybody. I strolled about the station in the early light of a clear, soft day and speculated on this matter of national temperaments. What a pity, I thought, if Holland were ever annexed by Germany or France or any country and made to modify its individuality. Before I was done with it I was inclined to believe that its individuality would never be modified, come any authority that might.

The balance of the trip to Amsterdam was nothing, a matter of two hours, but it visualized all I had fancied concerning Holland. Such a mild little land it is. So level, so smooth, so green. I began to puzzle out the signs along the way; they seemed such a hodge-podge of German and English badly mixed, that I had to laugh. The train passed up the center of a street in one village where cool brick pavements fronted cool brick houses and stores, and on one shop window appeared the legend: "Haar Sniden." Would not that as a statement of hair-cutting make any German-American laugh? "Telefoon," "stoom boot," "treins noor Ostend," "land te koop" (for sale) and the like brought a mild grin of amusement.

When we reached Amsterdam I had scarcely time to get a sense of it before I was whisked away in an electric omnibus to the hotel; and I was eager to get there, too, in order to replenish my purse which was now without a single penny. The last mark had gone to the porter at the depot to carry my bags to this 'bus. I was being deceived as to the character of the city by this ride from the central station to the hotel, for curiously its course gave not a glimpse of the canals that are the most charming and pleasing features of Amsterdam—more so than in any other city in Holland.

And now what struggles for a little ready money! My bags and fur coat had been duly carried into the hotel and I had signified to the porter in a lordly way that he should pay the 'busman, but seeing that I had letters which might result in local invitations this very day a little ready cash was necessary.

"I tell you what I should like you to do," I observed to the clerk, after I had properly entered my name and accepted a room. "Yesterday in Berlin, until it was too late, I forgot to draw any money on my letter of credit. Let me have forty gulden and I will settle with you in the morning."

"But, my dear sir," he said, very doubtfully indeed and in very polite English, "I do not see how we can do that. We do not know you."

"It is surely not so unusual," I suggested ingratiatingly, "you must have done it before. You see my bags and trunk are here. Here is my letter of credit. Let me speak to the manager."

The dapper Dutchman looked at my fur coat and bags quite critically, looked at my letter of credit as if he felt sure it was a forgery and then retired into an inner office. Presently a polished creature appeared, dark, immaculate, and after eyeing me solemnly, shook his head. "It can't be done," he said.

He turned to go.

"But here, here!" I called. "This won't do. You must be sensible. What sort of a hotel do you keep here, anyhow? I must have forty gulden—thirty, anyhow. My letter of credit is good. Examine it. Good heavens! You have at least eight hundred gulden worth of luggage there."

He had turned and was surveying me again. "It can't be done," he said.

"Impossible!" I cried. "I must have it. Why, I haven't a cent. You must trust me until to-morrow morning."

"Give him twenty gulden," he said to the clerk, wearily, and turned away.

"Good Heavens!" I said to the clerk, "give me the twenty gulden before I die of rage." And so he counted them out to me and I went in to breakfast.

I was charmed to find that the room overlooked one of the lovely canals with a distant view of others—all of them alive with canal-boats poled along slowly by solid, placid Hollanders, the spring sunlight giving them a warm, alluring, mildly adventurous aspect. The sense of light on water was so delightful from the breakfast-room, a great airy place, that it gave an added flavor to my Sunday morning breakfast of eggs and bacon. I was so pleased with my general surroundings here that I even hummed a tune while I ate.

CHAPTER L
AMSTERDAM

AMSTERDAM I should certainly include among my cities of light and charm, a place to live in. Not that it has, in my judgment, any of that capital significance of Paris or Rome or Venice. Though greater by a hundred thousand in population than Frankfort, it has not even the forceful commercial texture of that place. The spirit of the city seemed so much more unbusinesslike,—so much slower and easier-going. Before I sent forth a single letter of introduction I spent an entire day idling about its so often semicircular streets, following the canals which thread their centers like made pools, rejoicing in the cool brick walks which line the sides, looking at the reflection of houses and buildings in the ever-present water.

Holland is obviously a land of canals and windmills, but much more than that it is a land of atmosphere. I have often speculated as to just what it is that the sea does to its children that marks them so definitely for its own. And here in Amsterdam the thought came to me again. It is this: Your waterside idler, whether he traverses the wide stretches of the ocean or remains at home near the sea, has a seeming vacuity or dreaminess of soul that no rush of ordinary life can disturb. I have noted it of every port of the sea, that the eager intensity of men so often melts away at the water's edge. Boats are not loaded with the hard realism that marks the lading of trains. A sense of the idle-devil-may-care indifference of water seems to play about the affairs of these people, of those who have to do with them—the unhastening indifference of the sea. Perhaps the suggestion of the soundless, timeless, heartless deep that is in every channel, inlet, sluice, and dock-basin is the element that is at the base of their lagging motions. Your sailor and seafaring man will not hurry. His eyes are wide with a strange suspicion of the deep. He knows by contact what the subtlety and the fury of the waters are. The word of the sea is to be indifferent. "Never you mind, dearie. As it was in the beginning, so it ever shall be."

I think the peace and sweetness of Amsterdam bear some relationship to this wonderful, soporific spirit of the endless deep. As I walked along these "grachts" and "kades" and through these "pleins"—seemingly enameled worlds in which water and trees and red brick houses swam in a soft light, exactly the light and atmosphere you find in Dutch art—I felt as though I had come out of a hard modern existence such as one finds in Germany and back into something kindly, rural, intellectual, philosophic. Spinoza was, I believe, Holland's contribution to philosophy,—and a worthy Dutch philosopher he was—and Erasmus its great scholar. Both Rembrandt and Frans Hals have indicated in their lives the spirit of their country. I think, if you could look into the spirits and homes of thousands of simple Hollanders, you would find that same kindly, cleanly realism which you admire in their paintings. It is so placid. It was so here in Amsterdam. One gathered it from the very air. I had a feeling of peaceful, meditative delight in life and the simplicities of living all the time I was in Holland, which I take to be significant. All the while I was there I was wishing that I might remain throughout the spring and summer, and dream. In Germany I was haunted by the necessity of effort.

It was while I was in Amsterdam this first morning that the realization that my travels were fast drawing to a close dawned upon me. I had been having such a good time! That fresh, interested feeling of something new to look forward to with each morning was still enduring; but now I saw that my splendid world of adventure was all but ended. Thoreau has proved, as I recalled now with some satisfaction, that life can be lived, with great intellectual and spiritual distinction in a meager way and in small compass, but oh, the wonder of the world's highways—the going to and fro amid the things of eminence and memory, seeing how, thus far, this wordly house of ours has been furnished by man and by nature.

All those wonderful lands and objects that I had looked forward to with such keen interest a few months before were now in their way things of the past. England, France, Italy, Germany, London, Paris, Rome, Berlin, Canterbury, Amiens, St. Peter's, Pisa—I could not look on those any more with fresh and wondering eyes. How brief life is, I thought! How taciturn in its mood! It gives us a brief sip, some of us, once and then takes the cup away. It seemed to me, as I sat here looking out on the fresh and sweet canals of Holland, that I could idle thus forever jotting down foolish impressions, exclaiming over fleeting phases of beauty, wiping my eyes at the hails and farewells that are so precious and so sad. Holland was before me, and Belgium, and one more sip of Paris, and a few days in England, perhaps, and then I should go back to New York to write. I could see it—New York with its high buildings, its clanging cars, its rough incivility. Oh, why might I not idle abroad indefinitely?

   * * * * *

The second morning of my arrival I received a telephone message from a sister of Madame A., Madame J., the wife of an eminent Dutch jurist who had something to do with the International Peace Court. Would I come to lunch this day? Her husband would be a little late, but I would not mind. Her sister had written her. She would be so glad to see me. I promptly accepted.

The house was near the Ryks Museum, with a charming view of water from the windows. I can see it now—this very pleasant Holland interior. The rooms into which I was introduced were bluish-gray in tone, the contents spare and in good taste. Flowers in abundance. Much brass and old copper. Madame J. was herself a study in steel blue and silver gray, a reserved yet temperamental woman. A better linguist than Madame A., she spoke English perfectly. She had read my book, the latest one, and had liked it, she told me. Then she folded her hands in her lap, leaned forward and looked at me. "I have been so curious to see what you looked like."

"Well," I replied smilingly, "take a long look. I am not as wild as early rumors would indicate, I hope. You mustn't start with prejudices."

She smiled engagingly. "It isn't that. There are so many things in your book which make me curious. It is such a strange book—self-revealing, I imagine."

"I wouldn't be too sure."

She merely continued to look at me and smile in a placid way, but her inspection was so sympathetic and in a way alluring that it was rather flattering than otherwise. I, in turn, studied her. Here was a woman that, I had been told, had made an ideal marriage. And she obviously displayed the quiet content that few achieve.

   * * * * *

Like Shakespeare, I would be the last one to admit an impediment to the marriage of true minds. Unquestionably in this world in spite of endless liaisons, sex diversions, divorces, marital conflicts innumerable, the right people do occasionally find each other. There are true chemical-physical affinities, which remain so until death and dissolution undo their mysterious spell. Yet, on the other hand, I should say this is the rarest of events and if I should try to formulate the mystery of the marital trouble of this earth I should devote considerable percentages to: a—ungovernable passion not willed or able to be controlled by the individual; b—dull, thick-hided irresponsiveness which sees nothing in the emotional mood of another and knows no guiding impulse save self-interest and gluttony; c—fickleness of that unreasoning, unthinking character which is based on shallowness of soul and emotions—the pains resulting from such a state are negligible; d—diverging mental conceptions of life due to the hastened or retarded mental growth of one or the other of the high contracting parties; e—mistaken unions, wrong from the beginning, based on mistaken affections—cases where youth, inexperience, early ungovernable desire lead to a union based on sex and end, of course, in mental incompatibility; f—a hounding compulsion to seek for a high spiritual and intellectual ideal which almost no individual can realize for another and which yet *may* be realized in a lightning flash, out of a clear sky, as it were. In which case the last two will naturally forsake all others and cleave only the one to the other. Such is sex's affection, mental and spiritual compatibility.

But in marriage, as in no other trade, profession, or contract, once a bargain is struck—a mistake made—society suggests that there is no solution save in death. You cannot back out. It is almost the only place where you cannot correct a mistake and start all over. Until death do us part! Think of that being written and accepted of a mistaken marriage! My answer is that death would better hurry up. If the history of human marriage indicates anything, it is that the conditions which make for the union of two individuals, male and female, are purely fortuitous, that marriages are not made in heaven but in life's conditioning social laboratory, and that the marriage relation, as we understand it, is quite as much subject to modification and revision as anything else. Radical as it may seem, I predict a complete revision of the home standards as we know them. I would not be in the least surprised if the home, as we know it, were to disappear entirely. New, modifying conditions are daily manifesting themselves. Aside from easy divorce which is a mere safety valve and cannot safely (and probably will not) be dispensed with, there are other things which are steadily undermining the old home system as it has been practised. For instance, endless agencies which tend to influence, inspire, and direct the individual or child, entirely apart from the control and suggestion of parents, are now at work. In the rearing of the *average* child the influence of the average parent is steadily growing less. Intellectual, social, spiritual freedom are constantly being suggested to the individual, but not by the home. People are beginning to see that they have a right to seek and seek until they find that which is best suited to their intellectual, physical, spiritual development, home or no home. No mistake, however great, or disturbing in its consequences, it is beginning to be seen, should be irretrievable. The greater the mistake, really, the easier it should be to right it. Society *must* and *is* opening the prison doors of human misery, and old sorrows are walking out into the sunlight where they are being dispelled and forgotten. As sure as there are such things as mental processes, spiritual affinities, significant individualities and as sure as these things are increasing in force, volume, numbers, so sure, also, is it that the marriage state and the sex relation with which these things are so curiously and indissolubly involved will be modified, given greater scope, greater ease of adjustment, greater simplicity of initiation, greater freedom as to duration, greater kindliness as to termination. And the state will guarantee the right, privileges and immunities of the children to the entire satisfaction of the state, the parents, and the children. It cannot be otherwise.

*   *   *   *   *

Mynheer J. joined us presently. He was rather spare, very waxy, very intellectual, very unattached philosophically—apparently—and yet very rigid in his feeling for established principle. The type is quite common among intellectuals. Much reading had not made him mad but a little pedantic. He was speculatively interested in international peace though he did not believe that it could readily be established. Much more, apparently, he was interested in the necessity of building up a code or body of international laws which would be flexible and binding on all nations. Imaginatively I could see him at his heavy tomes. He had thin, delicate, rather handsome hands; a thin, dapper, wiry body. He was older than Madame J.,—say fifty-five or sixty. He had nice, well-barbered, short gray whiskers, a short, effective mustache, loose, well-trained, rather upstanding hair. Some such intellectual Northman Ibsen intended to give Hedda.

CHAPTER LI
"SPOTLESS TOWN"

AT three o'clock I left these pleasant people to visit the Ryks Museum and the next morning ran over to Haarlem, a half-hour away, to look at the Frans Hals in the Stadhuis. Haarlem was the city, I remember with pleasure, that once suffered the amazing tulip craze that swept over Holland in the sixteenth century—the city in which single rare tulips, like single rare carnations to-day, commanded enormous sums of money. Rare species, because of the value of the subsequent bulb sale, sold for hundreds of thousands of gulden. I had heard of the long line of colored tulip beds that lay between here and Haarlem and The Hague and I was prepared to judge for myself whether they were beautiful—as beautiful as the picture post-cards sold everywhere indicated. I found this so, but even more than the tulip beds I found the country round about from Amsterdam to Haarlem, The Hague and Rotterdam delightful. I traveled by foot and by train, passing by some thirty miles of vari-colored flower-beds in blocks of red, white, blue, purple, pink, and yellow, that lie between the several cities. I stood in the old Groote Kerk of St. Bavo in Haarlem, the Groote Kerk of St. James in The Hague—both as bare of ornament as an anchorite's cell—I wandered among the art treasures of the Ryks Museum in Amsterdam and the Mauritshuis and the Mesdag Museum in The Hague; I walked in the forests of moss-tinted trees at Haarlem and again at The Hague; my impression was that compact little Holland had all the charm of a great private estate, beautifully kept and intimately delightful.

But the canals of Holland—what an airy impression of romance, of pure poetry, they left on my mind! There are certain visions or memories to which the heart of every individual instinctively responds. The canals of Holland are one such to me. I can see them now, in the early morning, when the sun was just touching them with the faintest pearls, pinks, lavenders, blues, their level surfaces as smooth as glass, their banks rising no whit above the level of the water, but lying even with it like a black or emerald frame, their long straight lines broken at one point or another by a low brown or red or drab cottage or windmill! I can see them again at evening, the twilight hour, when in that poetically suffused mood of nature, which obtains then, they lie, liquid masses of silver, a shred of tinted cloud reflected in their surface, the level green grass turning black about them, a homing bird, a mass of trees in the distance, or humble cottage, its windows faintly gold from within, lending those last touches of artistry which make the perfection of nature. As in London and Venice the sails of their boats were colored a soft brown, and now and again one appeared in the fading light, a healthy Hollander smoking his pipe at the tiller, a cool wind fanning his brow. The world may hold more charming pictures but I have not encountered them.

And across the level spaces of lush grass that seemingly stretch unbroken for miles—bordered on this side or that with a little patch of filigree trees; ribboned and segmented by straight silvery threads of water; ornamented in the foreground by a cow or two, perhaps, or a boatman steering his motor-power canal boat; remotely ended by the seeming outlines of a distant city, as delicately penciled as a line by Vierge—stand the windmills. I have seen ten, twelve, fifteen, marching serenely across the fields in a row, of an afternoon, like great, heavy, fat Dutchmen, their sails going in slow, patient motions, their great sides rounding out like solid Dutch ribs,—naïve, delicious things. There were times when their outlines took on classic significance. Combined with the utterly level land, the canals and the artistically martialed trees, they constitute the very atmosphere of Holland.

*   *   *   *   *

Haarlem, when I reached it, pleased me almost as much as Amsterdam, though it had no canals to speak of—by comparison. It was so clean and fresh and altogether lovely. It reminded me of *Spotless Town*—the city of advertising fame— and I was quite ready to encounter the mayor, the butcher, the doctor and other worthies of that ultra-respectable city. Coming over from Amsterdam, I saw a little Dutch girl in wooden shoes come down to a low gate which opened directly upon a canal and dip up a pitcher of water. That was enough to key up my mood to the most romantic pitch. I ventured forth right gaily in a warm spring sun and spent the better portion of an utterly delightful day idling about its streets and museums.

Haarlem, to me, aside from the tulip craze, was where Frans Hals lived and where in 1610, when he was thirty years of age, he married and where six years later he was brought before the Burgomaster for ill-treating his wife, and ordered to abstain from "*dronken schnappe.*" Poor Frans Hals! The day I was there a line of motor-cars stood outside the Stadhuis waiting while their owners contemplated the wonders of the ten Regents pictures inside which are the pride of Haarlem. When I left London Sir Scorp was holding his recently discovered portrait by Hals at forty thousand pounds or more. I fancy to-day any of the numerous portraits by Hals in his best manner would bring two hundred thousand dollars and very likely much more. Yet at seventy-two Hals's goods and chattels—three mattresses, one chair, one table, three bolsters, and five pictures—were sold to satisfy a baker's bill, and from then on, until he died fourteen years later, at eighty-six, his "rent and firing" were paid for by the municipality. Fate probably saved a very great artist from endless misery by letting his first wife die. As it was he appears to have had his share of wretchedness.

The business of being really great is one of the most pathetic things in the world. When I was in London a close friend of Herbert Spencer told me the story of his last days, and how, save for herself, there was scarcely any one to cheer him in his loneliness. It was not that he lacked living means—he had that—but living as he did, aloft in the eternal snows of speculation, there was no one to share his thoughts,—no one. It was the fate of that gigantic mind to be lonely. What a pity the pleasures of the bottle or a drug might not eventually have allured him. Old Omar knew the proper antidote for these speculative miseries.

And Rembrandt van Ryn—there was another. It is probably true that from 1606, when he was born, until 1634, when he married at twenty-eight, he was gay enough. He had the delicious pleasure of discovering that he was an artist. Then he married Saskia van Uylenborch—the fair Saskia whom he painted sitting so gaily on his knee—and for eight years he was probably supremely happy. Saskia had forty thousand gulden to contribute to this *ménage*. Rembrandt's skill and fame were just attaining their most significant proportions, when she died. Then, being an artist, his affairs went from bad to worse; and you have the spectacle of this other seer, Holland's metaphysician, color-genius, life-interpreter, descending to an entanglement with a rather dull housekeeper, losing his money, having all his possessions sold to pay his debts and living out his last days in absolute loneliness at the Keizerskroon Inn in Amsterdam—quite neglected; for the local taste for art had changed, and the public was a little sick of Hals and Rembrandt.

As I sat in the Kroon restaurant, in Haarlem, opposite the Groote Kerk, watching some pigeons fly about the belfry, looking at Lieven de Key's meat market, the prototype of Dutch quaintness, and meditating on the pictures of these great masters that I had just seen in the Stadhuis, the insignificance of the individual as compared with the business of life came to me with overwhelming force. We are such minute, dusty insects at best, great or small. The old age of most people is so trivial and insignificant. We become mere shells—"granthers," "Goody Two-Shoes," "lean and slippered pantaloons." The spirit of life works in masses—not individuals. It prefers a school or species to a single specimen. A great man or woman is an accident. A great work of art of almost any kind is almost always fortuitous—like this meat market over the way. Life, for instance, I speculated sitting here, cared no more for Frans Hals or Rembrandt or Lieven de Key than I cared for the meanest butcher or baker of their day. If they chanced to find a means of subsistence—well and good; if not, well and good also. "Vanity, vanity, saith the preacher, all is vanity." Even so.

From Haarlem I went on to The Hague, about fifty minutes away; from The Hague, late that evening, to Rotterdam; from Rotterdam to Dordrecht, and so into Belgium, where I was amused to see everything change again—the people, language, signs,—all. Belgium appeared to be French, with only the faintest suggestion of Holland about it—but it was different enough from France also to be interesting on its own account.

After a quick trip across Belgium with short but delightful stops at Bruges, that exquisite shell of a once great city, at Ghent and at Brussels, the little Paris, I arrived once more at the French capital.

CHAPTER LII
PARIS AGAIN

ONCE I was in Paris again. It was delightful, for now it was spring, or nearly so, and the weather was pleasant. People were pouring into the city in droves from all over the world. It was nearly midnight when I arrived. My trunk, which I had sent on ahead, was somewhere in the limbo of advance trunks and I had a hard time getting it. Parisian porters and depot attendants know exactly when to lose all understanding of English and all knowledge of the sign language. It is when the search for anything becomes the least bit irksome. The tip they expect to get from you spurs them on a little way, but not very far. Let them see that the task promises to be somewhat wearisome and they disappear entirely. I lost two *facteurs* in this way, when they discovered that the trunk was not ready to their hand, and so I had to turn in and search among endless trunks myself. When I found it, a *facteur* was quickly secured to truck it out to a taxi. And, not at all wonderful to relate, the first man I had employed now showed up to obtain his *pourboire*. "Oh, here you are!" I exclaimed, as I was getting into my taxi. "Well, you can go to the devil!" He pulled a long face. That much English he knew.

When I reached the hotel in Paris I found Barfleur registered there but not yet returned to his room. But several letters of complaint were awaiting me: Why hadn't I telegraphed the exact hour of my arrival; why hadn't I written fully? It wasn't pleasant to wait in uncertainty. If I had only been exact, several things could have been arranged for this day or evening. While I was meditating on my sins of omission and commission, a *chasseur* bearing a note arrived. Would I dress and come to G.'s Bar. He would meet me at twelve. This was Saturday night, and it would be good to look over Paris again. I knew what that meant. We would leave the last restaurant in broad daylight, or at least the Paris dawn.

Coming down on the train from Brussels I had fallen into a blue funk—a kind of mental miasma—one of the miseries Barfleur never indulged in. They almost destroy me. Barfleur never, in so far as I could see, succumbed to the blues. In the first place my letter of credit was all but used up—my funds were growing terrifyingly low; and it did not make me any more cheerful to realize that my journey was now practically at an end. A few more days and I would be sailing for home.

When, somewhat after twelve, I arrived at G.'s Bar I was still a little doleful. Barfleur was there. He had just come in. That indescribable Parisian tension—that sense of life at the topmost level of nervous strength and energy—was filling this little place. The same red-jacketed musicians; the same efficient, inconspicuous, attentive and courteous waiters; Madame G., placid, philosophic, comfy, businesslike and yet motherlike, was going to and fro, pleasingly arrayed, looking no doubt after the interests, woes, and aspirations of her company of very, very bad but beautiful "girls." The walls were lined with life-loving patrons of from twenty-five to fifty years of age, with their female companions. Barfleur was at his best. He was once more in Paris—his beloved Paris. He beamed on me in a cheerful, patronizing way.

"So there you are! The Italian bandits didn't waylay you, even if they did rob you, I trust? The German Empire didn't sit too heavily on you? Holland and Switzerland must have been charming as passing pictures. Where did you stop in Amsterdam?"

"At the Amstel."

"Quite right. An excellent hotel. I trust Madame A. was nice to you?"

"She was as considerate as she could be."

"Right and fitting. She should have been. I saw that you stopped at the National, in Lucerne. That is one of the best hotels in Europe. I was glad to see that your taste in hotels was not falling off."

We began with appetizers, some soup, and a light wine. I gave a rough summary of some things I had seen, and then we came to the matter of my sailing date and a proposed walking trip in England.

"Now, I'll tell you what I think we should do and then you can use your own judgment," suggested Barfleur. "By the time we get to London, next Wednesday or Tuesday, England will be in prime condition. The country about Dorchester will be perfect. I suggest that we take a week's walk, anyway. You come to Bridgely Level—it is beautiful there now—and stay a week or ten days. I should like you to see how charming it is about my place in the spring. Then we will go to Dorchester. Then you can come back to Bridgely Level. Why not stay in England and write this summer?"

I put up a hand in serious opposition. "You know I can't do that. Why, if I had so much time, we might as well stay over here and settle down in—well, Fontainebleau. Besides, money is a matter of prime consideration with me. I've got to buckle down to work at once at anything that will make me ready money. I think in all seriousness I had best drop the writing end of the literary profession for a while anyway and return to the editorial desk."

The geniality and romance that lightened Barfleur's eye, as he thought of the exquisite beauty of England in the spring, faded, and his face became unduly severe.

"Really," he said, with a grand air, "you discourage me. At times, truly, I am inclined to quit. You are a man, in so far as I can see, with absolutely no faith in yourself—a man without a profession or an appropriate feeling for his craft. You are inclined, on the slightest provocation, to give up. You neither save anything over from yesterday in the shape of satisfactory reflection nor look into the future with any optimism. Do, I beg of you, have a little faith in the future. Assume that a day is a day, wherever it is, and that so long as it is not in the past it has possibilities. Here you are a man of forty; the formative portion of your life is behind you. Your work is all indicated and before you. Public faith such as my own should have some weight with you and yet after a tour of Europe, such as you would not have reasonably contemplated a year ago, you sink down supinely and talk of quitting. Truly it is too much. You make me feel very desperate. One cannot go on in this fashion. You must cultivate some intellectual stability around which your emotions can center and settle to anchor."

"Fairest Barfleur," I replied, "how you preach! You have real oratorical ability at times. There is much in what you say. I should have a profession, but we are looking at life from slightly different points of view. You have in your way a stable base, financially speaking. At least I assume so. I have not. My outlook, outside of the talent you are inclined to praise, is not very encouraging. It is not at all sure that the public will manifest the slightest interest in me from now on. If I had a large bump of vanity and the dull optimism of the unimaginative, I might assume anything and go gaily on until I was attacked somewhere for a board bill. Unfortunately I have not the necessary thickness of hide. And I suffer periods of emotional disturbance such as do not appear to afflict you. If you want to adjust my artistic attitude so nicely, contemplate my financial state first and see if that does not appeal to you as having some elements capable of disturbing my not undue proportion of equanimity." We then went into actual figures from which to his satisfaction he deducted that, with ordinary faith in myself, I had no real grounds for distress, and I from mine figured that my immediate future was quite as dubious as I had fancied. It did not appear that I was to have any money when I left England. Rather I was to draw against my future and trust that my innate capabilities would see me through.

It was definitely settled at this conference that I was not to take the long-planned walking tour in the south of England, lovely as it would be, but instead, after three or four days in Paris and three or four days in London, I was to take a boat sailing from Dover about the middle of April or a little later which would put me in New York before May. This agreed we returned to our pleasures and spent three or four very delightful days together.

It is written of Hugo and Balzac that they always looked upon Paris as the capital of the world. I am afraid I shall have to confess to a similar feeling concerning New York. I know it all so well—its splendid water spaces, its magnificent avenues, its varying sections, the rugged splendor of its clifflike structures, the ripping force of its tides of energy and life. Viewing Europe from the vantage point of the seven countries I had seen, I was prepared to admit that in so many ways we are, temperamentally and socially speaking, the rawest of raw material. No one could be more crude, more illusioned than the average American. Contrasted with the *savoir faire*, the life understanding, the philosophic acceptance of definite conditions in nature, the Europeans are immeasurably superior. They are harder, better trained, more settled in the routine of things. The folderols of romance, the shibboleths of politics and religion, the false standards of social and commercial supremacy are not so readily accepted there as here. Ill-founded aspiration is not so rife there as here: every Jack does not consider himself, regardless of qualifications, appointed by God to tell his neighbor how he shall do and live. But granting all this, America, and particularly New York, has to me the most comforting atmosphere of any. The subway is like my library table—it is so much of an intimate. Broadway is the one idling show place. Neither the Strand nor the Boulevard des Capucines can replace it. Fifth Avenue is all that it should be—the one really perfect show street of the world. All in all the Atlantic metropolis is the first city in the world to me,—first in force, unrivaled in individuality, richer and freer in its spirit than London or Paris, though so often more gauche, more tawdry, more shamblingly inexperienced.

As I sat in Madame G.'s Bar, the pull of the city overseas was on me—and that in the spring! I wanted to go *home*.

We talked of the women we had got to know in Paris—of Marcelle and Madame de B.—and other figures lurking in the background of this brilliant city. But Marcelle would expect a trip to Fontainebleau and Madame de B. was likely to be financially distressed. This cheerful sort of companionship would be expensive. Did I care to submit to the expense? I did not. I felt that I could not. So for once we decided to be modest and go out and see what we could see alone. Our individual companionship was for the time-being sufficient.

Barfleur and I truly kept step with Paris these early spring days. This first night together we revisited all our favorite cafés and restaurants—Fysher's Bar, the Rat Mort, C———'s Bar, the Abbaye Thélème, Maxim's, the American, Paillard's and the like,—and this, I soon realized: without a keen sex interest—the companionship of these high-voltage ladies of Paris—I can imagine nothing duller. It becomes a brilliant but hollow spectacle.

The next day was Sunday. It was warm and sunny as a day could be. The air was charged with a kind of gay expectation. Barfleur had discovered a neo-impressionist portraitist of merit, one Hans Bols, and had agreed to have his portrait done by him. This Sunday morning was the first day for a series of three sittings; so I left him and spent a delicious morning in the Bois. Paris in spring! The several days—from Saturday to Wednesday—were like a dream. A gay world—full of the subtleties of social ambition, of desire, fashion, love-making, and all the keenest, shrewdest aspects of life. It was interesting, at the Café Madrid and The Elysée, to sit out under trees and the open sky and see an uninterrupted stream of automobiles and taxis pouring up, depositing smart-looking people all glancing keenly about, nodding to friends, now cordially, now tentatively, in a careful, selective social way.

One evening after I returned from a late ramble alone, I found on my table a note from Barfleur. "For God's sake, if you get this in time, come at once to the Abbaye Thélème. I am waiting for you with a Mrs. L., who wants to meet you." So I had to change to evening clothes at one-thirty in the morning. And it was the same old thing when I reached there—waiters tumbling over one another with their burdens of champagne, fruit, ices, confitures; the air full of colored glucose balls, colored balloons floating aloft, endless mirrors reflecting a giddy panorama, white arms, white necks, animated faces, snowy shirt bosoms—the old story. Spanish dancers in glittering scales, American negroes in evening clothes singing coon songs, excited life-lovers, male and female, dancing erotically in each other's arms. Can it be, I asked myself, that this thing goes on night after night and year after year? Yet it was obvious that it did.

The lady in question was rather remote—as an English-woman *can* be. I'm sure she said to herself, "This is a very dull author." But I couldn't help it. She froze my social sense into icy crystals of "yes" and "no." We took her home presently and continued our rounds till the wee sma' hours.

CHAPTER LIII
THE VOYAGE HOME

THE following Wednesday Barfleur and I returned to London via Calais and Dover. We had been, between whiles, to the races at Longchamps, luncheons at Au Père Boivin, the Pré Catalan, and elsewhere. I had finally looked up Marcelle, but the concierge explained that she was out of town.

In spite of the utter fascination of Paris I was not at all sorry to leave, for I felt that to be happy here one would want a more definite social life and a more fixed habitation than this hotel and the small circle of people that we had met could provide. I took a last—almost a yearning—look at the Avenue de l'Opéra and the Gare du Nord and then we were off.

England was softly radiant in her spring dress. The leaves of the trees between Dover and London were just budding, that diaphanous tracery which resembles green lace. The endless red chimneys and sagging green roofs and eaves of English cottages peeping out from this vesture of spring were as romantic and poetic as an old English ballad. No doubt at all that England—the south of it, anyhow—is in a rut; sixty years behind the times,—but what a rut! Must all be new and polished and shiny? As the towers and spires of Canterbury sped past to the right, gray and crumbling in a wine-like air, something rose in my throat. I thought of that old English song that begins—

"When shepherds pipe on oaten straws—"

And then London once more and all the mystery of endless involute streets and simple, hidden, unexplored regions! I went once more to look at the grim, sad, two-story East End in spring. It was even more pathetic for being touched by the caressing hand of Nature. I went to look at Hyde Park and Chelsea and Seven Kings. I thought to visit Sir Scorp—to cringe once more before the inquiring severity of his ascetic eye; but I did not have time, as things turned out. Barfleur was insistent that I should spend a day or two at Bridgely Level. Owing to a great coal strike the boat I had planned to take was put out of commission and I was compelled to advance my sailing date two days on the boat of another line. And now I was to see Bridgely Level once more, in the spring.

After Italy and Holland, perhaps side by side with Holland or before it, England—the southern portion of it—is the most charmingly individual country in Europe. For the sake of the walk, the evening was so fine, we decided to leave the train at Maidenhead and walk the remaining distance, some five or six miles. It was ideal. The sun was going down and breaking through diaphanous clouds in the west, which it tinted and gilded. The English hedges and copses were delicately tinted with new life. English robins were on the grass; sheep, cows; over one English hamlet and another smoke was curling and English crows or rooks were gaily cawing, cheered at the thought of an English spring.

As gay as children, Barfleur and I trudged the yellow English road. Now and then we passed through a stile and cut diagonally across a field where a path was laid for the foot of man. Every so often we met an English laborer, his trousers gripped just below the knee by the customary English strap. Green and red; green and red; (such were the houses and fields) with new spring violets, apple trees in blossom, and peeping steeples over sloping hillsides thrown in for good measure. I felt—what shall I say I felt?—not the grandeur of Italy, but something so delicate and tender, so reminiscent and aromatic—faintly so—of other days and other fames, that my heart was touched as by music. Near Bridgely Level we encountered Wilkins going home from his work, a bundle of twigs under his arm, a pruning hook at his belt, his trousers strapped after the fashion of his class.

"Well, Wilkins!" I exclaimed.

"W'y, 'ow do you do, sir, Mr. Dreiser? Hi'm glad to see you again, Hi am," touching his cap. "Hi 'opes as 'ow you've had a pleasant trip."

"Very, Wilkins, very," I replied grandiosely. Who cannot be grandiose in the presence of the fixed conditions of old England. I asked after his work and his health and then Barfleur gave him some instructions for the morrow. We went on in a fading light—an English twilight. And when we reached the country house it was already aglow in anticipation of this visit. Hearth fires were laid. The dining-room, reception-hall, and living-room were alight. Dora appeared at the door, quite as charming and rosy in her white apron and cap as the day I left, but she gave no more sign that I was strange or had been absent than as if I had not been away.

"Now we must make up our minds what particular wines we want for dinner. I have an excellent champagne of course; but how about a light Burgundy or a Rhine wine? I have an excellent Assmanshäuser."

"I vote for the light Burgundy," I said.

"Done. I will speak to Dora now."

And while he went to instruct Dora, I went to look after all my belongings in order to bring them finally together for my permanent departure. After a delicious dinner and one of those comfortable, reminiscent talks that seem naturally to follow the end of the day, I went early to bed.

When the day came to sail I was really glad to be going home, although on the way I had quarreled so much with my native land for the things which it lacks and which Europe apparently has.

Our boasted democracy has resulted in little more than the privilege every living, breathing American has of being rude and brutal to every other, but it is not beyond possibility that sometime as a nation we will sober down into something approximating human civility. Our early revolt against sham civility has, in so far as I can see, resulted in nothing save the abolition of all civility—which is sickening. Life, I am sure, will shame us out of it eventually. We will find we do not get anywhere by it. And I blame it all on the lawlessness of the men at the top. They have set the example which has been most freely copied.

Still, I was glad to be going home.

When the time came the run from London to Folkstone and Dover was pleasant with its fleeting glimpses of the old castle at Rochester and the spires of the cathedral at Canterbury, the English orchards, the slopes dotted with sheep, the nestled chimneys and the occasional quaint, sagging roofs of moss-tinted tiles. The conductor who had secured me a compartment to myself appeared just after we left Folkstone to tell me not to bother about my baggage, saying that I would surely find it all on the dock when I arrived to take the boat. It was exactly as he said, though having come this way I found two transfers necessary. Trust the English to be faithful. It is the one reliable country in which you may travel. At Dover I meditated on how thoroughly my European days were over and when, if ever, I should come again. Life offers so much to see and the human span is so short that it is a question whether it is advisable ever to go twice to the same place—a serious question. If I had my choice, I decided—as I stood and looked at the blue bay of Dover—I would, if I could, spend six months each year in the United States and then choose Paris as my other center and from there fare forth as I pleased.

After an hour's wait at Dover, the big liner dropped anchor in the roadstead and presently the London passengers were put on board and we were under way. The Harbor was lovely in a fading light—chalk-blue waters, tall whitish cliffs, endless squealing, circling gulls, and a bugle calling from the fort in the city.

*   *   *   *   *

Our ship's captain was a Christian Scientist, believing in the nothingness of matter, the immanence of Spirit or a divine idea, yet he was, as events proved, greatly distressed because of the perverse, undismissable presence and hauntings of mortal thought. He had "beliefs" concerning possible wrecks, fires, explosions—the usual terrors of the deep, and one of the ship's company (our deck-steward) told me that whenever there was a fog he was always on the bridge, refusing to leave it and that he was nervous and "as cross as hell." So you can see how his religious belief squared with his chemical intuitions concerning the facts of life. A nice, healthy, brisk, argumentative, contentious individual he was, and very anxious to have the pretty women sit by him at dinner.

The third day we were out news came by wireless that the *Titanic* had sunk after collision with an iceberg in mid-ocean. The news had been given in confidence to a passenger. And this passenger had "in confidence" told others. It was a terrible piece of news, grim in its suggestion, and when it finally leaked out it sent a chill over all on board. I heard it first at nine o'clock at night. A party of us were seated in the smoking-room, a most comfortable retreat from the terrors of the night and the sea. A damp wind had arisen, bringing with it the dreaded fog. Sometimes I think the card room is sought because it suggests the sea less than any place else on the ship. The great fog-horn began mooing like some vast Brobdingnagian sea-cow wandering on endless watery pastures. The passengers were gathered here now in groups where, played upon by scores of lights, served with drinks and reacted upon, one by the moods of the others, a temperamental combustion took place which served to dispel their gloom. Yet it was not possible entirely to keep one's mind off the slowing down of the ship, the grim moo of the horn, and the sound of long, swishing breakers outside speaking of the immensity of the sea, its darkness, depth, and terrors. Every now and then, I noticed, some one would rise and go outside to contemplate, no doubt, the gloominess of it all. There is nothing more unpromising to this little lamp, the body, than the dark, foggy waters of a midnight sea.

One of the passengers, a German, came up to our table with a troubled, mysterious air. "I got sumpin' to tell you, gentlemen," he said in a stage whisper, bending over us. "You better come outside where the ladies can't hear." (There were several in the room.) "I just been talkin' to the wireless man upstairs."

We arose and followed him out on deck.

The German faced us, pale and trembling. "Gentlemen," he said, "the captain's given orders to keep it a secret until we reach New York. But I got it straight from the wireless man: The *Titanic* went down last night with nearly all on board. Only eight hundred saved and two thousand drowned. She struck an iceberg off Newfoundland. You, gentlemen, must promise me not to tell the ladies—otherwise I shuttn't have told you. I promised the man upstairs. It might get him in trouble."

We promised faithfully. And with one accord we went to the rail and looked out into the blackness ahead. The swish of the sea could be heard and the insistent moo of the fog-horn.

"And this is only Tuesday," suggested one. His face showed a true concern. "We've got a week yet on the sea, the way they will run now. And we have to go through that region—maybe over the very spot—"

He took off his cap and scratched his hair in a foolish, thoughtful way. I think we all began to talk at once, but no one listened. The terror of the sea had come swiftly and directly home to all. I am satisfied that there was not a man of all the company who heard without feeling a strange sensation. To think of a ship as immense as the *Titanic*, new and bright, sinking in endless fathoms of water. And the two thousand passengers routed like rats from their berths only to float helplessly in miles of water, praying and crying!

I went to my berth thinking of the pains and terrors of those doomed two thousand, a great rage in my heart against the fortuity of life—the dullness or greed of man that prevents him from coping with it. For an hour or more I listened to the vibration of the ship that trembled at times like a spent animal as a great wave struck at it with smashing force.

It was a trying night.

I found by careful observation of those with me that I was not the only one subject to disquieting thoughts. Mr. W., a Chicago beef man, pleased me most, for he was so frank in admitting his inmost emotions. He was a vigorous young buck, frank and straightforward. He came down to breakfast the next morning looking a little dull. The sun was out and it was a fine day. "You know," he confided genially, "I dreamed of them poor devils all night. Say—out in the cold there! And then those big waves kept hitting the ship and waking me up. Did you hear that smash in the night? I thought we had struck something. I got up once and looked out but that didn't cheer me any. I could only see the top of a roller now and then going by."

Another evening, sitting in the deepest recesses of the card room he explained that he believed in good and bad spirits and the good spirits could help you "if they wanted to."

Monsieur G., a Belgian, doing business in New York, was nervous in a subdued, quiet way. He never ceased commenting on the wretchedness of the catastrophe, nor did he fail daily to consult the chart of miles made and course traveled. He predicted that we would turn south before we neared the Grand Banks because he did not believe the captain would "take a chance." I am sure he told his wife and that she told every other woman, for the next day one of them confided to me that she knew, and that she had been "stiff with fear" all the night before.

An Englishman, who was with us making for Calgary gave no sign, one way or the other. The German who first brought us the news was like a man with a mania; he talked of it all the time. An American judge on board talked solemnly with all who would listen—a hard crab of a man, whose emotions found their vent in the business of extracting information. The women talked to each other but pretended not to know.

It took three days of more or less pleasant sailing to relax the tension which pervaded the whole vessel. The captain did not appear again at table for four days. On Wednesday, following the Monday of the wreck, there was a fire drill—that ominous clanging of the fire-bell on the forward deck which brought many troubled spectators out of their staterooms and developed the fact that every piece of hose employed was rotten; for every piece put under pressure burst—a cheering exhibition!

But as the days passed we began to take heart again. The philosophers of the company were unanimously agreed that as the *Titanic* had suffered this great disaster through carelessness on the part of her officers, no doubt our own chances of safely reaching shore were thereby enhanced. We fell to gambling again, to flirting, to playing shuffle-board. By Saturday, when we were passing in the vicinity of where the *Titanic* went down, only much farther to the south, our fears had been practically dispelled.

It was not until we reached Sandy Hook the following Tuesday—a hard, bright, clear, blowy day, that we really got the full story. The customary pilot was taken on there, out of a thrashing sea, his overcoat pockets bulging with papers, all flaring with headlines describing the disaster. We crowded into the smoking-room for the last time and devoured the news. Some broke down and cried. Others clenched their fists and swore over the vivid and painful pen pictures by eye witnesses and survivors. For a while we all forgot we were nearly home. We came finally to quarantine. And I was amused to see how in these last hours the rather vigorous ardors of ship-friendship that had been engendered by the days spent together began to cool—how all those on board began to think of themselves no longer as members of a coördinated ship company bound together for weal or woe on the bosom of the great deep, but rather as individuals of widely separated communities and interests to which they were now returning and which of necessity would sever their relationship perpetually. I saw, for instance, the American judge who had unbent sufficiently after we had been three days out to play cards with so humble a person as the commission merchant, and others, begin to congeal again into his native judicial dignity. Several of the young women who had been generally friendly now became quite remote—other worlds were calling them.

And all of this goodly company were so concerned now as to whether they could make a very conservative estimate of the things they were bringing into America and yet not be disturbed by the customs inspectors, that they were a little amusing. What is honesty, anyhow? Foreign purchases to the value of one hundred dollars were allowed; yet I venture to say that of all this charming company, most of whom prided themselves on some form of virtue, few made a strictly honest declaration. They were all as honest as they had to be—as dishonest as they dared be—no more. Poor pretending humanity! We all lie so. We all believe such untrue things about ourselves and about others. Life is literally compact of make-believe, illusion, temperamental bias, false witness, affinity. The so-called standards of right, truth, justice, law, are no more than the wire netting of a sieve through which the water of life rushes almost uninterrupted. It seems to be regulated, but is it? Look close. See for yourself. Christ said, "Eyes and they see not; ears and they hear not." Is this not literally true? Begin with number one. How about *you* and the so-called universal standards?

It had been so cold and raw down the bay that I could scarcely believe, as we neared Manhattan Island that it was going to be so warm and springlike on land as it proved. When we first sighted Long Island and later Long Beach it was over a thrashing sea; the heads of the waves were being cut off by the wind and sent flying into white spindrift or parti-colored rainbows. Even above Sandy Hook the wind made rainbows out of wave-tops and the bay had a tumbled surface. It was good to see again the stately towers of the lower city as we drew near—that mountain of steel and stone cut with its narrow canyons. They were just finishing the upper framework of the Woolworth Building—that first cathedral of the American religion of business—and now it reared its stately head high above everything else.

There was a great company at the dockside to receive us. Owing to the sinking of the *Titanic* relatives were especially anxious and all incoming ships were greeted with enlarged companies of grateful friends. There were reporters on hand to ask questions as to the voyage—had we encountered any bodies, had we struck any ice?

When I finally stepped on the dock, gathered up my baggage, called a few final farewells and took a taxi to upper Broadway, I really felt that I was once more at home. New York was so suggestively rich to me, this spring evening. It was so refreshing to look out and see the commonplace life of Eighth Avenue, up which I sped, and the long cross streets and later upper Broadway with its rush of cars, taxis, pedestrians. On Eighth Avenue negroes were idling at curbs and corners, the Eighth Avenue type of shopkeeper lolling in his doorway, boys and girls, men and women of a none-too-comforting type, making the best of a humdrum and shabby existence. In one's own land, born and raised among the conditions you are observing, responsive to the subtlest modifications of speech, gesture, expression, life takes on a fresh and intimate aspect which only your own land can give after a trip abroad. I never quite realized until later this same evening, strolling out along Broadway to pay a call, how much one really loses abroad for want of blood affinity and years and years of residence. All the finer details, such as through the magnifying glass of familiarity one gains at home, one loses abroad. Only the main outlines—the very roughest details—stand revealed as in a distant view of mountains. That is why generalizations, on so short an acquaintance as a traveler must have, are so dangerous. Here, each sight and sound was significant.

"And he says to me," said one little girl, strolling with her picturesque companion on upper Broadway, "if you don't do that, I'm through."

"And what did you say?"

"Good *night*!!!"

I was sure, then, that I was really home!

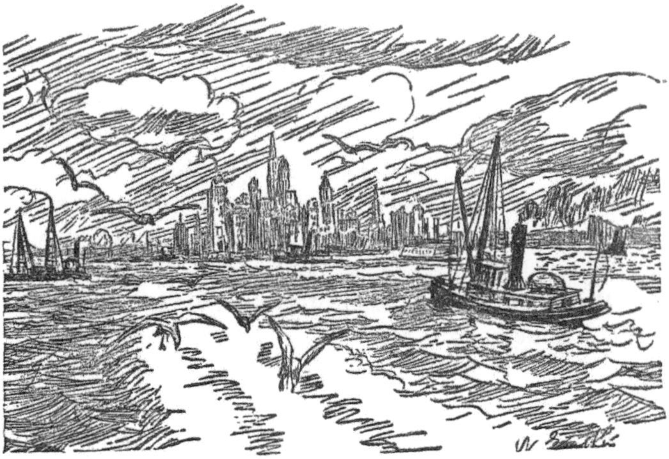

Milton Keynes UK
Ingram Content Group UK Ltd.
UKHW030726080824
446708UK00009B/194

9 789357 966658